The First 50
Super Bowls

The First 50 Super Bowls

How Football's Championships Were Won

ED BENKIN

Foreword by MIKE CURTIS

McFarland & Company, Inc., Publishers
Jefferson, North Carolina

LIBRARY OF CONGRESS CATALOGUING-IN-PUBLICATION DATA

Names: Benkin, Ed, author.
Title: The first 50 Super Bowls : how football's championships were
    won / Ed Benkin ; foreword by J. Michael Curtis.
Other titles: First fifty Super Bowls
Description: Jefferson, North Carolina : McFarland & Company,
    Inc., Publishers, 2018. | Includes bibliographical references and
    index.
Identifiers: LCCN 2017048276 | ISBN 9781476670577 (softcover :
    acid free paper) ∞
Subjects: LCSH: Super Bowl—History. | Football—United States—
    History.
Classification: LCC GV956.2.S8 B46 2018 | DDC 796.332/648—dc23
LC record available at https://lccn.loc.gov/2017048276

BRITISH LIBRARY CATALOGUING DATA ARE AVAILABLE

ISBN (print) 978-1-4766-7057-7
ISBN (ebook) 978-1-4766-3072-4

Front cover photograph of the Vince Lombardi Trophy
by Jerry Coli (Dreamstime)

Printed in the United States of America

McFarland & Company, Inc., Publishers
    Box 611, Jefferson, North Carolina 28640
    www.mcfarlandpub.com

To my wonderful daughters,
Lauren and Jessica,
who inspire me every day with their smiles,
their generous hearts and their love

Acknowledgments

I would like to thank my literary agent and longtime attorney, Lloyd Z. Remick, Esq., of Zane Management and his staff of attorneys who made this publication possible with all of their hard work.

I would also like to thank the host of media relations staffs across the National Football League along with various NFL alumni organizations who helped me coordinate more than 100 interviews for this extraordinary project.

Lastly, I would like to thank NFL Films, whose ability to tell the stories of the Super Bowl has left a lasting impression on generations of football fans.

Table of Contents

Foreword
by Mike Curtis

When I first began playing pro football, there was no Super Bowl. However, the Super Bowl was born thanks to a rivalry between two leagues.

I was a proud member of the Baltimore Colts of the National Football League for most of my career. I came to Baltimore in 1965 even though I was also drafted by Kansas City of the American Football League. I chose the NFL and eventually became a linebacker after being drafted as a fullback. The Colts had several NFL rivals, but the rivalry between the NFL and the AFL was football's biggest battle. The leagues began getting into bidding wars for players and the competition was just as fierce off the field as it was on the field.

In 1966, the two leagues finally made peace and agreed to a merger. It would also give the leagues an opportunity to go head-to-head before the merger was completed four years later. When the idea of a championship game between the leagues' top teams frist came up, it wasn't even called the Super Bowl. It was called the AFL-NFL World Championship game.

The Green Bay Packers represented our league proudly in the first two games as they made the NFL the true world champion. We would have our opportunity to represent the NFL in Super Bowl III and were expected to win easily against the New York Jets. Unfortunately, we became the victims of one of sport's biggest upsets, as the underdogs from the AFL came away victorious.

The pain from that loss still lingers, but the game changed the Super Bowl forever. The media attention, coupled with the drama of the outcome, made it the most important game in pro football since the Colts beat the Giants for the 1958 title. The Super Bowl would become the most hyped sporting event in America and would grow to what is almost an unofficial national holiday.

Today, the Super Bowl is not only pro football's biggest game, but it is an event followed by millions of people. Even non-football fans remember where they were when special Super Bowl moments occurred. Today, the Super Bowl is one of the most watched television events in the world and the game of football has grown thanks to its popularity. Today's players continue to make memories that last a lifetime for fans across the world.

The Super Bowl is also part of American culture. A look back at Super Bowls is a time warp through the generations. Fans of past Super Bowls during my time now get to share their Super Bowl memories with the generations that followed. The Super Bowl has also featured some of the greatest teams ever to play the game. Teams such as the Packers of the '60s, the Steelers of the 70s, the 49ers of the 80s, the Cowboys of the 90s and the Patriots of the new millennium have taken their place among Super Bowl dynasties.

Some players become famous simply because of one play in a Super Bowl. Such was the case with our kicker, Jim O'Brien, two years after we lost to the Jets. The Super Bowl also has its superstars as the best of the best rise to the occasion when the game is on the line.

The players and coaches who have told their Super Bowl stories give every reader a chance to go inside the game and inside the locker room. There are also stories about some of the amazing events surrounding the big game along with personal stories of players dealing with both victory and defeat.

The Super Bowl has come a long way since its early days when two proud leagues battled to see who would be the champion of pro football. Today's Super Bowls feature the best from the AFC and NFC as millions of people around the world watch the final chapter to a season. However, it all began with the story of two leagues and men who played with pride and passion for the game.

As for me, I was able to experience the thrill of winning a Super Bowl two years after our defeat when the Colts beat the Cowboys in Super Bowl V. I was fortunate enough to make an interception at the end of the game which helped set up our game-winning field goal. While some Super Bowls are more memorable than others, every Super Bowl has its share of stories written by the men who played and coached the game.

I hope you enjoy this look back at 50 years of Super Bowl memories. I was proud to be a Baltimore Colt and to be one of the many who would help pave the way to making the Super Bowl America's biggest sporting event. The game may end, but the memories last a lifetime.

Mike Curtis played 14 seasons in the NFL (1965–1978) for the Baltimore Colts, the Seattle Seahawks and the Washington Redskins.

Preface

My introduction to football came on a rainy day in Orchard Park, New York.

I lived in the Buffalo area from age three to 12. When I was five years old, I went to my first NFL game in September of 1974. The Buffalo Bills took on Joe Namath and the New York Jets on a stormy and windy day at Rich Stadium. Thanks to Mother Nature, neither team completed a pass until the fourth quarter. Buffalo won, 16–12.

While there were less stormy trips to other games, my passion for the NFL grew rapidly. It remained when I returned to the Philadelphia area in 1981. As pro football continued to skyrocket as America's favorite game, my passion for history carried over to the world of pro football. Hearing the voice of John Facenda with his brilliant work on NFL Films quickly drew me into the quest for knowledge of the story of the NFL. One story which caught my attention from the beginning was the Super Bowl.

In the days when the likes of cable TV and ESPN were in their infancy, there were often regular showings of highlights from Super Bowls past. To see how the game grew from a war of leagues to the most watched sporting event in the country is a remarkable story. As each Super Bowl passed, I could remember watching the games with family and friends and understood how the Super Bowl was also a journey of generations.

I followed my passion for sports into my adult life and have been fortunate to fulfill my life's ambition to work as a sports broadcaster. In 2004, I was hired by KYW News Radio in Philadelphia and also became a part of Sports Radio WIP in the city several years later. Among my many duties each year is to cover the Philadelphia Eagles. From the draft to the end of the season, I have the opportunity to spend much of my time covering the NFL.

The opportunity for freelance writing throughout my career planted a seed to someday tell the story of the Super Bowl. I realized that each Super Bowl was a story within itself and continued to be fascinated by the stories from America's biggest game. Family members would jokingly quiz me to find out how fast I could identify scores and other moments from past Super Bowls. When it came time to tackle this project, I knew there was more to each Super Bowl than what could be found in a highlight reel.

With the help of a host of NFL alumni, media members and other sources, I decided to embark on this quest to bring the reader inside the game in a way the stories of the Super Bowl had never been told. I also wanted the stories for this project to be original. All of the interviews for this book were conducted exclusively by me to give you, the reader, a fresh perspective on the stories from the Super Bowl.

I was both honored and humbled to hear so many incredible stories from the 102 former players and coaches that we spoke with for this book. From players such as Jerry Kramer and Len Dawson who took the field for Super Bowl I to modern day heroes such as Adam Vinatieri and Malcolm Butler, this book gives the reader an inside look at Super Sunday unlike any other. We did not want this to be a story about every three-yard gain, which could easily be found on the Internet. We wanted to give the reader a brand new perspective on the Super Bowl. Whether it's a game involving a massive blowout or a heart stopping finish, each chapter is a special story about the biggest sporting event of the season.

The NFL has its own story to write every year and the climax arrives on the last Sunday of the season. However, the Super Bowl is more than just the last game of a five-month NFL campaign. It is an event which grabs the attention of both football and non-football fans. The famous commercials, lavish halftime shows and the celebration of America preceding the game has made the Super Bowl must see TV. It is also the ultimate reality series because the script is written by the participants every Super Bowl Sunday.

I hope you enjoy this journey through the first half century of Super Bowls as told by the men who made the game what it is today. From its humble beginning to its current status as the most watched event of the year, there is truly no other event like the Super Bowl.

The First 50 Super Bowls

I
PLENTY OF SEATS AVAILABLE

Peace was finally at hand in pro football.

After six years of war, the National Football League and American Football League agreed to a merger in 1966. The merger would take place in 1970, but the two leagues would finally have the chance to settle the score on the field.

With the creation of the AFL-NFL World Championship Game (later to be called the Super Bowl), the winners of both leagues would meet to decide a true world champion. On January 15, 1967, the NFL's Green Bay Packers and AFL's Kansas City Chiefs made history as they took the field at the Los Angeles Coliseum for the first ever Super Bowl.

Most considered the AFL to be an inferior league and the Packers were a heavy favorite to win. For the Chiefs, it was an opportunity to finally prove the AFL was on equal footing with the older league, something Kansas City Quarterback Len Dawson was well aware of as the Chiefs arrived in Los Angeles.

"It was an opportunity for the American Football League to play against the National Football League," said Dawson. "It was exciting."

Exciting was hardly the word Vince Lombardi was using. There was tremendous pressure on the Packers' legendary coach heading into the game. NFL owners were not only expecting a win, but a rout. While Lombardi was tense leading up to the game, he tried to keep his players shielded from the outside pressure and the predictions of a blowout. Lombardi kept the Packers out of Los Angeles until the end of the week and Offensive Guard Jerry Kramer believes their time away from the city may have left the Packers overconfident.

"We were up in Santa Barbara away from the media," said Kramer. "We were playing poker and having a pretty good time. Quite frankly, we did not respect the Kansas City Chiefs as much as we should have. They had pretty good football players."

Lombardi would remind the players of the importance of the game as the week progressed. Fines for breaking team rules were raised to as much as $5,000. Even with the escape to Santa Barbara, Lombardi's legendary intensity was in full force during practice. Linebacker Dave Robinson knew his head coach was feeling the heat.

"There was a lot of pressure put on us by Vince Lombardi," said Robinson. "He was feeling pressure from the National Football League. You could tell he was nervous with the way he talked and the way he walked and the way he hollered in practice. That week, there was no laughing or joking. He was dead serious."

There was a different type of pressure on Kansas City. While the Chiefs were a heavy underdog going into the game, it was the first opportunity for the AFL to prove it belonged on the same field with the best from the NFL. One player who seemed to relish the moment was Fred "The Hammer" Williamson. The Chiefs Cornerback ushered in the age of pre-game trash talking by vowing to use his forearm to neutralize the Green Bay receivers.

"It's the personality of The Hammer," said Williamson. "It is to intimidate and make them think more about me than the game. It's a game of intimidation. That's what the game is about."

Williamson wasn't worried about his comments serving as motivation for the Packers. However, Kansas City Head Coach Hank Stram asked The Hammer to tone down his rhetoric as game day drew closer.

"Hank said you can't talk about the Packers and you can't talk about what you're going to do," Williamson said. "I said that's my style. That's me. They know we're here. We can't hide out from these guys. I'm telling you what I'm going to do to them."

While The Hammer continued to talk, the Packers shrugged off Williamson's brash predictions. Robinson said the coaches were more concerned with findings ways to exploit the talkative defensive back.

"The guys laughed about them," Robinson said. "Our coaches made light of it. They kept showing us what the thought were his weaknesses."

Green Bay Running Back Jim Taylor was all business as he prepared for what would be his last game as a Packer. Taylor claims Lombardi did what he had to do to keep his team focused and the comments by Williamson were far from intimidating to a team which had just captured its second straight NFL title.

"That's chin music," said Taylor. "We were a little more mature and a little more developed. We had already been in championship games. Talk's cheap. That's B.S. Smell it, but don't sample it."

There was also a battle off the field between two television networks. NFL Commissioner Pete Rozelle had agreed to let both CBS and NBC televise the game. CBS had been broadcasting NFL games, while NBC was the AFL's broadcast home. In the days leading up to the game, tempers flared between the two television crews. By the end of the week, a fence had been placed between the CBS and NBC trucks.

As kickoff drew closer, the pressure continued to mount for Lombardi. The Green Bay Coach was interviewed by Frank Gifford for CBS before the game, and Gifford told Kramer Lombardi was shaking throughout the interview.

"A great deal of the pressure was on him," said Kramer. "I said, 'damn, if he's this nervous, I'm nervous.'"

It was clear that many fans did not think the AFL belonged on the same field as the NFL. Thus, the first Super Bowl was the only one which did not sell out. It did not even come close. Only about 61,000 of the 94,000 seats at the Coliseum would be filled. Fans were urged to move to better seats. One of those fans was a ten-year-old named James Lofton, who would later play in three Super Bowls with the Buffalo Bills.

"You want popcorn or you want a hot dog when you are ten years old," said Lofton. "We sat up pretty high and every quarter, we moved down a little bit. The stadium was only 60 or 65-percent full. By the fourth quarter, we were close to midfield about 20 rows up."

One person who appeared to have similar apathy towards the game was Max McGee. The Green Bay wide receiver was planning on retiring after the game and wasn't expected to see any snaps, so he was more than happy to spend a night on the town the previous evening … and morning. McGee broke curfew with little fear of Lombardi's wrath or the thought of missing playing time.

Green Bay had the first possession of the game, but a pair of sacks by the Chiefs on Quarterback Bart Starr forced the Packers to punt. Kansas City would also be forced to punt on its first possession and Green Bay would take over on its own 20. Early in the drive, a shoulder injury to Green Bay Wide Receiver Boyd Dowler thrust McGee into action. Despite a busy Saturday night on the town, McGee made history as he hauled in a 37-yard touchdown catch from Starr. It was the first score ever in a Super Bowl, and it gave the Packers a 7–0 lead. McGee made the catch by reaching with one hand behind his back before sprinting into the end zone and Robinson said one of the most famous touchdowns in Super Bowl history was actually a mistake.

"He went back to try and knock the ball down so the defender couldn't intercept it," said Robinson. "He said the ball just kind of stuck in his hand and he took it and went in for a touchdown."

While McGee's "mistake" resulted in the first touchdown of the game, it was especially frustrating for Williamson. The Hammer was forced to watch helplessly from the far side of the field as Cornerback Willie Mitchell was beaten on the play.

"Max McGee runs like he's in cement," said Williamson. "He's got concrete on his shoes. He comes in and scores two touchdowns against Willie Mitchell because Willie Mitchell was intimidated. All of a sudden, he's in front of Max McGee, someone he's watched since he was twelve years old."

The Chiefs would tie the game in the second quarter on Dawson's touchdown pass to Curtis McClinton, but the Packers answered on the ensuing drive as Taylor scored the first rushing touchdown in Super Bowl history to put Green Bay up, 14–7. The Chiefs would cut the lead to 14–10 before the half as Dawson moved his team to the Packers' 24. Dawson completed all four of his passes on the drive, which ended on a Mike Mercer field goal. After 30 minutes, the game was far from the blowout that many had predicted. Kramer insists there were no signs of panic in the Green Bay locker room at halftime.

"We were very business-like," said Kramer. "I don't think we were terribly emotional. There were some blocking assignments that had been missed and we were going over a few things, but it isn't funny anymore. We had ourselves a ball game with a hell of a football team. I think we got more serious."

While Dawson was confident heading into the game, he knew the challenge he and his teammates faced going toe-to-toe with Lombardi's Packers. By halftime, Dawson's confidence was rising.

"I felt much better at halftime than I did before the game," Dawson said. "I was in the National Football League for five years. I was well aware of the talent that they had on that football team. At halftime, we felt that we had an excellent chance to put more points on the board."

Meanwhile, The Hammer was not convinced many of his teammates were as confident as their quarterback.

"The heads were down," Williamson said. "I didn't really have a lot of respect for some of the players the way they were talking and the way they were thinking to each other. We had six or seven all-pros on that team. The guys who were all-pros were stand-up guys."

Throughout the history of the Super Bowl, there is often one play in a game which proves to be the most significant. In Super Bowl I, the play came on the opening drive of the second half. Green Bay's Willie Wood intercepted a Dawson pass and returned it 50 yards to the Kansas City 5-yard line. Robinson was one of three hard-charging Packers who rushed Dawson on the errant throw.

"We had shut the run down completely," Robinson said. "We didn't blitz in the first half at all. In the third quarter, every passing situation was a blitz. We felt if we could stop the pass, the game was over."

Elijah Pitts scored on the Packers next play, and the Chiefs would never recover.

"We had to throw the football," said Dawson. "We're leading right into the hands of that great defense that the Packers had."

A second touchdown catch by McGee along with another scoring run by Pitts closed out the scoring in Super Bowl I. To add insult to injury for the Chiefs, Williamson's prediction was reversed as he was knocked out of the game late in the fourth quarter. Williamson was lunging to tackle Green Bay's Donny Anderson, but the running back's knee accidentally caught Williamson on the head. The Hammer had been hammered and Williamson received little sympathy from the Packers.

"Everybody wanted a shot at the Hammer to shut his big mouth up," said Robinson. "Donny Anderson got him, and our bench just erupted in laughter and joy. We didn't really take the Hammer seriously. If he intended to strike fear in the hearts of the Packers, he did exactly the opposite thing."

"I thought it was appropriate," Kramer said. "He was nothing but a big mouth. There were giggles all around."

Williamson considers the injury a freak accident, maintaining he did his job as a defender before getting knocked out.

"I took out Fuzzy Thurston," said Williamson. "Then I went to Donny and I took him out. It was a five-yard loss. Everybody went down. I was the only one who didn't get up because his knee hit me on the helmet and put me to sleep for a minute."

The Packers had lived up to their high expectations for Super Bowl I. Despite a pressure-packed week heading into the game, Lombardi did what he had done so many times in the past. He had his team ready to play football.

"We were a team that really stayed focused," said Taylor. "Lombardi kept us on track on both sides of the ball. We came to play football. We really weren't worried about the papers and all of the clippings."

The defeat would not be easily forgotten by the Chiefs, who would get a chance for redemption in Super Bowl IV. Williamson would not be a part of Kansas City's next Super Bowl team as his time with the Chiefs ended after the following season. Williamson has no regrets about his brash trash talk before Super Bowl I despite the result of the game.

"The hype started there," said Williamson. "I was the Pied Piper. The press followed me around. They came into my hotel room, and I was prepared for that."

While the Chiefs were left to ponder their place in football history, the victorious Packers had upheld the NFL's honor in the league's first meeting with their AFL rivals.

"I think it was a combination of relief and business," said Kramer. "We did our job. We played well. There was a certain relief that we had won the game. It was satisfaction, relief, and a combination of things."

For the Packers, it proved to be just another day at the office and plenty of seats were available for anyone who wanted to see it.

II
THE LAST 30 FOR THE OLD MAN

The real drama of Super Bowl II took place off the field.

Few expected the AFL's Raiders to beat the NFL's Packers. After disposing of the Chiefs in Super Bowl I, Green Bay was a heavy favorite in the second meeting of NFL and AFL champions.

But the Packers were about to lose their soul.

Rumors were running rapid leading up to the game that Packers Coach Vince Lombardi would be coaching his last game on the Packers' sideline. The man who built a dynasty on a snowy NFL outpost in Wisconsin was finishing up one of his most challenging seasons ever. Green Bay was aging and wounded and many thought its number was finally up in 1967. However, the Packers persevered and arrived in Miami for Super Bowl II as three-time NFL champions. It took a herculean effort in the NFL Championship as Green Bay survived both the Cowboys and record cold in the "Ice Bowl" which ended with a dramatic drive for a touchdown in the final minute. Packers Lineman Jerry Kramer still considers the drive the signature moment in Green Bay's dynamic dominance of the 1960's.

"The final drive in the Ice Bowl was probably my finest moment as a football player," said Kramer. "Everybody on the team elevated their performance. There is something about the human spirit that is capable of incredible performance when they make up their mind and are emotionally charged."

Lombardi was the man who drove that emotional spirit in his team and it was hard for anyone in a Green Bay uniform to imagine having any other man as their leader. Yet, the rumors continued to spread about a Lombardi retirement. Kramer and his teammates were looking to keep their focus on the game even though they were well aware of the situation. After a team meeting during the week, one sentence by Lombardi punctuated what many players had feared.

"I felt pretty strongly that this might be his last game," Kramer said. "He goes over the schedule and finishes and walks away from the podium. He stops after about ten steps and turns around and comes back to the podium and he says 'this may be our last time together.'" "I looked at Bart (Starr) and said 'what the hell is this about?'"

Just like the previous Super Bowl, the AFL was given very little chance to win even though the league would, on paper, be well-represented. The Oakland Raiders rolled through the regular season with a 13–1 record and blasted the Houston Oilers, 40–7, in the AFL title game. Oakland appeared to be a worthy opponent for the gritty but aging Packers and several Raiders were eager to prove the AFL belonged on the same field with the NFL's best. The league was still smarting over the Packers' 35–10 win over the Chiefs in Super Bowl I and the Raiders were determined to write a different script in Miami. Oakland Defensive Back Rodger Bird knew the Raiders were confident heading into Super Bowl II, but Bird also knew they would be facing a legendary team on the other side of the field.

"We had a very good football team," said Bird. "We were lucky to have a quarterback like Daryle Lamonica. He led us to the Super Bowl and was a great quarterback. We felt good about our chances but we were up against Green Bay. They were a great team."

Lamonica had certainly done his part leading Oakland to the AFL Championship. The man known as "the Mad Bomber" threw for 3.228 yards and 30 touchdowns during the season. The Raiders Defense was also dominant and featured one of the most feared pass rushes in football.

"We were a physical football team," Bird said. "Most teams in the AFL were very similar. We passed quite a bit. We were very confident."

Despite Oakland's bravado, Green Bay would be more than ready to win its second straight Super Bowl title. After surviving the hell that was the Ice Bowl in their NFL Championship win over the Cowboys, a business trip to sunny Miami was welcomed by many of the Packers.

But Linebacker Dave Robinson said Lombardi made the players aware the trip was indeed about business.

"We still thought it was going to be easy," said Robinson. "That's when Vince came up to us and started getting on us about what could happen. He brought the team back to reality real fast. That was Vince Lombardi. You can't take it easy."

Oakland was still dealing with the stereotype of the AFL being an inferior league. Even Kramer admitted the Packers looked at their two NFL playoff opponents as the tougher foes before they even reached the Super Bowl.

"We thought it was going to be the easier game of the playoffs," Kramer said. "The Rams maybe would be the toughest because they had beaten us a few weeks before. The Cowboys would be next and the Super Bowl would be the easiest of the three."

While the Packers thought less of the Raiders than their NFL opponents, Kramer said there were no issues with motivation by the time they took the field at the Orange Bowl.

"The game itself was businesslike and professional," said Kramer. "You want people to know you're a hell of a football team and you're a hell of an organization. You're playing for your pride and your team and your coach and history. There's enough there to get you emotional and to get you to perform at a high level."

In Super Bowl I, the underdog Chiefs hung tough through the first two quarters before the Packers pulled away in the second half. This time, Green Bay would make quick work of their AFL opponent. The Packers' defense shut down Oakland's offense in the first quarter as they Raiders were forced to punt on their first two drives. Green Bay was able to put points on the board on its first possession as a Don Chandler field goal provided the only points of the first 15 minutes. After Chandler's second field goal early in the second quarter, Green Bay's defense quickly forced a three and out. The Packers got the ball back and needed just one play for the game's first touchdown. Bart Starr connected with Boyd Dowler for a 62-yard scoring pass. It was 13–0 in favor of the NFL Champions and Green Bay appeared ready to run away with Super Bowl II.

"They were doing some shifting," Bird said. "Because of that, they had Boyd Dowler open going down one side. Myself and Howie Williams just failed to pick him up. That was an easy pass for Green Bay."

Oakland would cut the lead to 13–7 on Lamonica's 23-yard touchdown pass to Bill Miller. Just as the Raiders were gaining momentum, a fumble by Bird on a punt set up Chandler's third field goal of the game. The Packers led, 16–7, at halftime and Oakland would never recover.

"I had returned 44 punts that year without dropping one," Bird said. "But all the punters that were kicking were right-footed. When the ball came down, it went the opposite way that I was quite used to."

As the Packers headed into the locker room, they realized they would be playing their last half of football for Vince Lombardi. Jerry Kramer wanted both himself and his teammates to dedicate the last 30 minutes to the man who made the Packers a dynasty.

"Vince would let the captains talk to everyone at halftime," Robinson said. "Jerry Kramer said it in the halftime talk. He said to play the last half for him."

Green Bay finished off Oakland early in the second half. A 35-yard pass to Max McGee set up a two-yard touchdown run by Donny Anderson. Another Chandler field goal put the Packers up, 26–7. Green Bay's defense added a score on Herb Adderley's 60-yard interception return. Lamonica would throw his second touchdown pass of the game to Miller less than two minutes later, but Oakland would get no closer. The Packers' 33–14 victory marked the third straight title for the franchise, with the last two ending in Super Bowl victories for Lombardi.

"He wanted that third consecutive title," Kramer said. "He drove us because that set us apart. That made us a different champion. No one had ever won three in a row. I felt he was the force behind us. He was the emotion. He was the drive. He was the energy. He was the reason we were there."

Several Packers planned to carry their coach off the field after time expired. The defensive captains were hoping to carry out the task, but they still had business to take care of in the closing seconds.

"We talked about carrying him off the field," said Robinson. "But when the game ended, we were on the field because Oakland had the ball when the game ended."

With the Green Bay defense on the field, Kramer and fellow lineman Forrest Gregg literally seized the moment.

"Coach starts to walk of the field after the game is done," said Kramer. "Forrest said 'Jerry, let's grab him.'"

While the Packers carried Lombardi off the field and into football immortality, the Raiders were forced to deal with the AFL's second straight Super Bowl defeat. For Bird, a phone call from the legendary owner of the Raiders would ease the pain of his second quarter fumble.

"Al Davis called me at about two o'clock in the morning," said Bird. "He told me he just wanted to talk to me about the Super Bowl. He said 'I apologize to you for not being aware of the fact that their punter was left-footed. We take all of the responsibility for the fumble of that punt.'" He just wanted to apologize for not having somebody to punt left-footed in our practices. That's the kind of guy he was. He wanted to cross the T's and dot the I's."

Lombardi would step down as head coach shortly after Super Bowl II, but the desire to be on the sidelines returned. Lombardi became the head coach of the Washington Redskins in 1969, but he would never get the chance to build the type of championship team he had in Green Bay. Lombardi died of cancer in 1970.

Kramer and his teammates continued to express their love for Lombardi before and after his death. Kramer recalled an interview with CBS' Tom Brookshier in which he revealed the side of Lombardi which few outside the Green Bay locker room understood.

"People don't know Coach Lombardi," said Kramer. "They don't understand him. They don't know him. We know him. We understand him and we love him. This is a beautiful man."

Shortly after Lombardi's death, the Super Bowl Trophy was renamed "The Vince Lombardi Trophy."

III
THE GAME THAT CHANGED THE GAME

The third edition of the Super Bowl was expected to be another mismatch.

Vince Lombardi's Packers had blown past the AFL's Chiefs and Raiders in the first two Super Bowls. Even with a merger on the horizon, few believed the best from the AFL could stay close with the National Football League champions. The 1968 Baltimore Colts were being hailed by many as one of the greatest teams of all time. Don Shula's squad had rolled through the regular season with a 13–1 record. The lone Baltimore loss came against Cleveland, but the Colts avenged their defeat by walloping the Browns, 34–0, in the NFL Championship game. After freezing the Browns in chilly Cleveland, the Colts were off to sunny Miami for the third edition of the Super Bowl. The event had been anything but super in the first two years and the Colts were an 18-point favorite against the AFL-Champion New York Jets. Players such as Safety Rick Volk admitted it was hard to ignore the lofty predictions heading into Super Bowl III.

"Our team went down for that Super Bowl and it was just going to be more of a fun-type week," said Volk. "But this was Super Bowl III. We were favored to win by a lot, so I don't think we were focused on what we were really there for. We were thinking more about where we were going to go to dinner and who we were going to eat with more than the New York Jets."

One Colt who never lost his focus was Linebacker Mike Curtis. The man known as "Mad Dog" was one of the most ferocious players of his era, but even Curtis understood why it would have been easy to get caught up in the notion that the AFL champs did not belong on the same field as the NFL representative.

"I think so," said Curtis. "The Jets, in a different league, did not look as good as we were."

The Jets didn't exactly storm through the 1968 season. New York finished 11–3, with one of their losses coming against last-place Buffalo. However, Quarterback Joe Namath and his teammates rallied at the end of the season and came away with a hard-fought victory over Oakland in the AFC title game. The Jets were on their way to the Super Bowl, but were viewed as uninvited guests to the Colts coronation. New York Cornerback Randy Beverly could feel the lack of respect from the rival league.

"They had always looked down upon our league," said Beverly. "But what had happened was our league became the league that people wanted to watch because of our scoring. We didn't have any boring games. They were all high-scoring, exciting games and the fan base was starting to look our way."

As the two teams prepared for Super Bowl III, the Jets were hardly interested in the pregame predictions. The AFL representatives continued to watch film on the Colts and Namath believed his team's short passing game coupled with the chance to run at the softer right side of the Baltimore front line was a formula for success. Meanwhile, the New York Defense was not expecting to see Johnny Unitas. The legendary quarterback was sidelined in the preseason with an injury and Shula had turned to Earl Morrall to guide the offense. Morrall played well throughout the season and Shula did not see any reason to make a change due to the team's success.

Beverly and the rest of the Jets weren't as impressed as the rest of the football world.

"We never thought that they were great from an offensive standpoint," said Beverly. "We saw a lot of flaws. We didn't see any speed, and that's the one thing we had in our league."

The Jets kept their confidence to themselves until three days before kickoff. Namath was at the Miami Touchdown Club and one inebriated Colts fan was happy to remind the New York Quarterback how badly the Colts were going to beat the Jets on Sunday. After hearing all week how his team had no chance, Namath had heard enough. He shot back at the fan by guaranteeing the Jets would win the game. Namath's guarantee would go public the next day, but the Colts insist they did not need Namath's brash prediction for motivation.

"We just thought that was Joe Namath's background," Curtis said. "I can't imagine he'd say we would beat them. I think he was saying they were going to work hard enough to beat us."

"We just sort of brushed it off as Joe Namath spouting off," Volk said. "We weren't really concerned about it. We didn't like the way he was spouting off and mouthing off, but that was Joe. He was confident they could do it. He didn't have anything to lose."

Namath's guarantee was not well received by Jets Head Coach Weeb Ewbank, who believed the last thing the Colts needed was bulletin board material. However, Beverly and the rest of Namath's teammates felt a sense of relief after hearing about the quarterback's guarantee.

"We were all mumbling pretty much to ourselves the same thing that Joe said," Beverly said. "It's just that none of us could say that, but Joe could. We all felt the same exact way and we said 'Way to go, Joe.'"

Namath had plenty to prove as the Jets took the field for Super Bowl III. The Jets' signal caller had thrown more interceptions (17) than touchdowns (15) during the season. Now, his reputation was on the line against one of the most powerful teams in football history. Namath's guarantee also generated an interest in the Super Bowl, which had been lacking in the first two championship games. It was the birth of true Super Bowl hype.

Namath and his teammates did not get off to a fast start. After the Jets were forced to punt on their opening series, Morrall quickly moved his offense deep into Jets territory. The drive stalled and Lou Michaels came on to attempt a 27-yard field goal. With his brother, Walt, watching from the opposing sideline as an assistant coach with the Jets, Michaels pushed his attempt wide to the right.

It would be an omen for what was to come for the Colts.

Late in the first quarter, the Colts recovered a fumble on the Jets 12-yard line. On the third play of the second quarter, Morrall's pass bounced high into the air off the shoulder pads of Tom Mitchell and was intercepted in the end zone by Beverly.

"It deflected just enough that Mitchell couldn't get his hands up quick enough to pull the ball in," said Beverly. "It actually hit his shoulder pads then it popped up. From that moment on, I was just tracking the ball and trying to find it."

Baltimore had twice been denied scoring opportunities deep in Jets territory. The game was still scoreless, but Beverly could begin to see frustration settling in for the Colts as the second quarter progressed.

"We felt their frustration," Beverly said. "What they didn't feel, we were telling them on the field. In the open field, they were moving the ball. Once they got down in the red zone, our defense stiffened up. We knew how to play with our backs against the wall."

Baltimore's Sam Ball had been part of an offense that had moved the ball effectively throughout the opening quarter. The right tackle was already getting the feeling that the Football Gods were not in the Colts' corner that afternoon.

"We got inside the red zone," Ball said. "We could not make the scoreboard light up. Michaels missed field goals and Earl Morrall hit guys right in the chest and the ball bounced up in the air."

The Colts had been denied twice. Now, it was New York's turn. Namath led the Jets on a 12-play, 80-yard drive. Matt Snell gave the AFL its first ever Super Bowl lead with a four-yard run as the Jets went ahead, 7–0.

"We weren't chasing anymore," Beverly said. "We were now in protection mode, and we played a lot looser. We weren't uptight. Now, let's continue on and let's give the ball back to Joe."

While many of the Colts were stunned, Volk was dazed for a different reason. As a result, the safety was a step late pursuing Snell as the New York running back ran towards the end zone.

"Matt Snell dazed me and I went out of the game for a while," Volk said. "I came back in and played, but I wasn't really playing my game. I didn't really know what was going on too well. I was sort of out of it."

On the ensuing drive, Baltimore blew another scoring opportunity as Michaels missed again from 46-yards out. The Colts had another chance on their next drive, but Morrall was intercepted on the Jets two-yard line by Johnny Sample. The Colts had one more chance in the final seconds of the half after reaching the Jets 41-yard line.

The Colts called a trick play that had worked during the regular season. Morrall handed off to Tom Matte, who ran right before passing it back to his quarterback. Morrall was supposed to throw the ball to Jimmy Orr near the end zone. Orr was wide open for what would have been an easy touchdown, but the quarterback did not see Orr. Morrall instead threw over the middle in the direction of Jerry Hill. Jim Hudson came up with New York's third interception of the half and the jubilant Jets went to the locker room with a 7–0 lead. Meanwhile, the Colts had squandered five scoring chances in the first half.

Morrall's decision to not throw to Orr is still puzzling to this day. Some believe Morrall did not see Orr because of the Florida A&M Band. The band was standing behind the end zone getting ready for the halftime show and the band's blue uniforms could have camouflaged Orr from Morrall's view. It mattered little at the time as the Colts had squandered their best scoring opportunity of the game.

"Earl was supposed to throw it to Jimmy Orr," Ball said. "The only one close to Jimmy was the tuba player. He threw it across the field to Jerry Hill and they intercepted that ball. We just couldn't grab our ass with both hands offensively as far as getting on the board."

"I knew Jimmy was behind me," said Beverly. "He passed me in order to get to where he was. I didn't believe he could throw the ball that far. We were kind of baiting him in and trying to figure out if he could throw it that far. We watched the guy in warm-ups and we watched him on film. With a couple of the passes, you could actually read 'Duke' on the ball."

While the New York offense had only scored once, Namath was frustrating Baltimore with Ewbank's strong game plan. Namath's quick passes had offset the Baltimore blitz and the ability to run to the right side of the Colts' defensive front was paying dividends. The runs to the right also meant the Jets were running away from Curtis and talented Defensive Lineman Bubba Smith.

"I eventually drifted off the line more towards the middle so I could pursue the running back," Curtis said. "We were stronger on our left side than we were our right side."

"They probably wanted to get rid of the ball a little quicker," said Volk. "We had a pretty good defense with our front four. They controlled the ball running and throwing and we really couldn't do much. They had us off-guard. They were just one step ahead of us."

The Jets had the momentum to start the second half and Namath and Company would completely control the third quarter. The Colts received the opening kickoff, but Matte fumbled on the first play from scrimmage. A 32-yard field goal by Jim Turner made the score 10–0, and the Jets would hold the ball for twelve of the fifteen minutes of the period.

"I think that was very important," Beverly said. "We were used to playing high-powered offenses. Conditioning was excellent. I think that we were in better shape than they were. They were breathing heavy. A lot of that is frustration and not focusing on what they were doing. They were making a lot of mental mistakes."

The frustration began to grow for the Colts, who entered the final period trailing, 13–0, after another Turner field goal.

"They were in the hole and they realized that and were very frustrated," said Beverly. "They were talking to themselves. We were watching them and following them around. They were just kind of arguing amongst themselves and so we knew we had them. Once a team starts to argue player to player, you know there's something wrong."

Desperate for a spark, Shula replaced Morrall with Unitas late in the third quarter. Unitas could not move the Colts on his first drive and another Turner field goal early in the fourth quarter increased New York's lead to 16–0.

"I had always wanted to play against him," said Beverly. "When he came in, I said now is my opportunity. It was something I had wanted to do for a long time. I was excited that he was coming in because I wanted to play against him."

Unitas' second drive ended with another big play in the end zone by Beverly. The cornerback stepped in front of Orr and had his second interception of Super Bowl III.

"It was kind of a bait situation," Recalled Beverly. "I knew his arm wasn't the arm that is was at one time where he could pinpoint it and get it where he wanted it. He laid it out in front of the receiver so that he could run under it. He couldn't throw that bullet right into his chest. That gave me the opportunity to just come underneath and cut in front."

Unitas was finally able to move his offense, but only after another long drive by Namath and company chewed more time off the clock. Baltimore's Jerry Hill scored from 1-yard out to cap off a 14-play, 80-yard drive. The Colts were finally on the board but still trailed, 16–7.

"We had always been able to come back," said Volk. "Whenever you had

Johnny U on your team, you always felt that if you were down, you were going to come back and win. I think we were still confident we were going to win the game."

But time was on the side of the Jets, who were 3:19 away from pro football immortality. The Colts were given one last reprieve as they recovered an onside kick and Unitas trotted back onto the field. Johnny U completed three straight passes as Baltimore moved to the New York 19, but followed with three incompletions to set up a fourth down. With time running out and his kicker struggling throughout the day, Shula elected to go for the first down. Unitas' pass sailed towards the far left corner of the end zone, but there was double coverage on Orr. The ball landed well past the Baltimore receiver and New York took over with 2:21 to play. The Jets were able to kill most of the clock before punting to the Colts with eight seconds left. When the final seconds ticked away, the Jets as well as the entire AFL erupted in a jubilant celebration.

"We were such underdogs," Beverly said. "No one thought of us winning the game. We just said 'Wow, it's over and we won. We're the champions.' It didn't hit until about two weeks after we got back home. We started reading the newspapers and people started calling."

Super Bowl III was much more than a New York Jets victory. It had given the AFL its first chance to claim equality with the NFL as the merger between the two leagues drew closer. It also was, in many ways, the birth of the Super Bowl as it is known today. Between the media attention leading up to the game and the significance of New York's win, pro football and its biggest game had changed forever.

"We can say that we are the reason that the league did come together," Beverly said. "We were the pioneers that I think brought football to the point of where it is today."

It was a different story in Baltimore, the victims of one of the greatest upsets in sports history.

"I was so tired," said Ball. "I gave every ounce of energy in my body to help us win, and I was so embarrassed. The invincible Baltimore Colts had beaten Cleveland, 34–0, in Cleveland and then we go down and lose to an AFL team."

Baltimore would go on to win Super Bowl V, but it would prove to be a consolation prize after the humiliation of Super Bowl III. Despite having a team that many believed was ready to take its place among the game's all-time best, the Colts are still forced to relive their Super Bowl III nightmare on a regular basis.

"I don't want to get into losing the Super Bowl," Curtis said. "It's not a relaxing thought."

The Jets spent the following season being treated as conquering heroes throughout the AFL. They were congratulated by their opponents as their place in pro football history grew larger each season. Even today, new generations of fans have learned about "The Guarantee" and how on one Sunday in Miami, the rebels from the AFL became world champions.

"To be a part of history is really outstanding," said Beverly. "I love it. Usually, the two weeks prior to the game, they'll show my highlights every once in a while. Even though I'm not in a game, I'm still there."

IV
THE AFL GETS EVEN

The war between the leagues was about to end.

After making peace with the AFL in 1966 and agreeing to a merger, the NFL was ready for a new era. The merger with the AFL would be complete at the end of the 1969 season and the AFL and NFL would become one league.

But the AFL still had one more game to play.

Super Bowl IV would take place in New Orleans, with the Kansas City Chiefs representing the AFL in its final game. The Chiefs were not only motivated to win a world championship and pull the AFL even with the NFL, but they were also looking for redemption. Three years earlier, the Chiefs left the field at Super Bowl I bruised and beaten. It would be a wound that remained fresh as Kansas City prepared for Super Bowl IV thanks largely to the words of former Packers Coach Vince Lombardi. After Green Bay's victory in Super Bowl I, Lombardi said the Chiefs were a tough football team but didn't compare with the teams in the NFL. Lombardi's words were still in the minds of many Chiefs before Super Bowl IV.

Quarterback Len Dawson never forgot.

"A lot of the guys were really upset about it," said Dawson. "They didn't forget it. They kept bringing it up after that game and at Super Bowl IV as well. We were in the game for a while, but we got another shot."

The Minnesota Vikings would be the NFL's representative. Despite the Jets' victory over the Colts in Super Bowl III, many still considered the AFL inferior to the NFL. Thus, the Vikings, led by their talented front four on defense and Quarterback Joe Kapp were a huge favorite. However, players such as defensive lineman Jim Marshall insist they did not take the Chiefs lightly heading into the contest.

"Absolutely not," said Marshall. "We looked at it as football. It doesn't make any difference what league or what division that you're in. You know you have to go out and do your best."

The Chiefs didn't need any extra motivation, but their quarterback needed to get past another round of adversity. Dawson had already dealt with both a knee injury and the death of his father during the season. The week of the Super Bowl, a report surfaced tying Dawson to a federal gambling investigation in Detroit. The quarterback would be cleared of any wrongdoing, and Dawson insists he was able to deal with the distraction despite facing questions about his innocence throughout the week.

"I didn't do anything wrong," Dawson said. "So I slept all right all week long. I didn't put that in my mind because I had a job to do. I couldn't have a lousy game because people would say 'maybe it's true about him.' I was all right. My teammates knew I was all right. There was nothing to it, so we just went about our business getting ready for that football game."

The Chiefs were a confident group as they prepared to face the best the NFL had to offer. Kansas City Coach Hank Stram was one of the most innovative coaches of his time. An offense filled with multiple formations coupled with a defense that featured five future Hall of Famers was about to hit the Vikings with something they had never seen in the NFL. Kansas City Linebacker Jim Lynch couldn't wait to get a crack at the NFL champion.

"There was a definite confidence," said Lynch. "I felt like we had a big advantage going into that game from a defensive standpoint."

Dawson roomed on the road with Safety Johnny Robinson. After a week of film session and preparation, Robinson made it clear to his roommate the defense would take care of business against the Vikings.

"He said he had looked at the film all week long," Dawson said. "And he said 'we might shut them out.' To me, that really helped knowing I could make a mistake but that the defense could overcome that."

Dawson was also salivating at the chance to put the creative Kansas City offense on the field against the famed "Purple People Eaters."

"I couldn't wait," said Dawson.

Before the Chiefs and Vikings took the field, the pregame festivities featured an ominous sign for Minnesota. A hot air balloon with a Viking mascot fizzled and crashed into the stands. It would signal how the day would go for Minnesota on the field. The Vikings barely got off the ground.

The game began to take shape in the opening quarter. After forcing the Vikings to punt on the opening drive, the Chiefs took the lead on a 48-yard field goal by Jan Stenerud. The soccer-style placekicker with the booming leg was the type of weapon rarely seen in the early days of the Super Bowl and Dawson saw a look of bewilderment from the Vikings when Stenerud connected from long distance.

"I looked at the sideline of Minnesota," Dawson said. "And they were like 'what's this?' That was a big plus for us to know we had a kicker that could make big kicks. He was a real weapon."

Stenerud would add two more field goals in the second quarter to increase Kansas City's lead. After Stenerud's third field goal, Minnesota's Charlie West fumbled the ensuing kickoff, and the Chiefs recovered on the Minnesota 19-yard line. Five plays later, Stram called for a "65 toss power trap," and Mike Garrett rushed into the end zone from five yards out.

The Chiefs led, 16–0, at halftime. Their defense was equally impressive as they held the Vikings to 24 yards on the ground over the first two quarters. Minnesota had also failed to convert a third down in the first half and Lynch could sense Minnesota was already on the verge of extinction.

"The game was going according to schedule," said Lynch. "They kind of came up against an immovable object. We're up 16–0. I'm not saying there was a celebration in the locker room at halftime by any stretch of the imagination, but it was certainly going about the way we thought it was going to go from a defensive standpoint."

Marshall insists the Vikings were ready for the multiple looks from the Kansas City offense, but simply couldn't find a way to stop the Chiefs.

"I think we were very well prepared for it in practice," said Marshall. "We knew pretty much what they were going to do, but they executed very well. We couldn't overcome their offense like we wanted to."

The Vikings finally got on track at the start of the third quarter. After forcing the Chiefs to punt, Kapp led Minnesota on a 10-play, 69-yard drive capped off by a Dave Osborn touchdown run. However, it took just one series for the Chiefs to respond and put the game away. Kansas City took the ball on the ensuing possession and marched to the Minnesota 46-yard line. Dawson hit Otis Taylor on a short pass and Taylor broke through Earsell Mackbee's attempted tackle and raced into the end zone to put the Chiefs up, 23–7. Kansas City was in command and Dawson knew the Vikings' chances to rally against the Chiefs' Defense were extremely remote.

"I didn't think there was any way," Dawson said. "Not with the people that we had. Once they're falling behind and they've got to throw all of the time, then that plays right into the hands of our defense."

Meanwhile, Dawson and Company continued to frustrate the Minnesota Defense. Marshall and his defensive linemates faced a host of double teams and Dawson was picking apart the Minnesota secondary with his short passing game.

"There was a lot of that," Marshall said. "We certainly didn't do as well as we wanted to do. It just happened to be one of those situations that we couldn't overcome."

The rest of the half only furthered the nightmare for Minnesota. The punishing Kansas City defense gave Kapp the biggest beating of his career and eventually sent him to the sidelines with a shoulder injury.

"The Minnesota Vikings had great football players and were a great team," Lynch said. "Kapp was really a tough guy. Arron Brown had one of the best games he ever had. He wound up doing the damage to Joe Kapp."

All that was left was for the Chiefs to run out the clock. Much to the surprise of many of the football "experts," the Chiefs had dominated the team from the supposedly superior league.

"I certainly don't think we were surprised that we won the game," said Lynch. "I think we had a real satisfaction with the fact that we did win the game. There was a quiet confidence that we had."

For the Vikings, it would be the first of four Super Bowl defeats over the next eight years. Marshall would see more of the NFL's greatest defenses in the coming seasons and had plenty of praise for the defense he watched from the opposing sideline in Super Bowl IV.

"I had a great deal of respect for them," said Marshall. "I had even more after that game. They played very well."

In the midst of the wild celebration in the cramped Kansas City locker room, Dawson was informed he had a phone call from the president.

"My response was 'the president of what?'" Dawson said. "He said it was the President of the United States. I did have the opportunity to talk to him. I didn't know he was such a great football fan."

The call from President Nixon concluded a remarkable day for Dawson, who was named the game's MVP. The Chiefs were world champions on the day the AFL ceased to exist.

"We were the stupid stepchild of professional football for several years," said Dawson. "It was the NFL that was really the real professional football. When that ended with the four Super Bowl games, it was 2–2. After that, we were on an equal basis with the National Football League."

V
O'BRIEN KICKS THE COWBOYS

Jim O'Brien was not a big fan of artificial turf.

The Baltimore Colts kicker had struggled kicking on the plastic surface during the regular season. O'Brien and the Colts would take the turf at the Orange Bowl to battle the Dallas Cowboys in Super Bowl V, and the rookie was hoping it wouldn't come down to a last-second field goal try.

"It was pretty marginal compared to today's true turf and all the other surfaces they have," said O'Brien. We didn't practice on it, we didn't kick on it and we didn't play on it. Houston, New England and Miami were the only teams we played that had artificial turf."

O'Brien was hardly the center of attention heading to the first Super Bowl since the NFL-AFL merger. Baltimore was one of three teams which agreed to move to the newly formed AFC made up largely of former American Football League squads, so this would be the first Super Bowl without an original AFL team. Super Bowl V was also about redemption. The Colts were back in the championship game just two years after being stunned by the Jets in Super Bowl III. Some thought a victory over Dallas would wipe away the memory of the loss to New York, but many Colts such as Linebacker Mike Curtis admitted Super Bowl III was a scar which would never completely fade away.

"Not really," said Curtis. "It's a whole different story. We lost when we were a lot stronger. It doesn't heal the wound from a game that you should have won hands down."

The Cowboys had little sympathy for Baltimore. Dallas had been one of the most successful NFL franchises in the years leading up to this Super Bowl, but earned a reputation of being "Next Year's Champions" by coming up short in the post-season. The Cowboys had narrowly lost to Green Bay in the 1966 and 1967 NFL Championship games, and also lost playoff games to Cleveland in 1968 and 1969.

Defensive Lineman Bob Lilly had lived through every playoff disappointment. Lilly and his teammates were determined to write a different ending in Super Bowl V, but the Cowboys almost wore themselves out with a week of intense practices before heading down to Miami.

"We went out that first week and tried to kill each other on the practice field," Lilly said. "By the time we went down to Miami, we were tired. We'd already given it all we got in practice."

While the Super Bowl was still in its infancy, there was still plenty of hype heading into Super Bowl V. The Colts had experienced the outside distractions heading into a Super Bowl. Lilly and the Cowboys got their first taste of it in Miami.

"We prepared really well," said Lilly. "We were not prepared for all the phone calls and all the people that wanted tickets and who came by the hotel and knocked on your room. We had no security."

There was no denying the pressure felt by both sides. A loss by Dallas would add to the excruciating list of post-season failures. A defeat for Baltimore would leave the Colts as losers of two of the first five Super Bowls. Baltimore Safety Rick Volk knew what was at stake in Miami.

"There's pressure on you in that game," Volk said. "We had been there before and they hadn't been there before. They had that going against them a little bit. We had some pressure because we had lost before, and now we needed to win it. This might have been our last chance."

One player who knew it would be his last chance was Baltimore's Sam

Ball. The offensive lineman had little left to give other than his heart due to a host of injuries. Ball had been relegated to backup duty after entering the season as a starter, and the veteran knew his body could not take another season of football.

"I tore cartilages in both knees," said Ball. "I tell people it was probably the most courageous year of my career. With my right cartilage, I heard it pop against the Oakland Raiders. Against the Denver Broncos, my own guard ran into me and I hurt my left knee. My ankles were shot, too."

The Colts and Cowboys both hoped to put together a dominating performance to erase their past failures. Instead, Super Bowl V became a carnival of errors, with the two teams combining for a record eleven turnovers. The first came on the Colts' second possession. Cowboys Linebacker Chuck Howley intercepted a Johnny Unitas pass and returned the ball to the Baltimore 46-yard line. The Cowboys were forced to punt, but a fumble by Ron Gardin set up a Dallas field goal by Mike Clark. Another field goal by Clark at the start of the second period made it 6–0, but the Colts would pull even on their next possession. A 75-yard pass to John Mackey tied the game at six, but it was a controversial score for Baltimore. The pass to Mackey was first tipped by Baltimore's Eddie Hinton. The ball then glanced off the fingertips of Dallas Defensive Back Mel Renfro and into the hands of Mackey. The pass would have been nullified if Renfro had not touched it, since one offensive player could not touch a pass that went to another without a defender also making contact with the ball.

"It was a fluke play," Volk said. "But it was good for us. The refs made the right call. Mel Renfro happened to just tip it. You see the ball flutter. It was legal and it was the right call."

O'Brien's extra point was blocked, and the Cowboys looked to quickly recover from what they felt was a questionable call on the Mackey touchdown.

"Mel Renfro was in the vicinity," said Lilly. "As far as we could tell looking at the play, he didn't come within six to eight inches of the ball. They gave them the touchdown, but we were still playing with them and our offense finally started moving the ball a little bit."

A Unitas fumble in the second quarter set up Dallas' first touchdown drive. Duane Thomas hauled in a seven-yard touchdown pass from Craig Morton, and the Cowboys led, 13–6. Unitas was knocked out of the game on the ensuing drive with a rib injury while throwing an interception, so the Colts would turn to Earl Morrall to lead the way the rest of the game. Morrall received much of the blame for Baltimore's loss in Super Bowl III, so the Colts were happy to see their popular teammate get a second chance.

"Earl Morrall was a great guy," said Curtis. "Everybody liked him. There wasn't any letdown, that's for sure. In practice, he would be just perfect. He was also a good guy because he never criticized anybody on the team."

On the other side of the ball, the Dallas Defense had to adjust on the fly with the arrival of Morrall.

"We knew he was a pretty good quarterback," said Lilly. "But I think he was a little hotter than John. Maybe it was because we were watching films with John. Earl was a little bit different quarterback. I think it changed the tone of the game a little bit."

In keeping with the tone of the contest, the Colts fumbled the opening kickoff of the second half. The Cowboys were poised to put the game away as they moved the ball to the Baltimore one-yard line. However, Thomas was hit by Curtis and fumbled just short of the goal line. The Colts recovered, and players on both sides believe it may have been Dallas' day if Thomas had reached the end zone.

"I think so," Lilly said. "I think so because our defense was that good. We could have probably settled into a running game and not thrown the ball quite as much, but that's football. You never know for sure."

But did the Colts recover the fumble? The first player to emerge from the pile with the ball was a Cowboy.

"Dave Manders covered the ball and they gave the ball to them," Lilly said. "That wasn't one of those plays where there was any question about it, but it's the way it worked out."

Morrall's quest for redemption hit a roadblock early in the fourth quarter. Another Howley interception in the end zone to start the final period denied the Colts a chance to tie the game. Morrall would move the Colts into Dallas territory on his next drive, but a fumble by Hinton rolled into the end zone for a touchback. It was the seventh turnover of the game for Baltimore, but a Dallas miscue three plays later would open the door for the Colts. Morton was intercepted by Volk, who raced 30 yards to the Dallas three-yard line.

"I just happened to be there," Volk said. "Craig had to get it over Roy Hilton's hands. You've got to make that play, which I was able to do. Ted Hendricks was in my way and I had to hurdle over him. I started going towards the pylon."

Tom Nowatzke scored on a 2-yard run, and O'Brien's second try at an extra point tied the game at 13–13 with 7:35 remaining.

"I stopped thinking about missing," O'Brien said. "I just concentrated. I was really nervous on the first extra point. It caused me to be a little slow starting my routine. Somebody got through the one side prematurely as well. Usually, when you start thinking about it, it's not going to be a good thing."

The final mistake of the game proved to be fatal for Dallas. Curtis intercepted Morton with just over a minute remaining and returned the ball to the Cowboys' 28-yard line. Two plays later, O'Brien came onto the field to attempt a 32-yard field goal. Nine seconds remained on the clock.

"Everybody asks what I was thinking," said O'Brien. "To be honest with you, I was thinking about keeping my head down. Then, I just kind of went blank. I concentrated probably more on that kick than I had anything in my whole life."

While O'Brien was focusing, his teammates were asking for help from a higher power.

"I was like everybody else on the sidelines praying," said Ball. "I was saying 'C'mon, Lord, we lost one of these already. Let him kick it.'"

Snapper Tom Goode sent the ball to Morrall, who placed the ball down perfectly for O'Brien. The rookie blasted the kick through the uprights, and the Colts were World Champions.

"He knocked that through straight as an arrow," Recalled Volk.

"Thank God I made it," O'Brien said. "It was a lot of pressure. Luckily at the time, I had Earl Morrall to calm me down. He said 'just pop it' and that's what I did, and it worked out well."

The kick set off a celebration for the Colts, while the Cowboys had again fallen short in the biggest game of the year. Lilly vented his frustration by tossing his helmet across the field after O'Brien's kick.

"That's when I set one of my Super Bowl records with a 44-yard helmet toss," Quipped Lilly. "I'd really never done anything like that before or since. One of the young Baltimore Colts brought my helmet over. I said, 'Young man, I'm sorry I did that. It was a poor example.' He said 'I don't blame you.'"

Despite the victory, many Colts believe the loss in Super Bowl III still overshadows the result of Super Bowl V. However, Volk believes the emotional pain would have been much greater with a loss to the Cowboys.

"We were able to come back and win Super Bowl V," said Volk. "If we had lost that game, then these two games would have been bad. By being able to win Super Bowl V, we sort of redeemed ourselves. It made the Jet loss more acceptable."

The win would be the last championship for the Colts in Baltimore. It was also the end for Ball, who had played his last game in the NFL.

"I couldn't believe the good lord let us play for the Super Bowl one more time in my life," said Ball. "George Blanda played for 16 years and never won a Super Bowl. I was elated that we won, but I knew when I got on the bus that it was the last time I'd put a helmet on."

For Dallas, it was another year of coming up short. Lilly and the Cowboys were "Next Year's Champions" yet again.

"It was devastating because we were a pretty good team that year," Lilly said. "It's just a shame, but we got over it."

Meanwhile, O'Brien never gets tired of seeing his game-winning kick.

"It puts a smile on my face," O'Brien said. "I do enjoy it. It's fun to see it. It's history."

VI

THIS YEAR'S CHAMPIONS

Before they were America's Team, they were Next Year's Champions.

After struggling through the early years of expansion, the Dallas Cowboys had emerged as perennial contenders. However, the Cowboys could never win the one game that mattered most.

Dallas' brief history was littered with championship failures, including two close losses to Green Bay in back-to-back NFL title games. In January of 1971, the Cowboys took the field for Super Bowl V, but watched Jim O'Brien's kick sail through the uprights in the closing seconds to give Baltimore the victory. As the 1971 season progressed, the Cowboys did not appear to be Super Bowl bound. Dallas started the season at 4–3 and embroiled in a quarterback controversy. However, Tom Landry made Roger Staubach his permanent starter in Week 8 and sent Craig Morton to the bench.

"The team really got divided," said Staubach. "Craig Morton was really a good quarterback, and I was coming into my own. Something had to be done as far as telling the team who the quarterback was. Fortunately, I got that opportunity."

Calvin Hill was one of three talented runners in the Dallas backfield. For Hill, the naming of Staubach as the starter provided relief for both himself and his teammates.

"There were guys who were for Roger and there were guys who were for Craig," said Hill. "I think the biggest thing was we finally settled on one guy."

Dallas won its final seven regular season games and advanced to Super Bowl VI. The Cowboys would get yet another chance to erase their painful past, and the upstart Miami Dolphins were standing in their way. Former Colts Coach Don Shula took over a franchise that had struggled since its AFL expansion days. It took Shula just two years to lead the Dolphins to Super Sunday, and the coach with the iron jaw would get his second chance at a title after watching the Jets upset his Colts three years earlier.

Larry Little was part of a Miami offensive line that was quickly becoming one of the best in the NFL, but he soon realized the Cowboys were better prepared to deal with the Super Bowl spotlight.

"We were still a young football team," said Little. "We were very happy to be playing in a Super Bowl. They had lost the year before. They were Super Bowl-worn and we were not."

Miami's Paul Warfield also knew experience would be a factor in Super Bowl VI. The wide receiver had done plenty of playoff damage to Dallas during his days in Cleveland, but Warfield and his Dolphin teammates were getting their first taste of Super Bowl hype.

"The Super Bowl is so overwhelming," said Warfield. "Even in its infancy years of Super Bowl VI, it was still a big game. By that time, it was built as the biggest game. A team that's there for the first time and does not have a tradition of great winning and not experienced is most apt to lose."

The Cowboys took a far different approach to their Super Bowl preparation than the previous year. Landry gave the team more days off leading up to the game, and Dallas' Bob Lilly knew he would deal with fewer distractions in New Orleans than he did in Miami a year ago.

"We had security at the hotel," Lilly said. "They turned the telephones off at ten o'clock. That was before cell phones, so we didn't have any problem with that."

"We had been to the Super Bowl the year before," Hill said. "We knew how to act during that week. We had been through that. We accepted it and knew how to handle it."

Even with a different approach, there was still the matter of taking care of business on the field, and Lilly knew the Dolphins were a dangerous opponent despite their lack of Super Bowl experience.

"The Dolphins were awesome on film," said Lilly. "We actually were in awe of their running game and their power and their speed. Their offensive line was great, and although they called their defense the No Name Defense, it was a great defense."

Staubach had earned his chance to lead the Cowboys into this Super Bowl, but the quarterback knew what was a stake for both himself and the franchise. After waiting his turn behind Morton, Staubach was now being entrusted to take the helm of a team which had spent much of its years with Don Meredith under center.

"I was a nervous wreck," Staubach said. "I did feel like I was quarterbacking Meredith's team. I didn't sleep at all the night before."

Cliff Harris was playing in just his second season with the Cowboys. The safety remembers the sense of determination by his veteran teammates who weren't about to let another championship opportunity slip away.

"We came into it with a real calm mind but with a lot of intensity," Recalled Harris. "That was brought to us by all the years of playoffs the

Cowboys had been beaten. I think there was a maturity of that group that didn't get overwhelmed."

While much would be made of the NFL's "Cold Weather Super Bowl" in January of 2014, there was quite a chill in the air in New Orleans for Super Bowl VI. The temperature at kickoff was 39 degrees, but it was a cold start for the offenses on both sides. Neither team could generate a scoring drive on their first possessions. On Miami's second opportunity, the Dolphins moved towards midfield, but Running Back Larry Csonka gave up his first fumble of the season. The Cowboys recovered at their own 48-yard line, and the tone was set for Super Bowl VI. Miami Safety Dick Anderson admitted a Csonka fumble was something the Dolphins did not expect to happen in the Super Bowl.

"I don't think it changed our mental attitude at all," Anderson said. "But when Csonka doesn't fumble ever and he starts off the game that way, it certainly wasn't the kind of start you would like in the Super Bowl. Deep down, maybe it took some wind out of our sails."

"I think that might have set the tone a little bit," Lilly said.

The Cowboys turned the fumble into a field goal and an early 3–0 lead, but it could have easily been 7–0 as Staubach threw short to Duane Thomas on third and goal instead of finding an open Mike Ditka in the end zone.

"Ditka was wide open," Recalled Staubach. "He came over and started yelling and chewing me out for not throwing the ball to him. The next series, he dropped pass over the middle. He came back to the huddle and I said 'nice catch, Mike.'"

The Dolphins would continue to go backwards as Bob Griese was sacked for a 29-yard loss on the next possession by Lilly. It was the longest negative play in Super Bowl history.

"You could see the resolve Bob Lilly had," Harris said. "You saw the intensity he had going after Griese. He would not let him escape. It certainly set a tempo for us."

Late in the second period, Dallas drove 76-yards on nine plays. Staubach found Lance Alworth from seven yards out, and the Cowboys increased their lead to 10–0.

"The first touchdown thrown to Allworth was one of the biggest thrills I've ever had," said Staubach.

The Dolphins would mount a late drive in the closing seconds of the half, and Garo Yepremian's field goal cut the Dallas lead to seven at halftime. The Cowboys had dominated the first half, but headed to the locker room with a slim seven-point lead.

"You should be relieved," said Anderson. "I just know that we were still in the game. Being down only by seven having not played very well in the first half, we still had the confidence we could go out and win the game."

The Cowboys put together a championship drive to start the second half. Dallas went 71 yards on eight plays, with seven coming on the ground. The last came from Thomas from three yards out to push the Dallas lead to 17–3.

"We had an excellent game plan," said Staubach. "They didn't change a whole lot. We could have thrown the ball more, but our running game was so good. The running game kept the defense off the field, and our defense was ready to play."

The Dallas Defense continued to frustrate Miami in the second half. It was a particularly difficult day for Warfield, who was stifled by a unique game plan by the Cowboys. Cornerback Mel Renfro blanketed Warfield on the outside, while Safety Cornell Green shadowed the shifty receiver when he lined up inside.

"It was an interesting scheme," Warfield said. "Tom Landry was a defensive genius. He used that genius to become innovative in so many respects. We were not in a position as a young football team to make the necessary adjustments. What they did in that ball game with their coverage scheme made it very difficult for us to have any success throwing the football."

Still, the Cowboys were in no mood to put the champagne on ice. They had been to the altar before only to come away empty when victory was within reach. Midway through the fourth quarter, a Chuck Howley interception return put the Cowboys on the Miami nine-yard line. This time, Staubach found Ditka in the end zone from seven yards out. Dallas led, 24–3, with 11:42 remaining, and the long wait for a championship was finally about to end for Lilly and his teammates.

"There was no sense of comfort until the very end," said Lilly. "We started getting a little bit giddy toward the end when we knew we had it."

The Cowboys put together another long drive, which chewed up much of the fourth quarter clock. Hill tried to put the icing on the cake with just under two minutes remaining, but fumbled attempting to dive into the end zone from just outside the goal line. Hill had battled a knee injury throughout much of the season, and was not 100-percent healthy on Super Bowl Sunday.

"I was really on one leg," Recalled Hill. "I tried to jump up, but I had no pop."

The inability to score the touchdown did not damper Hill's enthusiasm as he returned to the sidelines. All that was left to vanquish the ghosts of the Cowboys' past was to watch the final seconds tick away.

"The most exciting part of it is when they're counting down," said Hill. "You see the clock in the last minute and it's like a countdown for a rocket ship. When the gun goes off, you're the best team in the world. That's a great feeling. It's like Christmas."

As the final gun sounded, Landry was lifted onto the shoulders of his players. After coming tantalizingly close to the top of the mountain, the Cowboys could finally call themselves World Champions. For the less-experienced Cowboys, the fulfillment of watching their veteran teammates savor the moment put Super Bowl VI into its proper perspective.

"I don't know if I fully understood the full impact of the emotion that they felt," Harris said. "I wasn't there the years before. I knew there was incredible emotion that was finally released that day."

"It was the most fun I had being in a locker room," Staubach said. "They weren't much older than me, but they had been with the team a lot longer. It just was a big deal to take the weight off their shoulders. Saying you can't win the big game is a lousy tag for an athlete."

The Cowboys finished with 252 rushing yards. The Dolphins became the only team not to score a touchdown in a Super Bowl. Miami would get its second chance a year later, but this game would be a lessoned learned for Shula's squad going forward. Left Guard Bob Kuechenberg knew the Dolphins had met their match against a more experienced opponent.

"Dallas was a very mature team and a very talented team," said Kuechenberg. "In the end, they won the game going away and rightfully so. They were better than we were that year."

The Cowboys has echoed the same sentiments in previous years. This time, the Cowboys were "This Year's Champions."

"It was like dropping a hundred-pound weight off your back," Lilly said. "It was such a relief as well as joy. We got rid of that stigma that we can't win the big one and we were champions. It was pure joy. We were absolutely elated. We would have a Super Bowl ring for the rest of our lives."

VII
PERFECTION

For the 1972 Miami Dolphins, the road to perfection began with the quest for redemption.

A perfect season was far from the minds of the Dolphins as they walked off the field after Super Bowl VI. Don Shula's squad had suffered a 24–3 defeat at the hands of the Dallas Cowboys. Miami had been thoroughly beaten in its first Super Bowl appearance, and Shula had suffered his second loss on Super Sunday. The Miami head coach had also been at the helm of the Colts when they were upset in Super Bowl III. When the team gathered for training camp in July, Shula sent a clear message to his players. Wide Receiver Paul

Warfield remembered how his head coach talked about never finishing second again.

"That was the very first theme that he talked about for at least a minimum of 30 to 45 minutes," said Warfield. "Everybody remembered that dull feeling that we had. We had an outstanding season, but the season doesn't mean anything if you don't win the Super Bowl. The Super Bowl is everything in the National Football League."

Guard Larry Little remembered how the sting of the Dolphins' Super Bowl loss along with Shula's message carried over into the 1972 season.

"You saw that film," said Little. "Shula said 'You guys will never have this feeling again.' It just stuck in our craw all year. We knew we had a really good football team, but we didn't know how good we really were until everything started happening for us."

Miami used its motivation to put together the greatest season in NFL history. It began with ten straight victories and an AFC East title. It was at this point of the 1972 campaign when Guard Bob Kuechenberg realized perfection was possible.

"Jim Langer and I were both out lifting weights," Kuechenberg said. "I asked him in between bench presses when we were going to lose a game. I asked which one it was going to be. He said, 'Not this week, dammit. Pass me the weights.' All of a sudden, you're 14–0 and the real season begins."

The "real season" was the post-season, and victories over Cleveland and Pittsburgh propelled Miami into Super Bowl VII. Awaiting the Dolphins in Los Angeles were the Washington Redskins, who were making their first Super Bowl appearance. The "Over the Hill Gang" had surprised the football world, as a group made up largely of grizzled veterans captured its first NFC Championship. One key member of the Washington Defense was Cornerback Mike Bass, who had narrowly missed a chance to be part of the Packers Super Bowl II squad. The rookie was cut by a legendary head coach, but Vince Lombardi gave Bass a second chance in Washington in 1969.

"So much of playing in this league is being in the right place at the right time," Bass said. "Green Bay cut me on the last cut before the season started. Coach Lombardi pulled me aside and said 'Don't give up. You can play in this league.' That's what kept me going."

Lombardi died of cancer after his first season in Washington. George Allen took over in 1971 and turned the Redskins into a Super Bowl team in 1972. Allen's enthusiasm along with his willingness to take a less tyrannical approach made him popular with his players.

"Coach Allen was tense about everything," said Bass. "He was a different breed of cat. He was a players' coach. We all really loved him. He treated us fairly unlike a lot of other coaches in the league at the time. He respected us as experienced ball players. We had a lot to do with preparing game plans."

Several of Miami's wins during the season came in close contests, and some still wondered if the Dolphins were deserving of their unbeaten record. The odds makers were not convinced. Despite coming away victorious in their previous 16 games, the Dolphins were underdogs heading into Super Bowl VII. Many Miami players believed the betting line provided extra motivation.

"Absolutely it did," said Kuechenberg. "It was unbelievable that here we are 16–0 at this point, and were playing a Redskins team who is 13–3. They lost to three teams that we had beaten, and we were three-point underdogs. That was an insult. That was incentive."

"It didn't matter what they thought about us," said Warfield. "They thought we were still an old AFL team, which most of the media did."

For Anderson, it was nothing different than what they had seen during the season.

"You looked at the betting lines in '72," Anderson said. "There weren't more than one or two games where we were favored. Why should the Super Bowl be any different?"

It the early history of the Super Bowl, the team with the most experience usually prevailed. The Dolphins had not only suffered a loss the previous year, but had dealt with the distractions of the biggest game of the season. Bass and the Redskins were dealing with Super Bowl hype for the first time.

"It was festive," said Bass. "It was also very, very new to us. We enjoyed the experience. I don't know if any of us, even Coach Allen, were prepared for distractions. Coach Allen emphasized we really had to have blinders on to avoid the distractions, but I'm sure some of the distractions had an effect on us."

Most of the first quarter was a defensive struggle. Each team punted twice before Miami began to move the ball late in the period. Shula shifted from his usual conservative game plan and Quarterback Bob Griese was able to connect on two key passes. The first went to Warfield and put Miami on the Washington 34-yard line. Three plays later, Griese found Howard Twilley for a 28-yard scoring strike in the final second of the first quarter.

Griese's Super Bowl start was his first since the fifth week of the regular season. The quarterback broke his leg in Week Five and was replaced by Earl Morrall. Griese returned in relief of Morrall in the AFC Championship game, and Kuechenberg and company noticed the difference with the man from Perdue under center.

"It did matter," said Kuechenberg. "Earl started 11 of the 17 games. While he did a great job, when you have Bob Griese in there, it's smooth kind of like Cassius Clay. With Earl in there, it was more like Joe Frazier. You had to physically beat them because it wasn't going to be as easy."

While Miami's offense had drawn first blood, its defense continued to terrorize Washington Running Back Larry Brown. The game plan for Shula and Defensive Coordinator Bill Arnsparger was to shut down Brown and force Quarterback Billy Kilmer to take to the air. Brown rushed for 1,216 yards during the regular season, but Miami's defense limited the dangerous back to 72 yards on 22 carries. Brown suffered an afternoon of punishment, and a hit by Anderson in the second quarter separated Brown from his helmet.

"That was indicative of how he felt," Anderson said. "He had been hit so many times."

Fittingly, the Miami defense would set up the second score of Super Bowl VII. Nick Buoniconti's interception with less than two minutes left in the half put the Dolphins on the Washington 27-yard line. Griese completed his sixth pass in six attempts as he connected with Jim Mandich at the two-yard line. Two plays later, Jim Kiick powered into the end zone, and the Dolphins' ended a dominating first-half performance with a 14–0 lead. Miami was two quarters away from its first Super Bowl title, but Little knew they had to maintain a high level of play against the Redskins.

"We knew they were a good football team," Little said. "They had some talent over there, but we just knew we had to go back out in the second half and do what we were supposed to do and run the football like we did."

Meanwhile, there was little panic in the Washington locker room.

"There was nothing drastic," Bass said. "We had all been in this situation before. We didn't panic or anything of that sort. We felt we could come out the winner of the game. We always felt the offense or the defense would make a couple of plays and turn it around."

After gaining only 72 yards in the first half, Washington began to move the ball at the start of the third quarter. Kilmer led the Redskins deep into Miami territory, but Curt Knight missed a 32-yard field goal. Washington had squandered its best scoring chance of the game, and Miami maintained its superiority in the trenches. Defensive Tackle Manny Fernandez was leading the way with a dominating performance, and would finish the game with 17 tackles.

"They thought Lenny Hauss could block Manny one-on-one," recalled Anderson. "Huge mistake. They didn't realize Manny was so much stronger than Lenny, and he tossed him around like a sack."

Miami nearly put the game away late in the third period after reaching the Washington five-yard line, but Brig Owens' end zone interception kept Washington's faint hopes alive. The Redskins drove deep into Miami territory at the start of the fourth period. With the ball on the ten-yard line, Kilmer threw for Jerry Smith in the end zone. Smith was open, but Kilmer's pass hit the goalpost on its path to Smith and fell harmlessly incomplete. On the next play, Jake Scott intercepted Kilmer, and it appeared Washington's fate was sealed.

After Scott's interception, Miami moved to the Washington 34-yard line. When the drive stalled, kicker Garo Yepremian was sent in for a 42-yard field goal attempt. Yepremian had the chance to put the ultimate exclamation point on a perfect season.

"We're going to kick the field goal to make it 17–0 on the 17th victory of the year for us," said Warfield.

Bass was ready in case Yepremian's kick didn't clear the line of scrimmage.

"My job really was that of what you call the spy-man," Bass said. "My job was actually to be there if the ball was blocked on an extra point or a field goal."

The little kicker's attempt was blocked and the ball deflected back to Yepremian, who had no intention of falling on the football. A pass attempt slipped out of Yepremian's hands and deflected into the air. Bass grabbed the deflection and raced into the end zone. Garo's Goof had put the Redskins back in the game with 2:07 remaining.

"Garo picked it up and tried to throw it," recalled Bass. "Nerves can play a part. He couldn't grip the ball. I just happened to be there at the right time. I caught the ball as a defensive back at its highest point. The one thing I could not let happen was have Garo Yepremian tackle me. I would never live that down."

While much of America laughed at Yepremian's failed pass attempt, his teammates were hardly in a jovial mood on the sideline.

"People may laugh about it now," Kuechenberg said. "We were not laughing at that point. To me, it was purely an act of cowardice. Garo was one of the best field goal kickers in the game, but he just panicked. All he had to do was fall on it."

"He was scared shitless," Anderson said. "He didn't know how to fall on a ball. He wasn't a football player. He was a great kicker. He was just scared and didn't know what to do. It was sad. It could have been 17–0 at 17–0, but the Gods wouldn't have it."

"Garo came to the sidelines," said Little. "If 50 guys could kill, he would be dead right then."

Washington got the ball back with 1:14 remaining, but the Miami Defense was able to put the game away. As the clock hit zero, Shula's Super Bowl demons were vanquished forever, and the Dolphins were undefeated world champions with a 14–7 victory.

"I remember being on the field very distinctly when time was running down," Warfield said. "We were in the huddle and I peeked at the scoreboard in the Coliseum, and it was flashing 'The Dolphins Are Super.' It was a great, great feeling."

Bass and the rest of the Redskins would not get another chance at a Super Bowl. By the time Washington reached Super Bowl XVII ten years later, all of the 1972 Redskins were off the roster. Bass would play three more seasons and finish with 30 career interceptions. However, the former Redskin knows he will be forever linked to Yepremian's ill-fated pass attempt. Bass and Yepremian remained friends and were teammates on the Lions in 1967. The two were able to raise money for charity together before Yepremian's death in 2015. Meanwhile, Bass still enjoys reliving his touchdown at Yepremian's expense.

"We've done some things for Wounded Warriors," Bass said. "Even though I haven't made a living off that play, it's enjoyable to watch."

Despite decades of dynasties in the NFL, only the 1972 Dolphins can make the claim of perfection. One urban legend has the remaining players from the 1972 squad enjoying a toast each time the last unbeaten team falls in the NFL each season. Little insists rumors of gloating by the players are overblown, but says they are still able to savor their perfect season.

"We don't do things that people say we do," Little said. "They call us a bunch of grumpy old men, but we're not a bunch of grumpy old men. We're a bunch of happy old men. Someone will eventually do it one day and if they do, so be it. We still know we were the first team to do it."

For now, Kuechenberg's stationary symbolizes Miami's amazing accomplishment.

"It's unique," Kuechenberg said. "On my letterhead, it says '1972. Perfection is immortal. Imperfection is ... just that.'"

VIII
MIAMI MASTERY

Perfection wasn't enough for the Miami Dolphins.

The 1972 Dolphins became the only unbeaten team in the modern NFL era, but the 1973 edition of the South Florida franchise appeared more powerful than the team that made NFL history. Despite losing two games, the Dolphins average margin of victory was greater than the previous season. The Dolphins also played a tougher schedule in 1973, and Miami's "No Name Defense" held opponents to 14 points or less. As Miami prepared to face the Minnesota Vikings in Super Bowl VIII, it appeared Bob Kuechenberg and his teammates would be a tougher test for the NFC Champion than in the previous year.

"We ended up losing two games," Kuechenberg said. "We were not perfect in our record, but it was a better team because we were more mature. We were still a very young team. We were a year more mature for the Viking game."

Players such as Kuechenberg and Larry Little were part of one of the best offensive lines in the NFL. Little agreed that Miami's performances in 1973 were more dominant than in the '72 season.

"We were a better football team in 1973," said Little. "Not because of the losses, but because of the way we dominated the teams we played."

While the Dolphins were making a record-setting third straight Super Bowl appearance, Minnesota was back in the championship game for the second time in five years. In Super Bowl IV, the Vikings were blown out by the Chiefs in the final title game before the AFL-NFL merger. Many of those same Vikings were still on the roster which headed to Houston to face the Dolphins. Among those returning were the dominating defensive linemen known as "The Purple People Eaters." One of the mainstays was Alan Page, a former teammate of Kuechenberg's at Notre Dame.

"I had a special plan ready for Alan Page," Kuechenberg said. "I had really studied Alan's film very, very closely. I knew more about Alan Page than Alan knew about himself. I was going to block Alan Page man-to-man no matter where he went."

However, the Miami coaching staff had other ideas. Offensive Line Coach Monte Clark reviewed film on Page with Kuechenberg in the days leading up to the game. Clark wanted Kuechenberg to block Page the conventional way, but the lineman was convinced it would be a recipe for disaster.

"I saw a little change in Alan's stance," Kuechenberg said. "Monty wanted me to block him by the book. I told Monty that you see what he does when you block by the book. I told him to at least ask the boss."

"The boss" was Don Shula, who made it clear to Kuechenberg he would be blocking Page by the book. Meanwhile, Shula was also dealing with a significant injury to his top receiver. Paul Warfield entered Super Bowl VIII with a tender hamstring, and most believed the graceful wideout would be limited against the Vikings.

"It was bad," said Warfield. "Unfortunately, during the week of practice in Houston, I was running a change of speed pattern for me. As I attempted to shift gears, I pulled a hamstring muscle. It did not work from that point until I took the field Sunday for the ball game. I knew I was very limited in what I could do."

The Vikings had Joe Kapp at quarterback when they lost Super Bowl IV. In Super Bowl VIII, the Minnesota offense would be led by Fran Tarkenton, who gave opposing defenses nightmares with his mobility. However, Dick Anderson and his defensive teammates took the same approach to Tarkenton and the Vikings as they did with every other offense they had faced during the season. Anderson credited his defensive coordinator for the success of the No Name Defense.

"The key to our defense was Bill Arnsparger's brilliance," said Anderson. "We had great communication with him. He was a non-emotional guy who really understood the game and what we could do."

After entering the Super Bowl as an underdog the previous year, Miami was favored to beat Minnesota. The Dolphins took the opening kickoff and would set the tone for the day with a crisp ten-play, 62-yard touchdown drive. Miami's powerful rushing attack was fueled by cross blocking and misdirection which left Minnesota's "Purple People Eaters" lost in the backwash of Miami's offensive line. Larry Csonka barreled into the end zone from five-yards out, and Miami had a 7–0 lead.

The tone was set for Super Bowl VIII.

"We knew about the Purple People Eaters going into the game," Little said. "But we knew what kind of offensive line we had. We knew if we did what we were supposed to do, we could handle those guys up front."

The Vikings would go three and out on their first drive, and the Miami machine would put together another impressive march to the end zone. But early in the drive, Page stuffed Running Back Jim Kiick for a loss. Kuechenberg vented his frustration toward his coaches on the sidelines.

"Jim Kiick and Alan Page arrived at the ball at the same time," said Kuechenberg. "He took Kiick down for a loss. That's when I lost it. I just turned to the sideline and looked at Shula. I was seeing red."

Kuchenberg threw out the textbook and dominated his former college teammate the rest of the day despite playing with a broken arm. Kuechenberg had suffered the injury in the regular season and played with a cast throughout the end of the '73 campaign.

The Dolphins finished up their ten-play drive with a one-yard run by Kiick. It was 14–0, but there was a sense the Vikings were already at a point of no return. Minnesota Defensive Lineman Jim Marshall admitted the first two touchdowns were staggering blows for the Vikings.

"I think so," Marshall said. "Any time you can have drives like that, it's hard to overcome. They scored each time. When you have long drives like that, it takes a lot out of a defense."

The Miami Defense was also doing its part. The Vikings totaled 25 yards on offense in the opening quarter. After the Dolphins increased their lead to 17–0, Minnesota moved the ball into Miami territory for the first time. Tarkenton was faced with a 4th and 1 on the Miami 6. Oscar Reed ran right, but Nick Buoniconti jarred the ball loose. Jake Scott recovered the fumble, and the Dolphins headed to the locker room with a 17–0 lead. There was still one half to play, but there was a sense the outcome was inevitable.

"We don't lose if they don't score," Anderson said. "In almost all of those games in those years, somebody stepped up and made a great play that changed the course of the game or really sealed the deal."

The game was being decided in the trenches. The Miami offensive line was having its way with one of the greatest front fours in NFL history.

"They played very well," said Marshall. "They gave us a lot of different blocking angles and took advantage of the aggressiveness we had shown during the season. I'm sure that's what the purpose of their blocking scheme was."

"They couldn't stop us," Little said. "They couldn't stop the run. We only threw the ball seven times the whole game. We knew we would dominate that defensive line going into the game. All we had to do was go out there and execute."

The Dolphins domination continued at the start of the second half. A sack on third down by Manny Fernandez finished off another three and out for the Vikings to open the third quarter. Miami's first drive began at the Minnesota 43. Faced with a third and five, it was time for Warfield to test his tender hamstring.

"It was important for me to play," Warfield said. "The Minnesota Vikings would not be taking any chances. They would give me the kind of coverage scheme that we anticipated. That would be important for our run game knowing that on any given play, I would receive some form of double coverage."

The plan for Warfield and Griese was to find a way to get the graceful wide receiver away from the double coverage. Warfield would first have to elude Cornerback Bobby Bryant as he lined up to the left. Griese took the snap and looked right, then immediately turned to the left and fired a pass down the sidelines. The ball arrived before Bryant could get help in the secondary, and Warfield made a leaping 27-yard reception.

"Bob was calling the play," said Warfield said. "He made it work. Bobby Bryant is coming up to jam me. His hands dropped. He did not try to jam me. He is looking to the inside of the field as he sees Bob Griese look away to the other side of the field. Bob turns and throws the ball to me. There's nobody over there. I just hoped I had enough leg power to catch it."

Warfield's catch put the Dolphins on the 11. Miami moved to the two and appeared ready to put the game away. Csonka got the call and plowed into the end zone despite the fact the play nearly ended in disaster for Miami.

"Bob forgot the snap count," said Little. "Csonka didn't know it, but we just ran the play anyway and scored. That's how good we were."

Miami entered the fourth quarter with a 24–0 lead. Minnesota finally got on the board early in the period as Tarkenton capped off a 57-yard drive with a four-yard run. The Vikings successfully fielded an onside kick after the score, but an offside penalty nullified the play. It summed up another frustrating Super Sunday for Minnesota.

"We were just outplayed," said Marshall. "I think that's the only thing that you can say."

The Dolphins spent much of the fourth quarter chewing up the clock with their rushing attack. The Miami offensive line continued its domination, and Page's frustration boiled over late in the period.

"Griese handed the ball off to Mercury Morris," said Kuechenberg. "Instead of chasing Mercury, Alan smacked Griese. I smacked him and we threw a few punches at each other, and he got ejected. He went from being the NFL MVP to the only player ever ejected in a Super Bowl."

All that was left for the dominant Dolphins was a curtain call. With time winding down, Shula decided to pull many of his starters one by one so they could savor the moment of a second straight Super Bowl title.

"You start to bring you key players out," Kuechenberg said. "He gave them a hug as he got to the sideline. Shula brought Csonka out, and then called me out and gave me a big old hug on the sidelines."

Csonka was named the game's MVP with a 145-yard rushing performance. Shula's Dolphins became the second franchise to win back-to-back Super Bowls and did so in convincing fashion.

"That was probably one of the easiest games we played all year," said Little.

The vanquished Vikings became the first team to lose two Super Bowls. Minnesota had been the unwilling victim of a Miami machine that had methodically taken the Vikings apart in pro football's biggest game. It would be the last Super Bowl victory for this group of Dolphins, and their second title left no doubt as to their place as one of the greatest teams in NFL history.

"We were truly a professional football machine," said Warfield. "We understood how you won, what it takes to win and what you needed to do. We were able to do those things every Sunday afternoon at one o'clock. We were not going to beat ourselves. We became, in my mind, a machine."

IX
BIRTH OF A STEEL DYNASTY

The Pittsburgh Steelers had waited a long time for success.

Founded in 1933, the Steelers were a franchise with a history of losing.

Before the AFL-NFL merger, Pittsburgh had never won a championship. Everything changed in the early 1970's as the Steelers began to assemble one of the most talented teams in the history of the game. Pittsburgh's rise towards the top of the football world came faster than many expected. Few believed the 1974 Steelers would get by the Raiders in the AFC title game, but Pittsburgh punched its ticket to the Super Bowl in Oakland and headed to New Orleans with the hope of wiping away 42 years of frustration.

It was a much different story for the Minnesota Vikings, who were making their third Super Bowl appearance. The Vikings had been completely dominated by both the Chiefs in Super Bowl IV and the Dolphins the previous year in Super Bowl XIII. Minnesota believed lessons learned from its two previous Super Bowl failures would pay off against the Steelers. However, the two Super Bowl defeats added extra pressure on Bud Grant's squad. While the Steelers were making their first trip to the Super Bowl, Head Coach Chuck Noll made sure his players had their share of time on Bourbon Street to keep them loose for their upcoming battle with the Vikings. Safety Mike Wagner and his teammates hardly seemed phased by the Super Bowl spotlight.

"I think we were definitely loose," said Wagner. "Coach Noll changed our curfew pattern where we didn't have a curfew. He wanted the players to enjoy what they could of the week. We still had business to take care of, but the only night we had curfew was the night before the game."

Guard Gerry Mullins also credited Noll for his decision to let the Steelers enjoy the nightlife of New Orleans as they prepared for the biggest game of their lives.

"Chuck Noll had a big part in taking some of the pressure off of us," said Mullins. "We had curfews, but we had pretty much a free reign to do what we wanted after we did our work at practice. He kept everybody loose."

Many believed points would be hard to come by in Super Bowl IX. The Vikings were led by the famed "Purple People Eaters" on their defensive front. Carl Eller, Alan Page and Jim Marshall often dominated the line of scrimmage and the Vikings had allowed just 24 points in their first two playoff games. Meanwhile, Pittsburgh's "Steel Curtain" was also wreaking havoc on opposing offenses. In an era of conservative offensive game plans and punishing defenses, Mullins knew the Steelers would be in for a tough fight in the trenches.

"The passing game wasn't open like it was today," Mullins said. "We had a pretty successful year running the football. Our goal was to not make a lot of mistakes and try to grind it out."

The Steelers feared they would be missing one of their key contributors on defense. Defensive Lineman Dwight White spent much of the week in the hospital battling pneumonia. Most expected White to sit out the Super Bowl. Wagner knew better.

"That was our first Super Bowl," Wagner said. "There was no way he was going to let anything stop him from being on that football field with a chance to play for a championship. He did the right thing. He spent most of the week trying to recover and get healthy."

The two defenses would also get help from Mother Nature. Super Bowl IX was originally going to be the first indoor Super Bowl, but the game was switched to Tulane Stadium since construction of the Superdome was not yet complete. The Astroturf field was water-logged from heavy rain the night before and gusty winds along with temperatures in the mid 40's did not set the stage for an offensive shootout.

The first quarter went according to plan with both defenses setting the tone. Pittsburgh was able to move into field goal range twice, but a miss by Roy Gerela and a botched snap kept the Steelers off the board. The Vikings faired much worse offensively, as the Steel Curtain neutralized the Minnesota attack. Minnesota gained just 27 yards in the first quarter and picked up only one first down. Vikings Quarterback Fran Tarkenton was one of the top quarterbacks in the game and his scrambling abilities often frustrated his opponents. On this day, Tarkenton would have very little room to run or throw.

"We really challenged their offensive game," Wagner said. "The first thing they wanted to do was try to establish the running game. But as far as Tarkenton, who made a career out of scrambling, it's amazing when you look at the replays of the game that he just was not effective. That gave us a lot of encouragement."

Minnesota's offense finally put together a drive in the second quarter, but Fred Cox missed a 39-yard field goal. Pittsburgh would punt on its next possession and the stage was set for the first score of Super Bowl IX.

Fittingly, it came from the defense.

With the ball on the Minnesota seven, Tarkenton's pitch back to Dave Osborn went past the arms of the running back. The ball rolled into the end zone where Tarkenton fell on it to prevent a touchdown. However, the ailing White rushed in to tag Tarkenton for a safety. Pittsburgh led, 2–0 and the early score by the defense did not exactly boost the spirits of the Vikings.

"It seemed to us the Vikings were much more uptight," said Wagner.

The Vikings threatened to take the lead late in the half as they drove into Pittsburgh territory with 1:17 remaining. Tarkenton threw deep for John Gilliam, who was hit by Glen Edwards as the ball arrived. The ball deflected into the air and was intercepted by Mel Blount and the 2–0 Pittsburgh lead was the lowest halftime score in Super Bowl history.

"Glen just clocked him," said Wagner. "The ball bounced up about 20 feet in the air, and Mel Blount intercepted it."

The Steelers knew there was still plenty of work to be done, but confidence remained high in the Pittsburgh locker room after 30 minutes of football. Mullins also understood the Minnesota Defense was once again playing at a high level.

"They had an outstanding defense," said Mullins. "They dominated in the NFC throughout the decade. We knew what we were going up against. Some things don't always work the first time around. They played a great game on defense as well."

The Vikings were very much alive as they headed to the locker room, but veterans such as Marshall had been a part of two frustrating Super Bowls. While the score was much closer in this championship game, the Steel Curtain was overshadowing the Purple People Eaters.

"I had great respect for their defense," Marshall said. "They played great. We were not so great."

Marshall and the defense had actually done their part to keep Minnesota well within striking distance, but another mistake on offense would open the door for Pittsburgh. The Vikings received the second half kickoff, but Bill Brown fumbled and the Steelers recovered on the Minnesota 30-yard line. Running Back Franco Harris rushed 24 yards to start the drive for Pittsburgh. Two plays later, Harris ran left and followed a crushing block by Mullins on Linebacker Wally Hilgenberg for a nine-yard touchdown run.

"That was a 35 special," Mullins said. "We had a trap and I turned the corner and saw Wally running at full speed to try and bust up the play. I just went down low on him and basically took him out. That allowed Franco basically to walk in. Obviously, that was a huge momentum boost for us. It was probably the turning point of the game for us."

With the Steel Curtain dominating much of the game, the nine-point lead seemed almost insurmountable. Despite facing a swarm of Steelers all afternoon, Tarkenton valiantly tried to keep his team in the game. Later in the quarter, Minnesota reached the Pittsburgh 45-yard line, but Tarkenton was once again denied by White. The lineman deflected Tarkenton's pass and Joe Greene picked off the deflection for another interception. The turnover added to the nightmare Marshall was forced to witness as the Minnesota Defense watched the offense crumble against the mighty Steelers.

Despite Pittsburgh's defensive dominance, the Vikings would get another scoring chance early in the fourth quarter. A pass interference penalty put Minnesota five-yards away from the end zone, but Chuck Foreman fumbled and Greene recovered to deny the Vikings' offense its best scoring chance of the day.

"They decided to attack Joe Greene that game by running right at him," Wagner said. "There was a tremendous pile and all of a sudden, Joe Greene pops out of the pile and he's got the football. I think it was the tone set that the Steeler Defense was going to play really tough, physical football."

Just when it seemed as if the Vikings were finished, Matt Blair blocked Bobby Walden's punt. Terry Brown recovered in the end zone and despite a missed extra point, the Vikings were suddenly three points down with over ten minutes remaining.

It was time for Pittsburgh's offense to step up.

Bradshaw led the Steelers on a 66-yard drive that took 6:47 off the clock. It ended with a four-yard touchdown pass to Larry Brown with 4:31 remaining. With the Pittsburgh Defense dominating much of the day, the offense was finally able to break through during the most important part of the game.

"We felt that we could handle what we needed to get done," said Wagner. "In the second half, our offense caught fire a little bit. It took a while for our offense to get fired up. When our offense put some points on the board, it just made it easier for us to continue."

It would be Wagner who would put the final nail in the Minnesota coffin. On the ensuing drive, the safety picked off Tarkenton's deep pass over the middle. The Pittsburgh running game ate up nearly all of the remaining time before Minnesota took over with 38 seconds left. The clock ran out on the Vikings as well as 42 years of frustration in Pittsburgh. Harris was named the game's Most Valuable Player after racking up 158 yards on the ground. It was a stark contrast to the Minnesota ground game as the Vikings were held to 17 rushing yards.

The Steelers were world champions for the first time in their history and the man beloved by players and coaches alike was no longer a lovable loser. Pittsburgh Owner Art Rooney was one of the most respected men in pro football. At long last, the man known as "The Chief" was able to savor a championship for his long-suffering franchise.

"The satisfaction besides winning a championship was seeing The Chief accept the Super Bowl Trophy," said Wagner. "He was very humble and he was very interested in all of the players. It was an open door policy."

The door had closed on the Vikings for the third time in Super Bowl history. Minnesota was now 0–3 on Super Sundays and Marshall and his teammates were forced to put another championship loss in the rear-view mirror. However, the pain of Super Bowl defeats lingers to this day.

"I put most of that stuff out of my mind," said Marshall. "It's painful memory. It gets stuck in that category."

There were cheers and tears for Rooney as he accepted the Vince

Lombardi Trophy from Commissioner Pete Rozelle. The players handed Rooney the game ball and the owner accepted his first championship with the same class he had exhibited throughout all of his years in pro football.

"There was his story of being in the league so long and not having winners or having situations where he got close but never made it," Wagner said. "It was just great to see The Chief accept that. I think, in his own way, he was excited. You couldn't tell, but he was very pleased. Everybody was happy for him."

"I think the highlight of the entire Super Bowl was seeing Mr. Rooney get that Lombardi Trophy," said Mullins. "He was so well-respected by everybody on our team. He was loved by everybody. We all knew about the futility of the organization for all those years. That got the monkey off Art's back."

Rooney and the Steelers were just getting started. The Steelers had set the table for what would be a dominant decade. Even as the Pittsburgh players celebrated their first Super Bowl title, Noll was already looking ahead.

"Noll congratulated us," recalled Wagner. "He said to enjoy this one but that we've got work to do. He said there was no reason why we couldn't win a couple more. Chuck was always pushing that envelope and reminding players that there's another challenge out there. I think Chuck set the tone."

X
SWANN SOARS FOR THE STEELERS

After years of suffering, the Pittsburgh Steelers suddenly had the opportunity to build a dynasty.

A franchise with a history of losing had wiped away decades of failure with a victory in Super Bowl IX. However, there was a sense that Chuck Noll's squad was just getting started. The core was in place for a long run in Pittsburgh and the Steelers once again made the trip to pro football's ultimate game. After reaching the Super Bowl the previous year, Safety Mike Wagner and the rest of his teammates were loose and confident as they arrived in Miami.

"It was the same approach for us," said Wagner. "It was a different environment. There was less contact with the fans and we were spread out with our families and friends."

The Dallas Cowboys awaited the Steelers in Miami. Dallas was making its third Super Bowl appearance in a year where few expected Tom Landry's team to contend. Despite several new faces on the roster, Dallas surprised the football world and became the first wild card team to advance to a Super Bowl. Even Quarterback Roger Staubach was a bit surprised to see the rapid growth of his team during the 1975 season.

"We really overachieved that year," said Staubach. "Our running game was not what it usually was. We didn't know what to expect in '75 and the thing that really worked for us was that we still had good athletes. We definitely overachieved that year. Coach Landry once said the '75 season was the best season we had."

The rookies would make an immediate impact in Dallas. One was Linebacker Randy White, who would eventually move to the defensive line and emerge as one of the most dominant lineman of his era.

"We had 12 rookies make that team," White said. "The Cowboys weren't picked to win the division and weren't picked to do much. We felt we brought some enthusiasm to some of the veterans that were there and we had some great veterans."

The veterans welcomed the newcomers as everything came together for Dallas late in the season. Cliff Harris had been part of the first two Dallas Super Bowls and the defensive back could sense the momentum building as the 1975 campaign progressed.

"It was one of my favorite years for the Cowboys," said Harris. "There was a time in the middle of the season where the press had given up on us and the fans had given up on us. We kind of internalized and motivated ourselves."

Harris would be making headlines leading up to the game. Pittsburgh Wide Receiver Lynn Swann suffered a concussion in the AFC Championship win over Oakland. Harris suggested getting hit again would be in the back of Swann's mind when he took the field for Super Bowl X.

"The press asked me what I was going to do and if I was going to take it easy on him," recalled Harris. "I said that if he came into my area, I'm going to knock him out. By saying I would do my best, I wasn't doing anything that I would have done with any other receiver. It theoretically fired up Lynn Swann."

The Cowboys had been fired up ever since their first playoff game in Minnesota. Staubach's "Hail Mary" pass to Drew Pearson in the closing seconds kept the team's championship hopes alive. The play was a lesson to the Dallas rookies such as Thomas "Hollywood" Henderson about the team's never say die attitude.

"I was sitting on the bench," said Henderson. "I was thinking whether I was going to spend my off-season in Oklahoma City, Austin or Dallas. I thought our season was over. I went from planning an off-season to going to a Super Bowl."

Even the veteran Steelers were getting help from some new faces. One of them was John Banaszak, a free agent defensive lineman who was making contributions on special teams.

"It was a tremendous experience," said Banaszak. "One of the reasons why I signed as an undrafted free agent with the Steelers was because I had never played on a championship team. There were 17 rounds in the draft back then and 475 players taken. I wasn't one of them. It really worked out to my benefit."

The stage was set for an intriguing Super Bowl on the tenth anniversary of the event. The underdog Cowboys would battle the defending champion Steelers in a game which would help skyrocket the already growing popularity of both teams. Dallas Wide Receiver Drew Pearson could sense the buildup as kickoff approached.

"We knew we were the team of destiny but that the Pittsburgh Steelers were the better team," said Pearson. "They were the favored team going in and we had to play that role of underdog. We had become the first team to take the wild card route to the Super Bowl."

Special teams would play a huge part of Super Bowl X and the tone was set on the opening kickoff. Henderson took a reverse and reached the Pittsburgh 44-yard line. Steelers Kicker Roy Gerela injured his ribs knocking Henderson out of bounds and the injury would affect the kicker all afternoon.

The Cowboys and Steelers were both forced to punt on their opening drives, but Pittsburgh punter Bobby Walden never got his punt airborne. Walden dropped the snap and the Cowboys brought him down on his own 29-yard line. It took Dallas just one play to capitalize as Pearson gathered in a 29-yard pass from Staubach over the middle and raced into the end zone.

"It gave us a lot of confidence and also let the Steelers know that we were ready to play," said Pearson. "To score that touchdown early in the game in the first quarter sent a message not only to our football team that we could play with these guys, but also sent a message to the Pittsburgh Steelers that these guys were pretty good."

"We knew they were going to run that play," Wagner said. "The issue is always what defense you're in when you run that play. We were in a two-deep zone, which means the safeties were over the top. Underneath, we had five players playing zone. You have Drew Pearson coming from our side and the players have kind of cleared off the zone on the other side."

It would be Swann who would rejuvenate the Steelers with the first of two miraculous catches. Swann soared over Cowboys Cornerback Mark Washington and tight roped along the sideline for a 32-yard gain at the Dallas 16-yard line. Shortly after Swann's soaring grab, Bradshaw hit Randy Grossman on a seven-yard scoring strike to tie the game at 7–7. The Steelers had used a three tight end set with Guard Gerry Mullins serving as the extra tight end.

"We were still basically a run-oriented team," said Mullins. "We had talent at wide receiver and the game had opened up, but we were trying to keep it close knowing that our defense was probably going to take us over the top."

Dallas regained the lead early in the second quarter as Toni Fritsch connected on a 36-yard field goal. The score remained 10–7 as the second quarter progressed despite another acrobatic catch by Swann. The receiver hauled in a 53-yard pass that is still considered one of the greatest catches of all time. Swann leaped into the air and deflected the ball, then made the catch while stumbling to the ground.

"He was just tough as nails," Wagner said. "The real beauty is just his athletic ability. I remember his first catch on the sidelines thinking 'Holy cow, this guy is so talented.' The poor defensive back had blanket coverage on all of those throws."

"I got to see those in person," recalled Mullins. "With the one on the sidelines, it was totally unbelievable how he stayed in bounds. Both of those were huge plays for us and put us in a position to get some points. Lynn's a great competitor and there was no concussion protocol back in the day. He just sucked it up and went out and played a super game."

The Steelers could not take advantage of Swann's high-flying heroics. Gerela missed a 36-yard attempt with 22 seconds left in the half, and the Cowboys headed to the locker room with a three-point lead.

The Pittsburgh Defense would give the offense another golden opportunity early in the third quarter. Cornerback J.T. Thomas intercepted a Staubach pass and returned the ball to the Dallas 25. Pittsburgh would be forced to settle for a field goal try, but Gerela missed again from 33 yards away. The miss would lead to the biggest emotional shift of Super Bowl X.

After Gerela's kick sailed wide of the mark, Harris came over to the kicker and mockingly put his arm around him and patted him on the head. Pittsburgh Linebacker Jack Lambert immediately came to Gerela's defense and threw Harris to the turf.

"The official didn't see it," Harris said. "Lambert came up from behind me. He should have gotten 15 yards."

The response by Lambert served as a fuse to the dynamite for the Steelers. It added extra fuel to the fire of Lambert, one of the most ferocious defenders in NFL history.

"Their defense was really good," recalled Staubach. "But Lambert was a fantastic leader. He was a tough son of a gun and he played over the top."

"My concern was Lambert was going to get thrown out of the game,"

Wagner said. "I told him I was glad he did that to Cliff because that was out of line, but we don't want you getting thrown out of the game. Players do use that to fire up their energy. I think the big message there was that we're not going to be intimidated."

Lambert stayed in the game and emerged as one of the top players of Super Bowl X. To this day, Harris regrets his taunt of Gerela.

"I know what made me do that," said Harris. "I was intense and fired up and he just happened to be standing beside me as I was trying to block it. Of course, it did worse for us."

"It was just the heat of the moment," Pearson said. "It was a situation that happened in that game and Cliff was a very emotional player and a very aggressive player. The Steelers throughout the whole football game were trying to intimidate us, but we fought back. That was just one incident."

It was an incident that raised the level of play of Pittsburgh's defense to an astronomical level. Even with an injury to star lineman Joe Greene, Pittsburgh continued to pressure Staubauch. The man known as "Roger the Dodger" would be sacked seven times in Super Bowl X.

The Cowboys still held a 10–7 lead heading into the fourth quarter, but the Steelers special teams came up with one of the game's most critical plays. Mitch Hoopes' punt in front of his own end zone was blocked by Reggie Harrison for a safety. The Dallas lead was down to one point.

"That was a part of a film study," said Banaszak. "We felt we had a shot at getting that thing. Sure enough, Reggie gets free and gets up the middle and blocks the darn punt. It was a big play, there's no question about that."

The Steelers followed the safety with a drive to the Dallas 12-yard line. The drive stalled, but Gerela finally came through with a 36-yard field goal to give Pittsburgh the lead. After the kick went through, Gerela jawed at Harris on his way back to the sidelines.

Dallas looked to regain the lead on the ensuing drive, but Wagner had a surprise for Staubach and Pearson. The Cowboys called for the same play that worked for a touchdown early in the game. This time, Wagner was ready after playing it safe on the play which had resulted in a first-quarter touchdown.

"It was just a matter of getting to a spot," Wagner said. "I said that I was jumping on this one this time. Otherwise, I'm just standing there watching it."

Wagner intercepted Staubach's pass and returned it to the Dallas seven-yard line. The Cowboys dug in defensively yet again, but another Gerela field goal increased the Pittsburgh lead to 15–10 with 6:37 remaining. Wagner's interception had kept the momentum going for Pittsburgh.

"Those turnovers certainly killed us," Pearson said. "The pressure they were putting on Roger really hurt us. We tried to run the same play I had scored the touchdown on early in the game. Roger should have thrown it short to Billy Joe DuPree, who was running an underneath clearing route. They read it well and picked off the play and that kind of turned the game."

After Dallas was forced to punt again, Swann would make another critical catch with the help of a heroic effort by Bradshaw. The Steelers' signal caller fired a 64-yard touchdown to Swann, putting the Steelers up, 21–10, with 3:02 remaining.

But Bradshaw paid a heavy price.

After dodging the first pass rusher, the quarterback received a blow to the head thanks to a hit from Larry Cole. Bradshaw threw a perfect strike to Swann before the hit, but was knocked out of the game with a concussion. While most of the Steelers were celebrating with Swann in the end zone, Wagner and Running Back Rocky Bleier ran to their quarterback's aid.

"I looked back and I saw him get hit," said Wagner. "If you hit somebody in the temple of the helmet, they're probably going to be knocked out. I was trying to see if he was going to be all right."

Harris arrived at Bradshaw at the same time as Cole. Harris hit Bradshaw around his waist as Cole delivered the head shot.

"It was a safety blitz," said Harris. "I hit him high enough that I wound up landing on top of him. In the booth, they said Cliff Harris knocked out Terry Bradshaw. I have seen that replay many times where Larry Cole hit him with his elbow right in the chin."

While Bradshaw headed to the locker room, Staubach was looking to get his team back in the game. The Cowboys put together a scoring drive which ended with a 34-yard touchdown pass to Percy Howard.

"We never felt we were out of it no matter what the situation or what the score was," said Pearson. "We get another chance to step back out on that field and hopefully create another miracle."

With 1:48 remaining, Dallas tried an onside kick, but Mullins recovered on the Cowboys' 42. The Steelers gained only one yard on three plays, but Noll elected to run the ball again on fourth down. The Cowboys stopped Bleier at the 39 and Staubach had one more chance with 1:22 remaining. After an adventurous afternoon on special teams, Noll decided to trust his defense in the waning stages of Super Bowl X.

"I was totally going berserk over that call at the time," Mullins said. "To me, that was just stupidity. Obviously, it worked out. I think we almost had a couple of punts blocked earlier."

"This is why we play the game," Wagner said. "The challenge was if I could help the defense to help protect the lead and win the game. It became a challenge and I think that's where great athletes thrive. You want to be tested by the best in those kinds of situations."

Staubach moved the ball to the Pittsburgh 38 with three seconds remaining. His final desperation throw was intercepted in the end zone by Glen Edwards, who caught the ball after it glanced off the fingertips of Wagner.

"Drew couldn't reach it and I was behind him," recalled Wagner. "I really thought I could catch it, honestly. It slipped off my finger and I thought 'okay, that's good.' and then I'm thinking 'uh oh' because you don't know where all the players are behind you at that point in time and you're wondering where the ball goes."

The clock was at zero, but Edwards decided to head out of the end zone and into the open field much to the dismay of his teammates.

"That was the first thing out of my mouth," recalled Mullins. "It was 'Hit the deck! Hit the Deck!' Roger Staubach was a tremendous competitor. If there were any seconds on the clock, we were always in jeopardy with him out there. We never took anything for granted until the clock showed all zeroes."

"I see Glen catch it and then he starts running out of the end zone," Wagner said. "The only way they could win is if Glen fumbled the ball. He's running down the field and I'm sitting there thinking 'please fall down or run out of bounds.'"

Edwards did eventually fall on the turf as Pittsburgh celebrated its second straight Super Bowl title. The valiant Cowboys had fallen short, but Dallas had done its part to make Super Bowl X an all-time classic. Staubach believed there was one major difference between the two teams.

"I think we didn't play to the Steeler toughness," Staubach said. "We played a good game and we were a good team, but the Steelers were a better team. I think we played them pretty tough under the circumstances."

The Cowboys headed back to their buses in defeat, but one rookie soon learned that playing in Dallas was a little different than most NFL cities. White was in for a surprise when he was asked to head off the bus and into a police vehicle.

"The buses were all full and we're in a bad mood," said White. "The PR guy told my roommate and me to ride in the police escort car. There's a guy sitting in the back seat with long hair and a hat and beard. This guy taps me on the shoulder and says 'I'm Willie Nelson. I'm a big fan.' I told him that I was a big fan of him."

White and the Cowboys would drown their sorrows during a country music extravaganza in the hours following Super Bowl X.

"Jimmy Buffett was there," White said. "So were Jerry Jeff Walker, Waylon Jennings, Willie Nelson and Ray Wylie Hubbard. I got to go on stage and sing 'Up Against the Wall Redneck Mother' with Willie Nelson, so I'll never forget Super Bowl X."

The Steelers didn't need a country concert following their victory. The only question was how many more championships would be won by one of the most talented teams in NFL history.

"There was no question that we respected the Cowboys," Banaszak said. "But going into that game, we felt like we were a better football team. It was intense. It was the most intense situation in my football career to that point. The 22 starters went out on the field and played their 'A' game and that's what it takes to win a championship."

XI
THE RAIDERS REIGN SUPREME

The Oakland Raiders had waited long enough.

The franchise which had been dominated by Lombardi's Packers in Super Bowl II had evolved into pro football's outlaws. While the renegade Raiders were happy to wear the black hat, they had also become one of pro football's most successful franchises. Oakland's record over the past eight seasons was 83–22–7, but John Madden's squad consistently came up short of reaching the biggest game of the season. The stretch included four straight losses in the AFC Championship game, with the last two coming against their rivals from Pittsburgh. This time, the Raiders were finally able to conquer the Steelers, and were on their way to the Rose Bowl in Pasadena for Super Bowl XI. After finally breaking through in the AFC title game, many believed Oakland was destined to capture its first world championship. However, Linebacker Phil Villapiano knew from past experience that victory was far from a sure thing.

"We were anything but relaxed," said Villapiano. "And we were usually one of the most relaxed teams out there. We had lost the AFC Championship four years in a row. We knew that anything could happen at any time."

Another successful franchise awaited the Raiders in Pasadena, but the Minnesota Vikings hadn't had any issues in the past when it came to reaching the Super Bowl. The Vikings would be making their record fourth Super Bowl appearance. However, Bud Grant's team had come up short in its first three trips to the big game. Minnesota had captured its eighth division title in nine seasons. The Vikings were once again led by Quarterback Fran Tarkenton and Running Back Chuck Foreman along with their highly-touted defensive front.

"We hadn't played the Vikings in years," said Villapiano. "We knew they had Tarkenton and they had Foreman and that defense. We were ready to play football and we were ready to play a perfect game that day."

To play the perfect game, the Raiders first needed to get past their Super Bowl jitters. Madden kept the team relaxed and focused even before they headed south to Pasadena. Defensive Lineman Otis Sistrunk said Madden made the difference leading up to Super Bowl XI.

"John prepared us really well the week before the Super Bowl," said Sistrunk. "We had two weeks before the Super Bowl. When we got to Pasadena, it was more business than it was pleasure."

"I give John Madden credit," Villapiano said. "He kept us together. He kept us grounded. He kept us focused. We knew we had to play our best game, and that meant everybody."

After a stalemate through much of the first quarter, Minnesota created the first scoring chance of the game. Vikings Linebacker Fred McNeill blocked Ray Guy's punt, and Minnesota took over on the Oakland three-yard line. The Vikings seemed destined to score the first points of the game, but Villapiano forced a Brent McClanahan fumble. Willie Hall recovered the loose ball, and the Vikings missed a golden opportunity to gain the early momentum in Super Bowl XI.

"You look back now," Villapiano said. "You say it was a big, big play. When I knocked the ball out of there, I felt my head go right through the ball. I knew it was loose. I grabbed McClanahan. I wouldn't let his arms up, so he couldn't get it."

The Raiders took over on their own two-yard line, and Super Bowl nightmares from the past were likely creeping into the minds of the Vikings.

"It does set off a lot of negatives in your mind," said Villapiano. "The Vikings are like 'Oh, no. We've been here three times before and had this happen to us.' Maybe it did add a little doubt to those guys, but it fired us up."

It was time for the Oakland offense to go to work. One of the top targets for Quarterback Kenny Stabler was Wide Receiver Cliff Branch. However, Branch knew he would draw enough attention from the Vikings to open up room for fellow wide receiver Fred Biletnikoff and Tight End Dave Casper.

"I had a phenomenal year," said Branch. "We knew the Vikings weren't going to let me beat them deep. Fred and Dave just had a phenomenal game. They got man-to-man coverage when I got the double coverage. Fred just got loose and had an MVP-caliber game."

The Raiders marched 90 yards and capped off the drive with a field goal early in the second quarter. Minnesota went three and out on the ensuing possession, and the Raiders took over and began their first march to the end zone. A catch by Biletnikoff put the Raiders on the Minnesota one-yard line, where Ken Stabler finished the drive with a touchdown toss to Casper. With 7:10 left in the first half, Oakland had a 10–0 lead. Jim Marshall and the rest of the Minnesota front four were already being neutralized as the Raiders began to establish superiority in the trenches.

"They did a great job," said Marshall. "They double-teamed us a lot which really hurt."

The Oakland offensive line was led by future Hall of Famers Gene Upshaw and Art Shell. The Raiders attacked the right side of the Minnesota front, where Shaw and Shell took control against Marshall and Alan Page.

"You're talking about two of the best in the business," said Sistrunk. "I practiced against these guys the whole time I was with the Raiders. You need a lunch when you practice against those guys."

While there was no debating the success of Shell and Upshaw, Marshall believes changes could have been made to the Minnesota game plan to alleviate the effectiveness of the Oakland offensive line.

"We had a scheme our defensive coach figured out," Marshall said. "He wanted to stick with it, and we weren't able to adjust to some of the things that they were doing. During the season, we were able to freelance a lot more than we were in the Super Bowl. They wanted us to be a lot more disciplined. I think that hindered our ability to overcome some of the things that we should have overcome."

After another Minnesota three and out, a punt return by Neal Cozie put the Raiders on the Vikings' 35-yard line. A pass to Biletnikoff at the one-yard line set up a touchdown run by Pete Banaszak, and the Raiders took a 16–0 lead into the locker room at halftime. It would mark the fourth time in four Super Bowl trips in which the Vikings finished the first half with no points.

"The Vikings had a very good ball club that year," said Sistrunk. "But once Kenny and everyone started putting points on the board, we knew all we had to do was stop Fran Tarkenton and the rest of those guys from getting into the end zone."

Despite a dominating first half, the Raiders had no plans to take their feet of the gas pedal over the final two quarters.

"We knew the game was far from over," Recalled Villapiano. "We knew we had to keep doing what we were doing. At halftime, it was business as usual as professionals. We were happy with the lead, but we weren't going to sit on it. We knew those guys could score."

Both offenses struggled at the start of the third quarter, but Oakland would move to the Minnesota 23-yard line with 5:16 left in the period. Another field goal by Errol Mann made the score 19–0. The Vikings finally reached the end zone on their next possession when Sammy White hauled in an eight-yard pass from Tarkenton. Minnesota had cut the Oakland lead to 19–7, and the Vikings were back in the game.

Oakland would now allow Minnesota to get closer. Minnesota got the ball back after forcing Oakland to punt, but Tarkenton was intercepted by Hall, and the Raiders moved in for the kill.

"A guy like Willie Hall should be in the Hall of Fame," said Sistrunk. "When he got that interception, we knew it was downhill after that. When Willie Hall got that interception, I knew we were almost home."

"He was one of the real unsung heroes," Villapiano said. "A lot of people don't talk about him. He did so many good things for us. When he intercepted that ball, we felt pretty good."

A 48-yard reception by Biletnikoff put Oakland on the Minnesota two-yard line. Banaszak plowed in for his second score of the day, and the Raiders' were 7:39 away from their first Super Bowl title.

"John told us not to let up," Sistrunk said. "When you've got somebody down, you kick 'em. We had Minnesota on the ropes and we had them down. All we had to do was put them away."

A play which summed up the day for both teams came just before the Hall interception. Tarkenton completed a pass to White over the middle, but a jolting hit by Jack Tatum with help from Skip Thomas separated White from his helmet. White held onto the ball, but the intimidating Raiders had delivered another blow to the Vikings.

"He didn't want to come back anymore," Villapiano said. "Wide receivers are pretty and they can run, but they don't like to get hit. When you get a hit like that from Jack Tatum, you're done for the day."

Oakland's defense would strike one more blow as Willie Brown's 75-yard interception return with 5:43 remaining increased the lead to 32–7. A late Viking touchdown made the final score 32–14. After coming close so many times, the Raiders were Super Bowl champions.

"We had been knocking on the door," said Branch. "It was just a great joy to finally get it accomplished. It was a relief and a joyful celebration. We finally finished the deal."

The victory was also satisfying for Madden and Owner Al Davis. The two future Hall of Famers had built one of the top franchises in football. After falling short of the Super Bowl after decades of winning seasons, Madden and Davis were finally on top of the football world.

"I think the whole team was happy for John and Mr. Davis," said Sistrunk. "Mr. Davis was one of the best owners in the NFL and John was one of the best coaches. Once we got to the big dance, we danced all night and we danced all day."

"We all know the reputation Al had in those days and the Raiders had," said Villapiano. "We were kind of on our own island. I think that's why a lot of people really liked to watch us play. We were the bad-ass team and the renegades. We had the reputation and deserved the reputation. That made it all so much more fun."

It was not fun for the Vikings, who had fallen flat in the Super Bowl for the fourth time. Many of the Minnesota players were on the field for all four defeats, and Marshall has tried to erase the memories of those not so Super Sundays for the Vikings.

"It was hard to lose," said Marshall. "You don't really think of it as single plays or what value they could have been. You think of the loss. I've kind of shredded all of the memory of all those losses. It was so painful, especially that last Super Bowl game against the Raiders."

Even with four Super Bowl losses, it is hard to tarnish what the Vikings accomplished during a remarkable nine-year period. Eight division titles and four trips to the Super Bowl are accomplishments that many franchises can only dream about. Marshall has tried to put his team's Super Bowl reputation in perspective, even though the pain still lingers from those four championship chances.

"There are guys who never had a chance to play in a Super Bowl game," said Marshall. "I hear that from a lot of my peers around the league. I think it's even worse to be on that big stage and not perform up to a standard that got you there. Whenever there's a winner, there has to be a loser."

The winners of Super Bowl XI were the Oakland Raiders. It was easy for Sistrunk to put his championship in perspective after becoming the first player to win a Super Bowl who did not play football in college.

"It was a great thrill for me making it to the Super Bowl," Sistrunk said. "That's something they can't take from you. If you've got the rung, you've got the ring. You're going to spend the money. The money's gone, but the ring with the title of Super Bowl Champion against the Minnesota Vikings will always stay with us."

XII
DEVASTATION BY DOOMSDAY

It would be Doomsday versus Orange Crush in Super Bowl XII.

The NFC-Champion Dallas Cowboys headed to New Orleans as the favorite. While Tom Landry's squad had plenty of offensive firepower, the Dallas defenders had been terrorizing offenses throughout the league in 1977. The "Doomsday Defense" looked to bring the franchise its second Super Bowl crown against a surprise party crasher from the AFC.

The Denver Broncos hardly had resume of Super Bowl representatives from the past. It took 14 years for the former AFL franchise to record a winning season. However, the 1977 Broncos were buoyed by their powerful

"Orange Crush" defense, and the Broncos went from NFL doormats to AFC Champions. Denver defeated Pittsburgh and Oakland in the post-season, so there was no denying the Broncos legitimacy on their march to Super Sunday. Denver's success painted the entire state of Colorado orange throughout much of the season, and Linebacker Randy Gradishar and his teammates were feeding off the energy from an entire region.

"The people throughout Colorado were just going nuts throughout the whole year," Gradishar said. "Everything was blue and orange. That whole thing of Orange Crush caught on."

While Denver was making its first Super Bowl appearance, Dallas would be playing in its fourth. The Cowboys lost to the Steelers in Super Bowl X four years after winning Super Bowl VI. Roger Staubach was in his first full year as a starter when the Cowboys captured their first championship, and it was clear the torch had been passed to a new generation of Cowboys.

"It was two different eras," said Staubach. "We had a lot of different players for that game. There were only a few of us from XII that were in VI."

While Staubach prepared to lead the Cowboys, the man under center for Denver was ready for some unfinished business. Craig Morton was the starting quarterback for Dallas when the Cowboys lost Super Bowl V. After Staubach took over the following season, it was clear Morton's days were numbered in Dallas. He was traded to the Giants in 1974 and arrived in Denver three years later. For the first time ever, a quarterback would face his former team in a Super Bowl. Both quarterbacks downplayed the matchup heading into the game, but Staubach admits there was added motivation to beat his former teammate.

"There was," Staubach said. "Craig Morton still had a lot of friends in Dallas. He was the MVP that year in the AFC. Losing to Craig would have made them say that they got rid of the wrong quarterback. That's a natural feeling, but I had a very good relationship with Craig Morton."

Drew Pearson wasn't surprised that Staubach was determined to come out on top against Morton, but the Dallas Wide Receiver said his quarterback kept his feelings on the matter to himself during Super Bowl week.

"There was motivation," said Pearson. "He would not tell you, me or coach Landry. You could not see that in him but knowing Roger and knowing the type of athlete he is and knowing how driven he is, he wanted to prove that the Cowboys made the right choice."

The two teams were already familiar with each other. Dallas defeated Denver, 14–6, in the regular season finale. Many of the regulars rested with playoff positioning already determined, but the tone was set for Super Bowl XII.

"It was another physical game," said Pearson. "Denver was a very good football team. They came in all fired up with all this Orange Crush stuff they were talking about. We knew one thing that they had was defense. They had some playmakers on offense, but the reason they got to the Super Bowl was their defense."

When Dallas traded Morton in 1974, the Cowboys received a pair of draft picks. One was used to select Randy White, who moved from linebacker to defensive line in 1977. The switch turned White into one of the most feared defensive players in football, and "The Manster" was hungry for a Super Bowl ring after falling shot his rookie season.

"You wanted a Super Bowl ring," White said. "I didn't care about anything else. I wanted a World Championship Super Bowl ring. I didn't know much about what it meant the rest of your life and still being remembered. I just wanted to win that football game and get a Super Bowl ring."

White was joined on the defensive line by Ed "Too Tall" Jones, Harvey Martin and Jethro Pugh. One of the linebackers behind this devastating front was Thomas "Hollywood" Henderson, one of the NFL's most outspoken players. Henderson became a force at strong side linebacker in 1977, and didn't believe Morton and his teammates could stand up to Doomsday.

"I don't think Craig Morton could beat us," said Henderson. "I think in '77, we had the best defense in football. We had no injuries and a tremendous group of men. I don't think they had a shot."

Cliff Harris had practiced against Morton during his early days in Dallas. The safety knew there was both a technical and psychological advantage going against his former teammate.

"That was a major factor knowing Craig Morton so well," Harris said. "I faced him every day in practice for years, and I know him as a person. That's a key point about this position that I played. It's really the understanding not just of the athlete you are facing but the person you are facing."

The Broncos knew Morton would have motivation of his own, but Gradishar also believed Denver's defense would have to once again make the difference if the Broncos were to pull off the upset.

"The sense was the defense was going to have to help win the game," Gradishar said. "Craig was humble enough that he certainly didn't make a big deal about it to us players. The reality is, from a human standpoint, there's a little bit extra."

But it would be more than just Staubach which presented a problem for Orange Crush. The addition of rookie Tony Dorsett gave the Cowboys a more powerful running game in 1977.

"We got Dorsett," Staubach said. "If you look at Dallas' running game in '74, '75, and '76, it wasn't as strong during those three years. When we got Tony again, we had a fantastic running game. We were really a much better team offensively in that '77 season than we were in '75."

When the Cowboys won Super Bowl VI in New Orleans, the temperature at kickoff was a chilly 39 degrees at Tulane Stadium. There would no concerns about cold conditions in this championship game. This would be the first Super Bowl to be played indoors, with the game taking place in the Louisiana Superdome.

The first half of Super Bowl XII featured a plethora of mistakes on both sides, but the Cowboys were able to avoid disaster. Dallas fumbled three times in the first quarter but each time, a hustling Cowboy was able to fall on the football. It was a different story for Denver, as the Broncos would give the ball away at a record pace.

On the Broncos second possession, Charlie Waters and White sandwiched Morton in the pocket. Morton made an ill-advised attempt at a short pass and Randy Hughes' interception put Dallas on the Denver 25. Five plays later, a three-yard run by Tony Dorsett gave the Cowboys a 7–0 lead.

It was just the beginning of the Denver turnover parade. On the next possession, Jones devoured Morton on a throw, and Aaron Kyle's interception set up an Efren Herrera field goal to put Dallas up, 10–0. Three more Denver turnovers in the second quarter prevented Morton and his teammates from gaining any kind of offensive momentum. The Cowboys also coughed up an opportunity when Billy Joe Dupree fumbled in Denver territory, but the mistakes were minuscule compared to those of the Broncos. By halftime, the Cowboys had a 13–0 lead, and the Broncos had committed seven turnovers. Four of the mistakes were interceptions by Morton, and the former Cowboy quarterback was lucky to be in one piece after the host of hits from the menacing Dallas front four.

"I don't think we had any more special info on Craig than we did anybody else," said White. "He wasn't the most mobile of quarterbacks. We knew one of the keys was to put pressure on Craig Morton, disrupt his timing and not let him throw the ball effectively."

"We definitely played with an over and above intensity level," said Harris. "I think one of the things that drove us so much was knowing Craig. He's a good guy. I don't dislike him, but we just wanted to beat him because he was a friend."

While the Dallas defense was having its way with Morton, the Broncos continued to self-destruct with a wave of mistakes.

"It was very frustrating," Recalls Gradishar. "We had eight turnovers in the whole game. You can't win a Super Bowl with eight turnovers. That turnover ratio certainly hurt us."

Thanks to the play of the Orange Crush defense, Denver was still within two scores at the start of the second half. The Broncos were finally able to hold onto the football on the opening drive of the third quarter, and a 47-yard field goal by Jim Turner cut the Cowboys' lead to ten. Later in the period, Butch Johnson's diving fingertip catch from 45 yards out put Dallas up, 20–3. It was a devastating blow for the Broncos thanks to a brilliant catch by Johnson and some quick thinking by Staubach.

"That was a big play," said Staubach. "We kind of took advantage of the things that we saw on film. I told Butch when he brought the play in that I'd be looking at him to throw it to if their weak safety stayed in the middle like we saw on film."

"They overplayed me on the play," Recalls Pearson. "It left Butch open on the post pattern with Roger adjusting that call figuring he would get that type of coverage in that situation."

While the Cowboys were celebrating their touchdown, their ever-stoic head coach was surprised to see Johnson change the pattern on the play to a deep post.

"Butch tells the story," Recalled Staubach. "Landry said, 'You were supposed to run in-route. What's going on out there?' Here we got a touchdown in the Super Bowl, and coach is almost chewing out Butch Johnson. He never said a word to me. Butch just said that Roger told me to run the post."

Rick Upchurch pulled the Broncos off life support with a 67-yard kickoff return. After another near-interception, Morton was replaced by the mobile Norris Weese, who led the Broncos to their first touchdown. Rob Lytle's one-yard run cut the Dallas lead to 20–10. Somehow, after seven turnovers and a quarterback change, Denver was still alive.

"It was 20–10," Gradishar said. "I remember talking with the defensive guys on the sidelines saying we still had a chance to win."

But the Cowboys were hardly shaking in their boots when Weese entered the game.

"I think the mistake the Broncos made when they brought Weese in was that they kept the running backs in to add protection," said Henderson. "It made me key and blitz. I think on one blitz, I almost killed him. I blitzed one time, and I thought they were going to call 911."

"There was no way Norris Weese was going to beat the Dallas Cowboys on that day," said Pearson. "Our defense ended up being more dominant in a very physical football game."

It was only appropriate that another Denver turnover finished off the Broncos. Weese fumbled on a hit by Martin with just over seven minutes remaining, and it took just one play on the ensuing drive for Dallas to wrap up its second world championship. It came from a perfect throw from someone other than Staubach. Running Back Robert Newhouse hit Goldie Richards on an option pass, and Richards' touchdown made it 27–10. The Cowboys had finally landed the knockout blow.

"He called it to the left," said Staubach. "When we practiced it, Newhouse had a hard enough time throwing it to the right, and he throws a perfect pass to Golden. That put the game away."

"We called them deceptives in Landry's school of thinking," Quipped Pearson. "We ran that fullback pass to the left to Robert Newhouse which caught them off guard. We had to come up with those kinds of plays to score against their defense, because they were physical throughout."

The Cowboys were fortunate to have the option play in their offensive arsenal. Staubach would have had a difficult time making a similar throw after suffering an injury early in the final period.

"I broke my top of my finger in the fourth quarter of that game," Staubach said. "I went in the locker room and they shot it and they took the blood out of it. It was swelled up. It was tip of my right finger, which was on my throwing hand. I had to get a pin in it the next day. I would have been out ten weeks if it wasn't the last game of the year."

In a day dominated by Doomsday, it was only appropriate White and Martin shared the Most Valuable Player award. However, White was more concerned with getting a Super Bowl ring than the MVP trophy as the final seconds ticked away in New Orleans.

"Harvey comes over and puts his arm around me," White said. "He said that we were co-MVPs of the game. I looked at him and I said 'Oh really? Good.' I didn't really know what that meant. It wasn't even on my mind. Then we got to go to New York and got the car."

White and Martin were part of a defense that stole the spotlight from Morton in Super Bowl XII, and White believes any one of the Dallas defenders could have taken home MVP honors. White was one of several Cowboys who would experience their first and only Super Bowl victory under the dome in New Orleans.

"We had been there and lost," said White. "Now, we had won. If you lose even though you're playing to be the world's best team, you feel like you're a loser. When you lose that game, it stays with you for a while. We were able to win one, and for the rest of your life, nobody can take that away from you."

"Greatest feeling in the world," Pearson said. "You have kids in your life. You get married and have those special moments in your life. As far as an athlete, this was the pinnacle. This is why I still get respect nowadays because you won that Super Bowl."

Staubach and Landry savored their second championship with a much different cast that came out on top in Super Bowl VI.

"Coach Landry was proud of the fact that he had a whole different team," said Staubach. "It was a good feeling to show that it wasn't a fluke that you won it once. For those eleven years I played, we never had a losing season. We always were in the thick of it."

There would be little consolation for the Broncos. A Cinderella season had been derailed by a Super Bowl nightmare in a turnover-filled disaster. However, the "Orange Crush" is still fondly remembered by Broncos fans across the country. While Denver would go on to have its share of Super Bowl success, Gradishar and his teammates were the first to put the spotlight on the franchise.

"We were very proud," said Gradishar. "That part of Bronco history. We take a lot of pride. People still remember that first Super Bowl. There's always a beginning. The excitement laid a new foundation for the Broncos. We were responsible in helping bringing that foundation."

The Broncos had come a long way in 1977, but the crown belonged to the Cowboys, and a Super Bowl title was hardly taken for granted by the victors.

"I was part of a 45-man team that won it all," Henderson said. "There's not that many human beings who can say that. It's one of my prouder accomplishments in my life as [a member of] a team."

XIII
BATTLE OF THE BEST

It had the feel of a heavyweight title fight.

In a decade full of talented teams, Super Bowl XIII would pit the top two franchises of the 1970's. The Pittsburgh Steelers were back in the Super Bowl after a two-year absence and were looking for their third title in five years. The Dallas Cowboys came to this Super Bowl as the defending world champions and were also looking for their third title of the decade. This would be the first Super Bowl rematch. The two teams had battled three years prior and had put together one of the best Super Bowls ever. This one appeared poised to top all of the others in a game which would feature 14 future Hall of Fame players and two future Hall of Fame head coaches. Dallas Wide Receiver Drew Pearson could sense the anticipation building throughout the week in Miami. He also knew this would be a better edition of the Cowboys than the one that lost to Pittsburgh in Super Bowl X.

"We knew they were chomping at the bit to get back to the Super Bowl," said Pearson. "But we felt we were on par with them this time. We felt we were just as good if not better than them. We had a phenomenal year offensively and defensively. We knew this was going to be a heavyweight fight."

Dallas Defensive Lineman Randy White was a rookie when the two teams met in Super Bowl X. Three years later, White was emerging as a dominant defensive player, but White knew he and his teammates would have their hands full with the Steelers.

"It was two great teams," said White. "It was a great game and a great matchup. Pittsburgh had a great team and we had a great team."

The Steelers had terrorized NFL offenses throughout the 1970's with a menacing defense. While the "Steel Curtain" still had the ability to dominate, new rules in the NFL allowed greater freedom for offensive players. One rule limited contact by defenders to within five yards of the line of scrimmage. It was nicknamed "The Mel Blount Rule" since the Pittsburgh Cornerback had emerged as one of the toughest defensive backs in the NFL. For Pittsburgh Guard Gerry Mullins, the new restrictions gave Quarterback Terry Bradshaw and his offensive teammates a better opportunity to light up the scoreboard.

"We had basically been a ball-control team in the first two," Mullins said. "Now, we had the weapons and Terry had the confidence. He could strike at any point in time. It was a different mindset. With the talent we had at wide receiver, we could score on anybody at any time."

The Cowboys were also putting up points with Quarterback Roger Staubach back at the helm. However, Dallas had added a powerful weapon to their offense the previous season. Tony Dorsett helped lead the Cowboys to a world championship his rookie year and the second year running back continued his torrid pace in his second season. Pittsburgh Safety Mike Wagner knew defenses around the league would have their hands full once Dorsett arrived in the NFL.

"I thought this was going to put the Cowboys in the Super Bowl," said Wagner. "Tony was just that kind of player. My biggest concern is how we were going to handle that offense with Tony Dorsett."

"We were a better team in '78," said Staubach. "Tony Dorsett was in his second year and (wide receiver) Tony Hill was getting more play. We were really good on offense and defense the whole season."

The Dallas Defense also had its share of stars. The unit known as "Doomsday" was second in the NFL in total yards allowed. One of the more flamboyant players on the Dallas Defense was Thomas "Hollywood" Henderson, a man who was never afraid to express himself.

"I came from a trash-talking family," said Henderson.

Henderson's trash talking was in full force before Super Bowl XIII. The linebacker offered his thoughts on the intelligence of Bradshaw, but insists it was spurred on by Cowboys Vice-President of Player Personnel Gil Brandt.

"He knew that I was pretty good with quips and talking trash," Henderson said. "He came to me and said 'Did you know that Terry Bradshaw wanted to go to LSU but couldn't get in because he couldn't pass the ACT or the SAT?' Gil looked at me and asked what I could do with that."

Henderson decided to use Brandt's information and turn it into a verbal swipe at Bradshaw.

"I came up with the line because I thought academically that Terry may be a little slow," said Henderson. "I came up with the line that Terry Bradshaw couldn't spell 'cat' if you spotted him the 'C' and the 'A.' This is based on Gil Brandt teeing it up for me."

The Steelers refused to get into a trash-talking competition with Henderson. Defensive Lineman John Banaszak was more concerned about stopping the likes of Staubach and Dorsett and had complete confidence in his quarterback.

"I can't remember us ever discussing something like that," said Banaszak. "We all read the quote from Hollywood Henderson. We knew what Terry Bradshaw could do on a football field. Terry Bradshaw was the offensive leader on the football team. Whether or not he could spell 'cat' if you spotted him the "C" and the "A" didn't really matter to us."

Super Bowl XIII got off the type of explosive start fans were anticipating. Dallas attempted to run a reverse, but the ball was fumbled and recovered by Banaszak on the Pittsburgh 47.

"We're on our heels and they try to gimmick us with a little reverse that I recovered," Banaszak said. "I think that changes the first half."

The Steelers moved to the Dallas 28. Bradshaw fired a touchdown pass to John Stallworth and Pittsburgh had drawn first blood. The Steelers forced the Cowboys to punt on the ensuing drive and Bradshaw followed by quickly moving his unit into Dallas territory, but Linebacker D.D. Lewis intercepted Bradshaw. The quarterback's troubles continued after Dallas was forced to punt. Bradshaw was sacked by Harvey Martin and fumbled the football. The Cowboys recovered and took over in Pittsburgh territory. On the final play of the first quarter, Staubach was hit by Wagner on an all-out blitz, but the quarterback was able to get the ball to Hill. The receiver raced 39 yards for a touchdown to tie the game at 7–7.

"We knew it wasn't going to be an easy football game," Banaszak said. "It was a classic battle between two teams that knew each other pretty well. We played them every year in the preseason. We knew an awful lot about the Dallas Cowboys. They knew an awful lot about us. The two teams went toe-to-toe against each other."

The Dallas Defense would make the next big play at the start of the second quarter. Pittsburgh moved the ball near midfield, but Bradshaw was hit by Henderson and Mike Hegman. With Henderson wrapped around Bradshaw, Hegman ripped the ball loose and ran 37 yards for a touchdown to give the Cowboys a 14–7 lead. Undaunted by the flurry of mistakes, Bradshaw struck back on the ensuing drive. A quick ten-yard pass to Stallworth turned into a 75-yard catch and run for a touchdown. Safety Cliff Harris trailed helplessly behind the play as Stallworth raced into the end zone. The veteran knew the challenge of stopping Stallworth and Lynn Swann would be more difficult in this Super Bowl with the new rules in effect.

"Stallworth and Swann were both great receivers," said Harris. "You change the defense and they went from a zone to a man-to-man to keep it simple. It made one of our stronger defenses a weaker defense."

The Cowboys put together another drive in the closing minutes of the half, but Staubach was intercepted by Blount, who took the ball to the Pittsburgh 29. Staubach threw in Pearson's direction after seeing coverage on Tight End Billy Joe DuPree.

"That was a big play," said Staubach. "Mel Blount came into the play. He told me afterwards he knew we were going to run that play and they were going to switch. Coach Landry said that our tight end was wide open and I told him somebody was on Billy Joe. When he saw the film later, he apologized to me."

Bradshaw quickly moved his offense back into Dallas territory. With 26 seconds remaining in the half, Bradshaw fired a seven-yard touchdown pass to Rocky Bleier. After a wild 30 minutes, the Steelers went to the locker room with a 21–14 lead.

"We had a tremendous offense," Wagner said. "We knew on defense we might give up 15, 20 or 25 points, but we knew our offense was going to put 25 or 35 points on the board. I think you saw it in the first half of that game."

Both defenses dug in early in the third quarter, but Dallas mounted a drive late in the period and reached the Pittsburgh ten-yard line. The Cowboys were faced with a third and three as Landry sent in a unique play. Reserve Tight End Jackie Smith entered the game.

"It was a play that we put in for short yardage and goal line the Friday before the game." recalled Staubach. "We put three tight ends in the game. Jackie was the third tight end and his job was to be a safety valve."

Staubach dropped back as Smith crossed over the middle in the end zone. Smith was wide open and Staubach threw to the future Hall of Famer, but Smith began to lose his footing as the ball arrived. The tight end dropped the football as he fell to the ground and the Cowboys were forced to settle for a field goal.

"We had never seen that play on defense," said Wagner. "They could have run that play ten times. We didn't know how to defend it, but he slipped. It had been raining slightly and it was wet. The ball was thrown behind him and his body was out of control, but there was a lot going on. The game wasn't decided by that."

Many fans point to Smith's drop after the game as one that may have cost Dallas the game. A touchdown would have tied the game at 21–21.

However, Staubach believes he should have made a harder throw as Smith crossed into the middle of the end zone.

"There is nobody near Jackie Smith," Staubach said. "If he would have stopped at the goal line, I would have drilled the ball to him. He was a safety valve. He didn't expect the ball to be there that quick. I think it shocked him."

Smith had joined the Cowboys after a long and successful stint with the Cardinals, but is remembered by many for the dropped pass in Super Bowl XIII. Players on both sides to this day are quick to defend Smith and believe a host of other factors ultimately decided the outcome of the game.

"Everybody pointed to that particular play after the game," Banaszak said. "It gave the impression that cost them the game. First of all, it would have only tied the game. Second of all, we still had another whole quarter to play."

"He gets way too much blame for that," Pearson said. "We sent Dorsett in motion and in doing that, we figured the linebackers would go with Dorsett and they did. Jackie was wide open. Roger takes blame for the incompletion because instead of firing the ball in there, he kind of took something off it. That may have thrown Jackie's timing off on that pass."

"It's the third quarter," said Staubach. "It's not like it's the last play of the game. There's still plenty of time. I think it's one of the worst accusations that I've ever seen in football to accuse a guy of costing us a game."

Smith's drop was the beginning of a chain of events that turned the tide of Super Bowl XIII. It began early in the fourth quarter when Bradshaw lobbed a deep pass downfield for Swann. Dallas Defensive Back Benny Barnes got his feet tangled with Swann as he fell to the ground. Barnes was called for pass interference, and the Steelers had the ball on the Cowboys' 23-yard line.

"I signaled that I wanted to run a safety blitz because I thought I could get Bradshaw," said Harris. "I was just a fraction away from him. Chuck Noll knew where I wasn't. There was a weakness. I was a free safety and if he threw it there, that was my position."

The call still haunts many of the Cowboys to this day who believe no flag should have been thrown on the play.

"Fred Swearingen was the official who threw the flag late," Staubach said. "He was in the middle of the field. If you see the film of that, the referee that is right on the play is signaling incomplete pass. The competition committee said if you throw the flag and someone sees the play better than you, you can pick the flag up, but those things happen."

The Steelers quickly took advantage of their opportunity. A sack was nullified by a delay of game penalty, but Henderson followed through with a hit on Bradshaw. Franco Harris came to his quarterback's aid and the usually calm and quiet running back began jawing at Henderson.

"He just touched me on the shoulder and said something," Henderson said. "I called him a powder puff. I told him he should be playing with girls because he blocked like a bitch. He was just soft to me."

Harris was anything but soft on the ensuing play. The running back burst through the middle for a 22-yard touchdown run. To add to the Cowboys' frustration, Safety Charlie Waters had a chance to tackle Harris but accidentally collided with Umpire Art Demmas. However, Harris was clearly motivated as he raced into the end zone.

"There could have been a penalty on Henderson," recalled Wagner. "Franco, in particular, really took issue. Franco went to the huddle and said 'Give me the ball.' You rarely see him get worked up. You watch the angle from the end zone and you see the determination with him running for those yards. That was a huge play."

"He was a guy that talked softly but carried a big stick," Mullins said. "You didn't want to get him upset if you were the opposition."

The misery continued for Dallas on the ensuing kickoff. Kicker Roy Gerela slipped and the ball bounced to White at his own 24. White had a cast on his left hand due to a broken bone and could not get a strong grip on the ball. White fumbled and Pittsburgh's Dennis Winston recovered the loose ball on the Dallas 18. On the play after the fumble, Bradshaw fired a high pass into the end zone where Swann made an acrobatic catch in front of a trailing Harris for another Pittsburgh touchdown.

"The team that's able to make the plays usually wins," White said. "The team that's not usually loses. Pittsburgh was able to make the big plays. It's not a whole lot more complicated than that."

"They were just fluky things that shouldn't have happened that would have certainly made a difference," said Harris.

Trailing 35–17, it appeared the cause was lost for Dallas, but Staubach refused to throw in the towel. "Captain Comeback" tried to rally his troops and the Cowboys put together an 89-yard scoring drive. Staubach connected with Billy Joe DuPree from seven-yards out to cut the Pittsburgh lead to 35–24. Dallas recovered an onside kick with just over two minutes remaining and Staubach went back to work.

"You've got a chance to win with him and the people around him," said White. "When Roger was there, we always believed if we could stop this team and get the ball back, we've got a good chance of winning the football game. We felt we would win most of them."

Staubach put together another scoring drive with the help of a pair of catches by Pearson for 22 and 25 yards. The receiver was hit by Wagner on the second catch and the jolt forced Pearson to the sidelines with cracked ribs. With 22 seconds to play, Staubach threw a four-yard touchdown pass to Butch Johnson. The score was 35–31, but the clock was the enemy of the Cowboys.

"We started making some plays and moving the football," Pearson said. "I think we just ran out of time. We made our move a little too late. We opened up our offense a little too late, but a lot of it has to do with the Steelers. We were up against one of the greatest defenses of all time."

"It's one of the things I truly respect Roger Staubach for," Banaszak said. "He was a competitor. There was no 'give up' in him or the Cowboys. They fought their way back into that football game. When they scored again, it got really hairy on the sidelines. We had to finish the game."

Dallas had one last chance, but an onside kick was fielded by Bleier. The Steelers ran out the clock and had their third Super Bowl title in five years. Two of their championships had come in epic battles with the Cowboys.

"Beating the Cowboys twice in two Super Bowls was real satisfying," Wagner said. "That's not to demean them at all. It's because they were a really great team. I never played on a losing championship team, so I can't imagine. They're the ones that probably sit there and go through the 'what ifs.'"

Many of the Cowboys reflect on what might have been to this day. A victory would have evened the number of Super Bowl titles in the 70's between Pittsburgh and Dallas at three apiece. The Cowboys of the 1970's are still fondly remembered by their fans, but the pain from Super Bowl XIII still lingers.

"I get together with Roger now," said Pearson. "We start talking about business or kids or family. The next thing I know, we're talking about that game. We felt we should have had that game and there's no question history probably would have been turned. They're all painful, but that loss to the Steelers that year in Super Bowl XIII was very painful and something we still talk about today as far as what we could have done."

"I wanted to win that game," said Harris. "I wanted to beat that team. I think we would have been defined as the team of the decade. It's not a personal thing for me. The one that I wished we could have won was Super Bowl XIII. It was an extraordinarily significant game. I don't think the pain has diminished too much from Super Bowl XIII."

For Henderson, there was more than a painful memory of a Super Bowl loss after his football career ended. The linebacker overcame a drug addiction and has been clean and sober since 1983. Henderson expressed regret about his comments towards Bradshaw before the Super Bowl and had the chance to apologize to the quarterback in person.

"I really felt bad about it," Henderson said. "I've been sober now for over 33 years. Right around my 15-year sober anniversary, Terry Bradshaw with CBS came to Austin to interview me. I pulled Terry to the side and said 'I really want to apologize for what I said about you. I was just trash-talking and I want to make amends to you about that.'"

At first, Bradshaw wasn't sure if Henderson was sincere, but realized Henderson's apology was heartfelt and thanked his former adversary.

In 2000, Henderson won $28 million in a Texas lottery. He created a charity to help young individuals in the East Austin, Texas area.

Meanwhile, the Steelers were enjoying their championship jackpot in the 1970's. They had become the dominant team of the decade with their victory in Super Bowl XIII. Even with the win, the Steelers credit the Cowboys for bringing out the best they had to offer on the football field.

"You always want to see if you can be challenged," Wagner said. "You want to be tested against the best. The other reality is you aren't always going to win. I always tell people the battle is on the football field. It's not in the stands and it's not in the parking lot and it's not in the media. The battle is on the football field. When that's over, let's respect effort."

The Steelers will always have the respect of one of the greatest quarterbacks ever to play the game.

"I would vote for the Steelers as the best team I've ever played against," said Staubach. "They just had it all together. I can't complain about losing to the Steelers. I hate to lose, but we lost to a great football team."

XIV
STALLWORTH SAVES THE STEELERS

The Los Angeles Rams were the party crashers in their own backyard.

While most teams have to travel far from home to play in the Super Bowl, the Rams only had to go 10.8 miles from Los Angeles to Pasadena. The Rose Bowl would be the sight of Super Bowl XIV, as the underdog Rams would take on the mighty Pittsburgh Steelers. Los Angeles had several strong seasons during the 1970's, but had fallen short of a Super Bowl berth until the 1979 campaign. It was an unlikely group of Rams that was set to face one of the greatest teams of all time. Los Angeles went 9–7 during the regular season, which was the worst record for any team to reach a Super Bowl. Rams Owner Carroll Rosenbloom died before the season opener. The Rams spent much of the year dealing with reports of a move to Anaheim. There were also a host of injuries, including one to Quarterback Pat Haden. The starter suffered a broken finger and was replaced by third-year backup Vince Ferragamo. Despite these obstacles, the Rams won the NFC West and two road playoff games to advance to the Super Bowl.

"It was a roller coaster ride of a season," said Ferragamo. "First, not being expected to be in the playoffs and then making it with a 9–7 record. When I started playing mid-season, we caught fire. We were playing our best ball at the end of the season. They were total team victories with offense, defense and special teams."

The Rams would have little time to celebrate their first trip to the Super Bowl. The Pittsburgh Steelers would once again be the AFC representatives and Chuck Noll's squad would be looking for its fourth Super Bowl title in six years. However, there were cracks in the Steelers' armor in 1979. Pittsburgh's star players were now grizzled veterans and age had caught up to some of the Steelers. However, Noll continued to push his players to another level during the season. John Banaszak was already entrenched as a starter on the defensive line, but injuries forced the former undrafted free agent to play nearly every position on the defensive front.

"He always had high expectations for his football team," said Banaszak. "I know that he had to know how good we were. There's no doubt about that. He would always push us a little bit harder. His message was that we could do this all over again. He was a masterful motivator."

Other players were motivated but forced into action out of necessity. Gerry Mullins had been a fixture at guard for the Steelers throughout the decade but lost his starting job in 1979. However, an injury resulted in Mullins being back into a starting role for Super Bowl XIV.

"That was sort of the tail-end of my career," said Mullins. "I was battling some injuries. I had pretty much been replaced by Steve Courson. I was sort of a backup at the time but then Steve got hurt, so I ended up starting that game."

Most believed the Steelers would have little trouble disposing of the Rams, but the Pittsburgh players were far from overconfident. Los Angeles had beaten Pittsburgh three times during the decade, including twice during their Super Bowl seasons.

"It takes great talent to get to that position," said Mullins. "If you try to underestimate anybody, then you're a fool. A few of our old assistant coaches were with the Rams, so we knew they were going to be well coached. They had some great players, especially on their defensive line."

"There were three former Steeler coaches on their staff," Banaszak said. "They knew us probably better than any other opponent we could have faced in that game. They knew our personnel because of the coaches and we knew going in it was going to be a tough game."

Ferragamo and the Rams did not think the Steelers would take them lightly, but used the blowout predictions from fans and the media as motivation leading up to kickoff.

"We were heavy underdogs but that worked to our advantage," recalled Ferragamo. "We were given no respect but people who knew us thought different. That gave us more incentive and fired us up, especially the veteran players we had on our team."

The Rams were also hoping to enjoy a rare home-field advantage for the Super Bowl with Pasadena so close to their home turf. However, the loyal legion of Pittsburgh fans were once again making their presence felt as a host of "Terrible Towels" were waving at the Rose Bowl.

"Playing at the Rose Bowl was special to us and especially the players from Southern California on our team," Ferragamo said. "The fan base was split about 50/50. The Steelers' fans travel well and made a lot of noise that day."

One Ram would not let a major injury stop him from playing in the Super Bowl. Defensive Lineman Jack Youngblood had been playing the entire post-season with a fractured fibula, but was on the field for the start of Super Bowl XIV.

The Steelers lived up to their pre-game billing as the favorite early in the game. After holding the Rams to a three-and-out on the games' opening series, the Steelers put together a drive that ended with a 41-yard field goal by Matt Bahr. However, the Rams quickly served notice the Steelers would be in for a struggle. A 39-yard run on the ensuing drive by Wendell Tyler put the Rams on the Pittsburgh 14. Los Angeles would move to the Pittsburgh one, where Cullen Bryant scored on a third-down run. The Rams had a 7–3 lead.

"The Steel Curtain defense was just that," said Ferragamo. "It was tough to break. We were able to do things that most teams could not do. We beat them up front with our All-Pro caliber offensive line. We were able to push them around some but they were fast and strong. Wendell got loose with Kent Hill pulling around end and broke into the open field. That play boosted our confidence even more and we were feeling good."

Pittsburgh came right back. A kickoff return by Larry Anderson set the Steelers up on their 47-yard line. Pittsburgh's drive would chew up the remaining minutes of the opening quarter. Early in the second period, a touchdown run by Franco Harris put the Steelers back up by three. However, the underdog Rams would answer again as Ferragamo kept his cool against one of the greatest defenses in NFL history.

"It was fun playing against one of the greatest teams of all time," recalled Ferragamo. "They had no weaknesses. In those days, they along with Dallas were really fast. The Steeler mystique was simply impressive, so going toe-to-toe with them was fun and exciting. We were kind of unpredictable because I was young and in my first season as a starter, so they virtually had no film to really study our tendencies."

Two drives resulted in Frank Corral field goals, with the last one coming in the final seconds of the half. The Steelers went to the locker room trailing by three against a team many thought they would blow out.

"We were behind at the half but we had played pretty well," said Banaszak. "It wasn't like we were overconfident going into that game. Two teams were going toe-to-toe with each other."

"There wasn't panic," Mullins said. "It was a veteran group at that particular point in time. With Terry back there, you're never out of it. You knew if you just kept plugging away, good things will happen for you."

A similar message was being sent by Noll, who had seen his team mount its share of second half comebacks. Both Noll and his players kept their cool as they prepared to return for the second half.

"There was no panic whatsoever," said Banaszak. "He knew we had played well in the first half. We didn't make as many plays as we probably could have early in that game, but there was a sense of confidence in his demeanor at that point. It certainly trickled down to the players."

Most teams would have been more than happy to lead the Pittsburgh Steelers at halftime in a Super Bowl. There were no complaints from the Rams, but Ferragamo wonders today if it may have worked as a disadvantage.

"We had the lead," said Ferragamo. "Looking back, I kind of wish the score had been reversed. I think if we could have had some trick plays in the second half and made a few more adjustments at halftime, we may have had an answer to their comeback."

Pittsburgh began the second half looking to knock out the scrappy underdogs. On the first drive of the third quarter, the Steelers went back in front on a 47-yard touchdown catch by Lynn Swann. However, the Rams answered with a quick counterpunch. Known for a conservative approach throughout much of the season, Los Angeles Head Coach Ray Malavasi realized he had to open up the playbook.

"Ray Malavasi was one of the main reasons why we did so well," Ferragamo said. "He always game planned an offensive plan best suited for the defense we would be confronted with. He knew what offensive sets and plays gave defenses the most trouble. He was a defensive minded coach and was responsible for designing our great defense that he was so proud of."

Ferragamo connected with Billy Waddy for a 50-yard pass on the ensuing drive and Malavasi followed with a unique play-call with the Pittsburgh Defense still reeling from the bomb downfield. Los Angeles went with a half-back option and Lawrence McCutheon threw a 24-yard touchdown pass to Ron Smith. Corral missed the extra point attempt, but the Rams were back on top, 19–17, and one of the great upsets in Super Bowl history was within their grasp.

"The one trick play did work with Lawrence throwing the TD pass," said Ferragamo. If we had more of that and had more trick plays, I believed we could do it again."

The momentum swing carried over to the Los Angeles defense. Bending but not breaking, the Rams twice intercepted Bradshaw before the end of the third quarter. Eddie Brown had the first interception, and Rod Perry caught the second off a deflection at his own five-yard line. The Steelers also lost Swann to an injury, and the champs appeared to be on the ropes at the start of the fourth quarter.

But the Steelers kept their cool.

"We're on the sidelines in a real tight ball game," recalled Banaszak. "We've been in that situation before. This is a veteran football team that was on the verge of winning its fourth Super Bowl. I think that's what took over in the fourth quarter."

Early in the fourth, Pittsburgh was faced with a third down and eight own its own 27. Bradshaw fired deep and hit John Stallworth on a 73-yard bomb which put Pittsburgh back on top.

"Terry Bradshaw is facing a third and eight," Banaszak said. "I'm thinking that we're going to throw a possession pass here, get the first down and drive the ball down the field. Bradshaw doesn't do that. He reads the coverage and reads the blitz. He throws this freaking bomb and it's right on the money to Stallworth."

After an exchange of punts, the Rams had the ball back with 8:29 left in regulation. Ferragamo quickly moved his team into Pittsburgh territory and reached the 32-yard line with less than six minutes to play. However, Ferragamo tried to force a pass over the middle and Jack Lambert intercepted the ball deep in Pittsburgh territory.

"That interception was a result of an ill-advised play that I had never practiced," said Ferragamo. "I should have changed the play. Play-action was not fooling anybody at that time. This is where experience plays a role in games. It was one of the prettiest passes of the day that I threw, but to the wrong guy. If you ever have a doubt about something, don't do it. It was a lesson to remember."

The ball was back in Pittsburgh's hands and the Steelers were soon faced with a third down on their own 33. Bradshaw again found Stallworth deep, this time for a 45-yard completion to the Los Angeles 22-yard line. The Steelers finally put the Rams away with just under two minutes remaining as Harris crashed into the end zone from the one. Stallworth had made the big plays in the second half after Swann's injury and both receivers had carved their legacy into Pittsburgh's Super Bowl success.

"They were both great players and they were both Hall of Famers," said Mullins. "That just tells you about the talent of each one of those guys. When you get to the big games, the guys who step up and make the plays are the guys who get to the Hall of Fame."

Pittsburgh's dynasty was complete with its fourth Super Bowl title in six years as the Steelers walked off the field with a 31–19 victory. It is almost impossible for a team to find consolation after a Super Bowl loss, but the Rams gained the respect of football fans across the nation.

"Most people who saw us play do remember that Super Bowl," Ferragamo said. "For some time, it was one of the most entertaining Super Bowls. I will always be proud of my teammates, coaches, and the front office staff who, through the greatest adversity of losing our owner at the start of the year, midseason trades, moving the franchise and quarterback controversies, were still able to make it to the pinnacle game of the year. To be part of something never done before is still to this day as rewarding as ever."

While the Rams received praise for their effort, the Steelers enjoyed an all-too-familiar locker room celebration. Bradshaw was named the game's MVP with 309 passing yards. The Steelers had finished off the decade of the 1970's by putting a stamp on their dynasty.

"It was a pretty frustrating year for the Steelers because of all the injuries," said Banaszak. "There was an expectation level for a player when his opportunity came to him. There were a lot of guys who had opportunities to play and play well that season and I think that carried over to Super Bowl XIV."

XV
RAIDERS PLAY THE WILD CARD

The 1980 Oakland Raiders were the prefect wild card.

A proud franchise expected to be in a rare rebuilding year had defied the odds to reach Super Bowl XV. The Raiders had to get to the Super Bowl the hard way. They became the second wild card team to reach Super Sunday, and the first to have to win three games to advance. Oakland hardly looked like a Super Bowl contender early in the season after getting off to a 2–3 start. The Raiders also lost starting quarterback Dan Pastorini to a broken leg, and were forced to turn to Jim Plunkett. The former Heisman Trophy winner resurrected a disappointing career in 1980 as he led the Raiders to New Orleans for Super Bowl XV.

Plunkett was one of several Cinderella stories on a franchise with a reputation of successful second chances. Linebacker Rod Martin was a 12th round draft pick in 1977. The USC alum had been traded to San Francisco in the preseason as a rookie, but returned to Oakland later in the year after being cut by the 49ers. Martin took his game to a new level in 1980 as the Raiders put together an impressive playoff run. After winning in Cleveland in the Divisional Round, Martin began to believe the Raiders were destined to hoist the Lombardi Trophy.

"We just felt like we were a team of destiny," Martin said. "That's really what boosted us to keep playing good and motivated us to win the Super Bowl. We were all on the same page."

The Raiders would face the Philadelphia Eagles in Super Bowl XV. The game would be a rematch of a hard-fought regular season contest between the two teams. On a chilly November day in Philadelphia, the Eagles had pulled out a 10–7 victory as they sacked Plunkett eight times.

"We had a great game that day defensively," Martin said. "We figured we might see them somewhere else later down the road somewhere. We looked at the film and how we played them and just made a lot of adjustments."

Eagles Linebacker John Bunting was making his first Super Bowl appearance. The nine-year veteran was preparing for another tough contest after he and his teammates outlasted the Raiders in November.

"It was extremely physical," said Bunting. "We played great defense. We stopped the run and we got after the passer. We didn't score a lot of points. We won, 10–7. It was a physical game and a hard-fought game."

Eagles Coach Dick Vermeil had built the Eagles into a team with a blue collar reputation. It took five years for Vermeil to turn the franchise from division doormats into NFC Champions. As the head coach of USC, Vermeil led the Trojans to an upset victory over Ohio State in the 1976 Rose Bowl. Vermeil had kept the Trojans focused on the game with a series of long practices, and he wanted to take the same approach with the Eagles before the Super Bowl.

Eagles Wide Receiver Harold Carmichael wasn't surprised.

"We had been like that all year for every game ever since Dick came in," Carmichael said. "A lot of times, we would have meetings by the second training camp up until bed check."

While the Eagles went through their workouts and were forced to retreat to their hotel rooms for the evening, Oakland Coach Tom Flores let his players indulge themselves on Bourbon Street.

"Tom said that this is New Orleans and we're going to have a good time," Martin said. "We were not going to get the curfew on us the whole time. He let us be relaxed and go out to enjoy the festivities, but he told us the main reason why we were here was to win the Super Bowl. We didn't jeopardize what we came there to do."

Oakland Wide Receiver Cliff Branch could sense the optimism in the air throughout the week in New Orleans. He also believed the chance to unwind at night on the town only made things easier for the Raiders.

"We were a very confident team," said Branch. "From Day One, they had curfew every night. We didn't have curfew until the night before the game. We were a very loose and confident group of guys."

There were two more storylines away from the field as Super Bowl XV approached. Raiders Owner Al Davis had announced plans during the season to move the franchise to Los Angeles. Davis looked to make the move without league permission, setting up a lengthy court battle and intensifying Davis' feud with NFL Commissioner Pete Rozelle. Meanwhile, America was celebrating the end of a national crisis. Earlier in the week, 52 American Hostages were released from captivity in Iran after being held for 444 days. A large yellow ribbon graced the front of the New Orleans Superdome, and players from both sides wore yellow stickers on the back of their helmets.

"That was something we always thought about," said Carmichael. "It was great to see the hostages come back home and everybody was safe."

"We knew the game was going to be televised worldwide," recalled Martin. "The hostages had just gotten back. Both sides really wanted to honor them."

It would be Martin who would set the tone for the game on the first possession. Eagles Quarterback Ron Jaworski fired a pass which was intercepted by Martin, giving the Raiders the ball on the Philadelphia 30-yard line.

"It was play action," said Martin. "I wanted to just drop back into my zone and cover my zone. He threw it like a bullet straight on but apparently, he didn't see me coming out there. It was a situation where he thought he'd just drilled the ball in there. I just made a great cut and took the ball away."

It did not take long for the Raiders to cash in on their early opportunity. Plunkett moved his offense to the two-yard line. On third down, Plunkett stepped up to avoid the rush and found Cliff Branch open in the end zone. The Raiders had seized the early lead, and Bunting claims a mistake was made to allow Plunkett to escape the pass rush.

"We had an opportunity to stop them down there," said Bunting. "We had a huge blunder by one of our players. It was a big mental error that gave Plunkett the time to throw that touchdown pass to Cliff Branch. We had a three-man rush instead of a four-man rush, and one of our rushers would have been right in his face."

The Eagles were in an early hole and were also short-handed at wide receiver. Starter Charlie Smith was limited with a broken jaw, and number three receiver Scott Fitzkee was out with a leg fracture. Still, the Eagles were counting on a spark from their powerful running game led by Wilbert Montgomery. Martin knew stopping Montgomery was the key to stopping the Eagles, and the Raiders held the talented runner to 44 yards on the ground.

"We were determined to stop the running game first and force them to pass the ball," said Martin. "We played a 3–4 defense and Reggie Kinlaw did a great job on the center. He was controlling that part of their offense in the middle."

"They used a defensive blocking scheme that really slowed down our running game," Vermeil said. "They did a good job and they shut us down. I take my hat off to them."

Later in the period, Philadelphia was able to move into Raider territory. With the ball on the 40, Jaworski fired a touchdown pass to Rodney Parker in the ride side of the end zone, but Carmichael was flagged for an illegal motion penalty which nullified the score.

"It was really not so much of a turn," Carmichael said. "My shoulders went up. Normally, we would go to a certain spot. I was trying to go right on time with it, but I went a little too early."

The reeling Eagles would receive another major blow from the surging Raiders. On Oakland's next possession, Plunkett escaped the rush and lofted a pass down the far sideline for Running Back Kenny King. Philadelphia Cornerback Herm Edwards leaped in the air to knock the ball away, but the pass floated over Edwards' fingertips, and King ran 80 yards to put Oakland up, 14–0. It was a brilliant play by both Plunkett and King, but Vermeil believes the score should have been nullified due to an infraction by Guard Mickey Marvin.

"Carl Hairston breaks and is going to sack the quarterback," said Vermeil. "The offensive lineman grabs him by the facemask and pulls him to the ground right in front of the referee, and he didn't call it. It should have been called back."

Philadelphia finally got on the board on the ensuing drive. Tony Franklin's field goal cut the Oakland lead to 14–3, but the Eagles missed a golden opportunity on the ensuing kickoff. The Raiders' Keith Moody fumbled after being hit by Ron Baker, but Martin fell on the ball at his own 20.

"I went back to block for him," said Martin. "I heard this collision. The ball was right there, so I jumped on the ball and tried to save us. If they would have recovered the ball, they would have been close to the goal line."

Franklin had another opportunity in the final minute of the half after Jaworski missed an open Parker in the end zone, but Franklin's 28-yard attempt was blocked by Ted Hendricks. The Raiders had the lead and a host of momentum at halftime, while the Eagles were still trying to recover from their slow start.

"There was not enough energy," said Bunting. "I don't think there was a lot of hooting and hollering, but I don't think there were enough positive things going on in our minds at that point in time."

The Raiders picked up right where they left off when the second half got underway. Plunkett led Oakland on a six-play, 77-yard drive. Branch capped off the scoring march with a 29-yard catch, as he beat Philadelphia Cornerback Roynell Young near the left side of the goal line.

"It was a corner pattern that was called," Branch said. "When Jim Plunkett read the play, he thought I had single coverage. They really had double coverage on me inside with the safety and Roynell on the outside. When Plunkett threw the ball, Roynell Young was still on the outside, I had time to make the adjustment."

Oakland now had a commanding 21–3 lead, and Philadelphia's offense could not get into any kind of rhythm as the second half progressed. While the Eagles were clearly not at their best, the Oakland Defense was largely responsible for turning Super Bowl XV into a one-sided affair.

"We're the ones that made them out of sync," Martin said. "They couldn't figure out what we were doing defensively or offensively. Defensively, we just wanted to shut them down and make sure they wouldn't get any momentum going."

Martin's second interception ended an Eagles' scoring threat and led to a 46-yard field goal by Chris Bahr. After three quarters, Philadelphia trailed, 24–3. Early in the fourth quarter, Keith Krepfle capped off an 88-yard drive with an eight-yard touchdown reception. The Eagles finally had life, but Oakland put the game away on the ensuing drive. Another field goal by Bahr gave the Raiders a three-score lead with less than nine minutes to play. Martin added his Super Bowl-record third interception, and the Eagles finished with four turnovers in the defeat.

"You only have about a 15-percent chance to win a football game when you're minus-three in turnovers," Vermeil said. "We had beaten them earlier in the year without turning the ball over and played extremely well in Philadelphia."

The only drama remaining after Oakland's 27–10 victory was what would happen in the locker room. Rozelle and Davis were forced to put aside their legal battle as the commissioner presented the owner with the Super Bowl trophy. Both men handled the handoff with class, as Davis basked in his second championship in five years.

"We were concerned," Branch said. "Pete Rozelle presented the trophy to Al and all of the players were being boisterous. They were waiting for this moment to see how Al was going to receive the trophy. Al kept his cool. He wasn't going to take away from anything we accomplished on the field."

"We thought it was going to be smooth," said Martin. "It was just respectful. They both had respect for each other in that situation even though things were happening outside of football. It was up to Al Davis to take care of it. We were just out there on the field to play."

There was a clear winner in Super Bowl XV, but some wondered if a week of intense practices and strict curfews had an effect on the Eagles. Vermeil believes what took place off the field did not determine the outcome.

"That had absolutely nothing to do with it," said Vermeil. "But you need a reason for losing. I never made any excuses for losing. The Raiders were a better team that day, and so they beat us. When you lose a Super Bowl game, they're going to give you a reason you lost. They chose to say that I was too strict with them, but that's a total exaggeration and not the truth."

But while Bunting continued to stress his love and admiration for his former coach, he did admit the heavy workload during the week may have been a factor in the loss to the Raiders.

"I think there is no question we were a very tight team," Bunting said. "We went down there and had what amounted to a double-day session on picture day. I think we had the longest Friday practice we ever had for a Dick Vermeil-coached team. I love that man as much as I love anybody in the world, including my family, but we were a tired team and we were a tight team."

Bunting also knew getting back to the Super Bowl would not be easy. He would return as an assistant coach with Vermeil and the St. Louis Rams in Super Bowl XXXIV, but would never get another chance as a player.

"I was sitting on a stool in the shower room," said Bunting. "Roynell Young came up to me and said 'We'll be back here next year.' I looked up at him and I said 'You have no idea how hard it was to get here.'"

Plunkett was awarded the MVP award after throwing for 261 yards and three touchdowns. Many believe Martin could have shared the award with Plunkett. The linebacker said Branch was also worthy of MVP consideration, while the wide receiver would have been willing to cast his vote for both Martin and Plunkett.

"There should have been co-MVPs of Super Bowl XV," Branch said. "Rod had three interceptions. Plus, he had the fumble recovery on the kickoff return that kept Philadelphia from getting a first and goal. His play during that game was just phenomenal."

The play of the Raiders throughout the game left the Eagles, their fans, and even some young family members with a frustrating feeling after all was said and done in New Orleans.

"I walk out onto the field," Bunting said. "I see my son, Brooks, who is laying in the end zone. I walk over, and he's got the program open and a pen in his hand, and he's scratching out the faces of the Raiders. I just had to laugh my ass off."

But it was Martin and the Raiders who had the last laugh.

"We had such great camaraderie with our teammates," said Martin. "It showed on the field."

XVI
THE 49ERS COME OUT OF THE COLD

The 49ers and Bengals weren't exactly preseason Super Bowl favorites in 1981.

Both franchises finished 6–10 in 1980. Both were expected to improve, but few fans had visions of a San Francisco-Cincinnati matchup in Super Bowl XVI. But when the dust settled on the 1981 regular season, the 12–4 Bengals and the 13–3 49ers emerged as survivors of their respected conferences. San Francisco had to slay the proverbial dragon to reach the Super Bowl by defeating the Dallas Cowboys in the NFC Championship. Joe Montana's touchdown pass to Dwight Clark with 51 seconds remaining gave the 49ers a dramatic 28–27 victory, and sent San Francisco to suburban Detroit for the Super Bowl. The win was extra special for San Francisco Running Back Earl Cooper, who was quite familiar with the Cowboys.

"I grew up in Texas not far from Dallas," said Cooper. "I respected Tom Landry and the Dallas Cowboys. It made it sweet to be there and beat your childhood heroes. To beat them in the manner that it happened is something people are still talking about to this day."

The Bengals had come out of the cold in more ways than one to earn their Super Bowl berth. Cincinnati hosted San Diego in the AFC Championship in a game forever known as "The Freezer Bowl." The Bengals overcame the Chargers and a minus-nine temperature with a brutal wind chill to reach Super Sunday.

Cincinnati Quarterback Ken Anderson almost didn't make it onto the field.

"I've got my helmet on sitting on my hands and they've got those little slots you tuck your feet into," said Anderson. "There was a big roar and I stand up to see if there was a turnover and I had to go back in. My feet don't come out and I go down and the first thing that hits is my facemask. I'm seeing stars and thinking that I can't get knocked out of this game by falling off the bench."

Anderson would recover and lead his team to its first ever trip to the Super Bowl. The 1981 Most Valuable Player joined his teammates in frigid Pontiac, Michigan. For the first time ever, a cold weather site had been selected for the Super Bowl. The game itself would be played indoors in the

Pontiac Silverdome, but the cold climate kept many of the players indoors during their free time. San Francisco Free Safety Dwight Hicks questioned why this Super Bowl would be played in a city with a cold January climate, but was also quite familiar with playing at the Silverdome.

"You sort of ask yourself why this was done," said Hicks. "Who would want a Super Bowl in a cold weather city? People want to go out and party and do things with the spectacle that comes with the Super Bowl. But it was close to my alma mater and I had been drafted by the Detroit Lions, and they had cut me. Here I am a year and a half later playing in the Super Bowl on their turf."

The Bengals were led by Head Coach Forrest Gregg, who had been to the Super Bowl as a player with the Packers and Cowboys. The 49ers were piloted by Bill Walsh, and the head coach quickly set the tone for the week by dressing as a bellhop when the team arrived at their hotel.

"I didn't even recognize it was Bill," said Cooper. "I just walked right past him."

But Cooper understood the genius of Walsh both on and off the field.

"He set the mood just by being loose and being Bill," Cooper said. "Bill always had a joke. He was very humorous, but very serious at the s ame time. In his humor, he still was a teacher. He was still working for that edge."

The Bengals were looking for an edge of their own after arriving in Michigan. However, Gregg and his team practiced outdoors in frigid Cincinnati before arriving at the Super Bowl, and Anderson believes it had a negative effect on the team's preparation.

"We stayed in Cincinnati all week and practiced," Anderson said. "The conditions were just as brutal. It was tough to get a lot of work done in the cold."

Both teams would come out of the cold and indoors for this Super Bowl, and both would start the game with mistakes. The 49ers and Bengals turned the ball over fewer than any other teams in the NFL during the regular season, but both squads gave the ball away early. San Francisco's Amos Lawrence fumbled the opening kickoff, and Cincinnati took over on the 49ers' 26-yard line. The Bengals quickly moved the ball to the San Francisco five but after a six-yard sack, Anderson's pass was intercepted by Hicks. The safety returned the ball to his own 32, and the Bengals were denied a glorious opportunity to strike first.

"I think that changed the complexion of the game tremendously," Hicks said. "In football, momentum is something both teams try to get because it's hard to stop once you get it. It's hard to get back once it stops. I think it was a very crucial play in the game and I was fortunate enough that I made the play."

Big plays were nothing new to Hicks. The defensive back led the 49ers with nine interceptions in 1981.

"People always talk about players making big plays at big times," said Hicks. "Big players make big plays in crucial times. I always felt that I wanted to be the guy to make the play."

According to Anderson, Hicks was fortunate to be where he was to make the play.

"I saw Dwight Hicks a few years ago," said Anderson. "He said he blew the coverage. He said 'I was supposed to go with my man, and something just told me to stay where I was.' We made the right play call against the right defense, and he made a very intelligent play."

The 49ers took advantage of the turnover and marched to the first score of the game. A pass to Freddie Solomon put San Francisco on the one, and Montana finished the 68-yard drive with a touchdown run for the first points of Super Bowl XVI.

The Bengals moved the ball early in the second quarter, but were once again denied by a turnover. Anderson threw a pass to Cris Collinsworth at the San Francisco five, but Eric Wright stripped Collinsworth of the football. San Francisco took over on its own eight where Montana would put together another impressive drive. The 49ers went 92-yards and finished off the drive with an 11-yard touchdown catch by Cooper. The running back came out of the backfield and gathered in a short pass from Montana before racing into the end zone while plowing through two Cincinnati tacklers. The touchdown came on a play the 49ers hadn't run for Cooper since the 1980 season.

"We used that play my rookie year against the New England Patriots," said Cooper. "We scored from further out and I ran a deeper route. Everything happened on that play exactly the way Bill drew it up."

Once Cooper caught the ball at the five, he had a quick decision to make with several Bengals bearing down on him as he headed towards the end zone.

"I never doubted that I was going to catch the ball," Cooper said. "When I caught it and tucked it, it seemed like 1,001 things went through my mind. Do I run for the pylon or just turn it up? I planted my left foot, went straight up the field and there it was."

After crashing into the end zone, Cooper soared into the air and slammed the ball down with a left-handed spike. It was an iconic moment in Super Bowl XVI which would land Cooper on the cover of Sports Illustrated.

"I had a double windup spike," Cooper said. "I was a big fan of Drew Pearson. Drew Pearson hurt his knee on the double windup spike, so I just threw it down."

Cooper's touchdown gave San Francisco a 14–0 lead, and the 49ers would score again after forcing the Bengals to punt. Ray Wersching's 22-yard field goal increased the San Francisco lead to 17–0. A squib kick on the kickoff after the field goal by Wersching was fumbled by Cincinnati's Archie Griffin, and the 49ers recovered deep in Cincinnati territory. With just seconds left in the half, Wersching added a 26-yard field goal, and the 49ers went to the locker room up, 20–0. It had been a frustrating half for the Bengals, but Anderson claims there were few adjustments which needed to be made before the second half. It came down to execution and holding onto the football.

"The coaches really didn't say a whole lot," Anderson said. "We kind of just stewed a little bit and came out and got some points in the second half. We still had our chances in the game."

The 49ers were also well aware the game was far from over, and Cooper believes there were no issues of overconfidence as San Francisco braced for a Cincinnati surge in the second half.

"They were going to make a run," said Cooper. "They were going to make some plays. We just had to stick to our game plan and keep the ball moving."

The Bengals stormed out of the gate at the start of the second half and quickly marched to their first score. Anderson capped off the opening drive of the third quarter with a five-yard touchdown run to cut the San Francisco lead to 20–7. Later in the period, Cincinnati moved to the San Francisco three and appeared to be on the verge of another touchdown. The 49er defense dug in and came up with one of the greatest goal line stands in NFL history.

One of the Bengals' top offensive weapons was running back Pete Johnson, a 250-pound bulldozer who could overpower the game's top tacklers. Anderson handed the ball to Johnson for a two-yard gain, but the big back was stopped for no gain on his next attempt. On third and goal, Anderson passed to Running Back Charles Alexander on the right side, but Dan Bunz stopped Alexander just short of the end zone. The Bengals went back to Johnson on fourth down, but he was stuffed by Bunz, Ronnie Lott and Hacksaw Reynolds. The 49ers had held and swung the momentum back into their favor as the third quarter came to an end.

"That was a huge play," Hicks said. "Any time a team gets down there inside the red zone, the percentages of them scoring goes up. For us to make that play with their personnel having a running back who is 250 pounds on the goal line was unreal. We stop them and, again, the momentum is on our side. I thought we had the game well in hand at that point."

"We had a good offensive line," Anderson said. "We had been very successful all year in goal-line situations with Pete. They stopped us and ultimately, that was probably the turning point in the game for us."

Once again, the Bengals were able to rise from the dead just when it seemed their fate was sealed. After forcing a San Francisco punt, Cincinnati took over on its own 47 early in the fourth quarter. It took just seven plays for Anderson to get his team back in the end zone as Tight End Dan Ross corralled a four-yard touchdown pass. With 10:06 remaining, the Bengals had cut the lead to 20–14 and were one touchdown away from taking the lead in Super Bowl XVI.

"We knew we could move the ball," said Anderson. "We knew we could score points. It would have been very interesting to see what would have happened if we had scored in that first and goal situation."

The 49ers faced a third down on their next possession, but Montana made one of the biggest plays of the game by rolling right and connecting with Mike Wilson on a 22-yard pass. The 49ers followed with seven consecutive running plays as they took 4:41 off the clock. Wersching connected again from 40-yards out, and San Francisco had a 23–14 lead with 5:25 remaining.

"We had them backed up and it was a long yardage situation," said Anderson. "Montana rolls to the right and hits the big play for the first down. They ate up a lot of clock after that."

"It was big," said Cooper. "It gives you breathing room. We knew our defense was stingy and they weren't going to give up a whole lot of points."

Eric Wright intercepted Anderson on Cincinnati's next possession, and another Wersching field goal increased the lead to 26–14 with 1:57 remaining. Ross would catch his second touchdown pass with only 16 seconds to play, but the 49ers recovered the onside kick, and the first Super Bowl title for the Team of the 80's was secured.

"It's hard to believe," Cooper said. "I had to pinch myself. I think I was numb for a while. Brent Musburger tried to talk to me and I don't think I could get words out. It was so unbelievable that we had come so far, so fast and so quick to be Super Bowl champions."

The 26–21 victory gave San Francisco its first ever Super Bowl title. Cooper would be part of another San Francisco Super Bowl three years later before finishing his career with the Raiders. Now a teacher in Texas, Cooper will be remembered as one of the first members of the 49ers of the 1980's who paved the way for even greater performances in future Super Bowls.

"I was a young guy from a small town with 45 people in my graduating class," said Cooper. "The whole world is watching. It couldn't have been a bigger moment. The only thing bigger in life is the birth of my kid."

Anderson and the Bengals appeared to have the pieces in place to make another Super Bowl run, but Cincinnati's next Super Bowl appearance came seven years later with Boomer Esiason under center. Anderson would finally get a Super Bowl ring with the Pittsburgh Steelers serving as an assistant coach at Super Bowl XLIII, but the former quarterback still wonders what might have been in Pontiac.

"It's nice to have it," Anderson said. "It's a very gaudy ring, but I will say that the ring doesn't travel from Hilton Head to Cincinnati when I come up here."

Meanwhile, the 49ers were world champions and also well ahead of schedule with their coach's time frame for success.

"Bill Walsh asked the coaches their expectations of what our record would be," said Hicks. "Each coach wrote down on a piece of paper what it was. I think Bill Walsh wrote down that if we were 8–8, we'd be right on schedule. We were 16–3."

XVII
STINGING THE KILLER BEES

It was a sprint instead of a marathon to Super Bowl XVII.

A players' strike during the 1982 season lasted 57 days, resulting in a nine-game schedule and a 16-team playoff. The Washington Redskins and Miami Dolphins emerged from the "playoff tournament" and arrived in Pasadena for the Super Bowl. Both squads had not only survived the revamped post-season format, but had stayed together during their time off in the middle of the season. Miami Linebacker A.J. Duhe says the Dolphins were able to keep their chemistry intact during the labor dispute.

"It was like a high school season," said Duhe. "But the playing field was equal for everybody. I thought for us as a unit, we kind of hung together as one of the closest-knit teams during that strike season. We stayed fresh and we stayed current. We knew what had to get done and how to stay in shape. I think that had a big impact on us being successful."

Washington also remained focused throughout the bizarre 1982 campaign. Quarterback Joe Theismann organized workouts for the team during the strike, and the surprising Redskins finished 8–1 in the regular season. Victories over the Lions and Vikings propelled Washington into the NFC Championship where they vanquished their longtime rivals, the Dallas Cowboys, to advance to the Super Bowl.

"That game was bigger than life," Theismann said. "To be able to win that was great. The whole environment was just riveting. Then, we only had one week to get ready for the Super Bowl. We didn't have the usual two weeks. We're riding the crest of this wave, and let's ride this sucker right out to California."

Riding that wave on a short week would be difficult for some of the Redskins. Defensive Lineman Dexter Manley admitted the enormity of the win over Dallas was still fresh on the minds of many of the players.

"That was our Super Bowl," said Manley. "It was a great rivalry for the league."

Even with the glow of the victory over Dallas and the short week with a trip across the country, The Redskins were refocused when they arrived in California.

"It really wasn't hard," said Theismann. "The Super Bowl is the Super Bowl. It's the game that every person points to. You don't sit around as a kid saying 'Gosh, I hope I get to play in an NFC Championship game.'"

Theismann knew he was fortunate to even be a part of the Redskins in 1982. When Washington started the 1981 season at 0–5, Head Coach Joe Gibbs was reportedly ready to trade his quarterback.

"I was on my way to Detroit in a trade with Eric Hipple," said Theismann. "Fortunately, Eric had a great game, and I want to thank him very much. The trade got nixed and I wound up staying in Washington."

The decision not to trade Theismann proved to be a wise one in the nation's capital. Washington won eight of its last 11 in 1981, setting up the Super Bowl run the following season. Theismann finished with the top passer rating in the NFC in 1982, but also had plenty of help from a bruising rushing attack. Washington Running Back John Riggins led way with 553 yards, and ran behind a powerful offensive line affectionately known as "The Hogs." Redskins Guard Russ Grimm recalled how his offensive coordinator first came up with the nickname.

"It was a term that was used one day by Joe Bugel in practice," Grimm said. "A reporter picked up on it and mentioned it in the paper. Some of the fans got wind of it. Next thing you know, we had a couple of guys show up with the hog noses and the dresses on calling themselves the Hogettes."

While Washington had the Hogs, Miami had the "Killer Bees" on defense. The nickname was created with six defensive starters having last names beginning with the second letter of the alphabet, but the Dolphins earned the "killer" portion of the name with a ferocious style of play. Miami allowed the fewest yards in the NFL, and Linebacker Kim Bokamper said it was a confident unit that arrived at the Rose Bowl.

"We knew they were going to try and run the football," Bokamper said. "They had a great offensive line, and we knew Riggins was going to be the guy who would get a lot of carries, but we were pretty confident. We played the Jets the week before and shut them out in the AFC Championship game. We felt pretty good about what we could do defensively."

"We weren't going to be able to just drop back and throw the football on a repeated basis," Theismann said. "They were just too good, too fast and too quick. Bill Arnsparger is one of the greatest defensive coaches in the history of football, and he had the players. We felt like we had to run the football."

The biggest concern for Miami was its passing game. Quarterback David Woodley led an aerial attack which was ranked last in the NFL, but Miami hardly looked like a team with a passing problem at the start of the game. On the Dolphins' second possession, Woodley connected with Wide Receiver Jimmy Cefalo on a 76-yard bomb and the Dolphins led, 7–0.

"It was a boost of energy," Duhe said. "Our adrenalin probably went up a notch. Then again, we know it's the Super Bowl and the team we were playing against was pretty damn good."

"It's a little bit of a shock there," Grimm said. "We'd been through it before when we were down a little bit, but it's a matter of staying with the game plan and the coaches were solid about keeping us on course."

A Woodley fumble would lead to Washington's first score. A hit from Manley jarred the ball loose from the Miami quarterback, and Dave Butz recovered at the Dolphins' 46. Washington settled for a 31-yard Mark Moseley field goal on the second play of the second quarter to cut the deficit to 7–3.

"I sacked David Woodley in the second quarter," Manley said. "That turned the game around. He fumbled the football and Dave Butz recovered and we started scoring."

Woodley shook off his fumble on the ensuing drive and led the Dolphins to the Washington three, where an Uwe von Schamann field goal put Miami back up by seven. The Redskins marched 80 yards on their next possession, and Theismann capped off the drive with a four-yard touchdown toss to Alvin Garrett. The game was tied at ten, but Miami would break the tie on the ensuing kickoff. Fulton Walker went 98-yards for the first kickoff return for a touchdown in Super Bowl history, and the Dolphins led, 17–10, at the half.

"We felt pretty good," said Duhe. "We knew, defensively, we were sound. We knew that was our bread and butter. We believed we could hold any team to a short number of points, and our offense would score enough to beat them. We played a lot of close games because of the style of defense we played."

Meanwhile, the Redskins were far from discouraged as they prepared for the second half. The long touchdown drive before Walker's return had helped the Washington offense settle into its game plan.

"It was only seven," Theismann said. "We were starting to run the football better. The game was settling in to our kind of football game."

The Redskins would strike again on their second possession of the third quarter. A 44-yard reverse by Garrett set up another Moseley field goal, and Washington pulled to within four. The teams traded interceptions, but it would be a defensive play by Theismann which would save the Redskins later in the period. With the ball on the Washington 18-yard line, a Theismann pass was batted in the air by Bokamper. The ball floated downward toward Bokamper's hands, and the Miami linebacker had a clear path to the end zone. However, a lunging Theismann reached out and knocked the ball away just before Bokamper grabbed it. Theismann had saved a touchdown, and likely the game, for his team.

"I felt like my feet were in cement," recalled Theismann. "You could read Pete Rozelle's name on the ball and you could see all the laces. It spun very slowly. I knew I couldn't get to the ball, so at the last minute I figured I should dive and try to get my arm up in between Kim's hands and try to knock it away."

"You felt you were watching one of the NFL Films in slow motion," said Bokamper. "The ball was up in the air and just hanging there. You didn't think it was ever going to come down. The ball hit my hands, and he stripped it from my hands. If I had dropped the ball, it probably would have been more painful, but the guy made a good play on the ball."

Duhe had initially forced Theismann into the errant throw. The Miami linebacker leaped into the air to the right of Theisamnn, forcing the quarterback to throw the opposite way. Duhe had batted down a pass which resulted in a touchdown the week before in the AFC Championship game, and was hoping a similar fate awaited his teammate as the play developed.

"We did put pressure on him," said Duhe. "It was sort of like my interception against the Jets. It was one of those moments where you almost see the ball in slow motion. Bo had that same opportunity and out of nowhere, the little man with the number seven on his back knocked it away."

A touchdown by Bokamper would have put Miami up, 24–13, and Washington would have likely had to adjust its offensive strategy in the fourth quarter.

"There was no way we would have won the football game," Theismann said. "We would have had to abandon our game plan. We would have had to throw the football."

"Joe Theismann made the best play of all," said Manley. "That was a heads up play and one of the key plays of the game."

One Dolphin who watched the play from the sidelines was Bob Kuechenberg. The offensive lineman was one of the last links to the champions from the 70's Super Bowls, and Kuechenberg knew his third Super Bowl ring was within Bokamper's grasp.

"That was the greatest play that Joe Theismann ever had in his career," said Kuechenberg. "We were up, 17–13, and it was still a tight ball game. "If he doesn't do that incredible effort, it's 24–13 and they can't give the ball to Riggins."

Washington went back to the basics in the fourth quarter The Redskins took over on their own 48 with 11:43 remaining, and it was time for Riggins and the Hogs to go to work. Washington ran three straight running plays, but the Redskins were just under a yard shy of a first down. On fourth down, Washington bypassed the punt and elected to go for the first down. There was only one possible option, and the rugged Riggins got the call. Riggins ran left, broke through the arm tackle of Don McNeal, and raced 42-yards for a touchdown. The man they called "The Diesel" had put Washington ahead, 20–17.

"We're leaving one DB for John," said Grimm. "If we block it right, we know we're going to get the first down. Very seldom did we ever break that play for a long gain. Usually, that was a play that would give us a two or three yard gain and we would be good to go."

Theismann watched the play develop after handing the ball to Riggins. His biggest concern was making sure his tight end wouldn't commit a penalty.

"Clint Didier comes in motion and Clint's outside of John," Theismann said. "As John breaks to the outside, I'm yelling at Clint 'Don't clip anybody!' Don hits him, and it's just like watching butter melt in a frying pan. He just sort of slid down him and off, and then Big John started that gallop towards the end zone."

As Riggins and the Hogs began to take over on offense, the Washington Defense shut down Woodley throughout the second half. The Miami quarterback did not complete a pass over the final two quarters, and the Dolphins gained only two first downs in the final 30 minutes. Woodley was lifted late in the game for veteran backup Don Strock, and Kuechenberg believes his head coach should have made the switch to Strock sooner.

"Shula waited too long to go to Don Strock," Kuechenberg said. "Hindsight is 20/20, and I certainly don't want to criticize Don Shula. But in my opinion, when you have a guy like Don Strock sitting on the bench, it's like having Earl Morrall on the bench behind Bob Griese. Shula always had a masterful backup quarterback behind his starter, but he waited too long to go to him."

But even Strock was left helpless as a spectator on the sidelines as the Redskins continued to run the football. The Dolphins were forced to punt again, and Washington ran the ball five straight times on its next possession to move the ball to the Miami 23.

"I've got the best seat in the house," said Theismann. "There's no amount of money you can pay for the seat that the quarterback has in a game like that. I get to see all of the blocking up front, and I get to see John run."

Theismann was more than just a spectator on the final scoring drive.

With 1:55 remaining, Theismann found Charlie Brown in the right side of the end zone from six yards out. The Redskins led, 27–17, and were on their way to their first Super Bowl crown. Theismann's pass had sealed the deal, but the quarterback knew the constant pounding of Riggins and the Hogs set up the passing play.

"It forces the defense out of things they want to do," said Theismann. "The linebackers have to come up a little more. It puts the corners on islands, and that's basically what we wanted."

"We had no possessions," Duhe said. "Our offense was going three and out, and they were doing those sustained drives. We probably were getting a little worn out. It was kind of the early stages of the 300-pound men coming at you."

Washington's defense forced Miami's offense to the sideline on four plays, and the Redskins ran out the clock. Riggins finished with 166 yards on 38 carries and was named the game's MVP. The vanquished Dolphins tipped their hats to the victors.

"John Riggins took over the game," said Kuechenberg. "It was much like the Dolphins ten years earlier."

"You've got Riggins going inside and you've got Riggins going outside," said Bokamper. "You're trying to cover both gaps. You'd throw an arm out there, and he'd just run through your arm tackle. It was frustrating, but I think the physical nature of that offensive line combined with a guy like John Riggins with the power that he ran really made it difficult."

Theismann admitted to coming close to tears as he gathered his offense in the final huddle of the game. The man who was almost traded away had a chance to savor the feeling of being a Super Bowl-winning quarterback. Theismann ran off the field holding the football in one hand and extending his index finger with the other.

"The emotions just flow out of you," said Theismman. "I always remembered Terry Bradshaw running off the field holding the football up after one of his Super Bowl wins. I always remembered Joe Namath running off the field waving that one finger. As I left the football field, it was really, in my mind, a split image. I don't even remember touching the ground."

The win was a profitable one for the Redskins as well. They earned $70,000 for the victory, which was significant in a year when players lost seven game checks because of the strike.

"My salary was $60,000, recalled Grimm. "I got $30,000 to play half a season. They told us that we had a chance to make $70,000 each if we just won another four games."

"My base salary in 1982 was $235,000," Theismann said. "I lost a bunch of that. You take $72,000 and take my base salary as one of the highest paid players, and you're talking 30–35-percent of my salary."

Gibbs took a congratulatory call from President Ronald Reagan in the Rose Bowl locker room. In a year when the league was divided by a strike, the united Redskins were Super Bowl champions.

"We played together as a team," Manley said. "We probably weren't the most talented team, but the coaches put us in a good position. Joe Gibbs spent the nights there. Joe Gibbs and his staff outworked our opponents."

"They had The Hogs," Duhe said. "They tried to stuff it down our throats. They weren't successful on a few drives but when they got the train moving, it was moving."

XVIII
THE ROUT OF THE REDSKINS

The Los Angeles Raiders didn't look like an underdog heading into Super Bowl XVIII.

While the Washington Redskins had earned the right to be favored in this Super Bowl, Los Angeles had been playing at a high level entering Super Sunday. The Raiders had crushed both the Steelers and Seahawks in the playoffs, and Tom Flores' squad was playing its best football of the season. However, Washington went 14–2, and both of its losses were by only one point. The rampaging Redskins set an NFL record with 541 points in 1983, and had a turnover ratio of plus-43. For players such as Quarterback Joe Theismann and Guard Russ Grimm, the 1983 Redskins were superior to the Super Bowl winning squad from the previous year.

"There wasn't a question in my mind as to whether we would win or lose," said Theismann said. "The question was how many points were we going to score against these guys. It had evolved to that. We were plus-43 in the giveaway/takeaway ratio. Put that into perspective today in football. If you get to 20 or 19, you should win the world championship."

"I tell people all the time that the '83 team was the best team I ever played on," said Grimm. "We lost two games that year, and both of them were by one point. The defense was playing well. We were plus-43 on the turnover ratio. It was unheard of."

One of Washington's wins in the regular season came against the Raiders in the nation's capital. The Redskins prevailed in a wild 37–35 contest, but the Raiders left the field knowing they could go toe-to-toe with a team many were calling one of the greatest of all time. Wide Receiver Cliff Branch also knew his team would have three key contributors on the field who were unable to play throughout most if not all of the regular season contest.

"We were very confident," Branch said. "We had played the Washington Redskins in Washington. I got hurt the first series after catching a 99-yard touchdown. We later acquired Mike Haynes, and Marcus Allen didn't play in the game."

Another Raider who entered the Super Bowl with confidence was Jack Squirek. The backup linebacker believed he and his teammates learned enough from playing the Redskins on the road to be ready for the rematch in Tampa.

"We respected the Redskins," Squirek said. "We knew they had a high-powered offense, and we knew we'd have to play well to beat then. I think the fact that we hung in there in a close game on the road, it taught our club that this team was beatable."

Playing on the road was nothing new to the Raiders. After a lengthy court battle between Owner Al Davis and the NFL, the franchise was allowed to move to the City of Angels in 1982. However, much of the team's work was still being done in Oakland.

"We still were a traveling team the whole year," said Branch. "We practiced in Oakland and we traveled down to L.A. to play the games and traveled to play the away games. In 1983, we finally moved down there and made the adjustment. I thought the change was good. It was an opportunity to play in the famous L.A. Coliseum."

One of the Raiders who helped his teammates get comfortable in their new home was Rod Martin. The linebacker grew up in Los Angeles, and Martin helped his team bond as the players began to settle in to their new surroundings.

"It was new to almost everybody," Martin said. "But I'm from L.A. I helped show which places to go. We just became closer as a unit. On Thursday nights, we all used to go out and have comradery night. It made us a strong unit and a strong team. We just took care of each other on the field and off the field."

Despite the move to Los Angeles, the Raiders continued to thrive on their renegade image. One of the most feared Raiders was Lyle Alzado, who threatened to "decapitate" Theismann during the game. The Washington quarterback took the comment in stride and later had the chance to see a softer side of Alzado at a Superstars competition in the Bahamas.

"There was a bunch of kids begging for food on the side of the road," recalled Theismann. "He wanted to give them money. There was a convenience store, and I said we should buy them a bunch of candy. We got these baskets of candy and everything, and we gave them to the kids. That was the Lyle Alzado I knew."

While Alzado gained a reputation as one of the most intimidating players in football, his teammates knew how valuable a player he was in the trenches.

"Lyle just tore up the offensive line," Martin said. "It was awesome to have him on our squad. We developed a relationship where we worked well together. We used to do some things out there that weren't called. He was a great teammate."

If the regular season matchup was an indication, Super Bowl XVIII had the potential to be a classic, but Washington Defensive Lineman Dexter Manley was confident his team would prevail as it did in the regular season.

"I thought the Raiders were a very talented football team," said Manley. "They had a lot of key people at key positions. They had Jim Plunkett and Marcus Allen and a nice offensive line, and they had a great defense. The Hogs were able to push those guys around. We ran the football on them and ate their lunch up and Joe Washington caught the winning touchdown on the two-yard line."

Washington had every reason to be confident heading into Super Bowl XVIII after putting together one of the greatest regular seasons in NFL history. However, Theismann sensed something was wrong as Super Sunday drew closer.

"My whole approach was that we were world champions and I'm going to go to Tampa and enjoy the Super Bowl experience," said Theismann. "I went out to dinners and did radio shows and TV shows. It was uncomfortable for me from the beginning. Adidas was making a new shoe for me that didn't fit. The weather was crummy. The entire week just didn't feel comfortable."

The Raiders felt differently during the week, and entered the Super Bowl brimming with confidence. Martin also knew Super Bowl XVIII would feature two talented football teams that represented the best in the NFL in 1983.

"They were the Super Bowl champions the previous year," said Martin. "They were the top dog to beat for everybody all year long. They were knocking people off during the season. We had a great game against them and we were Super Bowl winners one time as well. There was just so much talent on both teams."

The talent on special teams would set up the first critical play of Super Bowl XVIII.

After the Raiders punted on the game's first possession, the Redskins were forced to do the same. However, Jeff Hayes had his punt blocked by Derrick Jensen, who recovered the ball in the end zone for the game's first score. The Raiders had taken a 7–0 lead 4:52 into the opening quarter.

"It did give us a lot of momentum," Branch said. "During the first quarter, both teams were very conservative, and we were going against the wind in the first quarter. When Derrick Jensen got that blocked punt and recovered the ball in the end zone, that definitely gave us momentum."

"That was definitely deflating," Manley said.

A fumble on a punt by Ted Watts gave the Redskins the ball on the Los Angeles 42, but Washington came away empty as Mark Mosely missed a 44-yard field goal. The Raiders struck again early in the second quarter, and Branch made the two big plays on the drive. The receiver hauled in a 50-yard pass, and Plunkett found Branch again two plays later for a 12-yard touchdown. With 9:14 left in the half, the Raiders had seized a 14–0 lead.

"We got out of being conservative," said Branch. "We opened it up once we got the wind at our back. Now, we're up 14–0 and confident we can really open our offense up."

Mark Moseley's 24-yard field goal on the ensuing drive put Washington on the board. The Redskins would get the ball back with 12 seconds remaining in the half. With the ball on their own 12-yard line, Joe Gibbs ruled against running out the clock and asked Theismann to run another pass play.

"I walk to the sidelines," recalled Theismann. "Joe says 'I want to run rocket screen.' I said to him that I didn't feel good about putting the ball in the air backed up this far with such little time. He said that it worked against them last time and I'm thinking to myself 'You don't think they know that?' I start to walk away, and I turn around and Joe points to me and says 'Run it.'"

The play had indeed worked against the Raiders in the regular season matchup. A screen pass to Running Back Joe Washington gained 67 yards and set up a touchdown for the Redskins. Raiders Linebacker Coach Charlie Sumner had a hunch the same play was coming and sent starting linebacker Matt Millen to the sidelines.

Squirek got the call to replace Millen.

"I actually wasn't even paying attention," Squirek recalled. "Charlie grabbed me by the shoulder pad and says 'Get in there, quick!' He could see that the formation was going in. He said that everybody on our defense was going to be in a zone. He said 'Everybody will be in a zone except you. You're covering Joe Washington man-to-man.'"

Theismann dropped back and looked to his right before turning to the other side of the field. He floated the pass towards Washington, but Squirek stepped in front of the speedy back and intercepted the pass at the five. Squirek only needed to take five steps to reach the end zone, and his touchdown gave Los Angeles a commanding 21–3 halftime lead.

"I think I remember more about what happened before the play," recalled Squirek. "As he was coming out of the backfield, I was closing in on him. It was real quick. The ball came. I saw it and intercepted it."

Theismann has sensed disaster was on the horizon when the play was called. He realized as soon as the ball was released that his instincts were correct.

"I'm going back to the huddle thinking that I don't like this," Theismann said. "But Joe Gibbs is a world champion coach, my coach, and we won a lot of football games, so I'm all in. As soon as I turn, I see Jack start to break towards Joe. Just as the ball leaves my hand, I see Jack intercept it and go in the end zone."

It appeared Squirek's touchdown was an early knockout blow, but Washington finally reached the end zone on the opening drive of the second half. A nine-play, 70-yard drive ended with a one-yard touchdown run by Riggins, but a missed extra point kept the Washington deficit at 12. Los Angeles regained the momentum on the ensuing drive. A 38-yard pass interference penalty on Darrell Green moved the Raiders into Washington territory. Marcus Allen ran in from the five, and the Raiders were up, 28–9.

"We had a lot of great leadership with our veterans," said Squirek. "We made sure that we weren't going to let up in the second half. At halftime, the coaches and our veteran leadership all told us that the game was not over."

The Redskins had one last chance to get back in the game late in the third quarter. After recovering a fumble on the Los Angeles 36, Washington picked up eight yards on two plays. Joe Washington was stopped by Squirek on third down, and the Redskins were faced with a fourth and one. Riggins got the call, but Martin blew past Tight End Rick Walker. Martin and Safety Mike Davis stopped Riggins short of the first down, and the Raiders' domination was nearly complete.

"He lines up in front of me," Martin said. "I said 'Okay, it's time to go now.' He came off the line and I just got underneath him, stood him up and got rid of him. I hit Riggins and Mike Davis came up as well and Mike almost knocked me off because he hit him so hard."

Martin was hardly surprised that he was able to beat Walker on the play. In a meeting with two CBS broadcast legends before Super Bowl XVIII, the linebacker recalled some of his battles with the tight end during his college days.

"It was so ironic," said Martin. "The night before, John Madden and Pat Summerall had interviewed me about the game and different scenarios. They asked me about the tight ends. I said they were very good blockers, but I didn't think either one could block me, especially Rick Walker. He couldn't block me when I was at USC and he was at UCLA."

The play capped off a frustrating day for Riggins. The running back was held to 64 yards on 28 carries. Martin and the rest of the Los Angeles front seven had clogged the inside lanes where Riggins looked to run, and Nose Tackle Reggie Kinlaw controlled the middle of the line in the trenches.

"Reggie Kinlaw to me was the MVP of the Super Bowl," Theismann said. "Reggie Kinlaw controlled the interior part of that line, which is really where we hung our hat."

"We made sure he couldn't get outside of us," Martin said. "We wanted him to run in the middle. We had Matt Millen in there along with Reggie Kinlaw. Reggie was controlling the center and shutting off everything in the middle."

In a game where everything went right for the Raiders, it was fitting that a broken play provided the finishing blow. On the first play after the fourth and one stop, Allen ran left and was forced to reverse his field. The future Hall of Fame runner turned right and went 74 yards for a touchdown. Branch was Allen's escort as he threw the final block on the electrifying run.

"The play was supposed to go inside of the hole," Branch recalled. "Marcus jumped out of the hole when there was a safety there. Marcus saw that and he began to reverse his field. The guy couldn't make the tackle. When he turned, he looked like a rocket going through the hole. I turned on the jets and got a little nudge on Anthony Washington, and Marcus Allen was in the end zone."

Manley was forced to watch helplessly from the sidelines as Allen rocketed across the field. While the outcome of Super Bowl XVIII would have likely remained the same without Allen's 74-yard scamper, Manley believes he would have been able to prevent Allen from reaching the end zone.

"I came off the field to take a break," said Manley. "He ran in reverse and came back. I would have caught Marcus Allen. There's no question in my mind. If I was in on that play, he would have never scored that touchdown, but Marcus made a great run."

Los Angeles would add a field goal to make the final score 38–9. Theismann was sacked three times in the final period and fumbled once while throwing his second interception of the game. For Theismann and the defending champs, there was little consolation after suffering a humiliating defeat.

"It was the most devastating feeling," recalled Theismann. "I was at the Pro Bowl after the '82 season. Bob Baumhower and I were sitting under this palm tree. I turned to Bobby and I hated to ask him this question, but I asked him what it was like to lose the Super Bowl. He said it was the most devastating feeling in the world. You almost wish you hadn't gotten there because the hurt is so bad. I'll never forget saying to him I hope that I never experience that."

"They beat us in every facet of the game that day," Manley said. "I can't tell you why. They were a different football team from the regular season."

There was a different feeling on the opposite sideline, where the Raiders were savoring a dominating Super Bowl performance. It was the franchise's third championship in eight seasons. Branch was one of the few Raiders to be part of all three.

"The third was the most dominating of pro football games the Raiders played," Branch said. "We totally dominated all three games that we played. We averaged 30 points a game against the Steelers, the Seahawks and the Washington Redskins. It was just totally dominating in all three phases of the game during that Super Bowl run."

For the Redskins, a season of domination ended with one loud thud in Tampa. Washington's 1983 squad could have been remembered as one of the greatest teams of all time, but Grimm understands the result on Super Sunday is what most people will remember about the 1983 Redskins.

"You can't take anything out of that season if you end up with a loss," said Grimm. "You remember the one that you lost, and that sticks with you for a long time."

In addition to Allen's 74-yard run, Squirek's interception will live on as one of the most memorable plays in Super Bowl history. Theismann has been forced to live with the errant pass and finally decided to address the issue with his head coach several years later.

"I see Joe at this charity function," said Theismann. "I told him that something's been bothering me now and I've got to get it off my chest. I said 'You know that call you made in the Super Bowl? That was one of the worst calls I've ever seen in my life.' He said I was probably right, but said 'That throw you made was probably one of the worst I've ever seen, too.' We both just laughed about it."

The play also puts a smile on the face of Squirek. The linebacker played five years in the NFL before retiring in 1986, but one play cemented his name in Super Bowl glory.

"The feeling after that was just something you can't describe," Squirek said. "It was a dream come true. It was something you dream about as a kid playing in the backyard, scoring a touchdown in a Super Bowl. Probably about half the team ran out on the field and they were jumping on top of me. It's an indescribable feeling."

XIX
JOE COOL BEATS DAN THE MAN

Football's top gunslingers were ready for a showdown.

It was a Super Bowl made for a Hollywood script with the two best teams in football and two of the game's best quarterbacks. The 49ers came to Super

XIX with Joe Montana leading the way. The San Francisco signal caller was looking for his second Super Bowl crown in four years. Standing in Montana's way were Dan Marino and the Miami Dolphins. In just his second season, Marino was busy shattering single season passing records. In 1984, Marino became the first quarterback to throw for over 5,000 yards (5,084). The second-year quarterback also tossed a record 48 touchdown passes. It seemed as if much of the spotlight was shining on Marino.

Joe Montana and the 49ers noticed.

San Francisco rolled through the regular season at 15–1 and was a slight favorite heading into the game. However, players such as San Francisco Running Back Roger Craig believed much of America was betting on Marino and the 14–2 Dolphins.

"Marino had an MVP year that year," Craig said. "The media had pumped him up to just crush us. We're underdogs in our own back yard and we took offense to that. Our defense was really upset. They wanted to show him that he's not as good as he thinks he is."

The 49ers were literally in their own back yard. Super Bowl XIX would be played 35 miles outside of San Francisco in Palo Alto, California. For players like Safety Dwight Hicks, the road to the Super Bowl was a short drive from Candlestick Park instead of a long plane flight.

"We didn't have to fly anywhere," said Hicks. "It was like a home game to us."

Hicks and his teammates had played at a high level, but spent much of the season under the radar with the spotlight on the San Francisco offense. The 49ers allowed the fewest points during the regular season. It was a different story for the Miami Defense in 1984. The unit which reached Super Bowl XVII with the top-ranked defense in the NFL was far different than the Super Bowl XIX version. Injuries to players such as Linebacker A.J. Duhe helped lead to a decline in the Miami Defense and Linebacker Kim Bokamper knew the unit would have its hands full against the powerful San Francisco Offense.

"We weren't the same football team that we were two years ago," said Bokamper. "A.J. was hurt and we were playing with some guys that were good players but weren't quite as intuitive as some of the guys that were there before."

While San Francisco had reached the Super Bowl during the 1981 season, it seemed like an eternity for the players after a heartbreaking loss to the Redskins in the 1983 NFC Championship Game. Craig and his teammates left the field in Washington that day with a new attitude which was evident at the start of their 1984 campaign.

"The year before was where the attitude and the commitment was made by our team," said Craig. "We got beat in the NFC Championship game. We were getting beat 21–0 in the first half. In the second half, we came back and dominated. We tied the game up but got two pass interference calls out of the blue. They kicked a field goal and beat us. We were so heartbroken from that game that we made a commitment as a team that we weren't going to let anybody get in our way the next year."

It did not take long for one rookie to buy into the winning attitude of the 49ers. Offensive Lineman Guy McIntyre contributed on specials teams in his first year, and would go on to be one of the team's top offensive lineman as the decade progressed. McIntyre also learned about the competitive fire of his quarterback.

"Joe's a very competitive guy," McIntyre said. "Marino was in his second year. Joe was a veteran of a Super Bowl already. I'm sure, knowing Joe, he was glad to be the underdog. He was glad to go in like that. It just made for a perfect stage for him to do what he does, and that's to win."

One player who knew all about Montana's competitive nature was Earl Cooper. The former running back had been switched to tight end with the arrival of Craig. Cooper was a key contributor to San Francisco's first Super Bowl victory three years prior, and knew Montana had plenty of competitive fire despite his reputation as "Joe Cool."

"I never really saw him get flustered at anybody," said Cooper. "He was Joe Cool. Was he excited and competitive? Yes, but never mad at anybody."

For Craig, his first Super Bowl appearance was also a chance to take on the team and the coach he cheered for as a youngster.

"I was a Miami Dolphins fan growing up," Craig said. "I knew them all. Don Shula was one of my favorite coaches. Now, I'm out there playing against the team I liked growing up. It was a touching moment for me."

Shula's Dolphins featured two talented receivers in Mark Clayton and Mark Duper. The two combined for 144 receptions in 1984, but Hicks claims their mouths were as productive as their receiving talents leading up to the Super Bowl.

"Clayton and Duper were talking big time trash," said Hicks. "I'm thinking that they saw the film and they know what we can do. I think they were trying to convince themselves to pump themselves up. I looked at film as well and I knew we matched up against them."

It was also a Super Sunday for President Ronald Reagan, who was sworn in for a second term earlier in the day. Reagan did the coin toss via satellite from Washington. San Francisco won the toss and elected to receive, but was forced to punt after the drive stalled. Miami capitalized on its first possession as Uwe Von Schamann booted a 37-yard field goal.

It was Montana's turn on San Francisco's next drive. The 49ers quickly moved to the Miami 33, where Montana rolled right and found Carl Monroe, whose catch and run gave San Francisco a 7–3 lead. Marino came right back on the next drive with five straight completions, with the last one going to Dan Johnson for a two-yard touchdown. Miami led, 10–7, after one quarter and the much-anticipated Marino-Montana duel was living up to its hype.

The 49ers made a key adjustment on defense in the second quarter. Walsh switched to a 4–1–6 formation and was hoping the dime coverage would slow down Marino. It proved to be one of the most important strategic decisions of Super Bowl XIX, and Hicks and his teammates received a promise from their teammates in the trenches that they would do their part to get to the Miami quarterback.

"I can remember Lawrence Pillers and Fred Dean saying they only need three seconds," recalled Hicks. "They said that's all they needed to get to Marino. I had to cover Nat Moore. Marino went to Nat Moore on third downs a lot. Instead of covering him off, I just bumped him the whole game because our defensive line said they only needed three seconds."

Montana gave his defense another lead at the start of the period. Craig's eight-yard touchdown catch put San Francisco on top, 14–10, and the powerful 49er offense was just getting started.

"It was loud in that stadium," Recalled Craig. "We were just in sync. Joe was on fire and everybody played their roles. I can remember it was like a fast-paced game like an Olympic 100-meters. You could see ourselves pulling away. Every play was just intense."

San Francisco's new defensive scheme quickly forced a Miami punt, and Montana went back to work with another scoring drive. The quarterback capped off the march with a six-yard run into the end zone. San Francisco led, 21–10 with 6:58 left in the half, and the Dolphins could sense the game was already slipping away.

"I remember running in the game," recalled Bokamper. "I knew I could beat my guy inside but then Joe would just come around. He picks up yards and you knew it was that kind of day. They were a very, very good offensive football team."

The 49ers were also an excellent defensive team, and Hicks and his teammates were beginning to shut down the high-powered Miami passing attack. San Francisco forced a three and out on Miami's next possession and the 49ers had little trouble scoring their third touchdown of the quarter. Craig did his part on the drive with a 20-yard catch to move San Francisco into Miami territory. Craig would finish off the drive with a two-yard run to put the 49ers up, 28–10.

"We played every play 100 miles per hour," said Craig. "When we were marching down the field, things were going so fast. It was just amazing how we dominated. It's probably one of the best games I've played. I was in rhythm and I could do whatever I want. The linebackers couldn't cover me. I was so focused that I caught two one-hand passes."

Miami was finally able to get back on the board with a field goal in the final seconds in the half. It appeared San Francisco would take a 15-point lead into the locker room at halftime, but a bizarre incident on the ensuing kickoff gave Miami another chance. McIntyre fielded the kick inside his own 20 and decided to kneel down, but was encouraged to get up and run. The lineman was hit by Joe Carter and fumbled the football.

"I was in my usual spot," McIntyre said. "My hands were a little more heavily-taped. I wasn't really ready to receive a ball. The ball just happened to bounce right there in front of me and I'm in the middle of the field. You kind of felt the whole stadium say 'get up and run.'"

The Dolphins recovered, and von Schamann's third field goal as time expired cut the San Francisco lead to 28–16.

"I was kind of trying to run and hide under the nearest bench," said McIntyre. "Hacksaw Reynolds grabbed me when we were going off the field and said 'Don't worry about it. We're going to be all right.' But I thought if we lose this game by three points, I'm going to run out of the stadium."

McIntyre's mistake gave an emotional boost to Miami, but the Dolphins Defense was still searching for answers. It was an especially painful half for Bokamper, who cracked his sternum early in the first quarter.

"It was a painful game," Bokamper said. There are some games you play where you just never feel like you're getting a bite out of that team. They're just having their way with you. I look back on that football game and that's kind of the way I felt. It's a credit to their offense and what they were able to do and probably a little indictment on us."

The San Francisco Defense continued its strong play at the start of the second half. The Dolphins were quickly forced to punt after their opening drive and Montana put together a drive that set up a Ray Wersching field goal. The Miami offense was stymied yet again on its next possession, and Montana would follow with a drive that virtually ended any hopes of a Miami comeback. On third down from the Miami 16, Montana threw a short pass to Craig on the left side. The multi-talented back raced into the end zone to make the score 38–16. Craig became the first player to score three touchdowns in a Super Bowl, and the 49ers were on their way to victory.

As the second half rolled on, the fog rolled in. It was a rare occurrence in Palo Alto, but not in the city 35 miles north.

Fog never rolled into Palo Alto," Hicks said. "It would come in sometimes at Candlestick. Fog started to come into Stanford Stadium and I thought 'Wow! This is kind of neat.' It was like being at Candlestick."

"We very seldom get fog in Palo Alto," said Craig. "For some reason that night, they just wanted to remind everybody that they were in San Francisco territory. It was like a Twilight Zone atmosphere."

Marino was having a Twilight Zone–type evening as the San Francisco Defense dominated the second half. The Miami signal caller was intercepted twice in the final period, and the second-year quarterback with the golden arm spent much of the final two quarters on the ground thanks to heavy pressure from the San Francisco front line.

"We showed them a lot of different looks," Hicks said. "We showed them a four-man front and a 3–4 in the first half and they scored 16 points. In the second half, they didn't score, so that was a very effective game plan. I wish we would have started the game like that. I don't think the game would have been as close as it was."

But Hicks and his teammates were more than satisfied with their 38–16 victory. San Francisco had captured its second Super Bowl crown in four years, while Miami had suffered its second Super Bowl loss in three seasons.

"We just got beat by a better football team," Bokamper said. "It seemed like everyone they had was making plays. Joe Montana was Joe Montana. He was in his prime. It was Joe Montana versus Dan Marino, and there was no question Joe Montana was a better quarterback on that day."

San Francisco finished with 537 total yards. Montana threw for 331 yards and won his second Super Bowl MVP award. McIntyre had his first Super Bowl title as a rookie and would win two more before the decade was complete. McIntyre believes the 1984 49ers may have been the best of the San Francisco squads which dominated the 1980's and became the team of the decade.

"We had a real veteran offensive line and a veteran defensive line," McIntyre said. "We had a good mix of everything. These guys had been together and had played together. They knew what it took. It could be considered the greatest team of that dynasty era."

Montana had bested Marino, but the defense had done its part.

"Everybody looks at the offense," Hicks said. "Offense sells tickets. Defense wins championships. It's really true because if the team can't score on you, you have a pretty good shot at winning the game."

XX
THE BEARS SHUFFLE TO GREATNESS

For the Chicago Bears, winning Super Bowl XX seemed to be a mere formality.

Chicago had dominated the 1985 season. The Bears had what many considered the best defense of all time. These new Monsters of the Midway had rolled into the Super Bowl after posting a pair of playoff shutouts. The Chicago offense also had its share of top flight performers with the likes of Walter Payton and Jim McMahon. Almost no one could stop the Bears through 18 games. The 19th would give Chicago the opportunity to win its first ever Super Bowl title.

Dan Hampton was one of three future Hall of Famers on the Chicago Defense. After rampaging through the regular season at 15–1 and terrorizing opposing offenses, Hampton knew he and his defensive teammates had a chance to achieve football immortality.

"It was a record-setting year," said Hampton. "It was the most devastating defense the NFL has ever seen before or since."

The Miami Dolphins were the only team to defeat the Bears during the regular season. The Dolphins downed Chicago on a Monday night in Week 13. While Miami ruined the Bears' hopes for a perfect season, Chicago Linebacker Mike Singletary believes the Monday night meltdown was a turning point late in the season.

"The Miami game did so much," Singletary said. "It was like two seasons for us. There was the season up to the Miami game. After the Miami game, it was sort of getting shocked into reality. We were reading our own press lines. After the Miami game, we woke up. We wanted to make sure that we finished what we started."

Bears fans were hoping for another shot at the Dolphins in the Super Bowl, but Miami was upset by New England in the AFC Championship Game. Hampton and his teammates were also disappointed about missing out on a chance at revenge.

"Our team wanted to play the Dolphins to avenge the Monday night loss," said Hampton. "The Dolphins must have been looking ahead. They didn't take care of business. The Patriots came in there and ran the ball and beat them."

The Wild Card New England Patriots were the party crashers in New Orleans. Few expected New England to reach the biggest game of the year, but three straight road playoff wins propelled the Pats into their first ever Super Bowl. Despite their remarkable run, New England Quarterback Steve Grogan realized the spotlight was on the charismatic Bears in The Big Easy.

"I think we were probably a little jealous about all the attention they were getting," said Grogan. "But we were kind of used to flying under the radar having played those three games on the road. Nobody expected us to win those. We just went about our business and got ready to play the game."

Grogan had been a spectator throughout much of the year and wasn't expecting to play in the Super Bowl. The veteran suffered a broken leg during the season and watched from the sidelines as Tony Eason led the way in the AFC Championship. Grogan had recovered from his injury, but Eason was set to start against the Bears.

"They had put two screws in my tibia," Grogan said. "I had asked the doctor if the screws would break or come out, and he said no. Then I said 'Get me back on the field.' I dressed for the Miami game."

The Bears made the most of their time in New Orleans, and a unique injury to McMahon was making headlines. McMahon bruised his glute muscle against the Rams in the NFC Championship game. When a news helicopter flew over a Bears' practice during the week, McMahon responded by revealing his injury in order for people to get a closer look at his wound.

While Head Coach Mike Ditka had turned the Bears into an NFL power, his defensive coordinator was also getting plenty of accolades. Buddy Ryan's "46 Defense" had turned the Bears into the most dominating defense in history, and the defensive players were fiercely loyal to the outspoken Ryan. However, Ryan had agreed to leave the team after the season to become the head coach in Philadelphia.

"(Gary) Fencik came up to me on Thursday that week," said Hampton. "He said it was official that Buddy was going to take the job in Philly. He said 'Whatever you do, don't tell Singletary.' It was because Singletary would become an emotional wreck."

When the players met with Ryan the night before the game, he indicated his time in Chicago was coming to an end. The defensive guru always passed out notes to his players about what they needed to do the next day. There were no notes passed in the meeting the night before Super Bowl XX.

"Buddy didn't pull out any reminders," Hampton said. "He just turned around and said 'No matter what happens tomorrow, you guys will always be my heroes.' He starts choking up and crying and just ducks his head and walks out."

After Ryan left the room, Fencik told Singletary about Ryan's new job with the Eagles. The news left the linebacker in disbelief and forced him to come to grips with Ryan's departure on the eve of the biggest game of his career.

"I just didn't believe that Buddy would leave without telling me," said Singletary. "But he was smart enough to know I wasn't mature enough to handle him leaving. I probably would not have played very well if I really believed that going into the game."

After Ryan left the meeting room, the rest of the coaches tried to go about business as usual. Defensive Line Coach Dale Haupt wanted the players to watch game film, but their hearts and minds were consumed with the loss of Ryan.

"He started the projector and I couldn't take it," Hampton said. "We'd seen the same film 25 times. I kind of just stood up and kicked the projector table over. Mongo (Steve McMichael) jumped off the ground, grabbed the chair, and threw it against the chalkboard, and the four legs impaled into the chalkboard. It was like something out of a Spielberg movie."

The Bears were able to regain their focus as game time approached. Chicago was one victory away from taking its place as one of the greatest teams of all time. Instead of being overwhelmed by the moment, the players embraced their destiny. Singletary said there was silence in the locker room as the Bears reflected on their journey to football's greatest stage. The linebacker also remembers the emotions he felt as he and his teammates prepared to take the field.

"I can still remember it like it was yesterday," said Singletary. "We're standing there holding hands and there were those huge doors at the Superdome and the stadium in absolute pandemonium. It was so loud and the emotion was so thick that we could not even talk to each other. Tears were streaming down our faces. It was a magical moment before the game."

There was no magic for the Bears on their opening series. A fumble by Payton was recovered by Larry McGrew at the Chicago 19. Tony Franklin kicked a 36-yard field goal, and New England had the lead 1:19 into the game. It was the first time the Bears had been scored upon in the post-season.

"You take the broomstick and you poke the hornet's nest," Hampton said. "That's what that was. We're pissed off. I was livid."

The Patriots had the early momentum, but the loss of a key player on the drive would change the strategy of a New England Offense already facing overwhelming odds against the mighty Bears. The plan for the Pats was to use two tight ends for much of the game, but one was lost for the rest of the afternoon.

"Lin Dawson blew his knee out on a crossing route," Grogan said. "Our game plan against their 46 Defense was to basically put two tight ends on the field and try to chip and help block in the passing game and try to run the ball at them. When Dawson went out, it changed everything that we had planned on doing."

The domination by the Bears began shortly after Franklin's field goal. A 43-yard pass to Willie Gault on the ensuing drive set up a Kevin Butler field goal to tie the game. The Chicago Defense would set up the next score as a combined sack by Richard Dent and Wilbur Marshall forced a fumble on the New England 13. Butler would add another field goal to give the Bears their first lead.

Later in the period, New England Running Back Craig James lost the ball on a tackle by Dent. Chicago once again got the ball on the Patriots' 13-yard line, and Matt Suhey's 11-yard run on the second play of the drive increased the lead to 13–3.

The Bears were just getting started.

A 59-yard scoring drive was capped off by a two-yard run by McMahon. Leading the way with a block was William "The Refrigerator" Perry, the defensive lineman who captured the attention of America with his part-time work on offense. Perry had been used by the Bears in goal-line situations, and "The Fridge" eliminated McGrew on McMahon's touchdown run.

When the Patriots got the ball back, Coach Raymond Berry replaced a battered Eason with Grogan. Eason left the game having failed to complete a pass in six attempts, and the fierce Chicago pass rush appeared to have taken an emotional toll on the third-year quarterback.

"He kept trying to convince everybody that he wasn't worried about the pass rush," said Hampton. "That's wagging your finger in front of the security dog. You don't want to taunt us. I thought the more he tells us he's not worried about our pass rush, the more I think our pass rush has already gotten to him."

Chicago's defense would eventually force another punt. Butler added another field goal on the final play of the half, and Chicago's lead went to 23–3. Even the most diehard New England fans scattered among the over 93 million viewers believed the Patriots had little chance of getting back into the game.

"I think we took a breath and tried to figure out what to do," Grogan said. "We felt like we could go back out and at least get ourselves back in the game. They were so good defensively. It was not going to happen."

Meanwhile, the Bears had no intention of softening up in the second half, and knew Grogan would bring a veteran presence sorely needed by a New England offense which finished with minus-19 yards of total offense in the first half.

"We knew that Grogan was more than capable," said Hampton. "He had won a lot of games. We felt like he was more of a threat to us. When he came in, we were highly aware of the fact that he was a very good player and he was more than capable of scoring points on us."

The Chicago domination continued in the second half. The Bears picked up their fourth and fifth sacks of the game on New England's first series of the third quarter. A punt pinned Chicago on its own four, but McMahon engineered a 96-yard drive which began with a 60-yard catch by Gault. McMahon finished off the drive with his second score from one-yard out, and Chicago led, 30–3. The drive was one of many impressive moments for the Chicago Offense during the season, but McMahon and Company were forced to play a supporting role with the spotlight on Ryan's unit.

"I understand that they feel like the ugly brother in the family," Hampton said. "But that was part of the design. We wanted to be the alpha dogs. We wanted to be the leaders. Nobody was stopping them but the way things unfolded, that defense started doing things that were unordinary."

The alpha dogs would get the next touchdown as Reggie Phillips intercepted a Grogan pass and went 28-yards to make the score 37–3. The rout continued with another New England turnover as Marshall recovered a fumble. The Bears drove to the one, and Perry got the call for the carry. The Refrigerator barreled into the end zone like a bowling ball, using the helpless Patriots as pins.

With the outcome no longer in doubt, the Bears sent many of their second stringers into the game. Among those was second-year linebacker Ron Rivera, who would go on to coach the Carolina Panthers to Super Bowl 50.

"It was our chance to play," said Rivera. "Every opportunity we got during the season to play, we relished. That's one thing I'll always have. I played in a Super Bowl and won a Super Bowl. I was fortunate enough to win with a great group of men and coaches."

Irving Fryar caught an eight-yard pass from Grogan early in the fourth quarter as Chicago gave up its only touchdown of the post-season. Even with victory secured, many of the Chicago defenders were not happy to see the Patriots reach the end zone.

"We were the youngest team in the league," said Singletary. "We should be happy that we won, but we really wanted a shutout. They got the three points then they got the other points. It was just one of those things about the pride which we had in ourselves."

Fittingly, the Bears defense scored the last points of the game as a sack by Henry Waechter resulted in a safety. The Patriots got the ball back in the closing minutes, and even the gutsy Grogan knew it was time to run out the clock when he talked to Head Coach Raymond Berry on the sidelines.

"I tried reverse psychology on him," said Grogan. "There were about three and a half minutes left and it was 46–10. I said that I didn't see any reason to try and run anymore hoping he'd say to just run it and get out of here. He said 'That safety just about did it.' My mind is going 200 miles an hour wondering if he was thinking we still had a chance. He just smiled and winked at me and walked away on the sidelines."

The numbers in Chicago's victory told the story of its dominating performance. New England was held to 123 total yards, with only seven coming on the ground. The Bears recorded seven sacks and forced six turnovers. Dent was named the most valuable player as he forced two of the New England fumbles and picked up one and a half sacks. The offense was also dominant, as Chicago finished with 408 yards.

But once again, the defense stole the show.

"They were the best I'd ever played against," Grogan said. "I'd be hard pressed to tell you another one that was any better than that defense."

One of the early Super Bowl traditions involved players from the winning team carrying their coach off the field. When Super Bowl XX ended, the Bears prepared to take both Ditka and Ryan for a ride.

"I went up to McMichael," Hampton recalled. "I said me and Dent were going to carry Buddy off. I said 'I didn't want Ditka to get all pissy about it, so you and Fridge carry Ditka off because we have to play for him again next year.' We wanted to send Buddy off the right way."

It would be the last time Ditka and Ryan would coach together. Ryan moved on to Philadelphia, but neither man would ever win another Super Bowl. Their icy relationship in the Windy City didn't prevent the Bears from fulfilling their destiny.

"It was magical," said Singletary. "It was like having two parents that were very different but very effective."

As Chicago celebrated, the Patriots were left to lick their wounds after being battered by the Bears in one of the most lopsided Super Bowls ever played. Future generations of Patriots would enjoy a much different ending in Super Bowls, but Grogan and his teammates still take pride in being the first team from New England to play on Super Sunday.

"It was special to be the first ever to go there," said Grogan. "What I tell people is the weeks leading up to the preparation for the game were some of the most exciting in franchise history at that point. The two weeks before the Super Bowl was just something incredible. It was such a thrill to be a part of the game and all of the things leading up to it."

But even after a quarter of a century had passed since Super Bowl XX, the Bears would still prove to be intimidating to the Patriots.

"Richard Dent was inducted into the Hall of Fame in 2011," said Hampton. "I'm backstage right before the event starts. In the corner of my eye, I see Raymond Berry. Just as he gets to us, he kind of looks up and says 'Oh, shit, not you two again!' We all started laughing."

Some believe the 1985 Bears put together the greatest single season in NFL history. Many in the football world still reference the Bears when making a comparison to the highest level of excellence. They will also forever be remembered in Chicago and across the nation with a combination of domination and charisma which has yet to be duplicated.

"I am so grateful," said Hampton. "That team played with a vibe. We were the Second City no longer. We hadn't won anything in a long time. I am so grateful for the outpouring of respect. It's truly been amazing."

XXI
A Giant Performance

The New York Giants had seen their share of hard times.

One of the NFL's proudest franchises had slipped into oblivion since its success in the late 1950's. From 1964 through 1978, New York had only two winning seasons. Once a perennial contender, the team owned by Wellington Mara had become a punching bag for the rest of the NFL.

The franchise's fortunes would change under the leadership of Bill Parcells. After a 3–12–1 start in 1983, Parcells built New York into a playoff team. After two straight post-season appearances, the Giants rolled through the NFL in 1986 with a 14–2 record. Parcells led his team to its first Super Bowl, and third-year Linebacker Carl Banks understood the magnitude of the accomplishment for the players who had suffered through the lean years.

"You start to hear the stories about the Mara family and what they had to go through," Banks said. "You heard them talking about how tough it was in the stadium. George Martin and Harry Carson were part of the lean years, and they talked about how they got booed so much."

There was no booing from the Giants fans in 1986. Banks teamed with NFL MVP Lawrence Taylor, Harry Carson and Gary Reasons to form one of the league's best set of linebackers. While the Giants had talent on offense, Wide Receiver Phil McConkey knew the heart of the Giants came from the defensive unit.

"The tradition is so rich in its history of incredible players and toughness," McConkey said. "Our team was epitomized by toughness, and the toughness was started by the defense. The defense ran that team. They were some really tough people. If you wanted to be on that team, you had to be like them. Even if you were a 160-pound punt returner, you had to play with that same tenacity."

McConkey was not taking his first Super Bowl appearance for granted. At the beginning of the season, New York released the backup wide receiver and special teams standout. McConkey played four games with Green Bay before coming back to the Giants.

"It was a great feeling to be wanted by a team that had let you go," said McConkey. "It was so satisfying to be able to come back to the Giants and contribute and be with my buddies where it started."

Waiting for the Giants in Pasadena were the Denver Broncos, who were making their second Super Bowl appearance. Nearly all of the Broncos from

Super Bowl XII were no longer with the team, and the most noticeable change was at quarterback. John Elway forced a trade to Denver after being drafted first overall by the Colts in 1983. In his fourth season, Elway had led the Broncos to the Super Bowl with a victory over Cleveland in the AFC Championship. "The Drive" of 98-yards which forced overtime in Cleveland seemed to be the start of Elway's legacy.

This would be the second meeting of the year between the two teams. The Giants had beaten Elway and the Broncos, 19–16, in the regular season with the help of four Denver turnovers.

"We kind of got a feel for the way they like to play," said Banks. "They were a multiple formation team. John Elway was John Elway but seeing him up close and personal, you kind of got an idea of how he runs their offense. It was a good test for us in understanding how they approach the game."

Vance Johnson was one of Elway's top targets during the regular season. The speedy wide receiver was ready to take the field for Super Bowl XXI moments after the AFC title game.

"I was so excited," said Johnson. "The anticipation was so great. All I kept remembering was as I child, the very thing I wanted most was to grow up and be in a Super Bowl, which everyone told me was impossible. All of those thoughts crossed my mind from that flight back from Cleveland back to Denver."

Elway's quarterback counterpart in this Super Bowl would be Phil Simms. After being benched in his early years with Parcells, Simms emerged as the leader under center for the franchise. Despite Simms' success, the New York Offense was known for its running attack, but New York Center Bart Oates could sense before the game that his quarterback would be a key contributor in The Giants' quest for their first championship in 30 years.

"About five of us took a cab to the game," Oates said. "We took it about five hours before the game. We wanted to experience everything about it. Phil's down on the field and it's about three and a half or four hours before the game. He says 'Man, I feel great.' He just had this confidence. He said 'The ball feels terrific.'"

The Giants were favorites going into Super Bowl XXI after winning their first two playoff games by a combined score of 66–3. New York had shutout division-rival Washington in the NFC Championship, and McConkey knew the Giants would be ready when they took the field at the Rose Bowl.

"We were so prepared for that game," McConkey said. "We were prepared two days after we had beaten the Redskins. We were so ready to play that game to a point where we were over-ready."

Johnson was also ready for the biggest game of his life, but the Denver

Wide Receiver admitted being overcome with the emotion of playing in his first Super Bowl as kickoff approached.

"I remember standing on the sidelines and looking up into the stands," Johnson said. "All of a sudden, I became a nine-year-old with the big grown up football uniform on crying as I watched the jets go across the stadium. It was the most amazing feeling. I'll never forget it."

The Broncos would draw first blood in Super Bowl XXI. On the opening drive, Elway directed his offense to the New York 30-yard line. When the drive stalled, Rich Karlis booted a 48-yard field goal to give Denver the early lead. However, Simms would begin his amazing day on the Giants' first possession. He went 6-for-6 on a 78-yard touchdown drive, capped off by a six-yard throw to Zeke Mowatt. It was 7–3 New York, and Parcells' plan of attack was unlike the more conservative approach from much of the regular season.

"It was like him to go out of character," said McConkey. "That was the first example of it in a big game to go totally opposite what the tendencies were, and I think that caught Denver off guard."

The Broncos would strike back on their next possession. Starting from his 42-yard line, Elway completed three passes and was aided by a pair of 15-yard penalties against New York. With the ball on the Giants' four, Elway ran a draw up the middle and reached the end zone to give Denver the lead. Both teams had moved the ball in the opening period, but Denver's success had come against the top-ranked defense in the NFL.

"We thought we had the best offense at the time because we had Elway," Johnson said. "We thought we would put more points up in the Super Bowl than they did because we had a great game plan."

But the Denver game plan could not overcome the wave of mistakes committed in the second period. Elway hit Johnson on a 54-yard pass, and Denver quickly moved to the New York one. But Taylor, Banks and Carson all made stops to force a fourth and goal from the six. Karlis came on for a chip shot, but his 23-yard attempt missed wide to the right.

Late in the half, a pass from Elway to Clarence Kay was ruled incomplete. Instant replay was used for the first time in a Super Bowl to confirm the call, but another angle on the CBS broadcast showed the play should have been ruled a catch. The Giants cashed in on the missed call on the next play as Martin sacked Elway in the end zone for a safety.

"There was something about the air that came out of us when John Elway threw that ball to Clarence Kay," said Johnson. "He caught the ball and it was a foot off the ground, but they called it a dropped pass. We knew that was a big turning point."

The Broncos still had a chance to increase their lead as Elway drove his team to the New York 16-yard line. However, Karlis missed again from 34 yards out. The score remained 10–9 as the teams reached the half. The Broncos had the lead, but the Giants had the momentum.

"They had not taken advantage of the situations that they got," said Oates. "We felt very confident that we could win this game."

"I don't think anybody panicked," recalled McConkey. "We didn't play very well and we knew it. We knew we would play better in the second half. We were a confident team despite being down by a point."

The Broncos were dealing with a different scenario at the half. The players knew they had let too many opportunities slip away, and Johnson believes a former Super Bowl quarterback on the CBS broadcast may have had an effect on Elway at halftime.

"I remember sitting there looking at John Elway watching Terry Bradshaw talk shit about him on national television," Johnson said. "He was saying how he was going to choke and how he had choked in all of Stanford's big games. I was watching John's face just change."

Elway's anger likely increased from the sidelines at the start of the second half. New York was faced with a 4th and 1 on its own 46. Parcells called for a fake punt, and backup Quarterback Jeff Rutledge surged forward on a sneak for the first down. Four plays later, Simms hit Bavaro for a 13-yard touchdown, and the Giants were up, 16–10.

"We always had that in our game plan," said Banks. "Rut saw it, and I'm sure the coaches told him that if was there, take it, and he did."

"That was it," Oates said. "From there, it was basically over with."

The Giants forced a punt on the ensuing drive, and a 25-yard return by McConkey put New York on the Denver 36. The drive stalled, but a Raul Allegre field goal increased the lead to 19–10. Another three-and-out by Denver with the help of a deflected pass by Banks on third down put the New York offense back on the field. After moving the ball to the Broncos 45, a flea-flicker resulted in a catch by McConkey on the one. The excitable New York receiver went flying into the air and went upside down before landing just short of the goal line.

"There were very complex emotions going on in my head at that point," said McConkey. "That was basically the play that broke the game open. When Joe Morris scored on the next play, the game was essentially over. I was absolutely thrilled with that but then frustrated at the same time because something I had dreamed about was a yard away."

Morris' touchdown run increased the New York lead to 26–10, and the Giants were on the type of roll which propelled them to the best record in the NFL during the season.

"That was the nature of that year," said Oates. "We got into a really good rhythm with our offense. The defense was just stalwart and we had solid special teams. Offensively, it was just one of our best performances."

The New York Defense was also in a rhythm. On Denver's next possession, Elway was intercepted by Elvis Patterson. On third and goal from
the six, Simms threw for Bavaro in the end zone. The ball glanced off
Bavaro, but McConkey grabbed the deflection for yet another Giants touchdown.

"I saw the whole thing develop," said McConkey. "It deflected off him
when he got sandwiched between two defenders. I'll never forget the sensa-
tion of that ball tumbling end over end. It was like I was a little boy back in
Buffalo catching snowflakes in my mouth. The sense memory to this day is
so acute that I can see the grains on the football, and the logo is clear as
day."

McConkey leaped into the arms of Bavaro then raced to the sidelines
with both arms wrapped around the ball. After falling one yard short earlier
in the game, McConkey had his Super Bowl touchdown.

"I was pretty much out of my mind at that point," McConkey said. "I
was somewhere else. It was all an absolute white, light blur after it had happened."

"It was going our way then," Banks said. "Phil put it right where is was
supposed to be, and Mr. McConkey being Johnny on the Spot always shows
up and gets something falling out of the sky."

McConkey's touchdown increased New York's lead to 33–10 with 10:56
remaining. Johnson and his Bronco teammates had watched their Super
Bowl dreams unravel during a second half which snowballed against Denver.

"We were standing there watching this happen," Johnson said. "There
were things happening during the ball game, but they were all happening
against us. The Giants were breaking every record you can imagine. You had
a quarterback who didn't have near the abilities of Elway, and he's outperforming John like crazy. It was ridiculous. It didn't look like the Broncos that
had played all year long."

Simms was indeed outperforming Elway. The man who often went
unnoticed on a team with a dominant defense and a punishing rushing attack
was putting together a performance for the ages. Simms would finish 22-for-
25 passing for 268 yards in one of the most efficient Super Bowl performances
in history. After a Denver field goal, Simms led the Giants on another scoring
drive, which was capped off by Otis Anderson's two-yard run.

Elway would finally get the Broncos back in the end zone on the ensuing
drive. The quarterback connected with Johnson for a 47-yard score. Johnson's
catch was the 100th touchdown in Super Bowl history, but the receiver was
in no mood to celebrate.

"I was really frustrated because I wish I had gotten the ball more," Johnson said. "When I scored the touchdown, there was no excitement. I walked

off the field with my head down. There really was no cheering in the stands. I did hold onto the ball because I knew this was a moment I would never forget, but I knew it was too late for us to come back."

The Giants were in full celebratory mode after their 39–20 victory. Parcells was carried off by his players after receiving his traditional Gatorade dunking in the closing minutes. McConkey was ready to savor the moment, but noticed something peculiar on his way to the locker room. The wide receiver found a gun lying on the ground, which had likely fallen off the belts of one of the security personnel. McConkey held the gun in his hand near his helmet and located another security guard so he could turn over the weapon.

"CBS got flooded with calls about McConkey having a gun in his helmet," McConkey said. "I scored a touchdown to help our team win the Super Bowl and saved some lives. All in a day's work."

The Giants had their first championship in three decades, and there was a genuine appreciation by the players for all of the difficult years the franchise had overcome.

"You kind of understood the magnitude of what it meant to the community as we started to go on the run," said Banks. "As the reality started to settle in that this could be a special season, you started to read stories. You started to hear from fans and parents saying they had been suffering for so long."

It was a different story in the Denver locker room, where the Broncos were left frustrated by their mistakes. After a storybook finish in the AFC Championship game, Elway and his teammates had come apart on football's biggest stage.

"I don't think I had ever felt that way during a game," said Johnson. "Everything just fell apart right from the first snap."

But everything fell into place for New York, and the Giants had their first Super Bowl title.

"It was indescribable," said Oates. "I had played football since I was eight years old. You're sitting in that locker room after the game and watching the Super Bowl presentation and you know you were an integral part of it."

XXII
AMBUSHED

Doug Williams knew the questions would be coming.

The Washington quarterback and his Redskin teammates were getting ready for Super Bowl XXII in San Diego. It was the third Super Bowl appearance in six years for Washington, and the first with Williams under center. It had been a long road for Williams to Super Sunday. He spent his first five seasons in Tampa Bay and led the Buccaneers to the NFC title game in 1979. After leaving Tampa for the USFL, Williams returned to the NFL in 1986. He spent much of his time as a back-up in Washington, but Williams replaced the struggling Jay Schroeder late in the 1987 season. While Williams was looking for his first championship, he was also trying to become the first African-American quarterback to win a Super Bowl. Williams took the lessons he learned at Grambling from Coach Eddie Robinson as well as former African-American quarterbacks as he prepared for the wave of questioning on media day.

"It wasn't difficult for me," Williams said. "I was coached by a great individual that understood that no matter what you do, it was still football. I had my oldest brother, Robert, to talk to and James Harris, who was a quarterback in the league in 1969. I understood who I was. I knew what the color of my skin was."

Williams almost missed his opportunity in Washington. Just before the start of the regular season, The Redskins were set to ship the veteran to another team. Their head coach decided to call off the deal.

"I was going to be traded at the end of the preseason to the Raiders," said Williams. "Joe Gibbs changed his mind. He felt like somewhere along the line, I was the guy that's going to come in, and things were going to work out the way they did."

Williams and the Redskins would face the Denver Broncos, who were making their second straight trip to the Super Bowl. After losing to the Giants the previous year, the Broncos were hoping for redemption in San Diego. Denver was once again led by the rocket arm of Quarterback John Elway and a strong supporting cast of receivers. Rookie Ricky Nattiel joined Mark Jackson and Vance Johnson to create one of the top receiving triplets in the NFL. Things did not start out well during training camp, but Johnson decided to use a 1980's comedy hit as a nickname for the three wideouts.

"We weren't getting along during the preseason," Johnson said. Mark Jackson was my roommate and we were arguing that if we called ourselves The Three Amigos, we would be forced to get along. The Amigos thing caught on, and we had a fantastic year."

While the Three Amigos did enjoy a spectacular season, Johnson was sidelined with a groin injury during the playoffs. The injury caused internal bleeding and forced Johnson to miss the AFC Championship game. It was severe enough to again force Johnson to the hospital prior to the Super Bowl, but the receiver did not want to miss the shooting of a video with Jackson and Nattiel.

"I was extremely limited," said Johnson. "We ended up shooting our Three Amigos video. I snuck out of the hospital to go shoot the video. We were on horses riding through Washington Park. I had to sneak back in the hospital after that. The team didn't know anything about it."

One of Washington's standout stars was also forced to deal with an injury in 1987. Offensive Lineman Russ Grimm was moved to center before the season, and suffered a sprained knee in November. Grimm was healthy enough to suit up for the Super Bowl, but the longtime "Hog" would be limited to backup duty.

"It was tough," said Grimm. "I get moved to center and all of a sudden, I get injured. It was a struggle to get back, but you're still part of it. It was still enjoyable, but not as much as when you're a starter."

Williams had waited throughout much of the season to become a starter. Still, Williams knew there would be as many questions about the color of his skin as there would be about the Denver Defense. One longtime legend involves one question to Williams by a writer from Jackson, Mississippi. Many claimed Butch John asked Williams 'How long have you been a black quarterback?' Accounts say the actual question from John was 'Doug, it's obvious you've been a black quarterback all your life. When did it start to matter?'"

"It's kind of like when I was in elementary school," said Williams. "The teacher gives you something to say at one end of the room, and tells you to pass it along and it never came out that way."

The question went on to urban legend status and is often rehashed throughout future Super Bowls. John passed away in 2014 of cancer, and the twist of the writer's words lives on in the minds of many fans. Williams and John stayed in touch long after Super Bowl XXII.

"Butch and I talked about this before he passed away," Williams recalled. "He appreciated the way I handled the question and he understood how it came out. He also understood how I answered the question. It came out 'How long have you been a black quarterback?' But I knew that wasn't the way it was meant."

There was still business to take care of on the field, and the Washington Defense was looking for ways to shut down Elway. Redskins' Lineman Dexter Manley was supremely confident he and his teammates could pressure Elway into mistakes after combining with Charles Mann for 18 sacks during the season.

"We were excellent on defense," said Manley. "Our defense was way better than the Denver Broncos Offense. We knew we could put pressure on them and get to them, and there was no way they could stop the front seven pass rush."

Washington could not get a pass rush on Elway on Denver's first play from scrimmage. Manley lost his footing on the slippery surface in San Diego, and Elway had ample time to find a wide-open Nattiel downfield. The 56-yard strike gave the Broncos a 7–0 lead less than two minutes into the game. After the Redskins were forced to punt, Elway put together another scoring drive. A Rich Karlis 24-yard field goal increased Denver's lead to 10–0, and it appeared the Broncos were on their way to their first world championship.

"I thought it was over with," said Johnson. "We knew there was no way that we were not going to pull this one out."

The Broncos were in control early, and it appeared Williams' day may be done late in the first quarter. The quarterback fell victim to the slippery field conditions as he dropped back to throw.

"The grass in that area didn't get a lot of sun," said Williams. "I think they re-sodded the field. When I planted my right foot, it never stopped going back. I did the split and hyperextended my knee. When the trainers came out, I told them not to touch me because I wanted to be able to get up on my own. I walked off on my own power and for me, that's all I needed."

Williams returned early in the second quarter with his team still trailing, 10–0. What followed was one of the greatest quarters of football in Super Bowl history.

It began on Williams' first throw in the opening minute of the period. The quarterback connected with Ricky Sanders for an 80-yard touchdown. The Redskins were back in the game, but it was just the beginning of an offensive explosion.

"There's no doubt that was a spark," Williams said. "It was crazy because it was a simple play. It was just seven yards where you throw a quick hitch, but we also had built in there if the cornerback came up to press and had no help, it turns into a fade rout. Mark Haynes came up to press Ricky Sanders and did a Cardinal sin … he missed."

The Washington Defense quickly forced a Denver punt, and Williams marched his offense to the Broncos' 27. On third-and-one, Williams took a gamble which paid off with a go-ahead touchdown pass to Gary Clark.

"They had a blitz on," said Williams. "We knew we were in field goal range. As a quarterback, you've got a little gunslinger in you, and you take a shot. It was one-on-one with Gary Clark. We win."

Denver's offense moved into field goal range on its next possession. The drive stalled at the 26, but Karlis missed a 43-yard field goal to keep Denver's deficit at four. When the Redskins took over, it was time for the Timmy Smith show to begin. The rookie running back was making his first NFL start due to a series of injuries suffered by George Rogers. Smith burst through a huge hole and raced 58 yards for another Washington touchdown.

"The one thing that they were afraid of more than anything was the ground game with our offensive line," Williams said. "We got a chance to start running the football and once that started, it opened everything else up. The pass was going to be easy after that."

While the Washington Offense was rolling, Elway and the Broncos had hit a road block. The offense could not give its defense any time to recuperate, as another three-and-out sent Williams and Company back onto the field.

"We were able to get to John Elway and rattle his cage," Manley said. "He was not himself that day, but the media built him up so much so that he was like Superman. He can't do it by himself."

Williams wasn't doing it by himself, but he was taking the lead role in a record-setting performance. One of his top targets was Sanders, and Williams found his speedy receiver for his second touchdown catch of the quarter. The 50-yard reception increased Washington's lead to 28–10. Sanders had victimized Denver Safety Tony Lilly, who was left in the dust as he broke free for the catch.

"I got a chance to talk to Tony about that," recalled Williams. "He just got caught up. We were running the ball so well, and he got caught up on the play action. We faked the 60 counter, and Tony just came up to force the run and before he knew it, Rick was behind him."

The Broncos found themselves on the receiving end of a blowout after jumping out to an early lead. The stunning turn of events left many of the Denver players in disbelief.

"They were breaking records," said Johnson. "Their receivers were running all over the place. Doug was throwing the ball like crazy over the top of our cornerbacks and our safeties. It was just a nightmare."

Washington added one more score before the half, as Williams found Tight End Clint Didier in the end zone. The Redskins set a Super Bowl record for most points in a quarter, and Williams had thrown a record-breaking four touchdown passes in the period. It took just 15 minutes of football for Super Bowl XXII to change from a 10–0 Denver lead to a 35–10 Washington rout.

"We wanted to be cautious," Williams said. "We had scored 35 points, be they also had a guy who was known for being the comeback kid in John Elway. We didn't want to get overconfident. The defense came back out and they stood up."

It was hard for many of Williams' teammates not to be overconfident. Washington was one half away from its second Super Bowl title in six seasons.

"Joe Gibbs knew that we had this game," Manley said. "He was much more calm at halftime. He'd never sort of get too out of character as a head coach. I think (Assistant Head Coach) Richie Petitbon stayed on it and put more pressure on Elway. We made good adjustments."

Grimm spent much of the first half watching the offensive fireworks from the sidelines. The veteran lineman would get playing time in the second half, but was already preparing for a victory celebration with the team's equipment manager.

"Joe's talking at halftime," Grimm said. "He said that we had to treat this as 0–0. Meanwhile, we're telling Jay Brunetti to get the hats ready. We go out in the third quarter and score another touchdown, and it's 42–10. We're saying, 'Get the hats out.'"

The hats were ready early in the fourth quarter, when Smith added another touchdown from four yards out. The rookie finished with a Super Bowl record 204 rushing yards, but Smith was the beneficiary of a dominating performance by the Washington front line.

"Timmy Smith had holes as big as the Marriott Hotel," said Manley.

The Redskins were 42–10 winners, and Williams was named the game's Most Valuable player as he finished with 340 passing yards. Manley and the defense did its part as well, and the defensive lineman recorded two and a half sacks in the victory.

"We were a better football team," said Manley. "To win in the National Football League, you've got to get to the quarterback. We had a front seven that could get to the quarterback. It was just a matter of footing. It seemed to be slippery on the edges. All day long, we beat them on one-on-one matchups."

While the Redskins were celebrating, the Broncos were forced to deal with their second straight Super Bowl blowout. Denver had lost Super Bowl's XXI and XXII by a combined 51 points, and even many of their own fans were tired of seeing their team on football's biggest stage.

"We knew we were going to be going home," Johnson said. "The word was back at home was that they hoped we didn't go to the Super Bowl anymore. It was a pretty sad moment to have to know we were going home with two losses. You might want to say that we made it to two of them, but now you've got two losses in the Super Bowl and that's what they remember."

People will always remember what Williams did on that day in San Diego. After a long journey to the top of the football world, Williams was able to put his Super Bowl performance in perspective.

"Everybody doesn't get a chance to do it," said Williams. "There are Hall of Fame guys who never got a chance to win the ring. It doesn't happen every day. You've got to take advantage of it when you can."

Since Williams' trip to the Super Bowl, several other African-American quarterbacks have led their team to the biggest game of the year. Williams is a big reason why race is rarely the topic for future generations of quarterbacks.

"That's exactly where we should be right now," said Williams. "You don't worry about the color of your skin. Just the fact that person can play football."

XXIII
A DRIVE FOR THE AGES

The Super Bowl was due for a dramatic ending.

America's biggest game had turned into America's biggest blowout. Few believed Super Bowl XXIII would be any different thanks to the recent dominance by the NFC. Six of the last seven Super Bowls had gone to the National Football Conference representative, with two being claimed by the San Francisco 49ers. San Francisco was back for a third time and the 49ers were a clear favorite heading into the game.

However, a formidable foe awaited Bill Walsh's squad. The Cincinnati Bengals appeared to be the AFC's strongest Super Bowl representative since the 1983 Raiders. Cincinnati was led by Quarterback Boomer Esiason, who had thrown 28 touchdown passes during the regular season. Esiason was named the NFL's Most Valuable Player and the Bengals rolled into the Super Bowl after a 12–4 regular season. Esiason understood why the 49ers were favored by a touchdown heading into Super Bowl XXIII, but Bengals Head Coach Sam Wyche decided to use the point spread as motivation.

"I remember him talking about how no one is respecting us and using that tactic to try and get us motivated for this game," Esiason said. "When you take a look at the 49ers roster back then, they had Hall of Famers all over the place. It really was an up and coming team that was great offensively and opportunistic defensively against this juggernaut of a franchise that had all these great players."

San Francisco had a combined 28–4 regular season record in its two other Super Bowl years, but it had been a rough road to Super Bowl XXIII for this edition of the 49ers. The team started the season at 6–5 and appeared to be ready to come apart, but Running Back Roger Craig believes a players' only meeting turned San Francisco's season around.

"We went through a lot of adversity that year," Craig said. "Our record wasn't that good. People were saying there was no way we were going to make the playoffs. We called a team meeting and we kicked the coaches out of the room. We took ownership of our team."

San Francisco won four of its last five games and playoff victories over Minnesota and Chicago sent the 49ers to Miami for Super Bowl XXIII. Only the Bengals stood in the way of a third Super Bowl title for San Francisco in eight years. However, Wyche was quite familiar with the 49ers after serving as an assistant coach under Walsh for three seasons. San Francisco Offensive Lineman Guy McIntyre knew the 49ers would face a very difficult opponent on this Super Sunday.

"They kind of knew us and kind of knew what we did," said McIntyre. "They had some familiarity to us as far as our offense. That was a really good Bengals team. They had some great players over there defensively."

The Bengals suffered a crushing blow the night before Super Bowl XXIII. Fullback Stanley Wilson was caught using cocaine in his Miami hotel room. Wilson was one of Cincinnati's most valuable weapons on third down and Esiason said the loss of Wilson less than 24 hours before kickoff was devastating to the offense.

"Stanley Wilson was found in a drug-induced haze the night before the game," Esiason said. "Stanley was our go-to third down guy. He was unstoppable."

The weather conditions were perfect in Miami for a Super Bowl, but the condition of the field was a different story. Both sides would be dealing with a slippery surface at Joe Robbie Stadium, and Esiason believes it had an effect on both teams early in the game.

"The field conditions were horrendous," recalled Esiason. "It was maybe one of the worst fields ever to have played a Super Bowl on if not the worst. There was rain the night before and the morning of the Super Bowl. I think they left the drainage system on and the field was coming up in clumps. You would dig your foot in and you could easily twist your ankle."

A game that would end in dramatic fashion began with a pair of devastating injuries. The first took place three plays into the game when San Francisco Tackle Steve Wallace suffered a broken ankle. Eleven plays later, Cincinnati Defensive Lineman Tim Krumrie suffered one of the most gruesome injuries ever seen in football. Krumrie broke two bones in his left leg, as his ankle caught part of the field while he was trying to make a tackle. Both teams looked to recover after seeing two key players taken off the field with broken bones.

"It took us a little bit of time to get together and get our offense together," said McIntyre. "It was a hard fought game. You never know what's going to happen when you get into these contests and injuries play a big part of it."

"They were two catastrophic injuries for both teams," Esiason said. "I actually lay the blame on those injuries on the field conditions."

The 49ers were the first team to get on the board. Montana marched his team 73 yards on their second drive to the Bengals' 24-yard line, where Mike

Cofer booted a 41-yard field goal. San Francisco appeared ready to double its lead early in the second quarter, but a bad snap foiled a 19-yard attempt by Cofer. The missed field goal was the shortest in Super Bowl history. The game remained 3–0 until late in the first half. Cincinnati moved the ball to the San Francisco 16 and a 33-yard field goal by Jim Breech sent the teams to the locker room at halftime tied at 3–3. It was the first time two teams were tied after the first two quarters of a Super Bowl.

"It just took a little time," McIntyre said. "You never know how you're going to match up until you go out and play and they played us really good."

The Cincinnati Defense was impressive over the first two quarters, but Esiason was frustrated with the inability of the high-powered Cincinnati Offense to move the ball against the 49ers.

"We couldn't really get anything done in the first half," recalled Esiason. "We weren't able to run effectively and we weren't able to convert on third downs. Our passing game was average at best if not below average. It wasn't who we were as a team."

Many of the failed third down conversions came on plays which were meant for Stanley Wilson and Esiason and his teammates were wondering how different the game might have been if Wilson hadn't been overcome by his drug problem the night before the game.

"We had a handful of third and short situations that we were unable to convert for whatever reason," recalled Esiason. "That really was a very frustrating aspect."

Esiason came out strong on the first drive of the second half. The left-hander completed three of his first four passes as the Bengals moved into San Francisco territory. Breech added another field goal from 43 yards and Cincinnati had its first lead of the game. However, Esiason was intercepted on the Bengals' next possession as Bill Romanowski brought the ball to the Cincinnati 23. The Bengals' defense stiffened once again, but Cofer's second field goal tied the game at 6–6.

The tie was broken on the ensuing kickoff.

Stanford Jennings raced 93 yards for a touchdown to give Cincinnati a 13–6 lead. It was a special moment for Jennings involving more than just football. The touchdown came one day after the birth of his daughter, Kelsey.

"He was my roommate," said Esiason. "I remember Stanford saying 'My wife's got her sister and her mother and they're in the hospital and everybody's good.' He said Kathy wanted him to stay here so I told him 'You should stay here.' I remember Sam Wyche and everyone else saying 'That's for Kelsey!' It was one of the most special moments you could ever imagine any of us going through."

It was a special moment for the Bengals on the scoreboard as Cincinnati regained the lead, but the 49ers came right back on their next drive.

"It really was a great moment in that game," Esiason said. "All of a sudden, we truly felt like we had momentum on our side, but if you score via a kickoff return, there's got to be some collateral damage to that. The collateral damage is that the defense has to immediately go back on the field."

A 40-yard pass to Craig on the first play of the fourth quarter put San Francisco in the red zone. Montana then survived a brush with a disaster as he nearly threw his first Super Bowl interception, but Cincinnati's Lewis Billups let the potential turnover slip out of his hands. Given a second chance, Montana hit Jerry Rice for a 14-yard score, and Super Bowl XXIII was tied at 13–13.

San Francisco had a chance to regain the lead later in the period, but Cofer missed from 49 yards out. The Bengals took over and began a methodical march into scoring range. On fourth down, Breech connected on his third field goal of the day from 40 yards away. With just over three minutes remaining in Super Bowl XXIII, Cincinnati led, 16–13, and one of the greatest quarterbacks of all time would have a chance to put together one of the most exciting finishes in Super Bowl history.

"They were 12–4 that year," Craig said. "They had a great defense, but the one thing Bill Walsh prepares us for was a two-minute offense. No one ran a two-minute offense like Joe Montana. That's what we did. That was our thing. It was natural for us to do what we did."

"We knew we had enough time," said McIntyre. "We knew we had a quarterback that wasn't going to let the pressure of the moment get to him. We knew if we did our job and gave him the time that we had the receivers to get open and it would happen."

The Bengals were 3:10 away from their first ever Super Bowl victory, but Esiason knew there was plenty of time on the clock for Montana to work his magic.

"I think all of us were a little bit concerned," Esiason said.

Montana had a long way to go to either tie or win the game for his team. A penalty on the kickoff pinned the 49ers back on their own eight-yard line. With the pressure of a Super Bowl title on the line, Joe Cool lived up to his nickname. As the 49ers prepared for their final drive, Montana pointed out Comedian John Candy in the stands to his teammates, alleviating the pressure of the Super Bowl spotlight.

"That was the legend of Joe," McIntyre said. "He was able to detach himself from those pressure situations and to just look at it that we were going to do what we always do. It was just what we did in practice and was no different. Him saying what he did helped us all calm down."

"He'd always say things like that to keep us calm," Craig said. "That's what kept us really cool and calm. We were laughing. That's how calm we were."

Esiason was trying to stay calm on the sidelines as San Francisco prepared for its final drive, but representatives from a famous vacation resort were trying to get the quarterback ready for a commercial shoot at the end of what they expected would be a Cincinnati victory.

"I'm on the sidelines and I get tapped on the shoulder by a group that was representing Disney World," recalled Esiason. "These people want to know whether or not I know my lines for this commercial. They have no clue how big this moment is for me. They have makeup there."

Montana completed the first three passes of the drive before the two-minute warning to give San Francisco breathing room. After a pair of runs by Craig, another catch by Rice moved San Francisco into Cincinnati territory. Craig made the next big play as his catch and run brought the ball just outside the Cincinnati 35.

"Keep the chains moving," Craig said. "That's what my role was. We all had roles that we played and we just took it to the next level."

After Montana's only incompletion of the drive and a penalty, a catch and run by Rice moved the ball to the 18. Craig's next reception brought the ball to the ten.

"We didn't stress," recalled Craig. "We saw stress on the Cincinnati Bengals' faces. As we were moving down the field, they were stressing more and more and more. We got more and more confident as we got closer."

"We were known for running the two-minute drill," McIntyre said. "We practice that a lot of times and did a lot of situational stuff that prepared us. When you're in them, you just try to remember how we did it. We just methodically moved down the field."

After a timeout, Montana fired a pass between two defenders and into the hands of John Taylor in the end zone with 34 seconds to play. The 49ers had marched 92 yards to take a 20–16 lead and Montana had put together one of the greatest drives in football history.

"All you want to do is get the touchdown," said McIntyre. "You want to get the lead and then whatever time is left you turn it over to the defense. It was elation. It was exhaustion. It was everything. That's what it's all about. You know it's the biggest game of the year. All of that comes rushing in."

As the 49ers celebrated, Esiason realized his dream of being a world champion along with his trip to Disney World would fall 34 seconds short.

"I said that I guess I'm not going to Disney World," Esiason said. "With that, they ran to the other side of the field looking for Jerry Rice. You want to talk about adding insult to injury. That really explains in a nutshell how my Super Bowl went."

The 20–16 victory helped cement San Francisco's status as the Team of the 80's. Bill Walsh had won his third championship, but he would not be back for a chance at his fourth. Walsh had decided to retire after the season and his players did not know about Walsh's plans to step down. When Brent Musburger on the CBS Radio post-game show asked Walsh if it would be his final game on the sidelines, the coach became emotional. It was clear Walsh was ready to walk away.

"I don't know any of the players that knew," McIntyre said. "I had no idea. I was just happy for the moment and then the question was asked and that's when I found out. It was the furthest thing from my mind."

"He surprised everyone," said Craig. "I was shocked. I was happy then I was sad because he understood me as a coach and he got every inch out of me as far as my abilities and what I could do. He brought it to life."

As the 49ers celebrated another championship and prepared for life without Walsh, the Bengals will forever be haunted by "The Drive." It cemented Montana's legacy, but left the Bengals seconds short of their championship dream. It is a memory Esiason is forced to relive on a yearly basis.

"The brilliance of Joe Montana is evident now all these years later," said Esiason. "Literally every Super Bowl, I have an appearance with him somewhere. Every Super Bowl, he's got to talk about the final drive and I have to pain my way through it. He's good natured about it."

While Montana finished with 357 yards passing and two touchdowns, Rice's 11 catches for 215 yards earned the receiver MVP honors. Craig did his part with a combined 172 yards rushing and receiving. Craig said Super Bowl XXIII will always be his favorite as the signature moment of the San Francisco dynasty was on display in the final seconds.

"It just shows what we're all about," Craig said. "It's all about teamwork and it's all about coming together. Joe Montana let everyone touch the ball. It just showed the world what we're all about."

XXIV
PHENOMENAL 49ERS

The San Francisco 49ers were ready to end the 1980's with an exclamation point.

The 49ers dominated the decade and headed to Super Bowl XXIV looking for their fourth championship in nine seasons. San Francisco put together a 14–2 regular season and blew past the Vikings and the Rams in the playoffs by a combined score of 71–16. The 49ers rolled through their 1989 campaign without Bill Walsh. The head coach had stepped down at the end of the 1988 season, but assistant George Seifert took over for Walsh and kept the San Francisco machine rolling. The 49ers looked more powerful than the team which needed a last-minute touchdown to beat the Bengals in Super Bowl XXIII. Some were calling the 1989 49ers one of the best teams ever to take the field. Guard Guy McIntyre wasn't surprised to see how the team maintained its success despite the loss of one of the game's greatest coaches.

"It wasn't like George was a new personality that we had to get comfortable with," said McIntyre. "George had been around ever since I had been around. He wasn't like somebody off the street."

San Francisco was part of a decade in which the NFC dominated the AFC on Super Sunday. Only the Raiders of 1980 and 1983 had come away victorious from the American Football Conference and the gap between the two conferences appeared to widen even further in 1989. The Denver Broncos would represent the AFC in New Orleans, but the 11–5 Broncos were the only AFC squad to reach a double digit win total. Denver was making its fourth Super Bowl appearance and its third in four years. While San Francisco was 3–0, Denver was 0–3 on Super Sundays, with the margin of defeat increasing on each trip. This edition of the Broncos was an even bigger underdog. Few gave Denver a chance against mighty San Francisco. Quarterback John Elway went through an inconsistent season as he threw the same amount of interceptions (18) as he did touchdown passes. On paper, Super Bowl XXIV appeared to be a mismatch.

McIntyre and his teammates weren't paying attention to the pregame prognosticators.

"I never heard any of that," McIntyre said. "I don't remember any of it. Part of it was probably not listening to television and not buying into the reports. I don't remember listening to a lot of news reports."

Broncos Wide Receiver Vance Johnson had been a part of the last two Denver Super Bowls. While Johnson was happy to get another chance at the Vince Lombardi Trophy, he understood the enormous task at hand for himself and his teammates with the mighty 49ers waiting in New Orleans. A change in the practice routine during the week by Head Coach Dan Reeves did not appear to serve as an advantage.

"I don't even think if we knew we had a chance," Johnson said. "We changed the whole practice up. We had never gone to the Super Bowl and practiced in pads. Dan Reeves made us wear pads. He made us run. He also made us do a lot of hitting and we never hit before a Super Bowl. I think he was trying to change things up."

San Francisco Running Back Roger Craig noticed the change in the Denver routine and believed it would serve as another advantage for the 49ers.

"I can remember they were doing two-a-day practices," said Craig. "If you're not in shape by now, doing two-a-days is only going to wear you down late in the season."

The extra work in pads by the Broncos was intended to set a more physical tone for the game. The 49ers had proven throughout the decade they could take their physicality to high level, but the team from the west coast with Joe Montana at quarterback was more famous for its flashy offense.

"We love when you play physical with us," Craig said. "That's when we're at our best. People didn't figure it out. When you run the West Coast offense as efficient as the way we did, that's when we were at our best."

Despite predictions of a San Francisco rout, the game still had to be played. The Broncos needed to keep the contest close early or face annihilation at the hands of Montana and Company, but Denver went three and out on the first possession of the game. San Francisco took over on its own 34 and quickly marched to the Denver 20. Montana hit Jerry Rice in the end zone and the 49ers had the lead 4:54 into the opening period.

The Broncos were down, but not out just yet. With the help of a 27-yard catch and run by Bobby Humphrey on a shovel pass, Denver moved 49 yards before its drive stalled. David Treadwell kicked a 42-yard field goal to cut the San Francisco lead to 7–3, but the competitive phase of Super Bowl XXIV was about to come to an end. The next time Denver got the football, Humphrey fumbled and Chet Brooks recovered the ball for San Francisco on its own 46-yard line. Montana quickly went to work and put together a ten-play scoring drive. The quarterback finished the scoring march with a seven-yard pass to Brent Jones. The extra point was missed, but the 49ers had a 13–3 lead and there was a sense in the Superdome San Francisco was on the verge of blowing the game open.

"It did start to snowball," recalled Johnson. "We knew we couldn't make any kind of mistakes against that team."

The 49ers struck again on their first drive of the second quarter. This time, it was a 69-yard drive with the help of a key fourth down conversion by Tom Rathman. The fullback also caught three passes for 39 yards on the drive and capped it off with a one-yard touchdown run. Rathman had been an unsung hero for the 49ers for four seasons, but his teammates were more than happy to share the spotlight with their fullback.

"We knew how hard Tom worked," McIntyre said. "He was a very, very hard worker and a hard-nosed guy. When any of those guys who are not the main guys have a big game, it's great to have."

"I was really happy for him," Craig said. "You have a threat like that out of the backfield. It reminds me of when Wendell Tyler and I were in the same backfield together. They couldn't key on everyone. We had a lot of daggers."

One of the biggest daggers was Rice, who continued to find open space in the middle of the Denver Defense. Late in the first half, Rice hauled in Montana's perfect strike from 38 yards away. San Francisco went to the locker room up, 27–3, and the 49ers could already begin making room in their offices for another Lombardi Trophy.

"You could not help but admire and respect it," Johnson said. "Just being there was amazing. The game felt like it just lasted forever. Every time you turned your head, you were watching the big screen and Jerry was running into the end zone with another touchdown."

The nightmare continued for Elway and the Broncos in the third quarter. Elway's first pass was intercepted by Michael Walter. It took just one play for Montana to find Rice again from 28-yards out, and San Francisco increased its lead to 34–3.

"We felt like we were in control of the game," McIntyre said. "But you never know. That's why we went back out there and we got back to work. We didn't take it for granted that just because we were there, they were going to ease off or we were going to ease off."

On Denver's next possession, Elway threw another interception as Brooks picked up his second turnover of the game. Two plays later, it was John Taylor's turn to get into the scoring spree. Montana hit Taylor with a 35-yard pass. The 49ers were up by 38 with nine minutes remaining in the third quarter. Montana had thrown a Super Bowl-record five touchdown passes.

"We were so efficient on that game day," recalled Craig. "It was like taking candy from a baby. Everything was clean. We trained and prepared to the fullest. It was amazing. It's beautiful when you're in synch. It's almost like watching Larry Bird shooting threes or Wayne Gretzky getting a good slap shot in or Michael Jordan soaring through the air. When you're in synch, it's amazing."

Meanwhile, Elway and the Broncos were on their way to their third Super Bowl blowout loss in four years. The man with the golden arm was suffering another Super Bowl blowout.

"I remember looking at John's face," Johnson said. "I was just wondering if this is what he would be known for. Knowing the type of player John was there was no way he was going to hang it up until he won a Super Bowl."

Elway's time would come eight years later, but Super Bowl XXIV lived up to its expectations of a one-sided affair. San Francisco had scored on six of its first eight drives and the 49ers never took their foot off the gas pedal.

"You don't think about the fact that we scored on three drives," said McIntyre. "You think about another drive and another chance, so let's get it done."

Denver finally reached the end zone after San Francisco's sixth touchdown with the help of a penalty. Bill Romanowski was flagged for interfering with Clarence Kay in the end zone and Elway finished the drive with a three-yard run. San Francisco responded with yet another score on a drive which mercifully took nearly seven minutes off the clock. Rathman finished it off with a three-yard run to start the fourth quarter. Another turnover set up the final score of the contest when Elway fumbled after being sacked by Don Griffin. Danny Stubbs returned the fumble to the Denver one, and Craig followed with a touchdown to make the final score 55–10. It was the largest margin of victory in the history of the Super Bowl. The 49ers outgained the Broncos, 461–167. Elway was held to 108 yards passing, and Denver joined Minnesota in big-game futility by falling to 0–4 on Super Sundays.

"There was no one that was going to beat San Francisco," said Johnson.

Johnson would never get another chance at a Super Bowl. His final season was in 1995, two years before Denver's return to the championship game. While the pain of three Super Bowl defeats still lingers, Johnson also knows there is no shame in making three Super Bowl appearances.

"You're a darn good football team if you make it to three Super Bowls," said Johnson. "You've got to give credit to Dan Reeves because of the type of coach he was. Obviously, John Elway was one of the greatest of all time."

Johnson would later win a bigger battle off the field. His post-football life was marred by alcohol addiction which nearly ended Johnson's life. The former receiver was near death in a coma before recovering and has now dedicated his life to helping others facing addiction.

"Coming through this and being sober is a true victory in itself," Johnson said. "I would rather win this Super Bowl against addiction than any of the Super Bowls I ever participated in."

San Francisco's masterpiece forever cemented the 49ers as one of the great teams of all time. In what would be his last Super Bowl, Montana threw for 297 yards and no interceptions, keeping his four-game Super Bowl interception total at zero. Craig has tremendous respect for the rest of the NFL dynasties and believes it is hard to compare teams from different eras, but the 49ers proved to be one of the game's all-time great teams.

"You can't really compare eras," said Craig. "It's only your opinion. You can't really compare because it's different times. The Pittsburgh Steelers were great in their era. We dominated our era. The Cowboys dominated the 90's era and the Patriots have dominated the millennium. You can't really compare because they were different times."

Meanwhile, the elements of the San Francisco offense can still be found in today's NFL.

"We were ahead of our time," Craig said. "We were running a 21st century platform in the 80's. It's still powerful today. We were the founders of that and the innovators of that."

XXV
A STAR-SPANGLED SUPER BOWL

The silver anniversary Super Bowl was being overshadowed by a more important battle.

As the New York Giants and Buffalo Bills prepared for Super Bowl XXV in Tampa, the Gulf War was underway in Iraq. Hostilities began ten days before Super Sunday, and a mix of patriotism and anxiousness was in the air at Tampa Stadium. The level of security at the Super Bowl would be the most intense ever seen in the pre–9/11 world.

While the minds of many were on the conflict in the Middle East, there was still a game to be played. It would be a welcome distraction for a nation dealing with war for the first time in decades. However, players such as New York Linebacker Carl Banks could sense a vastly different atmosphere at his second Super Bowl appearance.

"The tensions were high," said Banks. "We were experiencing something that we had never experienced before as a nation. In the field of sports, we had never gone through that kind of a military security protocol. Everything we did that week was under the cloak of security."

Super Bowl XXV had all the makings of a classic matchup. The powerful New York Giants would face the high-flying Buffalo Bills in a game which matched a complete contrast in styles. The NFC Champion had won the past six Super Bowls, but the AFC was sending its strongest representative in several seasons. The Bills were powered by their fast-paced no-huddle offense. Buffalo destroyed the Los Angeles Raiders, 51–3, in the AFC Championship game. The Bills had also beaten New York at the Meadowlands earlier in the season. Buffalo seemed destined to claim its first Super Bowl title, but Quarterback Jim Kelly insists his team not arrive in Tampa overconfident.

"I definitely don't think we were overconfident going in," Kelly said. "I know I wasn't. As a quarterback, you always try and stay focused and keep in mind on what you're there for. I thought we were going into that game with a positive attitude, and I'm sure the Giants did, too."

Buffalo's 17–13 win over New York in December was a physical contest. The Bills lost Kelly to a knee injury in the victory, but the quarterback was able to return for the post-season. One of his top targets was Wide Receiver

James Lofton, who found it difficult to believe any of the Bills would have taken the Giants lightly.

"I don't think we were overconfident," said Lofton. "That year, the Giants were the toughest team that we had played. Defensively, they had a lot of standout players and a lot of stars who were still playing really well. We knew it was going to be a tough game."

There was clearly an absence of overconfidence with the Giants as well. Banks and his teammates had seen enough of Buffalo in their first matchup to know they would be facing a very talented team in Tampa.

"The NFC in general was supposed to be more physical," Banks said. "But Buffalo was built like an NFC team and in particular, an NFC East team. They had good, strong guys up front and a good running game and good quarterback. They were physical. We left that game knowing they were not a typical AFC team."

New York had lost Quarterback Phil Simms earlier in the season and had to survive a nail-biter in San Francisco to claim the NFC title. Matt Bahr's fifth field goal gave the Giants a 15–13 win and denied the 49ers a chance at a third straight Super Bowl crown. Jeff Hostetler had taken over for Simms at quarterback and added an extra dimension of mobility at the helm.

The Giants and Bills found different ways to win in 1990. Buffalo's offense looked unstoppable, and Kelly and his teammates put up points like a pinball machine. Meanwhile, the Giants won with power football and the top-ranked defense in the NFL. New York Defensive Coordinator Bill Belichick unveiled an entirely new look for his defense for the Super Bowl. It involved less pressure on the quarterback and more on the Buffalo receivers. However, Belichick admitted the scheme could set the dangerous Thurman Thomas free throughout the game. The Buffalo Running Back led the league in yards from scrimmage for the second straight year, so Banks admitted to being skeptical when the plan was revealed to the players.

"We would have taken another week to prepare for those guys," said Banks. "They were just a track meet. We just came out with a great strategy from Bill Belichick. We were insulted when he first came out and said he wanted Thurman Thomas to get 100 yards rushing, but then he told us why."

Buffalo was favored to win by a touchdown, but the Bills and their head coach, Marv Levy, were bracing for another tight contest with the Giants. They were also preparing with less time than most Super Bowl participants since the NFL did not have a bye week before Super Bowl XXV.

"We had squeaked out a 17–13 win against them," Levy said. "They had just come off a win over the San Francisco 49ers. We knew we were playing a good team. You didn't have the leisure to prepare as comfortably as you did during the course of a regular season game."

It was only appropriate that two teams wearing red, white, and blue took the field in Tampa. The pre-game ceremonies featured flag-waving fans and a memorable rendition of the national anthem by Whitney Houston. The Giants and Bills were ready to go to battle, but America was facing a far greater battleground in the Persian Gulf.

"I think it was an emotional moment for both teams," Banks said. "That national anthem started, you could feel chills go through the bodies of everybody in that stadium. It was the game that you wanted to win for America and play for America."

The Giants were able to hold the Bills to a rare three and out on the first possession of the game. Hostetler then moved the Giants into Buffalo territory, where Matt Bahr's 28-yard field goal gave New York the first points of the game. Hostetler have proven he could move the Giants on their opening possession, and Center Bart Oates and his linemates were well adjusted to the quarterback's style of play.

"Jeff was more comfortable on the move," Oates said. "We actually put in a lot of bootlegs and a lot of rollouts. Very seldom would we do a straight drop back."

The Bills quickly countered on the ensuing possession as Kelly hit Lofton for a 61-yard pass down the left sideline. Lofton was pushed out of bounds on the New York eight-yard line, but a deflection on the pass by Cornerback Perry Williams may have saved a touchdown.

"I've got a step and a half on him," said Lofton. "The ball was just slightly underthrown, but Jim put a lot of air under it. Everson Walls comes out and pushes me out of bounds inside the ten-yard line. Looking back on it, you wonder what I could have done to stay in bounds."

A first and goal on the eight was usually an automatic touchdown for these Bills, but the Giants forced Buffalo to settle for a 23-yard field goal by Scott Norwood. The game was tied, 3–3, after one quarter, and Banks was feeling confident with Belichick's game plan.

"We knew right away that is was going to work," said Banks. "It was exactly how Bill Belichick and his staff had scouted it. As long as they were going to continue to play the way they had played the previous nine games, we knew exactly what we had to do, and that was to really pound their receivers."

But Hostetler was taking a pounding of his own. Buffalo's defense pressured the Giants' signal caller throughout the first part of the second quarter. After a New York punt, Kelly directed his team 80 yards on 12 plays. Don Smith capped off the drive with a one-yard run to give Buffalo a 10–3 lead. The Bills' Defense would then increase the lead, but a heads up play by Hostetler prevented Buffalo from gaining an even bigger advantage. After tripping over Running Back O.J. Anderson, Hostetler was sacked in the end zone by Bruce Smith for a safety. Smith had his hand on Hostetler's wrist, but the quarterback kept a firm grip on the football and denied Smith the chance at a fumble which could have resulted in a touchdown. New York responded by forcing Buffalo to punt, and the Giants went back to the basics on offense despite trailing, 12–3.

"That was the key," said Oates. "We were able to stay with it and not let that be a negative."

Giants Coach Bill Parcells talked throughout week to his team about "shortening the game." The longer New York's offense was on the field, the less time the high-scoring Buffalo offense would be able to put up points.

"We wanted to get the offense back on the field as fast as possible and as much as possible," Banks said. "We wanted to really control the clock. In all honesty, time was not on our side as long as they had the football."

"The Giants did a fine job in the game," said Levy. "It's enough to handle all the changes and all the differences without dredging up more."

New York needed to move faster on offense late in the first half. The Giants took over on their own 12-yard line with 3:49 remaining, and Hostetler drove his team to its first touchdown of the night. Stephen Baker's catch with 25 seconds remaining in the half cut the Buffalo lead to 12–10. New York got the ball to start the third quarter and put together one of the greatest drives in Super Bowl history. The clock-chewing march stalled at the Buffalo 32, and New York was faced with a third and 13. Hostetler threw a short pass to Wide Receiver Mark Ingram, who broke five tackles and lunged for the first down to keep the drive alive.

"They threw about an eight-yard completion to Ingram," recalled Levy. "Two of our great defensive players, Darryl Talley and Nate Odomes, came to put the hit on him. They knocked each other off the tackle and he picked up the first down. That was the key play."

Five plays later, Anderson scored from the one to give New York a 17–12 lead. The 75-yard drive went 9:29, the longest scoring drive in Super Bowl history.

"You're in the moment," Oates said. "You just know that you're out there and you've got the ball. You can only go one play at a time, but it was to our benefit. We really needed to score and score on long drives. The longer they stayed off that field, the better it was for us."

Meanwhile, Kelly and the Bills had spent an eternity on the sidelines. The combination of the two scoring drives by the Giants sandwiched around a long halftime show had kept the Buffalo offense in hibernation.

"That was not the most fun time," recalled Kelly. "You want to be on the field because you knew how potent the offense was. You want to be able to help your team win. When you're on the sidelines, you're not doing anything to help. It was a great game plan. The best thing for them was to keep us off."

When the Buffalo Offense returned to the field, the New York defenders continued to punish their receivers. The increased pounding on the likes of Lofton and Andre Reed resulted in mistakes rarely seen in 1990 by the Bills.

"We knew we could really start to get into the heads of their receivers," said Banks. "They'd have some incompletions that they would normally complete. We had the right game plan defensively to get the ball back to our offense."

"You go from a 12 minute halftime to a 25 minute halftime," Lofton said. "There are all of those little quirks that you're not used to and you have to get under your belt. But once again, they were a great defensive team and they did a lot to stop us."

However, the Giants could not stop Thomas. On the first play of the fourth quarter, Thomas bounced off a tackler and raced 31-yards for a touchdown.

"We knew Thurman was the reason we were in that game," said Kelly. "He had some great runs. It was something as I stated before that I really should have ran the ball a little bit more."

The Bills had regained the lead, but the Giants responded with another methodical drive. New York marched to the Buffalo three where Linebacker Cornelius Bennett batted down a Hostetler throw on third down. Bahr kicked his second field goal of the game, and the Giants were up by a point after taking another 7:32 off the clock.

The teams traded punts before Buffalo got the ball back with 2:16 remaining on its own ten. Kelly had run the no-huddle offense to near perfection throughout much of the season. Now, he had a chance to run it one more time and give Buffalo its first Super Bowl title.

"It was a dream come true," Kelly said. "I was a little boy growing up in Pittsburgh. I put a magic marker number 12 on my jersey and I was pretending I was leading my team down the field to win a Super Bowl."

Kelly had a long way to go, but a 21-yard run by Thomas on third down moved the ball to the Buffalo 40. A mix of short passes and Kelly scrambles put the Bills just outside the New York 40, and Thomas made another run to the 29. With the clock ticking and no timeouts remaining, Kelly was forced to spike the football. Eight seconds remained, and Norwood trotted out to attempt a 47-yard field goal.

"You don't have a lot of time to think about it," Oates said. "It's going to go one way or another."

Norwood had been a very accurate kicker for the Bills over the years, but had struggled with long distance on grass fields. The Buffalo kicker went 1-for-5 in 1990 on grass from 40 yards or beyond, so the odds were not in Norwood's favor as he prepared for the kick of his life. While Levy watched with his team, he was already thinking ahead in case the kick went through, knowing the Giants would have time left on the clock.

"That was very strongly on my mind," said Levy. "There were eight seconds to go at the time and I knew even if he made the kick, there might be three or four seconds still up on the clock."

Norwood approached the ball and hit it solidly. The ball drifted upwards into the Tampa night and appeared headed inside the goal posts, but slowly began to hook towards the right. The ball sailed wide of the post and set off a wild celebration on the New York sideline, and the Giants savored victory in the closest Super Bowl ever played.

"We were exhausted and they were exhausted," recalled Banks. "If that kick would have went in, we would have had to have tipped our hat to him. It was one of those type of games, but we held them out of his range and that's why we won it."

"They were a better team," said Oates. "If that game had gone another quarter, they were going to catch up."

From his view from the sidelines, Kelly initially thought the kick had gone through, but soon realized Buffalo's fate as the Giants began to celebrate on the field.

"I thought for sure," Kelly said. "You look and you're thinking, 'Okay!' but I looked out and saw the guy who went to block the field goal jumping up. I realized it didn't make it."

Many of the Bills collapsed to the ground in shock. Some tried to console Norwood, who will be forever remembered for "Wide Right."

"It was a long kick," said Lofton. "It was 47 yards from the right hash. I'm just hoping that he hits the ball well, because you'd hate for a guy to shank it. He hit it really well. He hit the ball straight and true, but it just stayed outside the right upright and ended up wide right."

"It's a crushing feeling," Levy recalled. "Here it is with your whole season coming down essentially to one play. You've got a guy kicking who's won several games late with his kicks to get us there. It was a blow."

The classy Norwood answered every question from the media after the game without leaving until the post-game interviews were finished. The rest of the Bills did everything in their power to raise the kicker's spirits as a host of his teammates came up to him and accepted their share of the blame for the loss.

"That's unfortunately just the way it is," said Kelly. "Even from the quarterback's perspective if you win, you get too much credit. If you lose, you get too much of the blame. Unfortunately, when it comes down to one play, everybody's going to remember that. I know Scott was one of the main reasons we made it to that game. I will never, ever say he's the reason why we lost the Super Bowl."

As the Bills tried to come to grips with their shocking Super Bowl defeat, the Giants were celebrating one of the most remarkable performances in the history of the game. New York held the ball for 40:33. Thomas rushed for 135 yards in the defeat, while Anderson was named the MVP with a 102-yard performance. The Giants had their second Lombardi Trophy in five years.

"The first one is the dream come true," said Oates. "In the second one, nobody thought you could do it. We rang the bell. We had a backup quarterback and the oldest running back against a team that was just an offensive juggernaut. We just overcame the odds. Truly, it was a team game. We played as a team."

Banks also understood the extra significance of the game, with American military personnel watching a half a world away, and a country welcoming a much-needed diversion from war.

"I think they were both equally as good," Banks said. "But if you take XXV, the nation was watching and we were the moment of release for an entire nation on edge. I would say that had the most importance because this was the game that took everybody's mind off the military conflict that we were entering."

XXVI
CAPITAL PUNISHMENT

The Washington Redskins and Buffalo Bills were on a collision course during the 1991 season.

Washington had put together a dominating campaign. The Redskins finished 14–2, with the second loss coming in a meaningless game in Philadelphia at the end of the season. Washington led the league in points and allowed the second-fewest total during the season. The Redskins advanced to the Super Bowl with a 41–10 romp over Detroit in the NFC Championship. Washington was making its fourth Super Bowl appearance in ten years under Joe Gibbs, and the 1991 edition appeared to be stronger than any of the previous Super Bowl squads from the nation's capital.

For Buffalo, Super Bowl XXVI would be a chance at redemption. The Bills had suffered a heartbreaking defeat the year before after Scott Norwood's kicked sailed wide to the right in the closing seconds against the Giants. Buffalo's high-powered offense was at the top of its game throughout much of the season. However, the Bills barely survived in the AFC Championship game as they squeaked out a 10–7 win over Denver. Despite the scare from the Broncos, Head Coach Marv Levy had guided his team back to the biggest game of the year, and Levy was proud of the resiliency the Bills had shown throughout the season.

"They had that," said Levy. "The support they had from teammates, fans and everybody in the organization helped propel it, but they were an amazingly resilient, high character group of people."

Washington's offense was led by Quarterback Mark Rypien, who was enjoying the finest season of his career. Rypien had watched from the sidelines as a third-string quarterback four years earlier as the Redskins rolled to victory in Super Bowl XXII. This time, Rypien would be at the helm, and he learned from his first visit to the Super Bowl about taking care of distractions at the beginning of the week.

"The preparation for the game was important," said Rypien. "But taking care of the tickets, getting your family all straightened out, and getting everything you needed to do non-football wise helped. I think it was imperative for me to see something like that."

Russ Grimm knew all about Super Bowl preparation. The veteran offensive lineman was making his fourth appearance in football's ultimate game with the franchise. However, age and injuries had limited Grimm to just one start in 1991, and the longtime "Hog" knew he would be putting on his uniform for the last time in Minneapolis.

"I knew I was going to retire," said Grimm. "That year, I had played one game then I'm out two. I'd come back and play one then I'm out three. I started falling apart."

The Bills were hoping they would not fall apart under the Super Bowl spotlight. There was a sense of a more serious tone set by Buffalo throughout the week. After falling one point short in Super Bowl XXV, anything less than victory in Super Bowl XXVI would be a disappointment. Quarterback Jim Kelly tried to keep the moment in perspective as he prepared to face the mighty Redskins.

"We were in another Super Bowl," said Kelly. "We had another opportunity to win. We knew that was one of the games where we would have to play a perfect game. We knew the Redskins were peaking at the right time."

The Redskins didn't need any extra motivation, but Buffalo Defensive Line Coach Chuck Dickerson provided bulletin board material. Dickerson insulted Washington's offensive line. "The Hogs" were one of the best in the business, but Dickerson shouted insults about drooling, bad breath, and a Neanderthal-like appearance. Gibbs was happy to show the video to his team.

"It fired us up," Grimm said. "There's no question. To see some of the remarks and his facial expressions ... it was uncalled for."

"That was a point of contention that our guys took to heart," Rypien said. "Here's a group of guys that had their own name. When the opposing team's defensive line coach makes comments like that, it gives you a little bit of an added advantage. I think our guys said 'We'll make him eat his words.'"

The Bills were dealing with enough pressure heading into the game. They weren't happy Dickerson added an unnecessary distraction. Buffalo Receiver James Lofton knew the Redskins would likely use Dickerson's comments to their advantage.

"The Redskins were a really talented team," said Lofton. "Chuck Dickerson made some comments about The Hogs and their offensive line which, I guess, gave them a little extra motivation."

Still, Buffalo was a worthy Super Bowl representative after a 13–3 season. Rypien knew he would be facing one of the most talented teams in the NFL with one of the league's top defensive players.

"What a great and talented crew that they had," said Rypien. "They were very skilled, and they had their own sense of physicality, too. With Bruce Smith, whenever you played against him, you better make sure you knew where he was on the football field. This is a team that seemed to have a destiny, and that was getting to Super Bowls."

The Dickerson comments gave Washington an early advantage heading into the game. A misplaced helmet would give them another head start. Harry Connick, Jr., sang the national anthem before kickoff, and several of his band members were stationed by the Buffalo bench before the performance. A person from Connick's crew moved the helmet of Thurman Thomas, and the Buffalo running back could not find his head gear after Washington went three and out to start the game. Thomas missed the first two plays before his helmet was retrieved, but the incident would prove to be an ominous sign for Buffalo.

Despite the missing helmet, Buffalo had a chance to grab an early lead thanks to several miscues by the Redskins in the opening quarter. On Washington's second possession, Rypien moved his team to the Buffalo two-yard line. On third and goal, Rypien hit Art Monk in the back of the end zone, but the touchdown was taken away when a replay review showed Monk's right foot was out of bounds. Chip Lohmiller lined up for a 19-yard field goal, but a muffed hold on the snap closed the door on Washington's first scoring chance. The Bills had early momentum. Rypien was also dealing with pressure early in the game after being sacked only nine times during the season. One hit on the opening series sent Rypien to the ground. One week later at the Pro Bowl, Rypien would discover the hit had resulted in a cracked rib.

"The ball is out of my hand and I'm getting smoked," said Rypien. "I remember Jeff Bostic coming over and saying 'Don't worry, big fella. Everything's going to be fine. These guys have a lot of adrenalin going right now. We're going to wear them down.'"

The two teams would trade interceptions after the field goal miscue, with both turnovers coming on deflections. Kelly's pass went high over Andre Reed, and Brad Edwards' interception brought the ball to the Buffalo 12. Two plays later, Rypien's passed was tipped and picked off by Kirby Jackson. The surprised Redskins found themselves in a scoreless tie despite two trips deep into Buffalo territory.

"You kind of wonder if this is our day," Rypien said. "We felt good about what we were doing. We were moving the ball. As the game wore on, we kept doing the things that we were doing. In the second quarter, we kind of got on track."

Washington would finally capitalize on its third chance in the red zone. Early in the second quarter, Rypien hit Ricky Sanders for a 41-yard completion at the Buffalo 17. The Bills defense kept Washington out of the end zone, but Lohmiller's 34-yard field goal gave the Redskins the first points of the game. After forcing another three and out, Washington took over on it's on 49. It took just five plays for the Redskins to reach the end zone. Earnest Byner finished off the drive with a ten-yard catch, and Washington was up, 10–0. Kelly was intercepted by Darrell Green on Buffalo's next possession, and a one-yard run by Gerald Riggs increased Washington's lead. It was 17–0, and the Redskins' physical play on both sides of the ball was wearing down the Bills.

"I think it played a factor," recalled Rypien. "Anytime you came out of the NFC East during that era of football, you're going to be battle-tested in many ways. You had to be physical and you had to own both lines of scrimmage. I think we had of a bit of an advantage going in."

"That's where it always is," said Grimm. "Every now and then, you may have a phenomenal quarterback or a receiver make some big plays for you or a linebacker gets a sack and a fumble, but it's going to be won and lost up front 90-percent of the time."

Buffalo's frustration boiled over at the end of the half. Kelly finally got the Bills moving as the Bills reached the Washington 28-yard line, but a pass to Reed on third down fell incomplete. Replays showed Edwards hit the Buffalo receiver early, and an enraged Reed slammed down his helmet in disgust. Reed was flagged for unsportsmanlike conduct, and the penalty took Buffalo out of field goal range. It was a fitting end to a half in which the Redskins were in complete control, while the Bills were unraveling.

"He was such a pro," said Rypien of Reed. "He always had been a pro of pros. It just shows what the Super Bowl will do to you. You kind of lose your head at times. It's trying to keep focused even in the worst of situations that enables you to get to where you want to."

The Bills limped into the locker room trailing by 17 points. The team with the high-powered offense failed to score through the first 30 minutes, and was clearly in comeback mode at the start of the third quarter.

"It makes you change your game plan," Levy said. "You get behind and your offense doesn't balance up as well. I keep saying that the most important thing in making a quarterback great is a good defense. If you don't have a good defense, he has to play catch up. He's predictable and he gets blitzed."

Buffalo's fortunes went from bad to worse on the opening series of the second half. Kelly was intercepted by Kurt Gouveia on the first play from scrimmage. Riggs walked in from the two, and the lead went to 24–0.

The Bills were finally able to get on the board on their next possession. Kelly hit Don Beebe for a 43-yard gain, and Buffalo was in the red zone. The Redskins defense stiffened, and Norwood kicked a 21-yard field goal to make it 24–3. The Bills would get their first touchdown the next time they had the ball. A pass interference penalty put Buffalo on the one, and Thomas scored to cut the lead to 24–10.

"You start feeling good about yourself," said Kelly. "It's a 60-minute game. We'd been in games where we'd come back and won."

"We knew we had to score again," Rypien said. "We knew how good those guys were and what they could do in a short period of time. We had to put the accelerator to the ground and do what we had to do."

The accelerator was on the ground on Washington's next possession. Rypien finished off the Bills with a 30-yard touchdown toss to Clark. The Redskins went up, 31–10. Two more turnovers by Kelly (a fumble and his fourth interception) led to a pair of fourth-quarter field goals. The Buffalo quarterback would throw a pair of touchdown passes late in the period to make the final score, 37–24, but Kelly has little memory of his touchdown tosses. After being battered throughout the game, Kelly was hit scrambling out of the pocket and smashed his head against the turf. The courageous leader of the Bills would later learn he had suffered a concussion.

"I remember my brother," Kelly said. "From what I saw pictures of, he came down on the sidelines. I remember I think I said something like maybe they should have hit me a little bit earlier and I might not have thrown a couple of those interceptions."

While the Bills were left to pick up the pieces after another Super Bowl defeat, the Redskins had emerged as the clear winner. A dominating performance on both sides of the ball had given Washington its third Super Bowl title. Rypien was named the game's MVP after throwing for 292 yards. Grimm would retire with his third championship, but was happier for the players who were enjoying their first.

"I knew that was going to be my last year," Grimm said. "To go out like that was really enjoyable. Also, we had a lot of new guys like Mark Rypien and Earnest Byner that hadn't had a ring yet."

Buffalo lost Super Bowl XXV by one point, but Super Bowl XXVI was a blowout. While the Bills were frustrated with their mistakes, Levy tipped his hat to the victors.

"They were a great bunch," said Levy. "They were exceptionally well-coached with Joe Gibbs and a defensive coordinator like Larry Peccatiello. Larry had been on my staff at William and Mary many years before. You don't hear much about them since, but they were an outstanding group."

The Redskins won't argue with Levy's assessment. Some believe the 1991 team deserves to be in the same company with many of the top teams in Super Bowl history.

"It never really gets mentioned," said Rypien. "If they start looking at the numbers and looking at what we had attained that season ... not a lot of teams do that. In the history of the game, this team deserves the accolades."

The Hogs had the last laugh on Dickerson, who was fired shortly after the Super Bowl. Grimm followed through with his retirement plans and began his coaching career the following season.

"I went in and told coach I was going to retire," said Grimm. "He went through the roof. Back then, there was Plan A and Plan B. I told him to put me on Plan C. A couple of weeks later he asked if I wanted to coach the tight ends."

Injuries would hamper Rypien later in his career, but he will always be remembered for his spectacular season in 1991 and his MVP performance in Super Bowl XXVI.

"It's the thrill of winning the game when it matters the most," Rypien said. "There's not another game out there that means more than that. For our guys to play at a high level like that is just very rewarding."

XXVII
The New Kids on the Block

It took the Dallas Cowboys just three years to go from laughingstock to Super Bowl contender.

Dallas finished with a 1–15 record in 1989 during Jimmy Johnson's first year as head coach. In 1992, the Cowboys were off to Pasadena for Super Bowl XXVII. Dallas reached the Super Bowl after knocking off the favored San Francisco 49ers in the NFC Championship game. The Cowboys' impressive 30–20 victory at Candlestick Park sent one of the league's youngest teams to pro football's ultimate game. One of the players who celebrated was second year Defensive Lineman Leon Lett, who was thrilled for some of his more experienced teammates that had lived through the lean years.

"It was a great moment for our team," said Lett. "You look back on it with the players that were put together. There were veteran players with the infusion of some young players. For the older players who went 1–15, to have that opportunity to play that game in San Francisco was just awesome to be a part of that."

Another player who savored the moment was Defensive Lineman Tony Casillas, who believes the victory in San Francisco made believers out of many around the league … including themselves.

"We really didn't realize how good we were," Casillas said. "Jimmy was really good about making us pay attention to what was in front of us and not what was too far down the road. We had to beat San Francisco. I think we were just kind of this young colt that didn't realize how fast and how good and how powerful he really was."

Standing in the way of the Cowboys were the resilient Buffalo Bills, who became only the second team in NFL history to make a third straight Super Bowl appearance. After rolling through the AFC for much of the past two seasons, Buffalo had to go the long way to reach Super Bowl XXVII. The Bills had pulled off the greatest comeback in NFL history in the wild card round against the Houston Oilers. Buffalo followed "The Comeback" with wins in Pittsburgh and Miami before arriving in Pasadena. Some believed the Bills were a team of destiny, but the questions of potentially being a three-time Super Bowl loser were prominent for Buffalo in the days leading up to the game. Cornerback Larry Brown could sense the pressure mounting for the Bills as the week progressed.

"All the pressure was on Buffalo," said Brown. "We were the youngest team in the league and everyone talked about how Buffalo had been there before and that this was their time. I thought the pressure was more on Buffalo than it was on us and I think that helped us stay relaxed."

"They always ask which team has the most pressure on them," Casillas said. "I don't think we felt any at all. The Bills probably felt more pressure because they hadn't won yet. They had lost two in a row and they were playing a team they didn't know a whole lot about. I think there probably was more pressure on them."

The Bills had lost Super Bowl XXV by one point as Scott Norwood's potential game-winning kick sailed wide to the right. Buffalo was never even close in Super Bowl XXVI as they were blown out by the Washington Redskins. Now, the Bills would get a third chance as Quarterback Jim Kelly and the rest of his teammates arrived in Southern California hoping the third time would be a charm.

"Now we're doing it three years on a row," said Kelly. "That was, in itself, an amazing feat."

Kelly had been a spectator during the wild card comeback with a knee injury as backup Frank Reich led Buffalo to victory. Kelly returned for the AFC title game as he helped lead his team to the Super Bowl, but as the Bills continued to deal with questions about their previous Super Bowl failures, the Cowboys remained loose and focused.

"I just think it was work," said Lett. "We worked as hard as we did every week before that. Jimmy said we would treat every game like it's a normal game. We started that week preparing like it was going to be a normal game and not the Super Bowl. We knew it was the Super Bowl, but I think we prepared intensely and it was a great week of work. We were ready."

The sun-soaked Rose Bowl was a picturesque setting for the game. Former Buffalo Running Back O.J. Simpson did the honors on the coin toss and received a warm ovation from the crowd. The moment would come just 17 months before Simpson's life would change forever as he stood trial for one of the most famous crimes in history.

Simpson's former team would strike first in Super Bowl XXVII. Dallas went three and out on its first possession. Buffalo special teams ace Steve Tasker blocked Mike Saxon's punt to give the Bills the ball on the Dallas 16. With the help of a holding penalty against Brown on third down, the Bills crept closer to the end zone. Thurman Thomas forced his way through two Dallas defenders across the goal line and Buffalo had a 7–0 lead. Bills Coach Marv Levy had watched his team gain an early advantage one year after trailing throughout their loss in Super Bowl XXVI.

"We started out right," recalled Levy. "Steve Tasker blocks a punt and we get a touchdown out of it. Usually, that portends to some very good things."

While the Bills celebrated, the Cowboys had the early look of a team dealing with first-time Super Bowl jitters.

"We knew they were a great team," Lett said. "They could put some points on the board. We watched them come back against Houston, so we knew the type of team that they had. Early on, there were some anxious moments with guys getting after each other on the sidelines. We needed to calm down and settle down."

The Cowboys would indeed settle down with some help from the Bills. Later in the quarter, Kelly was intercepted by James Washington to give Dallas the ball on the Buffalo 47. Quarterback Troy Aikman finished the drive with a 23-yard touchdown pass to Tight End Jay Novacek to tie the game. Dallas would break the tie on Buffalo's next possession.

Kelly and his offensive teammates began the drive on their own ten-yard line. It would take just one play for Dallas to seize the lead. Kelly was hit by Charles Haley as he dropped back to throw. The ball glanced off the helmet of Lett and into the waiting arms of Jimmie Jones, who tumbled two yards into the end zone.

"It was in slow motion," recalled Lett. "I think it was a screen. Most of the time on the screen, the guard shows pass and your momentum gets you going forward. I kind of lost my balance and was getting my balance and seeing the ball floating over the top my head and then I see Jimmy Jones in the end zone getting ready to go celebrate. I can remember that moment very clearly."

The dazed Bills attempted to strike back on the ensuing drive as the second quarter began. A 40-yard pass from Kelly to Andre Reed moved Buffalo to the Dallas four. The Bills would reach the edge of the goal line on third down, but Kenneth Davis was stopped by Ken Norton inches away from the end zone. On fourth down, Levy gambled and went for the touchdown, but Kelly was intercepted by Thomas Everett. The Bills had come away empty and the momentum continued to build for the Cowboys.

"We knew they were going to try and run the football," Casillas said. "Thurman was one of the best running backs in the league. We became very bullet proof because they couldn't score on the goal line. I think physically, we really got into their heads. It starts to set in. The rigor mortis of doubt always starts to creep in your mind."

"You turn the football over the way we did that game," Kelly said. "It was like, what else could go wrong? You're not going to win any games if you do it that many times."

Kelly's day would be done on Buffalo's next possession. A hit by Ken Norton re-injured Kelly's right knee, and the man regarded as one of the toughest players in the league was sent to the sidelines for the rest of Super Bowl XXVII.

"It's heartbreaking to see players get hurt and to see Jim go down," said Levy. "But I don't think that there's ever, ever been a better backup quarterback than Frank Reich. He led the greatest comeback in pro football and the greatest comeback in college football at Maryland."

"Going there for me was a little bittersweet," Kelly said. "The sweetness was getting to three Super Bowls in a row and the bitter part was me getting my knee blown out in the second quarter."

Reich quickly engineered a scoring drive. Another long catch and run by Reed set up a Steve Christie field goal to cut the Dallas lead to 14–10. Buffalo's super sub appeared to be ready to lead another comeback, but the Dallas Defense stuck to its game plan despite the quarterback change.

"He wasn't as accurate as Jim," Casillas said. "We knew we had to continue to do what we were doing and we just kept bringing it. With that depth, he wouldn't be able to save the day."

It took only five plays for the Cowboys to strike again. A 38-yard run by Emmitt Smith put Dallas in the red zone and Aikman followed with a 19-yard touchdown pass to Michael Irvin. The Bills barely had time to recover from the latest Dallas score when the Cowboys forced another turnover. On the first play on the ensuing drive, Thomas caught a screen pass on the right side, but Lett swooped in and stripped the ball from the Buffalo back. The Cowboys had forced the fourth Buffalo turnover of the half.

"Coach Johnson constantly talked about getting guys on the ball," said Lett. "We did it in practice. That was just a situation where our pursuit of the ball was perfect on that screen pass. Thurman was a great cutback runner and he made a couple of cutbacks. I just happened to see the ball. He made a nice move on me and I had an opportunity to reach out and get the ball."

The Cowboys quickly took advantage as Aikman found Irvin again from 18-yards out. An interception by Brown on Buffalo's next drive prevented the Bills from drawing closer. Dallas had a 28–10 halftime lead and had taken complete control of Super Bowl XXVII.

"You can never relax against a team like that," said Brown. "This is the same team that came back and set a record against the Houston Oilers. The main thing we talked about was that this team could score and it could score fast. The goal was to step it up and play more aggressive than we did in the first half."

Meanwhile, the stunned Bills were staring at the prospect of their third straight Super Bowl defeat. A mistake-filled first half with five turnovers had left Buffalo searching for answers, but their wounded quarterback did not lose hope with two quarters of football remaining.

"There's no time during a football game when I thought I was going to be out of it," said Kelly. "I always thought that it didn't matter what we were down by. We could still come back."

The Buffalo offense would have to wait before getting an opportunity to cut into the lead. The Cowboys opened the second half with a 6:39 drive which ended with a Lin Elliott field goal. It remained 31–10 until the final play of the third quarter when Reich hit Don Beebe with a 40-yard touchdown. It was a touchdown that should not have counted since Reich crossed the line of scrimmage before unleashing the bomb to Beebe.

"I remember Jim Jeffcoat was really teed off about that one," recalled Lett. "He had a lot of things to say about that play. I just remember him going ballistic. They got back in it with that play."

"You couldn't worry about the officials," Brown said. "The play was over the line. You could not get caught up in that trap. You had to play Cowboy football. That was our focus the whole second half."

Dallas would finish off Buffalo in another flurry. Aikman threw a 45-yard touchdown pass to Alvin Harper. On Buffalo's next possession, Everett made his second interception of the game and put the Cowboys deep in Buffalo territory. Smith's ten-yard run made it 45–17, but the onslaught wasn't over. A high snap was fumbled by Reich and Norton scooped up the loose ball and ran into the end zone. With 21 quick fourth quarter points, Dallas had turned Super Bowl XXVII into a rout.

"We were fantastic during the season in winning the takeaway/giveaway," said Levy. "I had a statistic up that if you win the giveaway/takeaway regardless of who gained the most yards and if you win it by two or more, you're going to win 90-percent of the time. We had done it so well and yet we turned the ball over nine times in that game against the Cowboys."

The ninth turnover came in the closing seconds and would lead to one of the Super Bowl's most memorable moments. Reich fumbled and Lett recovered the football. The defensive lineman headed for the end zone for what would have been a record amount of points for a team in a Super Bowl. At the 12-yard-line, Lett began his celebration by holding the ball out with his right hand, but the speedy Beebe raced from the other side of the field. Beebe knocked the ball away from Lett just before he crossed the goal line. The play had no bearing on the inevitable outcome, but Lett will be remembered for his premature celebration and is constantly reminded of the moment even to this day.

"I didn't see him and we had a celebration planned," said Lett. "Jimmy Jones and I were going to do a hip hop dance. It was a great play and it goes down in history as one of the great follies."

While the Bills were beaten and heading for their third straight Super Bowl loss, Beebe's play served as an inspiration for people across the country. It also was a symbol of Buffalo's resiliency during one of the franchise's darkest moments.

"It really provided the example of what our team was all about," Levy said. "Frank Reich is sacked and fumbles and Leon Lett picks it up. Don Beebe sprints after him and goes all the way down the field and knocks the ball out on the one-yard line. That was the example of what those players were made of."

Lett would go on to be one of the Cowboys' key contributors during their dominance in the early 1990's, but the former defensive lineman is forced to live with the memory of the play. Lett has turned the moment into an opportunity to serve as a life lesson for himself as well as others he works with on a daily basis as an assistant coach.

"It was a great play," Lett said. "I always talk about it with the players that I work with now. It never ends, but for me it's always been a lesson to me to always finish. I get a chance to drill that home with every opportunity

I get with the players that I work with now. It also shows to never quit and I have a lot of respect for Don because a lot of guys would have just said 'forget it.'"

That respect has turned into a friendship with Beebe in the years following Super Bowl XXVII.

"I've had a chance to visit with Don Beebe over the years," said Lett. "I always wanted to know what made him chase. He's a tough guy and he's a prideful guy. I always give him a hard time because I think he missed a turnover when it was late in the game and I chased Steve Tasker down and got the ball out. I always tell Don I think he was jealous of my play. He had to return the favor."

Even with Lett's celebratory gaff, Dallas was back on top of the football world. The 52–17 victory capped a dramatic turnaround for a franchise that had hit rock bottom three years earlier.

"I'm not sure at that time we knew how talented we were," said Brown. "Here's a team that three years earlier went 1–15. After that game, we realized we've got something special here. That game really sealed the deal. We all had so much respect for Buffalo. We thought if we could do this to a team like that, I think this really gave us the confidence that we could build a dynasty."

The Bills were building a more infamous legacy. Buffalo had now lost three straight Super Bowls and the margin of defeat had grown each year. This time, Kelly had been forced into the role of spectator.

"You're the leader and the captain and the quarterback," said Kelly. "You're standing on the sidelines and there's nothing you can do."

It was a different story in the Dallas locker room, where a dynasty was just beginning.

"You celebrate the opportunity to win the big one," Lett said. "As the clock goes down and you're the Super Bowl champion, you just think about all the hard work and all of the ups and downs of the season. You see the emotions of the players and the coaches along with the entire organization. Everyone comes together and you're the last one standing. You're the king of the hill."

XXVIII
Jimmy's Last Roundup

The Dallas Cowboys had survived their share of bumps in the road during the 1993 season.

The defending world champions reached their second consecutive Super Bowl after rocketing to the top of the NFL in 1992. However, the road back to the Super Bowl wasn't easy for Jimmy Johnson's Cowboys. Dallas started the season at 0–2 as star Running Back Emmitt Smith staged a holdout due to a contract dispute. Smith returned, but had to heroically carry the Cowboys to the top seed in the NFC on the final day of the regular season. Playing with a separated shoulder, Smith picked up 229 total yards in a win over the Giants. Playoff victories over the Packers and 49ers sent the Cowboys to Atlanta for Super Bowl XXVIII and players such as Defensive Lineman Leon Lett were relieved to make it back to Super Sunday after a challenging season.

"It was tough for so many reasons," said Lett. "You had to start with the foundation and the hard work you have to put in after you win a Super Bowl. You have the opportunity to celebrate and re-commit and refocus. There were a lot of things going on that season. There was Emmitt's holdout and changes on the roster."

The coaching of Johnson was one of the major reasons why Dallas was back for a chance at a second straight title. Defensive lineman Tony Casillas credits Johnson for keeping his players focused throughout the 1993 campaign.

"Nothing was easy especially with the odds of getting back twice," said Casillas. "We were confident enough and knew to pay attention to detail and paying attention to the little things would prepare us. We were really prepared. Jimmy Johnson was the Bill Belichick of the '90's."

However, the players were not aware of a storm brewing between Johnson and Owner Jerry Jones. The two men had returned the Cowboys to glory, but the friction between them was becoming too much for both to bear.

"I think everyone thought that Jimmy and Jerry had this great relationship," Casillas said. "We didn't see what was going on in the bars or after the meetings. We didn't hear the comments in the whole relationship."

For the second straight year, the resilient Buffalo Bills awaited the Cowboys in the Super Bowl. Buffalo was making a record-setting fourth straight Super Bowl appearance, but had yet to claim football's top prize. The Bills were blown away by the Cowboys, 52–17, the previous year and America decided it had enough of Buffalo in the big game. As the season progressed, nearly everyone outside of Western New York was hoping anybody but the Bills would represent the AFC in the Super Bowl. Just like Johnson, Buffalo Coach Marv Levy kept his team's focus on football while the rest of the football world rallied against the Bills.

"We were grateful that we fought our way back," said Levy. "There were all kinds of rumblings outside. My concentration was with what was going on down on the field. We were just concentrating on winning. I can under-stand the fans saying they've seen the Bills there three times and they would like to see someone else. Certainly, fans all over the country would like to see their team there."

However, some Bills did use the "us against the world mentality" as motivation. As Buffalo finished off Kansas City in the AFC Championship, several fans unveiled a banner which read "We're back. Deal with it, America." As the final seconds ticked down, Quarterback Jim Kelly looked into an NBC camera and declared "We're Back" it a tone similar to one heard in the movie "Poltergeist." Buffalo's return to the Super Bowl was a horror movie to some, but the Bills players as well as their fans rejoiced in their history-making accomplishment.

"We had to have some motivation going into it," said Kelly. "It doesn't matter who you are or what your record was the year before. You start from scratch and you fight to get to that one game. That's why you play the game. You play it because you want that Super Bowl ring."

If the Bills failed in their attempt to get their rings, they would become the first professional sports team to lose four straight championship games. The Cowboys were a heavy favorite despite concerns over the health of their quarterback. Troy Aikman suffered a concussion in the NFC Championship game and there was no bye week leading up to Super Bowl XXVIII.

"I knew Troy had multiple concussions during his career," Casillas said. "I think we were really more concerned with his back than anything. It would have been a great question with the extensive protocol now if he would have played."

As the two teams prepared for the kickoff in the Georgia Dome, there were the typical pregame nerves being felt by players on both sides. However, it would be a breathing problem inside the dome which signaled to Casillas that Super Bowl XXVIII may be a bit more difficult than Super Bowl XXVII.

"We knew in that game it was going to be a little different," Casillas said. "I vividly remembered you could not breathe in that venue. It was very hard to breathe with all the smoke from the pregame show. When you first came out there, it didn't feel right. It had a different vibe to it."

Despite the vibe being felt by Casillas, the Cowboys would strike first. Kevin Williams returned the opening kickoff to the Buffalo 48 and Aikman moved the Cowboys to the 24. Eddie Murray's 41-yard field goal gave Dallas the first points of the game, but the underdog Bills would counter on their first drive. Kelly moved Buffalo 43 yards and into Dallas territory where Steve Christie blasted a Super Bowl record 54-yard field goal to tie the game at 3–3.

After Dallas was forced to punt, the turnover nightmare which doomed Buffalo in previous Super Bowls resurfaced. Thomas fumbled a shovel pass by Kelly and Darren Woodson recovered at midfield. Dallas once again moved into Buffalo territory, but the Bills' defense forced another field goal by Murray. It was 6–3 Dallas after one quarter, but the underdog Bills were making things difficult for Dallas.

"They had great players on that offense," recalled Lett. "It was tough because it would burn you out as far as your energy. You had defensive lineman having to turn and run. You had linebackers trying to cover Thurman Thomas. They were tough."

The Bills would get a big break on the ensuing drive. Buffalo was forced to punt, but a running into the kicker penalty on Dave Thomas gave the Bills a second chance. Kelly quickly moved his team into scoring position with a quick-rhythm, short passing attack. Thomas capped off the drive with a four-yard run, and the Bills had a 10–6 lead.

"I remember Thurman Thomas making a great move on me at the goal line," Lett said. "I thought I had him. I made a nice move to put myself in position to make the play. He made a great move on me to score the touchdown."

The team that nobody wanted in the Super Bowl had taken the lead in the second quarter and Buffalo hardly looked like the team that crumbled against the Cowboys the previous year. Still, Levy knew there was plenty of work to be done.

"You're feeling good about it," Levy said. "But you concentrate on what's going on in front of you."

The early troubles continued for Dallas before halftime. After moving the ball to midfield, Aikman was intercepted by Nate Odomes, who brought the ball back to the Dallas 48. With just over a minute to play, Buffalo quickly moved back into the red zone. Facing a third down on the nine, another shovel pass to Thomas resulted in no gain. It was no surprise to see how well the play was defended considering what the Cowboys had seen on TV earlier in the week. Jimmy Johnson saw footage of the play during a Buffalo practice and realized the Bills had not run the play in previous years. Despite the third down stop, Christie ended the half with his second field goal. The underdog Bills were leading 13–6 and were two quarters away from erasing the ghosts of Super Bowls past. Meanwhile, frustration was building for the Cowboys.

"I remember James Washington coming to me when we were on our way in," recalled Lett. "He was wondering what was happening. I was so teed up and pissed off about that play that I told him 'You just take care of your business.' I was so locked in on not making another mistake."

Once the Cowboys reached the locker room, the players settled down and attempted to refocus on the task at hand. For Brown, it was less about Buffalo's early success and more about Dallas doing what it was capable of doing in the second half.

"We felt there were opportunities that we gave up in the first half," said Brown. "We always focused on what we did. We didn't focus on what other teams did. We felt that we were prepared for every team that we played. We felt that if we played well, it didn't matter what the other team did."

The play that would change the course of Super Bowl XXVIII took place less than one minute into the third quarter. Thomas took a handoff as Lett charged into the backfield past Buffalo Center Kent Hull. Lett stripped Thomas of the football and Washington scooped up the fumble and ran 46 yards for a touchdown.

"They had gashed us on that play earlier," Lett said. "We knew it was coming. We talked about it. I think I got a good jump on the ball and I beat Kent on the back block. Thurman had just gotten the handoff, so I hit him as soon as he got it."

The game was tied at 13–13, but there was a sense the Bills were once again about to unravel under the Super Bowl spotlight.

"It just re-energized us," recalled Brown. "Buffalo had a look on their face as 'Here we go again.' One thing on a Jimmy Johnson team that was said was that the team that could overcome adversity would be the team that's going to win in the end. When you have adversity, it's how you handle it."

But the game was still tied. While many Bills appeared to be dealing with déjà vu, Levy believed it was still anybody's game with nearly a full half to play.

"It's 13–13," said Levy. "Every play isn't going to go your way. I don't think that type of mentality pervaded at all."

But the Bills would never recover from the Thomas turnover and the Cowboys quickly took over the game. After forcing a Buffalo punt, Dallas marched 64-yards on eight plays. Seven of the eight plays went to Smith, as he picked up 61 yards on the drive. He finished it off with a 15-yard run. The Cowboys were ahead, 20–13, after three quarters. For the Bills, it felt like 120–13.

"They kind of had that glassy-eyed look," recalled Casillas. "This is no disrespect to Buffalo, but I couldn't imagine four Super Bowls and coming out as the runner up every time. There comes a point when you're battling a team and you're giving it your best shot and look at where we were at. It creates a self-doubt and a 'here we go again' syndrome. You look over there and they've got their heads down."

Kelly was intercepted on the first play of the fourth quarter, as Washington retuned the ball to the Buffalo 34. Smith went back to work as he picked up 29 yards on three plays. On fourth and goal on the one, the league's MVP put the game away with another touchdown run. Dallas was up, 27–13, and the destiny of both franchises in the 1990's was sealed. The Cowboys had turned the game around with Washington's touchdown return along with a heavy dose of Smith throughout the second half.

"He took over so many games throughout the course of his career," Brown said. "Whenever he's running well, it's a great thing for us. It gives the defense a little more rest. Emmitt wasn't a guy that fumbled a lot. When 22 was doing well, it was going to be a good day for the Dallas Cowboys."

"That's the beauty about a great offensive team," said Casillas. "They can run the football. You start the fourth quarter on the sidelines and you look back up and there's 7:50 left in the game. That's what our offense did so many times to so many teams. That's a devastating blow right there."

A late field goal by Murray finished off the scoring. Smith added a Super Bowl MVP to his crowded trophy case as he finished with 132 yards on the ground. As the Cowboys celebrated their 30–13 victory in Super Bowl XXVIII, the Bills walked off in defeat for the fourth straight on Super Sunday. It marked the end of both a remarkable and heartbreaking run for Buffalo. As time has passed, the Bills are earning more praise for their remarkable run, but the sting of four straight Super Bowl defeats forever lingers.

"You wanted to be known as world champions," Kelly said. "Unfortunately, it never happened but the more we're removed from those four games, the more people realized what we accomplished."

"I keep hearing that from people," said Levy. "I hear it from fans and the media that it was an amazing accomplishment. Maybe they were being nice to me. We would love to have won one of them and we didn't. It turned out to be the impossible dream, but it is a game. I'll remember fondly those guys that I worked with and how resilient they were."

While it was the end of the run for the Bills, it seemed as if the Dallas dynasty was just beginning. All the pieces were in place with one of the NFL's top coaches and a host of talented players still in their prime.

But the coach was not sticking around.

The egos of Johnson and Jones could not co-exist going forward and Johnson parted ways with the Cowboys two months after the Super Bowl. The move came as a shock to many players who found it hard to believe Johnson would walk away from a budding dynasty.

"I don't think anybody had any idea," said Brown. "No one saw that coming at all. There was no indication that he was remotely thinking about leaving and we had no idea."

"It was sad," Casillas said. "It was pretty emotional. I know how hard Jimmy worked. I know what a fierce competitor he was. We were creating a dynasty and were starting to go towards that and to think how they couldn't co-exist, I was shocked. I never thought he was going to step down. I never saw the writing on the wall."

The Cowboys would still win one more Super Bowl in the 1990's, but many were left with a feeling of what might have been. Johnson moved on to Miami but never reached the Super Bowl with the Dolphins. In the end, Jones and Johnson did not enjoy similar success once their breakup was complete.

Meanwhile, the Bills were forced to deal with being the only team to lose four straight Super Bowls. For Kelly, the sting of football defeats took a back seat to the challenges he would face in his personal life. Kelly would lose his young son, Hunter, to Krabbe Disease and also survive a brutal battle with cancer. It put Kelly's Super Bowl losses in a far different perspective.

"One thing I realized now is that I don't have it that bad," said Kelly. "There are so many people who have it a lot worse than I do. I'm a blessed man. I'm just thankful to God that I'm here today."

A third Super Bowl title without Johnson two years later would cement Dallas as a dynasty, but it was Johnson who left a lasting impression on the road to victory in Super Bowl XXVIII.

"Jimmy Johnson came in before the season into our first team meeting," recalled Brown. "He said 'I know we can win another Super Bowl. The question is do we want to?' I think everybody bought in."

XXIX
NOBODY'S BACKUP

Steve Young was understandably out of patience.

The San Francisco quarterback and future Hall of Famer had spent much of his prime football years watching from the sidelines. Stuck behind Joe Montana for several seasons in San Francisco, some wondered if Young would ever get his chance to show off his vast variety of skills on football's biggest day. Young's time would finally arrive at Super Bowl XXIX.

The 49ers reached the Super Bowl for the first time with Young as their starting quarterback. After being stopped by the Cowboys in the NFC title game for two straight seasons, Young and his teammates finally broke through against Dallas. San Francisco's 38–28 victory served as vindication for Young and sent the 49ers to Miami for the Super Bowl. Bart Oates had been a part of a pair of championships with the New York Giants, but now stood under center for Young in San Francisco after leaving New York as a free agent. Oates had seen enough of Montana from the opposing sidelines to understand Young's frustration.

"He was one of the five greatest quarterbacks in NFL history," Oates said. "How do you follow somebody like that? It's impossible to really do it where people could really appreciate you. Steve's offensive numbers were better than Joe's, but Joe had four Super Bowls and Steve didn't have one."

Vanquishing the Cowboys was especially sweet for the 49er veterans who had been derailed by Dallas the previous two seasons. Rookie Fullback William Floyd was enjoying a trip to the Super Bowl in his first season in the NFL, but understood the excitement of his veteran teammates who had been foiled by the Cowboys in 1992 and 1993. Floyd also knew what it was like to be part of a championship team.

"I had just finished winning the national championship with Florida State in Miami," said Floyd. "I'm back in Miami again getting ready to play in the Super Bowl a year later. I almost expected that. When you win a championship, that's what you expect. That's kind of what the 49ers expected. They expected to be in the Super Bowl every year."

The 49ers appeared unstoppable and many believed the NFC Championship game was the "real" Super Bowl between the two best teams in football. Still, the AFC would have a representative in Miami, but it would not be the Buffalo Bills for the first time since 1989. The San Diego Chargers emerged as the party crashers of 1994. Despite an 11–5 record, few gave the Chargers a chance to reach pro football's ultimate stage. However, San Diego pulled off a comeback against Miami at home and went on to upset the Steelers in Pittsburgh in the AFC title game. The Chargers reached their first Super Bowl in franchise history and Wide Receiver Mark Seay and his teammates basked in their underdog status.

"It was very rewarding," said Seay. "It was something that a lot of us experienced all for the first time, but we were very confident. We knew if we could put points on the board, our defense would come through for us. I think that we surprised others more than we surprised ourselves."

Despite the Chargers' enthusiasm, it seemed as if San Francisco's biggest opponent in the week leading up to the game would be its press clippings. Most felt San Diego had no chance against the mighty 49ers. Floyd and his teammates kept their focus, but did allow themselves to find another competitor as they prepared for the Chargers.

"We didn't let any inside influences come in," said Floyd. "We were a focused football team. I don't think we had one ball dropped in practice that entire week. We were playing for perfection. We were playing to be the best 49er team that ever won a Super Bowl. We were not really playing against the Chargers, per say. We were playing against the other great 49er Super Bowl teams."

The Chargers were hardly offended by the predictions of a San Francisco blowout. Not only were Seay and his teammates used to being under-dogs, but they were also beaten soundly by the 49ers during the regular season.

"We didn't mind being the underdog," Seay said. "We were underdogs pretty much all year. That was nothing new and being a former 49er, I knew what kind of players they had over there. I knew what they were trying to do from when I was a part of their organization, which was to get to another Super Bowl and win it. That was an awesome team that they put together."

The 49ers spent the week praising the Chargers and showing San Diego plenty of respect. Privately, Oates knew he was about to get his third Super Bowl ring.

"That might be the only game I ever played in my career where I knew we were going to win," said Oates. "I just knew. There was no doubt in my mind that the outcome of the game was already determined. It was just a matter of what the final score was going to be."

While the two teams would have to play four quarters of football to determine the final score, it did not take long for San Francisco to strike first. Young hit Jerry Rice over the middle for a 44-yard touchdown and San Francisco had taken the lead just 1:24 into the game. Seay and his teammates barely had time to absorb the magnitude of the Super Bowl before falling into an early deficit.

"The Super Bowl is different," Seay said. "When Jerry caught that touchdown, that's when I knew this game was like no other game. We got routed against them in the regular season and then we see that first touchdown. That didn't help our confidence at all."

The stunned Chargers went three and out on their first possession and the 49ers quickly struck again. It took only four plays for Young to double the lead as he capped off the drive with a 51-yard pass to Running Back Ricky Watters. It was 14–0 San Francisco and only 4:55 seconds had elapsed in Super Bowl XXIX.

"They were stunned a little bit," Floyd said. "They had a huge mountain to climb. We played them in San Diego and we beat them pretty good. We had a lot of confidence going into that game. How could we let a team that we pretty much manhandled in the regular season beat us for the biggest prize in all of football?"

San Diego was able to strike back on its next possession. A drive which took seven minutes off the clock ended with a one-yard touchdown run by Natrone Means. It appeared to be a sign the Chargers had survived the quick strikes by San Francisco to start the game, but the 49ers quickly squashed any hopes of a competitive Super Bowl. The 49ers took nine plays to reach the San Diego five. Young threw a pass over the middle to Floyd at the two and the rookie lowered his head and barreled into the end zone to increase San Francisco's lead.

"We worked that play in practice about 20 times," said Floyd. "Actually, it worked out differently. You saw Ricky Watters score on that same play. He runs a flare route out to the sidelines. That same play was called. We ran a check down basically in the middle of the field. Steve read it and it worked out perfectly."

Later in the quarter, Young threw his fourth touchdown pass of the game as he found Watters from eight yards out. San Diego would add a field goal before the end of the half, but the 28–10 halftime score symbolized the San Francisco dominance over the first two quarters. The San Diego Defense and their star linebacker, Junior Seau, had been neutralized.

"It was cruise control," said Oates. "There was no pressure on the offensive lineman. They didn't have any exotic schemes. Junior was a terrific effort guy, but one guy's not going to make it happen."

The Chargers tried to find hope at halftime. San Diego had staged its share of comebacks during the season and Seay and his teammates were hoping they were saving their greatest comeback for the Super Bowl.

"We felt we could come back," Seay said. "Maybe they thought they had it in the bag. Most of our wins that year came in the second half. We had every reason to believe if we could do it against them we can come back in with some confidence."

But any faint hopes of a comeback were quickly crushed by the 49ers. The Chargers began the second half with a three and out and the 49ers' offense picked up right where it left off on its first possession. Young directed his offense on a 62-yard scoring drive with 53 of the yards coming through the air. Watters finished the drive with a nine-yard run to make the score 35–10. After stopping the Chargers on fourth down on the San Francisco 33, the 49ers struck again. Rice's second touchdown catch from 15-yards away made the score 42–10. Young had thrown his fifth touchdown pass of the game with 3:18 left in the third quarter. San Francisco was rolling and Oates was thriving under center in his third Super Bowl playing in an offense which was a different style than the power running Giants.

"It was a very different scheme," said Oates. "It was an open west coast offense with a lot of movement. Whatever they do, you counter it to their detriment. The Giants wants to play smash mouth. Basically, it was here is the play we are going to run and let's see if you can stop it."

San Diego got back in the end zone on the ensuing kickoff as Andre Coleman scored on a 98-yard return. The Chargers added the first two-point conversion in Super Bowl history and it would be Seay who would do the honors. The receiver caught a pass from Stan Humphries in the middle of the end zone to cut the deficit to 42–18.

"That was the first year it was implemented," said Seay. "I was the first one to do it. There only can be one person that can say they were the first. I take a lot of pride in that."

While Seay had his spot in the history books, Young was making his own history. The quarterback connected with Rice from seven yards out early in the fourth quarter for his record-setting sixth Super Bowl touchdown toss.

"It just worked out that we were the 49ers and we put 49 points on the board," said Floyd.

The Chargers would add one more touchdown, but San Francisco was a clear winner with a 49–26 victory. It was the fifth Super Bowl title for the franchise and Young finally had his moment at the top of the mountain. The quarterback mockingly asked his teammates to "get the monkey off his back" as he watched the end of the game from the sidelines.

"I was super-ecstatic for him," Floyd said. "A lot of other guys won their Super Bowls with Joe. I won mine with Steve. They were able to have Super Bowl wins with Joe sand Steve. With everything Steve went through, I was happy that I was a part of that."

Meanwhile, Floyd and the rest of the 49ers had plenty of time to savor the moment as the seconds ticked away. He also watched his head coach, George Seifert, savor his second Super Bowl crown.

"You're thinking about how you can get your family down when you see other families coming down," said Floyd. "You see how George responded. He was kind of wound up during the year and was able to loosen up at the end of the season. We poured a little water on him and I gave him a hug. It was fun to be a part of that and soak all that in."

As San Francisco celebrated, San Diego headed to the locker room trying to absorb their Super Bowl blowout. However, time has allowed Seay to put Super Bowl XXIX in perspective considering the caliber of the opponent on the other side of the field.

"There are teams playing right now," Seay said. "I believe that team would have beaten any team. They were that good. We got to the Super Bowl, which was a good thing, but we didn't get there at the right time."

Oates would play one more season before retiring. The decision to sign with San Francisco gave Oates the opportunity to win his third Super Bowl title and the former center is able to look back at his career and appreciate all he was able to accomplish.

"I marvel at it even to this day," Oates said. "I look back and look at this little kid that grew up in the southwest corner of Georgia and had a dream but not being a physically dominating guy. I got by and I learned to play the game and I got better as time went on. I was blessed with opportunities and to be at the right place at the right time."

Floyd would play three more years in San Francisco before finishing his career in Carolina. As a rookie, Floyd was hoping his Super Bowl title would be the first of many during his time in the NFL. Now, Floyd can appreciate how difficult it is to win a championship.

"I understood where I stood after my first year," Floyd said. "I was around some of the Bills like Bruce Smith, Cornelius Bennett, Thurman Thomas and Andre Reed. They went to the Super Bowl for four years and those guys were never able to get one and that was a great football team. Just being around guys like that put it in perspective for me how special winning that Super Bowl ring was."

It was certainly special for Steve Young, who was finally second to none.

XXX
A Soap Opera with a Happy Ending

"As the World Turns" had nothing on the 1995 Dallas Cowboys.

America's Team became America's greatest drama series. The Cowboys were an early version of reality TV, with enough plots and storylines for a drama bigger than the series named after their city. Despite the drama, the Cowboys found a way to reach the 30th edition of Super Sunday.

The Cowboys were seeking their third Super Bowl title in four years, but there was a different atmosphere around the 1995 edition of the franchise. Barry Switzer was in his second year as head coach and Switzer had spent much of the past two seasons trying to shake off comparisons of his coaching style to his predecessor, Jimmy Johnson. There were reports of a rift between Switzer and Quarterback Troy Aikman. The team went through a stretch of three losses in five games which included a blowout loss at home to San Francisco. The Cowboys also lost a game in Philadelphia in which Switzer's decision to go for a first down deep in Dallas territory late in the fourth quarter cost his team the game. Just when the masses were gathering at the gates like an angry mob, the Cowboys regained their footing and advanced to Super Bowl XXX.

Cornerback Larry Brown and his teammates were relieved to reach the Super Bowl after an eventful season in which everybody seemed to want a piece of the Cowboys.

"You're the hunted," said Brown. "You're the team everyone is trying to knock off now. You've achieved success after starting at the bottom. Now you're starting at the top where everybody knows who you are. You're the team that everybody wants to beat."

The Cowboys didn't need any extra motivation to reach Super Bowl XXX. Dallas was hoping for a third straight title in 1994, but the 49ers defeated Switzer's squad in the NFC Championship. San Francisco went on to win Super Bowl XXIX, leaving Cowboys such as Defensive Lineman Leon Lett wondering what might have been.

"We were so crushed not winning Super Bowl XXIX," said Lett. "I think there was that burning desire to go back and the expectations were we were going to go back."

"I think that bitter taste hurt everybody," Brown said. "It was probably the most painful loss that I've ever been a part of in Dallas. I think everybody wanted to show that we were still that dynasty. We had something to prove again."

An old Super Bowl rival awaited the Cowboys in Arizona. The Pittsburgh Steelers were back in the big game for the first time in 16 years. While the likes of Terry Bradshaw and Mean Joe Greene were long gone, the 1995 version of the Steelers appeared to be a formidable foe for the favored Cowboys. After falling just short of a Super Bowl berth the previous season, the Steelers broke through in 1995 with the NFL's second-ranked defense. The AFC hadn't won a Super Bowl in 12 years, but Pittsburgh appeared to be a very strong representative. However, Head Coach Bill Cowher's team had survived a mid-season slump and a close contest with Indianapolis in the AFC title game before advancing to the Super Bowl.

"We had reached a pivotal point," said Cowher. "We were 3–4 after seven games and we were able to reel off eight straight wins and get the number one seed. The game against Indianapolis came down to the final play and we find ourselves in Super Bowl XXX going against the Dallas Cowboys."

Dallas received a boost with the addition of Cornerback Deion Sanders. The flamboyant future Hall of Famer proved to be the perfect fit for the Cowboys after winning a Super Bowl the previous year in San Francisco.

"He had a totally different type of confidence," Lett said. "We were a blue collar, hard-working confidence. Deion was this new flag of confidence that was perfect. It was like starting over again."

The Cowboys were favored to extend the NFC's dominance. While the Steelers appeared to be a strong representative, Lett did not believe the Pittsburgh Offense was as dangerous as the high-powered Buffalo Bills, the team the Cowboys defeated in Super Bowl XXVII and Super Bowl XXVIII.

"We had played the Steelers the year before and we handled them pretty good," recalled Lett. "We knew they were a tough team but as far as talent, I don't think they were as talented as Buffalo on offense. Defensively, they were pretty good. We may have been a little overconfident. They were a better team I guess than we thought they were."

Most of the Cowboys knew what it was like to deal with the hype surrounding the Super Bowl. They were also prepared for the extended pregame ceremony and the emotional adjustment needed to be ready by kick-off.

"The Cowboys had been there in the years before that," Cowher said. "We came out of the locker room and we were all fired up, but you realize the pregame is about five to seven minutes longer than normal. By the time the game started, we were kind of deflated. The experience factor showed up early in that game."

The Cowboys took the opening kickoff to the Pittsburgh 26, but the Steelers snuffed out a reverse on third down and Chris Boniol came on to kick a 42-yard field goal to give Dallas a 3–0 lead. After forcing a three-and-out on Pittsburgh's first possession, Dallas got a boost on offense from one of their top defensive players. Sanders had the chance during the season to double as a receiver and a 47-yard reception by "Prime Time" put Dallas deep in Pittsburgh territory. Four plays later, Aikman hit Jay Novacek from three yards out, and the Cowboys had a 10–0 lead. The Steelers showed life on the ensuing drive as they moved the ball to the Dallas 36, but a high snap by Center Dermontti Dawson resulted in a 13-yard loss. Pittsburgh was forced to punt and it appeared the Cowboys were on the verge of burying the Steelers early.

"I think Dermontti didn't realize he was in the shotgun," said Cowher. "He thought he was still under center. You get into that game for the first time and it was the first time for pretty much everybody on that football team and I think it showed early."

The Cowboys appeared to land the early knockout blow on their next possession, but a 24-yard touchdown catch by Michael Irvin was nullified when the receiver was called for pass interference. Another Boniol field goal made the score 13–0, but Pittsburgh finally found its footing late in the first half. After converting on a fourth and one in Dallas territory, Quarterback Neil O'Donnell moved the Steelers to the Dallas six. O'Donnell hit Yancy Thigpen for a six-yard scoring strike before halftime and Pittsburgh was back in the game.

"I think there was no sense of panic," recalled Cowher. "I think we were a football team that year that had proven we had come back from a lot of deficits. We felt really good about the ability of our offense to score and to settle down on defense and not give up any big plays. I think we felt very good going into halftime particularly after getting that score."

Meanwhile, the Cowboys suddenly realized they would have their hands full against the scrappy underdogs from Pittsburgh. For Lett and his teammates, it was time to hit the reset button despite holding a six-point lead at halftime.

"We always went into the locker room like it was 0–0," said Lett. "We approached it that way every game. It was the mindset of the team and the mindset Coach Johnson first instilled in us. We knew we had it. They were tougher than we thought they were."

The Steelers appeared poised to take the lead early in the third quarter. Pittsburgh moved the ball to its own 48, but O'Donnell's pass fluttered into the hands of Brown. The Dallas defender returned the ball to the Pittsburgh 23 and Smith crashed in from the one two plays after the turnover to put Dallas up, 20–7. It appeared O'Donnell threw the pass right to Brown, but the cornerback credited the pass rush from his teammate for the errant throw.

"Charles Haley had a great pass rush," recalled Brown. "Charles hit his arm just as he was throwing the ball and it changed the path of that football. It looked like it sailed on him, but it was actually a great play by Charles Haley. It came right to me and the key was to catch it. Don't drop this ball."

It was a frustrating turn of events for the Steelers. Cowher believes the play could have resulted in a Pittsburgh touchdown to Ernie Mills on a crossing route if the pass was accurate.

"He might have walked in for a touchdown," Cowher said. "But he threw it over his head. He may have confused it with another route that was a little deeper. That was a tough one because we were driving again. It was a situation where we really had a chance to put some points on the board."

Things seem to go from bad to worse for the Steelers on the ensuing drive when they failed to convert on a fourth down near midfield. Pittsburgh's defense kept the Steelers in the game by forcing a punt and O'Donnell followed with a drive into Dallas territory.

"I just thought we settled in defensively," said Cowher. "We gave ourselves a chance and really that's all you can do. That's why I went for it on fourth down. I felt really good about our defense getting the ball back."

A sack on third down forced Pittsburgh to settle for a field goal. Norm Johnson's kick from 46 yards out brought the Steelers to within ten with 11:20 remaining.

Cowher decided it was time to gamble.

As the Cowboys sent in their return team, Cowher elected to try an onside kick. Deon Figures recovered the bouncing ball and Pittsburgh took over on their own 47-yard line.

"We had actually thought about an onside kick on the opening kickoff of the game," Cowher said. "It was something we had seen in our preparation. We thought it was going to be there. I just wanted to make sure looking at the two previous kickoffs we had that everything seemed in place."

The momentum had swung to the Steelers and after being in control throughout much of the game, Lett and the Cowboys were suddenly seeing their third Super Bowl title slip away.

"That was a high blood pressure moment," said Lett. "It was warm. We had to go right back out and there was a lot of stress on the defense. I could see the stress on a lot of the guys' eyes in the huddle."

Lett could also see the fiery Cowher on the other sidelines fueling his team with emotion after the kick. Also on display were the famed "Terrible Towels" being waved by the large contingency of Pittsburgh fans in the stands at Sun Devil Stadium.

"We never really looked at the other team," Lett said. "But I could see Bill Cowher going down the sideline getting them pumped up. I definitely remembered that and all of the Terrible Towels in the stadium. It felt like there were a lot more Pittsburgh Steeler fans in that stadium than Dallas Cowboy fans."

The Steelers quickly capitalized on their momentum. O'Donnell brought his team to the edge of the Dallas goal line and Bam Morris walked in along the right side. With 6:36 remaining, Super Bowl XXX was a three-point game.

"It was a very weird game," said Brown. "We felt early on we had control of that game. They had that onside kick which was a great call and all the momentum changed. It re-energized their offense. Now, we're in a dog-fight."

Dallas moved the ball on its next possession, but a six-yard sack by Levon Kirkland forced the Cowboys to punt. Pittsburgh was back on the move again with time winding down in regulation, but Brown would seal both the MVP award and another Super Bowl title for Dallas with his second interception of the game. Once again, it appeared O'Donnell's pass went right to Brown, but the defensive back believes he was simply in the right place at the right time.

"It was an all-out blitz," said Brown. "He went to a blitz check and I jumped the route and cut the receiver off. I played the route on that play. I could tell be the way O'Donnell's shoulder was facing that he was going to throw the slant route. I actually cut the receiver off and beat him to the spot."

"It was a blitz," recalled Cowher. "Honestly, I think Andre Hastings should have broken out. I think it was just a misread by both of those guys. That was the tough one. I think it was just a misinterpretation on Andre Hastings part. Neil thought he was going to go out and he threw it right to Larry."

Brown took the ball back to the Pittsburgh six. The finishing blow came from Smith, who scored for the second time in the game from four yards out. Dallas' 27–17 victory gave the franchise its third title in four years and its first under Switzer. A year of turmoil had turned into a season of satisfaction. For one year, Jones was vindicated for letting Jimmy Johnson walk away as the Lombardi Trophy returned to Dallas.

"It was drastically different," Brown said. "When Coach Johnson got to the Cowboys, his whole thing was to rebuild the entire program. He accomplished that. "By the time Barry got there, that mission had been accomplished. Everything was in place and it was about keeping it going. They had two very different jobs and they both did a great job."

Brown's two interceptions earned him the game's Most Valuable Player award. Lett wasn't surprised to see Brown have the biggest game of his career after a week of intense film study.

"I remember watching film with Larry Brown," said Lett. "Larry Brown was one of those guys that I didn't get to watch film with, but for Super Bowl XXX we were watching film late before the game. Early that morning, he was watching film and I was thinking 'Larry's really locked in.' It was great to see him make those plays."

As the celebration began, Jones and Switzer had the chance to hoist the Lombardi Trophy. For Brown, his play in Super Bowl XXX would be relived forever, but the cornerback wasn't worried about an individual award as his team celebrated yet another Super Bowl crown.

"I appreciated it more as I got older," said Brown. "We didn't have a team that worried about personal accolades. I don't think there's a player on that team that talked about an award they won. It was always about the team. Now that I'm older I'm a lot more grateful and appreciative, but I'm happier that our team won. We were able to put that third ring on as a team."

Cowher would have to wait ten more years before getting another opportunity for his ring. His Steelers received high praise for taking the heavily-favored Cowboys down to the wire, but the sting of defeat would linger for the head coach.

"It hurts a lot to get that far and to be that close," Cowher said. "It was just a special team. It was disappointing to have a journey that came so far to end in that kind of manner."

As the Steelers dealt with the franchise's first Super Bowl loss, the Cowboys had marked their place in history as the team of the 90's. It is difficult to compare Super Bowl dynasties from different eras, but Lett is aware he and his teammates have taken their place as one of the greatest teams of all time.

"We had a great team," said Lett. "We had great chemistry. We won some close games and we won games without all of our starters. That's what great teams are all about. We did it consistently and we did it together."

XXXI
THE LOMBARDI COMES HOME

For the Green Bay Packers, a trip to Super Bowl XXXI was the end of a long climb out of the abyss.

The proud franchise had built a dynasty in the 1960's and Vince Lombardi's Packers had captured the first two Super Bowl titles. Many consider Lombardi to be the greatest coach of all time and the Super Bowl Trophy bears the name of the former Green Bay coach.

But there would be no Lombardi Trophies in Green Bay throughout the 1970's and 1980's.

The franchise fell on hard times after Lombardi's departure. For the next 24 years, the Packers recorded only five winning seasons and won just one playoff game. Green Bay's fortunes finally changed in 1992 when Mike Holmgren took over as head coach. In the same year, General Manager Ron Wolf acquired Quarterback Brett Favre in a trade with Atlanta. The Packers became contenders and reached the NFC Championship game in 1995 before falling to Dallas. In the 1996 season, Green Bay reached the Super Bowl for the first time in 29 years. While some of the Packers had been through the growing seasons, Andre Rison joined the team early in the 1996 campaign. The talented wide receiver had been cut by the Jacksonville Jaguars and was eager to get another chance with one of football's most storied franchises.

"It was a great feeling to be part of something that will never be forgotten," said Rison. "There's the historic tradition the Green Bay Packers carried from Vince Lombardi and Bart Starr and Brett Favre and all of the great players that came through there. Just to be part of that family and that affiliation is overwhelming."

Standing in the way of the Packers were the New England Patriots, who were making their second trip to the Super Bowl. This was a far different cast than the team which was slaughtered by the Bears in Super Bowl XX. After winning two Super Bowls with the Giants, Head Coach Bill Parcells had turned the fortunes of the franchise around. The Patriots made a surprising run to Super Bowl XXXI, but Quarterback Drew Bledsoe and his teammates were heavy underdogs as they headed to New Orleans. However, Bledsoe had emerged as one of the NFL's top quarterbacks with a host of weapons to work with in 1996.

"I think expectations were low outside of the building," said Bledsoe. "For me, the addition of Terry Glenn was a really big step for us. Having Shawn Jefferson and Terry Glenn outside where we had some speed and could really stretch a defense really makes a difference on how you can approach offensive football. It freed up a lot for Curtis Martin."

Martin was emerging as one of the game's top running backs in his second season. He rushed for 1,152 yards and 14 touchdowns in 1996 and helped balance the New England attack. The Patriots appeared to have plenty of firepower to go against the league's top defense, so there was potential for Super Bowl XXXI to be closer than many were predicting.

But the Patriots were forced to deal with a major distraction involving their head coach.

A report surfaced stating that Parcells intended to leave New England after the Super Bowl to become the head coach of the New York Jets. The Patriots tried to focus on the Packers, but Bledsoe and his teammates were forced to deal with questions about the future of Parcells.

"It was a little bit disappointing," Bledsoe said. "To get to that game and to have the season that we had and to have so many people focused on Bill and whether he was staying or going was disappointing. I don't know if it necessarily was a distraction, but it was kind of disappointing to have that be the story rather than kind of this Cinderella season that we had to get into the game."

It was a far different atmosphere with the Packers, who welcomed the intense Super Bowl spotlight. Green Bay's roster was a unique combination filled with several veterans making their first appearance on Super Sunday. Rison says it proved to be a perfect mix.

"We had so many different characters on our team and different personalities," Rison said. "We had big personalities. We all respected each other and we had a great locker room atmosphere and a great atmosphere off the field. The comradery was superb."

Rison was also thrilled to be playing with Favre, a star quarterback in the prime of his career. For the second straight season, Favre was the NFL's Most Valuable Player after throwing for 3,899 yards and 39 touchdown passes. However, Green Bay also put together the top-ranked defense in the NFL with the help of veteran Reggie White. The defensive lineman had spent most of his career in Philadelphia, but left for Green Bay in 1993 with the hopes of capturing his first ever Super Bowl title. The combination of the offense, defense and special teams bolstered by return man Desmond Howard made the Packers a complete team, but Bledsoe's focus was on White and his defensive teammates.

"We knew that we had our hands full," said Bledsoe. "The thing that gets overlooked sometimes with Desmond Howard and Brett Favre being great players is that their defense was number one in the NFL that year. It was really an exceptional defense that we were playing against and we knew that it was going to be a great challenge."

The Packers appeared to be up for the challenge at the start of Super Bowl XXXI. New England picked up only one first down on the game's opening drive and was forced to punt. Green Bay struck quickly on its first possession with the help of Howard, who returned the ball 32 yards to the Packers 46 yard-line. On the drive's second play, Favre called an audible at the line of scrimmage. Rison ran past Cornerback Otis Smith and was wide open down the field. Favre's deep pass was caught by Rison near the New England 20 and the speedy receiver had a clear path to the end zone.

"We were playing with the MVP," said Rison. "That's like being on the court with Michael Jordan. We're on the field with Brett Favre. We knew we had a quarterback like that, so we never panicked when an audible was called."

It was the perfect call by Favre and Rison knew he would be wide open when the ball arrived.

"It's coming to me," said Rison. "All I could say to myself was 'Lord, please don't let it hit my helmet.'"

The next big play came from the Green Bay Defense. On the ensuing possession, Bledsoe fired to the left side, but Cornerback Doug Evans made a juggling interception and the Packers took over on the New England 28. Green Bay had to settle for a 37-yard field goal by Chris Jacke, but the lead was 10–0 with 8:42 remaining in the first quarter.

Bledsoe and his teammates kept their cool. On the next drive, the New England Offense got rolling.

"We did stay within our game plan," recalled Bledsoe. "We hit a long screen to Keith Byars and did some play action stuff. We stayed with the game plan and ultimately took the lead for a minute."

The screen to Byars went for 32 yards and the catch and run by the fullback sparked the offense. A pass interference penalty put the Patriots on the one and Bledsoe fired a touchdown pass to Byars to put New England on the board. The Patriots Defense quickly forced a Packer punt on the next possession and New England began the next drive at its own 43. On the third play of the drive, Bledsoe connected with Glenn for a 44-yard completion to the Green Bay four.

"We knew they had talent," Rison said. "We knew they were a great team. They had the Tom Brady of that era in Drew Bledsoe. We knew at any given time, those guys could strike. They had Terry Glenn. He was like my little brother away from the game. I always wanted him to succeed."

Bledsoe followed with his second touchdown pass, this time to Tight End Ben Coates. After falling behind by ten points in the first eight minutes, New England had seized the lead.

"It felt like we were right back in it," said Bledsoe. "I know we were heavy underdogs coming into the game, but we felt like we could move the ball and score some points against them."

Rison and his offensive teammates went back to work and the receiver wasn't surprised to see Bledsoe spark the Patriots after the fast start by Green Bay.

"Those guys got rolling," said Rison. "We had to find our way. Our defense really had played them great up until that point. The momentum changed just that fast. We regrouped as a team. We knew it would be a long game, but we were so confident."

That confidence was never more evident after one of the biggest plays of the game. In the opening minute of the second quarter, Favre fired a pass down the right sideline to Antonio Freeman. The receiver caught the ball in stride and raced 81 yards for a touchdown to put Green Bay back on top. There were still nearly three quarters of football to play but as Rison danced with Freeman in the end zone, the receiver believed his first Super Bowl ring was well within reach.

"We knew the game was over," Rison said. "We had taken their best shot. We knew the game was over. We just had to finish."

The game was far from over in the minds of the Patriots, but New England's deficit would grow before the end of the half. Jacke would add another field goal to increase the Green Bay lead to six. New England looked for a quick strike on the ensuing drive, but Bledsoe's deep pass was intercepted by Mike Prior. The Packers followed with a 74-yard drive which took nearly six minutes off the clock. Running Back Dorsey Levens did his part on the ground by picking up 31 yards on the drive. Favre finished the drive with a two-yard touchdown run and Green Bay went to the locker room at halftime with a seemingly comfortable 27–14 lead.

"We scored points in the critical moments," Rison said. "We scored points right before the half. The middle of the field was open and Dorsey started to get going. We didn't even play our best game."

The Packers had their way with the New England Defense in the first half. Bledsoe and the offense had moved the football against the powerful Green Bay Defense and the quarterback knew the offense had to stick with the game plan in the second half.

"They were a fast and athletic defense," recalled Bledsoe. "They were big and strong. We knew that going straight at them was going to be a problem. We had to give them some misdirection and play action and screens and make them run a little bit."

The Green Bay Offense would get the football to start the second half. Favre moved the Packers to the New England 37, but the Patriots stopped Levens on third and fourth down. After an exchange of punts, Bledsoe and the offense embarked on a 53-yard scoring drive. It took just seven plays for New England to reach the end zone and Martin's 18-yard run cut the Green Bay lead to 27–21. The Patriots had seized the momentum.

Desmond Howard would take it away with one of the most memorable plays in Super Bowl history.

On the ensuing kickoff, Howard fielded the ball at the one. The former Heisman Trophy winner burst up the middle of the field and was free after breaking a tackle at his own 30. Howard raced into the end zone for a 99-yard touchdown return. The Packers would add a two-point conversion to make the score 35–21. There was still 3:10 remaining in the third quarter, but Howard's touchdown changed the entire complexion of Super Bowl XXXI.

"You feel like we're back into it," Bledsoe said. "Then the next play they score again and that's deflating. When you play in the NFL where everyone is so evenly matched, if you can gain a significant advantage in the return game, it makes a huge difference. That was certainly the case in that game."

"They decided to kick to him," said Rison. "They got burned."

With 3:10 remaining in the third quarter, the Patriots were forced to make changes on offense. Down by two scores with just over a quarter to play, there would be less misdirection and play action. Bledsoe was forced to drop back on nearly every play and White was able to take advantage. The future Hall of Famer helped close out the game for the Packers. On New England's first possession after the Howard touchdown, White picked up a pair of sacks on Bledsoe.

"The biggest problem that team presented was with the one-on-one matchups," Bledsoe said. "When you've got arguably the most talented pass rusher coming off one edge, you really have to focus on that side. You're not going to block him one-on-one."

Rison and the rest of the offensive players were happy to see White rise to the occasion. The man known as "The Minister of Defense" was one of the most respected players in pro football and many around the NFL were hoping White would leave New Orleans with his first Super Bowl ring.

"It felt so good to see him rejoice," Rison said. "He definitely had Packer fans in his corner and Philadelphia fans in his corner. You saw him complete it. Reggie helped me pick the Green Bay Packers when I was available. "I felt comfortable with him in the locker room as a big brother and a teammate."

The Green Bay Defense dominated the final quarter as the Patriots were shut down on the offensive end. White picked up his third sack and Bledsoe was intercepted two more times as he desperately tried to rally his team from a two-touchdown deficit.

"Any defense has a significant advantage if they can make you one dimensional," said Bledsoe. "If they can get you into a situation where they know you have to throw and they can tee off and rush the passer, it's difficult against any defense. When you had the kind of talent the Packers had, it's blood in the water and the sharks are coming."

The Packers ran out the clock and celebrated their 35–21 victory. As time wound down, one of the Green Bay receivers came up to Favre and asked for the football. It was Don Beebe, a man who had been a part of four straight Super Bowl losses with the Buffalo Bills. The quarterback was happy to hand Beebe the ball.

Favre threw for 246 yards and Howard was named the game's Most Valuable Player. The Vince Lombardi Trophy was heading home to Green Bay, while the Patriots were simply heading home. Parcells was heading to North Jersey shortly after as he agreed to become the head coach of the Jets. Bledsoe would continue to put together an impressive career, but would be forced to watch from the sidelines as Tom Brady guided the Patriots to victory in Super Bowl XXXVI. He would never get another chance to play in a Super Bowl and Bledsoe claims he does not spend his time in retirement watching any rebroadcast of Super Bowl XXXI.

"You're fortunate enough to make it to that game," said Bledsoe. "If you don't win in terms of the emotions, it's harder than never making it at all. When you get that close to the ultimate goal and you don't achieve it, it really is a pretty bittersweet thing. That's quite simply why I haven't gone back and looked at it for a long time."

Meanwhile, the Lombardi Trophy returned to Wisconsin for the first time since the man the trophy was named after guided the Packers to Super Bowl glory. It is fair to say a Super Bowl championship in any city is special. It is also easy to understand the significance of what a Super Bowl title means to Green Bay.

"You get that as soon as you get around the fans," Rison said. "Once you play for the Packers, you understand that there's the NFL and then there's the Packers."

XXXII
THE BRONCOS BREAK THROUGH

For over a decade, the Super Bowl was not kind to the American Football Conference.

As the football world prepared for Super Bowl XXXII, the National Football Conference was once again a heavy favorite. The NFC Champion had captured the last 13 Super Bowls with the Raiders enjoying the last AFC victory in Super Bowl XVIII. The Green Bay Packers were expected to extend the streak in the 1997 season. The defending world champions appeared to be even stronger than the team which came away victorious in Super Bowl XXXI. Quarterback Brett Favre collected his third straight league MVP Award and Green Bay matched its 13–3 record from the previous season.

Nearly all of the Packers were looking for their second Super Bowl ring. Seth Joyner was looking for his first. The veteran linebacker had spent most of his career in Philadelphia with Buddy Ryan's "Gang Green" defense. Those Eagles never reached a Super Bowl. Packers General Manager Ron Wolf brought Joyner in during the off-season and the linebacker quickly settled in under Head Coach Mike Holmgren and Defensive Coordinator Fritz Shurmur.

"It was special," said Joyner. "The ultimate goal is always to get to the Super Bowl. While I was not able to get it done with my brothers in Philadelphia, for Mike Holmgren and Ron Wolf and Fritz Shurmur to give me an opportunity to get to a Super Bowl in Green Bay was pretty special."

Representing the AFC would be the Denver Broncos, who would be making their fifth Super Bowl appearance. The Broncos had been beaten in their first four attempts, with three coming during the NFC's winning streak over the AFC. The Broncos were blown out in all of their Super Bowl defeats, but this would be Denver's first Super Bowl appearance in eight years. The 1996 Broncos were expected to reach the Super Bowl after a 13–3 season, but Denver suffered a stunning playoff upset as they were beaten by a 9–7 Jacksonville squad. John Mobley was a rookie when the Broncos walked off the field in defeat and said the loss to the Jaguars stuck with Denver throughout the 1997 season.

"That Jacksonville loss was quite a deflating loss," said Mobley. "For us, it gave us axe to grind. We knew we had to come back with a different mindset and I think it made everybody a lot hungrier. That off-season, there was no other team that worked harder than we did. We knew we had lost an opportunity and we knew what it took to get there."

The Broncos avenged their loss to Jacksonville by blowing out the Jaguars in the opening round of the playoffs. Denver then won road games in Kansas City and Pittsburgh and headed to San Diego for Super Bowl XXXII. Despite sending one of their best teams ever to the Super Bowl, few gave the Broncos much of a chance against the mighty Packers from the NFC. Mobley and his teammates weren't complaining.

"It was the greatest thing ever," Mobley said. "Nobody gave us a chance. That whole week leading up to the game was all about the Green Bay Packers and what they did last year coming into the Super Bowl. We were an afterthought. Everybody counted us out."

The Packers were far from overconfident as they prepared for the

Broncos. For Joyner, the glare of the Super Bowl spotlight was overshadowed by his preparation for the game.

"It was a little overwhelming in the beginning," recalled Joyner. "Once you get past the first practice and you get past the first media day, it really turns into a normal work week because your schedule is pretty much the same."

Much of the media attention surrounded John Elway. The Denver Quarterback had been to three Super Bowls since his much-hyped arrival in the NFL, but all three ended in disaster. Elway had been the main weapon of the Denver offense in his early days, but the emergence of Running Back Terrell Davis gave the Broncos a much more balanced attack. Davis rushed for 1,750 yards and 15 touchdowns in 1997. Joyner knew the key to victory for the Green Bay Defense would be stopping one of the game's top rushers.

"The guy was tearing the league up rushing the ball," Joyner said. "We looked at the game and we felt like we were a bigger defensive unit and we fared extremely well against the run throughout the year. We felt like we could make the game one-dimensional if we could take T.D. out of the equation."

Joyner would be lining up behind his former Philadelphia teammate. Defensive Lineman Reggie White joined the Packers the previous season and earned his first Super Bowl ring. Joyner was thrilled to be reunited with one of the league's most respected players when he came to Green Bay.

"It was always great to play with Reggie," Joyner said. "People don't realize I played in the NFL for 13 years and for eight of those years I played right next to Reggie. That in itself was pretty special. To play right next to a guy who was such a great football player really enhanced my job."

There appeared to be a bad omen for Denver even before the game got underway. Former Washington Quarterback Doug Williams and former Redskins Coach Joe Gibbs participated in the coin toss. Williams had torn apart the Broncos in Super Bowl XXII as Washington rolled to a 42–10 victory.

There was more trouble for Denver on the field at the start of the game. The Packers took the ball into the end zone on the game's opening possession. Favre put together a 76-yard scoring drive and capped it off with a 22-yard pass to Antonio Freeman.

But if Broncos fans were suddenly having nightmares from past Super Bowls, the response by Denver soothed the nerves of many across the Rocky Mountains. Denver struck back on its first possession with the help of a 32-yard kickoff return by Vaughn Hebron. An Elway interception was wiped out by a holding penalty on the drive and Davis followed with a 27-yard run. Four plays later, Davis plowed in from the one and Super Bowl XXXII was tied at 7–7. There was still 5:39 remaining in the first quarter, but the touchdown served notice that this Super Bowl would not be a runaway for the NFC.

"That was huge," recalled Mobley. "When we responded that way offensively, I think the defense got a little nudge of momentum going back out on that field. We knew we could exploit them offensively."

The Packers moved near midfield on their next possession, but an interception by Tyrone Braxton gave Denver the ball on the Green Bay 45. Elway went back to his ground game as Davis pounded out 29 of the next 45 yards. The last yard came from Elway on the first play of the second quarter as he rolled right and easily crossed the goal line. Denver had its first lead and the strong blocking for Davis by the Denver offensive line was taking its toll on the Packers' defensive front.

"We knew they had big guys up front that got winded easily," said Mobley. "We wanted to make sure we kept an up tempo running game attack at them."

"You look at them as a smaller team trying to out-quick you," said Joyner. "You really don't grasp the speed with which they played. They did a lot of blocking where they were cutting players. It was before they eliminated the chop blocks, so you'd engage with one guy and another guy would come from another side."

Elway had walked into the end zone on his touchdown run thanks to a fake to Davis, but the Denver running back had another reason for not taking the handoff. Davis began suffering from a migraine headache and was forced to leave the game late in the second quarter.

"He'd had this migraine condition for a while," Mobley said. "We'd see him at practice from time to time sitting on the sidelines under the umbrella just putting water on his head. Once it happened, I thought we'd lost him for the biggest game of the season."

Davis would return in the second half after taking migraine medication, but both teams would score again before the first half ended. A sack by Safety Steve Atwater forced a Favre fumble and Neil Smith recovered for Denver. Jason Elam's 51-yard field goal increased Denver's lead to 17–7, but Green Bay would strike back in the final seconds of the first half. Favre took over on his own five-yard line with 7:38 on the clock. The Green Bay signal caller took his team on a 95-yard drive. It ended with 12 seconds remaining in the half as Favre threw a six-yard touchdown pass to Mark Chmura. The Broncos led, 17–14, but the Packers had momentum as they headed into the locker room.

"We tried to get our legs back under us," Joyner said. "We hadn't experienced giving up that type of yardage and giving up those types of points really at any point of that season. When you're used to playing a certain way you kind of get shocked by that."

The Broncos got a boost to start the second half with the return of Davis, but the running back fumbled on Denver's first play from scrimmage. The Broncos held Green Bay to a field goal, but Ryan Longwell's 27-yard kick tied the game at 17–17. The two teams traded punts as the period progressed, with one Denver drive starting on its own eight-yard line. Elway led his team on a 13-play, 92 yard drive and the 11th play of the scoring march would be one of the greatest in Elway's storied career. The quarterback rolled right and leaped into the air head first. He was met by three Packer tacklers who sent Elway spinning in mid-air. The future Hall of Famer landed on the Green Bay four and the inspiring run triggered an emotional boost throughout the Denver sideline.

"It sent goosebumps throughout my body," recalled Mobley. "It had the same effect on everybody. We were sitting down on the bench. All of a sudden, we see John scrambling. When he dove and got spun around and then got up, everybody was like 'Let's go. We've got this.' That was nothing but pure grit and determination."

Joyner was trailing on the play and took responsibility for allowing Elway to get free for his "helicopter" run.

"I was pretty pissed off at myself," Joyner said. "I was actually supposed to be spying him on that play and I kind of got caught up in the wash on the wrong side of the ball and he got away. I remember that play vividly. He kind of stepped like he was going to go to my right. When I stepped to go that way, I got too far up in the line and got caught up in the rush. He broke out to his right and got away from me."

Davis scored again two plays later and the Broncos had a 24–17 lead in the final minute of the third quarter. Denver had a chance to increase its lead when Freeman fumbled the ensuing kickoff, but Elway was intercepted in the end zone by Eugene Robinson. The Packers had the momentum back to start the final period.

Green Bay put together another impressive drive and Freeman redeemed himself with three catches on the four-play drive. The last grab was a 13-yard touchdown reception and the Packers had pulled even with 13:32 remaining.

"We hadn't been ahead since the first seven points of the game," said Joyner. "Once we pulled even, we kind of got things under control in a positive direction. Let's run the football and control the clock and control the game and get the lead and play great defense from there."

"There was never a point during that game where we felt we were going to lose," Mobley said. "I don't know what it was. There was some kind of strange aura that was in the air that we were going to win this game. Everybody knew it and everybody believed it. It did get touch and go for a while, but nobody ever panicked."

The two defenses tightened up and both sides were forced into a pair of punts. Denver got the ball back with 3:27 remaining on the Green Bay 49. The Broncos reached the 18-yard line where Davis got the call once again. The running back ran to his left and reached the one with 1:47 remaining. With a touchdown seemingly inevitable and time on the side of the Broncos, Holmgren instructed his defense to let Denver score so his offense would still have time to get a tying touchdown. Davis went through a hole the size of the Grand Canyon and the Broncos had a 31–24 lead.

"We understood why," Joyner said. "If you don't let them score, they're going to run the clock out and kick a field goal. The game is over and it's a wrap. We basically allowed them to score with the hope that the offense could take the ball and tie it up."

While the last run on the drive was a gift from the Green Bay Defense, the Denver Offense had worn down the Packers' massive front. The man in the middle was Tackle Gilbert Brown, who was listed at 340-pounds. Some believed it was a generous estimate for the large lineman.

"Big Gilbert Brown had enough," Mobley said. "By the third and fourth quarter, he was over there with an oxygen mask."

The NFC's Super Bowl winning streak was on the verge of ending, but the reigning MVP still had one more chance. Favre and the Green Bay offense started on their own 30-yard line with 1:39 left. Mobley and his defensive teammates would have to make one more stand.

Favre completed four straight passes to Dorsey Levens as Green Bay moved to the Denver 32. Favre's next pass fell incomplete. On third down, Favre's pass fell incomplete again, but an accidental collision between two teammates forced Atwater and Randy Hilliard out of the game.

"That was probably the tensest situation of the game," said Mobley. "We knew what Brett Favre and that offense was capable of. For us to lose two of our key players on defense in one fell swoop did create a sense of tension."

It was now fourth and six with 32 seconds left. Favre dropped back and looked for Chmura over the middle.

"It was a man to man," Mobley said. "It was a bomb blitz so we were bringing the house. That means I've got the tight end man to man. We'd practiced this play, but we never ran it with the bomb blitz on. I knew he was going to run an option route."

Mobley's reached Chmura before the pass arrived. The linebacker stepped in front of the tight end and batted the ball to the ground. The Super Bowl misery for both the Broncos and the AFC had come to an end in dramatic fashion.

"I kind of baited Brett," said Mobley. "I anticipated him breaking inside, so I jumped out and hurried to get myself back inside because the ball was going to be there as soon as he turned around. Luckily, I got back into position just in time to undercut it and get in front of him. That was it. That was history there."

The Denver sideline erupted with all eyes on Elway. The quarterback had put his Super Bowl ghosts to rest. Meanwhile, Mobley was in partial disbelief as he celebrated his title-clinching play.

"It started to hit me slowly," Mobley said. "It hit me that we just won the Super Bowl and I had just knocked down the last pass of the game to help the team win. As I'm jogging, it just finally hits me."

Elway came out to take a knee for the final play then leaped into the air with the football in his hand. After four Super Bowl blowouts and the shock of the Jacksonville loss from the previous season, the Denver Broncos had their first world championship.

"It was huge," said Mobley. "This is what guys play their whole lives for. They get to the pinnacle of making it to the NFL, but everybody wants to play in that game. The ultimate goal is to win a Super Bowl. There are so many great players that have come into this league that haven't had an opportunity to not just win one, but to play in one."

The Packers has lost a Super Bowl for the first time in franchise history as there would be no repeat for Favre and his teammates. Most had a chance to savor a Super Bowl victory the year before, but Joyner walked off the field in defeat in his first opportunity to win a championship.

"It was crushing for me," said Joyner. "Most of the guys had won it the year before. They understood the experience and felt the thrill of winning a Super Bowl. For me, to wait 12 years to get to that point and then lose it was unimaginable to say the least."

As the Broncos gathered onto the podium to accept their championship, Owner Pat Bowlen declared "This one's for John!" and handed the Lombardi Trophy to his quarterback. Elway thrust the trophy into the air in celebration. A career filled with memorable moments finally had a Super Bowl title to put at the top. For Elway and the Broncos, the wait was finally over.

"This is something they're going to cherish the rest of their lives," Mobley said. "It is amazing how with that one game, you create a lifetime of friends and fraternity amongst these people with that one memory."

XXXIII
Going Out on Top

For John Elway and the Denver Broncos, it was time for an encore. Denver had ended the long AFC drought as well as its own Super Bowl frustrations with a win over Green Bay in Super Bowl XXXII. In the 1998 season, the Broncos had the look of a team which was more than capable of a repeat. Denver stormed out to a 13–0 start and finished with a 14–2 record in the regular season. The Broncos rolled past Miami before downing the Jets in the AFC Championship. Denver was off to Miami for its second straight Super Bowl appearance and sixth in team history.

For Elway and most of his teammates, it was a chance for a second straight title, but one member of the 1998 Broncos has been denied of a ring by his current teammates. Seth Joyner was part of the Packers' squad which lost to Denver the previous year. Joyner was ready for another season in Green Bay, but the Packers traded the veteran linebacker to the Broncos at the end of training camp.

"That whole year was kind of weird," recalled Joyner. "I got traded to the Broncos the week before the first regular season game. To wind up playing on the team that just beat you in the Super Bowl was kind of weird within itself. That's the business of football."

Many believed the Broncos were on a collision course with Minnesota for the Super Bowl, but the high-scoring Vikings never made it to Miami despite a 15–1 regular season. Minnesota was upset by Atlanta in the NFC Championship game as the Falcons advanced to Super Bowl XXXIII. Despite duplicating Denver's 14–2 regular season record, the Falcons spent much of the season flying under the radar. It took the upset over the Vikings to make the rest of America take notice of the team known as the "Dirty Birds." Wide Receiver Terance Mathis and his teammates had plenty of confidence throughout the season after rolling past some of the NFL's top teams.

"We finished the season with a nine-game winning streak," said Mathis. "We beat the 49ers twice. We beat the Patriots and a good Chicago Bears team. We beat Peyton Manning and the Colts and a good Dolphins team. We were pretty good, but no one was giving us any credit."

The Falcons didn't mind being under the radar throughout much of the season. Mathis said the snub provided motivation and helped Atlanta reach its first ever Super Bowl.

"What happened during this period was that we found solace within each other," Mathis said. "You hear that old cliché where it's that 'us against the world' thing. That's how we took it. It was just us in that locker room and on that field and in that facility. We didn't care what anybody thought or what anybody said about us."

Even many of the Broncos were surprised to see the Falcons instead of the Vikings reach the Super Bowl, but Linebacker John Mobley and his teammates had a healthy respect for the NFC Champions as they headed to Miami.

"It was supposed to be the Minnesota Vikings," said Mobley. "When the Falcons upset them and got there, it's easy for a lot of teams to have a letdown and say that it's not the team we felt we had to gear up for. The coaches made sure we weren't going to fall for the banana in the tailpipe. They made sure we weren't going to have a lapse."

The Broncos were also dealing with a whole new world in Miami. When Denver reached the Super Bowl the previous season, they were a heavy underdog against Green Bay. This time, the Broncos were a clear favorite to bring home their second straight Lombardi Trophy. Mobley and his teammates chose to ignore the lofty predictions from the outside world.

"There wasn't a lot of TV watching," recalled Mobley. "He made sure we did things together as a team during the week that kept everybody away from the media. Whatever kind of speculation there was on TV, we were pretty much unaware of it unless we went upstairs and put on the TV."

Mathis and his teammates took a different approach as they prepared for their first Super Bowl. Atlanta was all business when it came time to prepare for the Broncos, but Mathis was also able to enjoy his week in Miami with his family.

"It was a blast," recalled Mathis. "I invited all of my family and my daughter was two weeks old at the time. I was in a whirlwind. We had just beaten the Vikings. Two weeks later, we were in the Super Bowl."

It was an extra special week for Mathis and his family after a difficult period during the bye week leading up to the Super Bowl.

"My mom had surgery for breast cancer," Mathis said. "The Super Bowl was secondary in that week for me. I was going to enjoy every minute of it. My wife and mom were there and my sisters were there. My grandparents and my other family members were there. It was a wonderful week."

It was also a week of speculation surrounding Elway. Many believed the future Hall of Fame quarterback would be playing his last game when he took the field for Super Bowl XXXIII. Mobley insists the rest of the Broncos knew nothing about Elway's plans and believed the quarterback was more than capable of playing for several more seasons.

"I don't think anybody knew other than him," Mobley said. "I thought this guy was going to play until he was 50. Just watching the way he kept his body up and the way he threw the ball, I thought he was going to play forever."

Elway looked more than capable of returning after the Super Bowl. The Denver Offense was ranked second in the NFL after racking up 501 points during the regular season. The efficiency of Elway and his teammates made the job of the defense easier throughout the 1998 campaign.

"The defense's best friend was the offense," said Joyner. "We averaged 31 points a game. That's never to take anything away from that defense but I know when you average that many points, it's a heck of a lot easier to play defense than when you're locked up at 0–0."

The other storyline for Super Bowl XXXIII involved Atlanta's head coach. Dan Reeves had led the Broncos to three Super Bowl appearances before being fired in 1992. After four years with the Giants, Reeves was hired by the Falcons and was set to face his former team in Miami. It had been a difficult year for Reeves, who underwent quadruple-bypass surgery in December. He returned for the final regular season game and led the Falcons to the Super Bowl.

"He was the rock," Mathis said. "He treated us like men. He told us we were grown men and to take care of our business. He took care of us and he respected us. We respected him and we played hard for each other and for him. There's always something that happens in sports that a team comes together. I think that was one of those moments for us. When Dan Reeves had his surgery, it brought us together."

The Falcons would get the ball first in Super Bowl XXXIII and a kick return by Tim Dwight put Atlanta on its own 37-yard line. The Falcons quickly moved deep into Denver territory thanks largely to the running of Jamal Anderson. The Atlanta back had rushed for 1,846 yards in the regular season and picked up right where he left off in the Super Bowl. The Falcons were on the eight-yard line facing third down, but Quarterback Chris Chandler was sacked by Bill Romanowski. Morten Andersen's 32-yard field goal gave Atlanta and early lead, but Mathis and his teammates were frustrated at the missed opportunity to reach the end zone.

"There was frustration," said Mathis. "I knew that if we scored there, it's a panic for the Broncos. We didn't pick up the blitz. The play was called for me and I was wide open. I looked and saw Chandler on his back. We settled for three and it was kind of deflating."

"We knew they could put points on the board," Mobley said. "It was good for us to only allow them to get three instead of a touchdown. We were pretty confident that once the offense got the ball, we'd be able to put points on the board. It was just a matter of keeping their offense out of the end zone."

The Denver Offense did indeed put points on the board after the Atlanta field goal. On Denver's first possession, Elway put together an 80-yard scoring drive with the help of a 41-yard catch and run by Rod Smith. Howard Griffith finished off the drive with a one-yard run as the Broncos took a 7–3 lead. The Broncos were still up by four late in the first quarter when Elway was intercepted by Ronnie Bradford. The turnover gave the Falcons the ball on the Denver 35. As the second quarter began, Anderson was stopped on third and one. Reeves gambled when the Falcons were faced with fourth down, but Anderson was turned back for a loss. The denial by the Denver Defense provided a huge momentum swing.

"It's basically them telling you that they think their guys are more dominant than you," Joyner said. "It's saying 'our manhood is up against your manhood and we're betting on ours.' That was a major turning point in the football game because it sent the message you aren't as good as you think you are and you're not more dominant than we are on this side of the ball."

"How many times is Jamal Anderson going to get stopped on fourth and less than a yard?" asked Mathis. "It wasn't too long after that when the big play happens."

The little plays happened first for Denver, resulting in a 26-yard field goal by Jason Elam. The big play would follow and virtually seal Atlanta's fate before the half came to an end. First, the Falcons would let an easy opportunity slip away. Atlanta marched back to the Denver eight, but Andersen missed on a 26-yard field goal attempt. When Denver got the ball back, Elway launched a pass to Smith downfield. The speedy receiver beat Safety Eugene Robinson for an 80-yard touchdown catch with just under five minutes to play in the half. Atlanta would get one last chance to reach the end zone before halftime, but the Denver Defense once again tightened up in the red zone. Andersen's second field goal brought the Falcons to within 11 at the half, but the Broncos appeared to be in control on both sides of the ball.

Joyner believed a Broncos' victory was a forgone conclusion.

"I just felt like this game was a wrap," recalled Joyner. "We were clearly the better team and they were clearly out and overmatched. The only thing that could have caused us not to win that football game was mistakes on our part."

The Falcons hardly felt they were out of the game. Mathis and his teammates had been down before during the season as well as in the NFC title game.

"We had been there before and there was no panic," recalled Mathis. "Plays that we had been making during the season were plays we weren't making that day. That was the most frustrating thing about it. I was having a decent game and you want to be in that situation. You want to be that guy to bring us back."

The Broncos left the door open for Atlanta after coming away empty on the first drive of the second half. Elam missed a 38-yard field goal and Chandler responded by moving his offense to the Denver 47. However, Chandler was intercepted by Darrius Johnson and the Denver offense came back onto the field. Mathis believes his quarterback may have still been feeling the effects of the sack he took on the opening drive of the game.

"I think Chris played with a concussion the whole game," Mathis said. "When Romanowski hit him, I think he was dazed for the game from there on out. Chris didn't miss plays. He didn't miss open guys like he was doing later in that game."

Another Elam miss would give the Falcons yet another opportunity and Chandler brought his team to the Denver 21. Once again, Denver's Defense forced a critical turnover as Darrien Gordon's interception off a deflected pass was brought back 58-yards to the Atlanta 24. It took the Broncos five plays to reach the end zone and Griffith scored again from the one on the opening play of the fourth quarter. Denver's lead swelled to 24–6 and Atlanta's missed opportunities deep in Denver territory resulted in an insurmountable deficit for the Dirty Birds.

"We weren't doing anything offensively," said Mathis. We turned the ball over three times in the second half and they got points on all three of them. It's 24–6 but it's still early in the fourth quarter. You're still thinking in the back of your mind that you can have it."

"We realized what their game plan was," Mobley said. "Our counter to it was pretty good. We bracketed Mathis who was killing us early and we were able to bottle up Jamal Anderson pretty good. Now, we just had to keep Chandler from hitting the big play on us."

Chandler threw his third interception of the game as Gordon's second pick was returned 50 yards to the Falcons' 48. It was the third consecutive Atlanta drive which ended in an interception. Elway hit Terrell Davis for a 39-yard gain and would score two plays later on a quarterback draw. The Broncos had a 31–6 lead with 11:20 remaining and Joyner's long wait for a Super Bowl ring was about to end.

"There were a lot of guys playing who realized I had been in the league for 13 years," Joyner said. "A lot of those guys were happy for me. They were happy for the fact that this guy was about to win a Super Bowl for the first time in a 13-year career."

The game may have been out of reach for Atlanta, but the Falcons were finally able to find the end zone. On the kickoff after the Elway score, Dwight raced 94-yards for Atlanta's first ever Super Bowl touchdown. Mathis would get the second touchdown for his team after another Elam field goal. He capped off a 76-yard scoring drive with a three-yard catch to cut the Denver lead to 34–19, but only 2:04 remained on the clock.

"It was a little too late but I do cherish it," said Mathis. "I kept the football. I have a big poster-size picture of it in my basement. It was the last touchdown of our season. It was the only receiving touchdown in the Falcons' history at the Super Bowl. You cherish it because there are many guys, including Hall of Famers, who have never played in a Super Bowl. I felt honored that I had an opportunity to play in a Super Bowl and had a chance to score."

The Broncos were able to run out the clock and Elway had a chance for a curtain call after taking a knee with just over a minute to play. Elway was named the game's MVP after throwing for 336 yards and one of the greatest quarterbacks in NFL history left the field for a final time. Elway announced his retirement three months after the Super Bowl.

The Broncos became only the sixth franchise to win back-to-back Super Bowls. Meanwhile, the Falcons were left with the same empty feeling which so many others have experienced on the losing end of America's biggest game.

"The tickertape comes down," Mathis said. "You go 'that's it?' It's the final game and you're walking off and you're watching them celebrate. It's just one of those empty feelings. At the end of the day, you get a chance to congratulate some guys on the other team then you've just got to suck it up."

The Broncos basked in another Super Bowl title. After going down to the wire with Green Bay the previous year, Mobley and his teammates had a chance to savor the moment throughout the final quarter.

"It was a little anti-climactic with the way the game went down," Mobley said. "We were really able to take it in and enjoy it while it was happening. It's something we weren't able to do in the previous one. I remember they took my helmet away from me and then me putting a hat on. We were sitting back just talking about how incredible it was."

It was incredible for Joyner, whose 13-year wait for a Super Bowl ring was over.

"I think it was difficult for it to settle in and to sink in," said Joyner. "I think it took a little time for it to sink in. You celebrate in the moment, but until you look back and reflect and think about your career and experiences and think about that day, you never really get to a point where you can really relish and really understand what was accomplished."

Despite the victory, Joyner had no plans to retire. He had served as a backup to the talented group of young Denver linebackers, but was hoping to get a chance as a starter again in 1999. Rams Coach Dick Vermeil brought Joyner into training camp the following summer, but Joyner was told he was being brought in to serve in a similar role as a mentor and a backup. Joyner decided to retire and missed an opportunity to be a part of the Rams' Cinderella season.

"I thought that if I couldn't compete for a starting job with the Rams then maybe it's time for me to call it a day," said Joyner. "I made the decision to retire after that workout and they go on to win the Super Bowl that year. I'm sitting home on Super Bowl Sunday miserable as all hell."

The Falcons had suffered defeat in their first Super Bowl, but a franchise which at times takes a back seat to the college game in Georgia had taken center stage. Mathis and his teammates had paved the way for future generations of Falcons.

"It gave Atlanta a sense of hope," said Mathis. "It gave Atlanta a sense of accomplishment. Georgia is a football state, especially with the University of Georgia. For us to do what we did is something we cherish. We started the terminology of the Dirty Birds."

The Broncos of the late 1990's aren't often mentioned as one of the all-time great teams. However, a 39–9 regular season record over three seasons along with two Super Bowl titles puts Mobley and his teammates in elite company. The linebacker believes it was about more than superstars and big plays which made the Denver Broncos two-time champions.

"Guys just gave it all up for one another," Mobley said. If they weren't all-pro players, they were all-pro players in the locker room off the field. I think that's what made that team what it was. Guys just wanted to win at any expense. It was about doing it all for the good of the team."

XXXIV
THE RAMS BY A YARD

The 1999 Rams rose from football purgatory to the top of the mountain.

The franchise has sunk to the bottom-dwelling section of the NFL since moving from Los Angeles to St. Louis in 1995. The Rams' win total dropped by one game each season from 1995 through 1998. The 1997 campaign signaled the arrival of Dick Vermeil as head coach. After spending 15 years away from coaching, the front office was hoping Vermeil's old school approach would turn the franchise around. However, it wasn't until Vermeil's third season that the Rams emerged as contenders, thanks largely to the surprising performance of Quarterback Kurt Warner. After taking over for the injured Trent Green in the preseason, the former grocery store worker led "The Greatest Show on Turf" to football's ultimate stage. The high powered St. Louis offense was the center of attention in Atlanta the week of Super Bowl XXXIV.

For Vermeil, this Super Sunday would be an opportunity for redemption. He had led the Eagles to Super Bowl XV, only to suffer a 27–10 loss to the Raiders. Vermeil brought a different perspective into this Super Bowl and was determined to keep his players loose with only one week to prepare for the game.

"I was much more relaxed going into a Super Bowl 19 years later," said Vermeil. "I think that's part of maturity, but we only had one week to prepare for the game, so maybe I didn't have enough time to screw it up."

John Bunting had played for Vermeil in Philadelphia, and was his co-defensive coordinator in St. Louis. Bunting could see the difference in his head coach heading into Super Bowl XXXIV.

"Dick obviously learned a lot from that experience," said Bunting. "The players went down to Atlanta and the staff stayed behind and developed a game plan. We arrived on that Tuesday on picture day and didn't even practice. We learned a lot from that experience in Super Bowl XV."

St. Louis rolled to a 13–3 record in 1999. One of the losses came at the hands of the Tennessee Titans, the AFC representative in this Super Bowl. The Titans also went 13–3, but needed to go the wild card route to reach Atlanta. After pulling off their "Music City Miracle" victory over Buffalo, the Titans beat the Colts and Jaguars on the road. Both teams were quite familiar with each other thanks to Tennessee's 24–21 victory over St. Louis on Halloween. It was on this day that players such as Rams' Linebacker Mike Jones realized the two teams had a chance to play again on Super Sunday.

"It was a great opportunity to play them earlier in the season," Jones said. "We went to their place and they jumped out on us. They really opened our eyes for what we needed to do. We knew if they played well and we played well, we may have another opportunity with them."

Rams Wide Receiver Ricky Proehl made the game-winning touchdown catch in the NFC Championship game. The veteran was well aware of the tough test Tennessee would present after seeing the Titans up close during the regular season.

"They had a physical defense," said Proehl. "They were a good football team. They caught our attention during the regular season with how they played against us. They were a tough, physical football team all the way around."

The matchup would feature the high-powered St. Louis offense against the menacing Tennessee defense. However, the other side of the ball also presented an intriguing matchup. The Rams' underrated defense had been the difference in an 11–6 win over Tampa Bay in the NFC title game. The Titans countered with Steve McNair, one of the most versatile quarterbacks in the NFL. Wide Receiver Kevin Dyson was happy to see his quarterback get a chance to shine on center stage.

"He always was the X factor," Dyson said. "That was a statement by him for what we as his teammates already recognized. He had his competitive spirit and a will to win. Since it was the Super Bowl, I think everybody else took notice."

Dyson was also happy to get another crack at the Rams. After beating St. Louis earlier this season, the receiver believed the Titans were more than capable of winning the rematch.

"We seemed to overcome a lot of adversity that year," said Dyson. "We were battle-tested. We faced the Rams early that year and played pretty well. We were confident."

Both teams were able to move the ball on their opening possession, but came up empty on field goal attempts. A botched snap denied the Rams three points, while Al Del Greco missed a 47-yard attempt for Tennessee. St. Louis was able to move the ball throughout the rest of the first half, but Warner paid the price. The Titans gambled with single coverage in order to pressure the St. Louis signal caller. Warner threw for 277 yards and took a beating at the hands of the ferocious Tennessee pass rush. The Titans kept the Rams out of the end zone, but Jeff Wilkins kicked three field goals to give St. Louis a 9–0 lead at halftime.

"It was frustrating," said Vermeil. "We dropped a touchdown pass. We got down in the red zone and didn't execute as well as we had all year. You give credit to Tennessee. They made it tough on us."

"We felt like we were dominating the football game," Proehl said. "But we only had three field goals to show for it. We just weren't executing and weren't hitting on all cylinders. We still felt confident in where we were."

The St. Louis offense was getting plenty of help from the Rams' defense. After keeping Tampa Bay out of the end zone in the NFC Championship, the St. Louis defenders limited Tennessee to 89 first-half yards.

"We got out to a good start," said Jones. "We felt comfortable playing against them. We had basically played six shutout quarters."

Despite being shutout in the first half, Dyson and his teammates were still confident heading into the locker room. Few teams had held "The Greatest Show on Turf" to nine points in a half, and Dyson knew the Titans weren't about to change their game plan for the final two quarters.

"It was nothing unfamiliar to us," said Dyson. "For me, I felt relieved considering the fact that they did only have nine points going into halftime. It could have been far worse and we really would have gotten out of our normal offense."

Tennessee's offense would face an even bigger deficit as the third quarter progressed. Warner and his teammates finally found the end zone as Tory Holt hauled in a nine-yard scoring strike, and the lead went to 16–0.

But the Titans didn't flinch.

"Tennessee stuck to their plan," said Jones. "They wanted to run the ball and do play-action passing. We were thinking they were going to be more wide open. We were on our heels against the run, and it caught up with us."

The Titans went right back to the basics on their next possession. They ran the ball seven times on a nine-play drive. George crashed in from one-yard out, and the lead was cut to 16–6. The Rams had the lead as the fourth quarter began, but the Titans had the momentum.

"They wore us down," Vermeil said. "We came out in the third quarter and scored, and then they banged on us and ate up the clock."

"They did a great job of controlling the clock," said Proehl. "They didn't get away from what they do and what got them there. It was very frustrating because they had some long drives and they were eating up the clock."

St. Louis was forced to punt on its next possession, and Tennessee put together another long scoring march. This time, the Titans went to the air as McNair connected on a pair of 21-yard completions. It was the start of a 13-play drive which ended on another touchdown run by George. With 7:21 remaining, The Rams' lead was down to three, and the long drives by the Titans were taking their toll on the St. Louis defense.

"We started getting tired," Jones said. "Guys started getting winded. They picked up the intensity. They actually changed the rhythm."

The Ram defenders were forced to get right back on the field after the offense went three-and-out on the next possession. Tennessee reached the St. Louis 25, and Del Greco got another chance. This time, the kicker split the uprights, and Del Greco's 43-yard boot had tied the game with 2:12 remaining. However, St. Louis would answer on the next play from scrimmage. Warner beat the blitz and hit Isaac Bruce for a 73-yard touchdown. The Rams were ahead, 23–16, but the quick scoring strike gave the Titans another chance.

"We scored late in the game on one big play," said Vermeil. "They get the ball back. It would have been better if we had taken five plays. If I had to do it over again, I would have said 'don't score right away.'"

"You go through your normal emotions," Dyson said. "Then, it comes right back. You get down, and you get right back up. That's just the nature of sports. I don't think any of us ever, ever doubted we were going down the length of the field."

The Tennessee offense took the field with 1:48 remaining. The stage was set for one of the greatest finishes in Super Bowl history.

The Titans marched from their own 12-yard line into St. Louis territory. They reached the 45 thanks to a McNair scramble combined with a facemask penalty. Tennessee would later face a critical third down on the 27. McNair pulled off a spectacular escape as he eluded two tacklers and hit Dyson for a first down at the ten. Six seconds remained, and the St. Louis defense had nothing left in the tank.

"They were gassed," said Dyson. "You could just tell. It's been well-documented. Even one of my teammates, Kevin Carter, who was on that Rams team, admits to it. It was a testament to the Rams and us that we all left it on the field. There was nothing left out there."

There was time for one more play. Dyson lined up to the right and went towards the area of the zone Jones was covering. Tight End Frank Wycheck went into the same area.

"The idea is that I am the bait and Frankie is the primary target," Dyson said. "The idea is if I make that immediate threat to him, Mike releases Frankie to the safety and there's a hole right behind where he left."

"We were basically in a match zone defense," said Jones. "I had all inside releases and any short releases. When the ball was snapped, I'm inside of Frank who is the number two receiver. I still have to look through him to make sure no one comes back into my area."

Dyson came back into the area and caught a quick pass from McNair just inside the five. Dyson turned towards the end zone, but Jones was able to adjust and grab Dyson by his legs. Dyson reached for the goal line, but fell one yard short. The play forever known as "The Tackle" preserved the victory for the Rams, and sent the Titans down to a heartbreaking defeat.

"I knew he was short," said Jones. "I knew where I was at on the field when I planted my foot. I believe I was at about the four, so I knew I didn't have to carry him that far. I knew if I got him on the ground, he was going to be short. That's what they teach you as a linebacker, to make sure you know where you're at."

The emotional Vermeil was forced to wait to see if the Rams were victorious. With chaos on the field, The St. Louis coach couldn't see what happened as the final play unfolded.

"I saw the pass play was going to be to the right side of the offense," said Vermeil. "I couldn't tell if he caught it, scored, or dropped it. I looked at the officials moving in to see what they were going to call. When I saw them cross their arms and wave no score, I knew we were world champions."

Jones and his teammates had held off the gritty Titans with one yard to spare, but exhaustion overpowered elation as the final gun sounded.

"It was relief," Jones said. "It was so funny, because the guys ran on the field. Everyone else hasn't been running up and down the field. Most of the eleven guys that were on the field were down on their knees. They threw their hands up, but there wasn't much of a celebration by those eleven guys. They had to get their breath."

"It could have gone either way," said Dyson. "If he doesn't get his body around to get his left hand on my left knee, I've got just enough to extend and get the final yard."

The Rams were Super Bowl champions for the first time in franchise history. It would be their only championship in St. Louis, with the Rams moving back to Los Angeles in 2016. Warner was named the MVP after throwing for 414 yards and surviving a tremendous beating by the Tennessee Defense. Jones and Dyson are forever linked to the final play, and the two have developed a friendship as well as a healthy respect for each other.

"We just happened to be the last two standing on the final play of the biggest game of all games," Dyson said. "I think Mike's very similar to myself. We're both team guys. It was hard to swallow initially. Seeing his humbleness through the whole thing helps me deal with it."

Vermeil was victorious on his second try at a Super Bowl. However, the victory in Super Bowl XXXIV didn't change the affection Vermeil still holds for his Super Bowl XV squad.

"It takes the same thing to get there and lose as it does to get there and win," Vermeil said. "Having done both, to win is a lot better. But I respect my losing team every bit as much, if not more, than my winning team. The whole process is what makes that game special."

Super Bowl XXXIV was indeed a special game, and Jones and Dyson will always be remembered for the finale.

"He's proud to be part of history and get his championship ring," said Dyson. "I'm proud to be part of history and wish I had a championship ring."

XXXV
PURPLE REIGN

The NFL entered the 21st century as a pass-happy, offensive minded league. But the first champions of the new millennium played winning football the old-fashioned way.

The Baltimore Ravens were anything but pass-happy. Baltimore rampaged through the AFC playoffs with one of the most dominating defenses in NFL history. The Ravens also relied on an offense with a strong running game and a passing attack which played it safe throughout much of the 2000 campaign. These were not Montana's 49ers or Aikman's Cowboys. They didn't need to be.

Baltimore Head Coach Brian Billick was an offensive coordinator in Minnesota when the Vikings were putting up record-setting offensive numbers. As a head coach in Baltimore, he realized he would need a different formula to win. The result was a record-setting defense which broke the NFL record for fewest points allowed in a season. The Ravens headed to Tampa to face the New York Giants, who were led by Billick's longtime friend, Jim Fassel.

"It always adds another dimension to it," said Billick. "When they were playing the Minnesota Vikings, who I had been with for nine years prior to coming to Baltimore, I knew I was going to play some friend whether it would be Denny Green or Jim Fassel."

It would not be Green thanks to a dominating performance by Fassel's squad in the NFC Championship. The Giants rolled past the Vikings, 41–0, in the most lopsided NFC title game ever played. One of the top players on the Giants was Safety Jason Sehorn, who believed winning with such ease against Minnesota may have actually hurt his team going into Super Bowl XXXV.

"I think we were extremely loose going in and probably overconfident just based on that victory over Minnesota," said Sehorn. "We were pretty loose and carefree, and I think that all changed when we got to Tampa. The practice schedule changed and the rules changed and the curfew changed."

Baltimore did not change its approach to game day. Its defense had shut down the high-powered Oakland Offense in a 16–3 AFC Championship victory. The Giants possessed a balanced attack with Running Back Tiki Barber and Quarterback Kerry Collins, but Billick knew stopping the run against New York would make the difference in the game.

"We had a great deal of confidence that they weren't going to be able to run on us," Billick said. "We knew they didn't know they weren't going to be able to run on us because no one did. We knew we matched up very well with them. If we could make it that one-dimensional game, it was going to be huge. That certainly was the difference in the game."

Sehorn was more concerned with the Baltimore Offense. On paper, it seemed as if stopping the run meant stopping the Ravens, but Sehorn knew Quarterback Trent Dilfer could make plays if the Baltimore ground game got off to a slow start.

"We felt Baltimore was a team run by their defense," said Sehorn. "They had an offense that didn't make mistakes. People said all week Dilfer was a manager, but he could throw the ball. They just didn't ask him to. They didn't ask him to wing it 35 of 40 times a game."

Dilfer wasn't planning on throwing 40 passes in the Super Bowl, but it would be two that would set up an early advantage for Baltimore. Both teams punted on their first two possessions, but a play before Baltimore's second punt would pave the way for the first score later in the period. On 3rd and 6 from the New York 46, Dilfer threw for Patrick Johnson in the end zone. The pass was overthrown, but Johnson was open on the play. It would be a pass pattern stored in the memory banks of Billick and Dilfer. Baltimore would get the ball on the New York 41 later in the period, and Billick was ready to try the same play. After a three-yard-gain, Dilfer threw deep again, and this time it was Brandon Stokley who was left one-on-one with Sehorn. With no help coming from the inside for the Giants safety, Stokley hauled in the first score of the game.

"It was a great matchup for us," Billick said. "We knew they would be leaning towards Shannon Sharpe, who was clearly our go to guy. Trent Dilfer did a magnificent job of seeing the one-on-one matchup. In fairness to Jason Sehorn, I think he was going to get help over the top."

"We felt like we'd take away Sharpe and one of their receivers and force them to go someplace else," Sehorn said. "We were double-teaming Sharpe and we were double-teaming the slot receiver, so the guy on the outside had a man-to-man."

On the touchdown, there were more than two players on Sharpe and Sehorn watched helplessly as Stokley hauled in the pass at the ten and went into the end zone. Free Safety Shaun Williams was trailing the play.

"They were triple-teaming Shannon Sharpe," said Sehorn. "I'm playing outside leverage, which leaves the whole middle of the field open. He threw a nice pass over the middle, and I'm trailing on the outside expecting somebody to be there, and there was nobody there."

The result was the worst case scenario for New York. The Giants were forced to play from behind against one of the game's greatest defenses. A series of events in the second quarter would increase the Baltimore stranglehold. Collins threw his first interception with just over ten minutes to play in the half. On the ensuing play, Dilfer was intercepted by Jessie Armstead, but a penalty nullified the 43-yard touchdown return by the Giants Linebacker.

"The deflating part was when Jessie Armstead's interception was overturned on a holding call on one of our lineman," Sehorn said. "You just never see that called."

Another long pass would set up Baltimore's second score later in the quarter. Dilfer hit Qadry Ismail with a 44-yard strike which led to a 47-yard field goal by Matt Stover. Late in the half, the Giants moved the ball to the Baltimore 29. A touchdown or a field goal before the half would have made the game a one-score contest, but Collins was intercepted by Chris McAlister near the goal line in the final minute. It was 10–0 at halftime, but the lead seemed larger with the way the Baltimore Defense was dominating the game.

"It was huge," Billick said of the interception. "It is a game of emotion. It is a game of ebb and flow. Anytime you can trample down what appears to be momentum or big play by a team, it's huge."

Collins would fare no better at the start of the second half. On the Giants first possession, Collins was intercepted by Kim Herring. Baltimore failed to capitalize as Stover missed form 41 yards out, but Collins' wasn't done throwing interceptions. His next one would set off one of the most remarkable sequences in Super Bowl history.

With just under four minutes to play in the third quarter, Duane Starks intercepted a Collins pass and returned it for a 49-yard touchdown. It was 17–0 and Collins had thrown his fourth interception of the game. It appeared the Giants were finished, but Ron Dixon brought his team back to life on the ensuing kickoff. Dixon raced 97 yards for a touchdown, and New York was finally on the board. Their momentum lasted until the next kickoff. Jermaine Lewis went 84 yards to put Baltimore back up by 17. The two teams had combined for three touchdowns in 36 seconds, and the scoring explosion set off a wave of emotions on both sidelines.

"We were going to get the ball offensively," said Billick. "We were really going to have to make something happen. To have a kickoff return for a touchdown, then kickoff to us and us maybe go three and out and put us in a tough position maybe is the match that's going to light the fire for the New York Giants."

"Very deflating," Sehorn said. "You think maybe we have a chance. We scored a touchdown and now we're back in the game and then we kick it off and they score a touchdown. You think maybe we don't have a chance. That was a huge swing of emotion."

That emotional swing along with a 24–7 lead for Baltimore proved to be too much for New York to overcome.

"Even though you fight it to the end," Billick said. "You kind of knew at that point the game was over."

The game wouldn't be officially over until time ran out in the second half. The Ravens added ten more points in the final period to finish off their 34–7 victory. Jamal Lewis scored on a three yard run, and Stover added another field goal with 5:28 remaining. Meanwhile, Collins and company could do nothing against Ray Lewis and the Baltimore defenders. The Giants never got past midfield in the final period and finished with just 152 total yards. Lewis was named the Super Bowl MVP as he led his defense into pro football immortality, while Collins finished with four interceptions and only 112 passing yards.

"They were going to pay a price coming over the middle," said Billick. "You kind of felt for Kerry Collins because he had to be a little hesitant. You could see where there was hesitation for Kerry Collins against a team where the last thing you want to do is drop back to pass when they know you want to drop back to pass."

Sehorn and his teammates had kept the Giants in the game early, but were forced to watch helplessly as their offense was shut down throughout the night. Despite the defeat, Sehorn couldn't help but be impressed by one of the most dominating defenses the NFL has ever seen.

"You respect what they did in a league that's offensive-minded," said Sehorn. "Most of the rules are set up for the offense. For a team to come out and have success that way is difficult. They weren't exotic. They didn't call crazy blitzes. They were so physical and they just beat you up."

Billick had the chance to take in the moment as time ticked away in the fourth quarter. With the Ravens in control, his primary decision in the final minutes was to find an escape path from the traditional Gatorade dunking. While Billick couldn't escape his bath, he was able to reflect on the greatest moment in his coaching career.

"It's surreal," said Billick. "Pretty much in that last quarter, we knew that was going to be it. It gives you the opportunity to let your mind wander a little bit about what's going on and that this is really something special. It did kind of put it in a surreal atmosphere in that you were really able to absorb what was going on."

Another man who enjoyed the moment was Art Modell. The Ravens' owner had dealt with a wave of criticism when he moved the franchise out of Cleveland after the 1995 season. Modell owned the Browns when they won the NFL Championship in 1964, but this was his first chance to hoist the Lombardi Trophy.

"The transition of the sale of the club was clearly put in place," Billick said. "We knew Steve Bisciotti was going to eventually take over ownership of the club. You could see the emotion and you could see what it meant to him. There wasn't one of us that wasn't just thrilled to death that we were a part of being able to give that to him."

The Ravens brought the city of Baltimore its first football title since the Colts captured Super Bowl V. Even the vanquished Giants knew they had been the unwilling victims of an all-time defensive performance.

"That defense was something else," Sehorn said. Seeing it firsthand, I can now say that was impressive."

But was it the greatest defense of all time? Many football fans still put the 1985 Bears at the top of the list, but Billick believes he can make a strong case for his unit. Breaking the scoring defense record and winning a championship fuels Billick's somewhat friendly argument.

"All we kept hearing all year long was it means nothing unless you win the Super Bowl," said Billick. "We did both, so I'm going to use that criteria. I'll sit and argue in a fun way and sit down and have a beer with anybody that doesn't want to argue that this isn't the single-season best defense in the history of the NFL."

XXXVI
THE PATRIOT WAY

As the 2001 NFL season was reaching its climax, America was still in mourning.

Super Bowl XXXVI would be played nearly five months after one of the darkest days in U.S. History. The September 11th terrorist attacks which brought down the Twin Towers and resulted in thousands of deaths put football in perspective during the season. After taking a week off due to the terrorist attacks, football returned to the gridiron as a grateful nation searched for an outlet to alleviate the sorrow. For players such as Patriots' special teams standout Larry Izzo, the return of the NFL provided relief for both fans and players.

"The country was just really taken back by all of the events at that time," said Izzo. "It was a very traumatic period for everybody and I think football gave people something to take their mind off that terrible time for our country."

As the season progressed, the Patriots and St. Louis Rams punched their tickets to Super Bowl XXXVI. However, the tragedy was still on the minds of players throughout the 2001 campaign. For people such as Rams Receiver Ricky Proehl, 9/11 hit home.

"It was devastating," Proehl said. "My parents grew up in the Bronx and my grandmother lived there. We had constant drives into New York City. The landmarks were the Empire State Building and the Twin Towers. That's what you saw on the Jersey Turnpike. For those to be gone was just crazy. It didn't seem real."

New England Quarterback Drew Bledsoe watched in shock with the rest of the nation as the towers fell. The league decided a week of mourning was needed, but Bledsoe had initially wanted to get back on the field sooner.

"My knee-jerk reaction after that happened was that we should get back out and play," recalled Bledsoe. "Obviously, that would have been the wrong decision in retrospect. I do think that sports in general and football in this instance does have a healing effect. It gave people something to get together for and something to cheer for and an outlet to get away from this horrible thing that had happened."

When the season resumed, Bledsoe suffered a sheared blood vessel in his chest in a game against the Jets which sidelined the quarterback for much of the season. In his place stepped Tom Brady, a rookie quarterback from Michigan who would begin his path to greatness. As Brady established himself as the starter, Bledsoe was forced into the role of spectator. Bledsoe continued to support Brady and the rest of his teammates but was understandably frustrated after losing his starting job.

"It was tough after being the guy there for close to a decade then getting hurt," Bledsoe said. "We finally get back to that game and you don't get to play. It was definitely bittersweet."

Brady had led the Patriots to a surprise Super Bowl run, but got plenty of help from his kicker. Adam Vinatieri booted a pair of crucial field goals in the snow to lead New England past Oakland in a divisional playoff. After disposing of Pittsburgh in the AFC Championship game, Vinatieri and the Patriots were on their way to the Super Bowl.

"It really was an interesting year," said Vinatieri. "The country just kind of stopped for a little while. We all grieved. It made you realize family values and how much your loved ones mean to you."

While the Patriots run to Super Bowl XXXVI was surprising to many, few were shocked to see the Rams reach the title game. St. Louis had won the Super Bowl two years prior and had reloaded after losing in the wild card round in 2000.

But the shadow of 9/11 continued to loom large for many players.

"It was an emotional year," said Proehl. "It's one of those deals where you remember exactly where you were, what time it was and then just being in shock. The whole year was predicated on 9/11 and I thought the league did a tremendous job."

St. Louis was a heavy favorite going into Super Bowl XXXVI. The Rams had put together a 14–2 regular season before defeating Green Bay and Philadelphia in the playoffs. St. Louis had also beaten the Patriots in the regular season, but Izzo believes there were positives to take out of their 24–17 defeat in the tenth game of the year.

"We played them at home and we were real competitive with them," Izzo said. "It was a tough game and we lost, but I think at about that point in the year, we thought we had a decent team going."

There was a patriotic theme leading up to Super Sunday in New Orleans. The pregame festivities featured songs and other events honoring America and those who were lost in the attacks. Former President George H.W. Bush participated in the coin toss along with Hall of Famer Roger Staubach.

But America was still a nervous nation.

"There still was this edge to everything," recalled Bledsoe. "If somebody really wanted to try and strike at the core of America, the Super Bowl was kind of an obvious place to try and do something. There was an edge to it that we certainly felt."

The Patriots had set the tone early by changing the Super Bowl pregame introductions forever. Instead of being introduced as individuals, the Patriots elected to take the field as a team.

"It represented what we were," said Izzo. "There were no stars on that team. Everybody had taken the 'do your job' mentality. If you do your job and everybody does their job to the best of their abilities, good things are going to happen."

"We felt like a band of brothers," Vinatieri said. "Going out as a group not only showed the Rams what they had to deal with but also the rest of the world that a group of men united is pretty hard to beat."

It was all about football once Vinatieri approached the ball for the opening kickoff. New England's defense was faced with the unenviable task of slowing down the powerful St. Louis Offense. The unit known as "The Greatest Show on Turf" racked up a league-leading 503 points. New England looked to set the tone early with a physical style of play preached by Belichick.

"Coach Belichick made a point that it was going to be our physical play that's going to win this game," Izzo said. "We were practicing in full pads in the heat down there. We were just grinding and then the game comes and we were ready to go."

The Rams were still able to strike first on their second drive. Jeff Wilkins hit a 50-yard field goal to put St. Louis up, 3–0. The score would remain 3–0 until midway through the second quarter when the New England Defense would put the Patriots ahead. Pressure by Linebacker Mike Vrabel forced an errant throw by Quarterback Kurt Warner and Cornerback Ty Law returned an interception 47 yards for a touchdown. The defense would set up another score late in the half. Proehl was stripped by Antwan Harris after a catch at the St. Louis 40. Terrell Buckley recovered and Brady hit David Patten on an eight-yard touchdown toss with 31 seconds left in the half. New England went to the locker room with a 14–3 lead and the stunned Rams were forced to regroup facing their largest deficit of the season.

"It was adjustments and getting back on track," Proehl said. "We knew that if we were at our best, no one could stop us. We felt like the whole defense was doing a good job. We had to do a better job of being more physical."

The halftime show was an emotional one as U2 took the stage. The Irish rock band played three songs while the names of the victims of the 9/11 attacks scrolled behind the performers.

"I still remember U2 playing in the halftime show," Izzo said. "You could hear it in the locker room. It was special to be a part of."

The Patriots were hoping to be part of something special after two more quarters of football. Both teams got off to a slow start in the second half, but the New England Defense once again set up a score late in the third quarter. Otis Smith returned another Warner interception to the St. Louis 33. The drive would stall, but Vinatieri came on for his first field goal of the game and his 37-yarder increased the lead to 17–3.

"I like having the opportunity to kick early in the game," said Vinatieri. "It just gets me into the game a little sooner. The shorter one earlier in the game probably helped out a little bit."

The Patriots appeared to put the game away on the Rams ensuing drive. A fumble on 4th and goal by Warner was returned 97 yards for a touchdown by Tebucky Jones, but a holding penalty on Willie McGinest gave St. Louis new life. Warner scored on a two-yard run with 9:31 to play to cut the New England lead to 17–10. A potential 24–3 lead had turned into a one-score game.

"They were a really good team and they started making some plays," said Izzo. "You kind of felt it getting a little bit away from you, but the sideline was still feeling like this was our game to win."

It was still 17–10 when the Rams took over on their own 45 with 1:51 to go. Warner completed two passes to move the ball to the New England 26. On the next play, Warner threw to his left and found an open Proehl inside the 15. Proehl cut back inside and streaked into the end zone and Super Bowl XXXVI was tied at 17–17 with 1:30 remaining.

"They were playing a lot of man coverage," recalled Proehl. "We had a go route and we did a switch release. I'm wide open down the sideline. I catch it and I feel the safety over the top. I got back and dove into the end zone. Now, it's a tie ball game."

There had never been an overtime period in a Super Bowl, but it appeared the Rams and Patriots would need extra time to settle the outcome. With 1:21 remaining and no time outs, New England took over on its own 17. Much of America, including FOX analyst John Madden, believed the Patriots should play it safe and run out the clock.

Brady and Belichick had other ideas.

"Tom had shown throughout the year that he was really different," Izzo said. "He had won a lot of games for us and shown he was everything we know he is now. He had something about him when it came to stepping up in crucial situations and have his wits about him when he was doing it."

The Patriots also had Vinatieri, one of the top kickers in the history of the game.

"We practiced the two-minute drill all the time," Vinatieri said. "I think every team does. That's kind of what it's built for. I think at that point, you've got plenty of time."

Three passes to J.R. Redmond moved the ball to the New England 41. After an incompletion, Brady found Troy Brown for a 23-yard reception, moving the Patriots closer to Vinatieri's range.

"They were getting out of bounds on every play," Proehl said. "It was so frustrating not having any control and to sit on the sideline and watch the emergence of Hall of Fame quarterback, Tom Brady."

Brady threw a six-yard pass to Jermaine Wiggins then rushed to the line of scrimmage to spike the ball. The clock stopped with seven seconds remaining. The ball was on the St. Louis 30 and Vinatieri came onto to the field for a 48-yard attempt. Vinatieri was in the same position as Jim O'Brien in Super

Bowl V and Scott Norwood in Super Bowl XXV. O'Brien made his game-winning Super Bowl kick. Norwood missed.

"I tried not to think about any of that stuff," said Vinatieri. "I just try to think that I've done this a million times before. I don't think about who's watching and how many people and what it's for. I just think that it's a 48-yard field goal. You've made it before. Try to make it again and block out all of the exterior circumstances."

As Vinatieri walked out for his field goal attempt, Proehl and the rest of the St. Louis offense could only watch helplessly after putting together the game-tying drive.

"It was the worst feeling in the world," said Proehl. "They get the ball on the 17-yard line with no timeouts. We just felt like we had them on the ropes at that point. We scored two touchdowns. We were back in this game, we were going to overtime and we're going to pull it off. We've done it all year."

But it would be Vinatieri who would get a chance at football immortality. The New England kicker approached the ball and blasted it towards the gap between the goal posts. The ball soared down the middle and split the uprights perfectly. The clock hit zero and the Patriots were Super Bowl champions with a dramatic, 20–17 victory.

"Sometimes you know right away and sometimes you have to look up," Vinatieri said. "That one was like a good golf shot when it leaves your club and you don't even really feel it. It just feels good and you just automatically know. That one left my foot and it felt really good. I looked up and I had my hands in the air cheering before it was even halfway to the uprights. I just knew it when I left my foot. I looked up and it was halfway there and was starting to celebrate. It wasn't going to go anywhere except for down the middle."

As the Patriots celebrated, the Rams left the field in shock. A team which was a two-touchdown favorite to capture its second Super Bowl title in three years had suffered a heartbreaking defeat. In Super Bowl XXXIV, the Rams had stopped the Tennessee Titans on the one-yard line on the final play. Proehl could now relate to the pain the Titans had felt two years prior.

"It puts things in perspective," said Proehl. "When we won two years prior against Tennessee, you were so caught up in the moment celebrating with your teammates. You don't even think about the other team. When you lose and you're sitting in that locker room, it makes you think what the Tennessee Titans went through. What a horrible feeling it is to lose."

Proehl and his teammates also had little time to absorb the stunning loss on the field as the league quickly prepared the podium for the victorious Patriots.

"You're like cattle," Proehl said. "They just steer you off and send you to the locker room because they've got to get the other team and get their families on the field. They get out the stage and then it's like a cattle call. They just run you off the field."

The Patriots were hardly in a hurry to leave the field. For Izzo and his teammates, the exhilaration of winning the Super Bowl on a last-second kick would last forever.

"You can't describe it," said Izzo. "You're running onto the field watching the winning field goal go in knowing that your team won. It's just the highest of the highs. It's like every little thing you think about as a kid growing up playing football."

Vinatieri had become the second kicker to connect on a game-winning Super Bowl field goal in the closing seconds. Vinatieri admits he hardly spends countless hours reviewing the kick, but will never forget the moment that will be forever remembered by generations of football fans in New England.

"I've only watched that kick maybe a handful of times," said Vinatieri. "It's always the same. I'm always turning to the sidelines fist pumping and screaming before its anywhere near the uprights and hitting the net."

As Brady began his run as one of the greatest quarterbacks in NFL history, Bledsoe moved onto Buffalo during the off-season. The quarterback was forced into a spectator role at Super Bowl XXXVI, but understood the impact the game had on a wounded nation. In the aftermath of 9/11, football had once again brought the country together.

There's a quote from Nelson Mandela," recalled Bledsoe. "Sport can create hope where there once was only despair. It's more powerful than governments in breaking down racial barriers. It laughs in the face of all types of discrimination."

XXXVII
Gruden Gets the Last Laugh

The Tampa Bay Buccaneers hardly possessed a rich history of winning.

Born out of expansion in 1976, the Bucs went through a host of miserable seasons. The franchise lost its first 26 games. Outside of an NFC Championship appearance in 1979, Tampa Bay was hardly a Super Bowl contender. The arrival of Tony Dungy as head coach in 1996 changed the fortunes of the franchise and once again brought the Bucs to the verge of a Super Bowl.

However, Dungy's Buccaneers could never reach pro football's ultimate game.

Enter Jon Gruden.

The fiery head coach took over for Dungy in 2002. The man known as "Chucky" added a new dimension to a team which had dominated on defense but struggled offensively. The result was a trip to Super Bowl XXXVII in San Diego. To reach Super Sunday, the Buccaneers had to get by a longtime nemesis in Philadelphia. The Eagles had beaten Tampa Bay the two previous seasons in the playoffs, but Gruden's Buccaneers overcame the cold, the odds, and an Eagles' squad that had dominated the Bucs the past two seasons. Cornerback Ronde Barber had been part of the Philadelphia failures in the past, and believes Tampa's win in The City of Brotherly Love on that cold January day changed the franchise forever.

"I don't want to diminish what we accomplished after that NFC championship game," said Barber. "But I don't think there's any question that everybody felt that was the major hurdle. That was the one we had to clear. Philly was the best team in the NFC that year. They were our nemesis."

Quarterback Brad Johnson had led the way for the new-look Tampa Bay offense. Johnson will always remember the feeling of walking off the field at Veterans Stadium victorious.

"That was our Super Bowl," said Johnson. "It was on the road. It was in the cold against a team we had nightmares against. We felt satisfaction from that."

The victory sent the Buccaneers to San Diego, where they would face the Oakland Raiders. Oakland had put together an impressive offensive show in 2002, and Quarterback Rich Gannon led the NFL in passing with 4,689 yards. The Raiders made it to Super Bowl XXXVII despite the loss of Gruden, whose rights were traded to Tampa before the start of the season. Much of the focus of this Super Bowl was on Gruden, who had a chance for revenge against the franchise that sent him packing before the 2002 campaign. Gannon insists the hype surrounding Gruden did not serve as a distraction, but felt his teammates created plenty on their own by spending more time on the town than preparing for the biggest game of their lives.

"We didn't handle it well," said Gannon. "We had half the players down there behaving themselves, and half of them running out late at night and partying. For an older team, that was a recipe for disaster."

Barber insists the Bucs were too busy getting ready for the Raiders on a short week to worry about the hype surrounding their head coach.

"That was the big story that week," said Barber. "It was a good story and it was the right story. I don't know if we looked at it as a way to take the attention off us. I think it just added another layer or another dimension to what was our Super Bowl run. We as a team had other things on our mind."

There was only one week between the conference championships and the Super Bowl, so both teams had little time to prepare. Despite flying from Philadelphia to Tampa and then cross-country to San Diego, Johnson believes the short week benefited the Bucs.

"I actually think us playing in the one week kind of helped us," Johnson said. "We were on high-performance mode at that time in the playoffs. We were rolling. I think there could have been a lull if there had been a two-week break."

Barber hardly wanted a long break from football after the emotional high of winning the NFC title game in Philadelphia. He got his wish when the coaches stayed behind on Monday and left one of Tampa Bay's defenders "in charge" of running practice the first day in San Diego.

"Simeon Rice was supposed to be in charge," Quipped Barber. "All of the coaches stayed. They didn't come until Tuesday night with the game plan. There was no anxiety. It was the complete opposite. We were on such a high beating Philly that we just stayed up there. We didn't have time to come down and realize where we were at."

Many believed the Bucs had an advantage thanks to Gruden's knowledge of his former team. Gruden even served as the practice quarterback during the week to better imitate Gannon's tendencies on the field. Barber believes it didn't matter who the practice quarterback was in the days leading up to the game.

"You can say what you want about John knowing the Raiders," Barber said. "Our defense was set up to beat a team just like Oakland. We couldn't write up a better offense to play against. It played right into our hands and it showcased itself in the first series of the game."

As Super Sunday drew closer, and even greater distraction awaited the Raiders. Center Barret Robbins went missing the day before the game after not taking his depression medication. An incoherent Robbins resurfaced later in the evening, but Head Coach Bill Callahan was forced to leave the starting center off the Super Bowl roster.

"We didn't know what was going on," Gannon said. "When he didn't show up for the walk through on Saturday or for the team picture or meetings, there was obviously concern. Once they found him, we didn't know if he was going to play. Eventually, we were told he wasn't able physically to play."

The loss of Robbins left a huge hole in the Oakland front line, and Gannon believes it was a serious setback to the entire offense.

"You're talking about a Pro Bowl center," said Gannon. "You're talking about the lines of communication not just in protection, but the checks in the run game assignments and the rules. It was a big loss because he was a Pro Bowl player that year."

By the time the Raiders took the field in sunny San Diego, Gannon could sense something was not right.

"We came out for pregame warmups," said Gannon. "It was very, very hot and humid. I can just remember guys coming out having a difficult time even catching their breath. We were a much older team on a short week and with the distractions and all that we had going on, it wasn't good."

Even after a week of controversy, Oakland managed to draw first blood. On Tampa's first possession, Johnson was intercepted by Charles Woodson, who brought the ball to the Tampa 36. However, a sack by Rice would force the Raiders to settle for a field goal. Oakland had the lead, but the Bucs already had the momentum.

"We didn't panic when something bad happened," Johnson said. "That was kind of our makeup. In the first quarter, there were a lot of nerves and a lot of energy. We couldn't get in the flow of the game, either them or us. In the second quarter, our offense kind of kicked into gear."

On the ensuing drive, the Buccaneers drove 58 yards on nine plays. Martin Gramatica's 31-yard field goal tied the game at three, and set the stage for a dominating second quarter. Dexter Jackson intercepted Gannon to set up another field goal, and Jackson would intercept another pass on Oakland's next possession. Later in the second quarter, Fullback Mike Alstott plowed in from the two to increase Tampa's lead to 13–3.

"We didn't take into account Gruden's ability to prepare them for some of our code words and some of our checks," Gannon said. "We had to change and make some adjustments. We really struggled in the first half. You combine that with turnovers and mistakes, it was uphill sledding the rest of the way."

The uphill climb got bigger for Oakland just before halftime. With 30 seconds remaining in the second quarter, Johnson hit Keenan McCardell with a five-yard scoring strike. The touchdown gave the Bucs a 20–3 halftime lead, and left Gannon and the Raiders searching for answers.

"They were fast," said Gannon. "They got up-field. We were big and slow. We had some problems initially handling Rice and (Warren) Sapp and some of the speed that they had. The other thing no one talks about is teams that had success against them had a lot of success running the football. We tried to run the ball in the first quarter a little bit, and we got stuffed."

If Gannon wanted answers during halftime, he would receive little help from the Oakland coaching staff.

"Halftime was a disaster," recalled Gannon. "It was handled poorly. We went into the locker room and nobody said anything for the first 15 minutes, which was a huge mistake. The coaching staff should have at least addressed the players. You have that long, extended halftime, and I think most players were just numb."

It was a much different story in the Tampa Bay locker room. The Bucs were brimming with confidence and hardly needed to make any major changes after a dominating first half. Barber even had a chance to enjoy the halftime festivities.

"I actually went into one of the video rooms," Barber said. "I watched the halftime show. There were very little adjustments. We got our rallying call and we did our adjustments and we still had 15 minutes. I watched halftime. It was pretty funny."

There were more smiles for the Buccaneers at the start of the second half. The Raiders punted on their first possession, and the Bucs would again find the end zone on the ensuing possession. An 89-yard drive ended with McCardell's second touchdown catch of the game, and Tampa's lead increased to 34–3.

"We came out in the second half and we stopped them," Johnson said. "Then we had an 89-yard drive. The second and third quarter is probably some of the best football that we've played offensively. We were flowing. It was definitely a knockout blow to a degree."

The Raiders weren't quite down for the count just yet. Oakland scored once in the third and twice early in the fourth to cut the Tampa lead to 34–21. Despite a forgettable evening, the Raiders had pulled to within two scores with 6:06 remaining.

"We were up 34–3," Johnson said. "This thing's over, but they got hot and we had some weird plays happen on us, too."

Despite the late surge by Oakland, Barber and many of the other Bucs were hardly in a state of panic.

"The second half was such a blur," said Barber. "We felt like it was over after the first half. Second-level guys were already playing into the third quarter. I don't know if we took our foot off the gas. We just played a lot more Cover 2. There was not going to be any miraculous comeback. There was no sense they were putting our lead in jeopardy."

The Buccaneers finished off the Raiders with a pair of turnovers in the final minutes. Derrick Brooks intercepted Gannon and went 44-yards for a touchdown. Another pick six from 50-yards out by Dwight Smith with two seconds remaining put an exclamation point on Tampa Bay's dominating 48–21 victory. Jackson's early interceptions earned the safety MVP honors.

"I honestly thought we had nine or ten guys that could have been the MVP of the game," said Johnson. "Dexter Jackson won it. He deserved it. But that's how many different guys played exceptional."

With victory in the bag in the final moments, several of the top Tampa players had the chance to savor the moment on the sidelines. However, Barber was still taking care of business on the field.

"I did not get to take it in," Barber said. "I was actually on the field. I played every snap in the Super Bowl on defense. It's funny, because I was one of the more tenured corners on the team. Brian Kelly was a year younger than me. I'm trying to get him to come back on the field. He was in the stands getting his wife and kids on the field."

While the Buccaneers celebrated the franchise's first world championship, the Raiders were forced to come to grips with a humiliating defeat. Their former coach had the last laugh one year after being cast off by Owner Al Davis.

"The worst decision Al ever made was trading away our head coach," said Gannon. "To get rid of John when we had so many good things going was a colossal mistake."

The mistake of letting Gruden go combined with a volatile mix in the Oakland locker room proved to be too much for Gannon and company to overcome.

"That was a dysfunctional group that somehow found a way to make it through the regular season and into a Super Bowl," Gannon said. "There were a lot of really good players on that team that were professional. It's hard when you have that imbalance on that team and not have everyone pulling the rope together."

For the Buccaneers, the Super Bowl storyline involving their coach remained off their radar until after the final gun.

"He never talked about beating Oakland because he was there," said Johnson. "He never once mentioned it. It was never about him saying we needed to beat his former team so he would look great. It was more of how we could be the best team we could be. When it was over, that's when the players recognized all of the story lines."

The Buccaneers had emerged from their early dark days of expansion to reach pro football's ultimate summit. A franchise with just three playoff appearances in its first 20 years of existence was no longer the butt of jokes around the league, and the veteran players who had lived through years of losing weren't about to take their championship moment for granted.

"We had a parade in Tampa," Johnson said. "We're all in convertibles and there's confetti falling. John Lynch got out of his convertible and started high-fiving the fans. Warren Sapp got out, and there was a time that they hugged. As awesome as it was for me and the city of Tampa, those guys had been there through the tough times. That was a pretty awesome moment."

To this day, Gannon still gets reminders of what went wrong the week before Super Bowl XXXVII. Gannon made a smooth transition off the field into the broadcast booth, and a trip to San Diego for a CBS telecast brought the former quarterback to his Super Bowl hotel. A hotel worker on the concierge level remembered Gannon from his Super Bowl XXXVII visit, and also remembered how much many of his teammates took over the town in the evening.

"She said she had never been so busy," said Gannon. "She said my teammates wanted more car services and more trips to the clubs and this and that. She said it was crazy. To hear something like that, even ten years later, it's hard. Then you find out more from coaches and staff members."

The memories are much different for Barber and his teammates, who will forever have a place in Florida football history.

"People didn't have pride in the organization," said Barber. "This was a town surrounded by a lot of great college football. I think that took precedence and sometimes still takes precedence, but there was a real palpable sense of greatness for once."

XXXVIII
LAST TEAM WITH THE BALL WINS

It was the budding dynasty versus the new kids on the block.

Super Bowl XXXVIII would pit the New England Patriots against the Carolina Panthers. New England would be looking for its second title in three years and appeared to have all the makings of the next NFL dynasty. Carolina was making its first Super Bowl appearance in its nine-year existence, and had rebounded from a disastrous 1–15 campaign two years prior. The Panthers went 11–5 and had to win two of their three playoff games on the road. After finishing off the Eagles in Philadelphia in the NFC title game, Carolina was off to Houston for Super Bowl XXVIII. Receiver Ricky Proehl had been part of two Super Bowl teams in St. Louis, and the veteran was happy to be a part of a history-making season with the Panthers.

"It was awesome," said Proehl. "You're part of history and part of something special. It was a young franchise that had done it the right way. It had a ton of talent, a great defense, and an underrated offense."

The Patriots were underdogs when they upset Proehl and the Rams in Super Bowl XXXVI. Bill Belichick's squad would be the favorites heading into Super Bowl XXXVIII, but New England hardly looked like a contender at the beginning of the season. Five days before the start of the 2003 campaign, Pro Bowl Safety Lawyer Milloy was cut over an issue regarding the restructuring of his contract. Wide Receiver Deion Branch was in his second season with the Patriots, but recognized the impact of the loss of one of the team's most respected players.

"We lose one of our captains over a financial dispute," said Branch. "Nobody saw that coming. It hit us pretty badly. The first game we played was in Buffalo, and he signed with the Bills."

Milloy and the Bills rolled to a 31–0 victory over the Patriots in the season opener, and New England seemed headed for an implosion. However, Belichick and his team moved past the opening day disaster and rattled off 12 straight victories to close out the season at 14–2.

"We got that one out of the way," Branch said. "I think Coach Belichick and his staff understood how it affected us. We didn't allow that to derail us off of our goal. We picked up the momentum and got things going."

Special Teams standout Larry Izzo said the emergence of Rodney Harrison helped soften the blow of Milloy's departure, but admitted it was still a bit of a shock to see Milloy heading out the door.

"It did get off to a rough start at the beginning," said Izzo. "There was some drama when one of your leaders is walking out of the stadium with a trash bag full of his locker."

The Patriots had displayed their resiliency during the 2003 season. Meanwhile, the Panthers' run to Super Bowl XXXVIII surprised much of the football world, and created a whole new generation of fans in the Carolina region.

"It was exciting to see the fans get on board," said Proehl. "You had so many implants from Charlotte that were Redskins fans or Falcons fans. They're becoming Panthers fans because we're winning. It was the birth of a franchise that was on its way."

The two teams had plenty of offensive firepower, but it would be the defenses which would control the tempo throughout much of the first half. The game was scoreless throughout the first 26 minutes, and the aggressive Carolina Defense was more than holding its own against Tom Brady and his high-powered offense.

"They pretty much were doing everything we thought they would do," said Branch. "We knew it was going to be a tough defensive game. Carolina had a great team with a great defense, and we had the same. It was just a tough-fought game early on."

New England was able to move the ball early and had one of the league's most reliable kickers in Adam Vinatieri, but the man who kicked the game winning field goal in Super Bowl XXXVI got off to a rocky start in Super Bowl XXXVIII. The Patriots advanced to the Panthers' nine on their opening drive, but Vinatieri pushed a 31-yard attempt wide to the right. Vinatieri would get another chance with 6:08 remaining in the half, but his 36-yard try was blocked by Shane Burton. The miss of a chip shot followed by the block forced Vinatieri to regroup mentally for the rest of the game.

"I still need to make that kick every time," said Vinatieri. "That's one of those that got away. The next one ended up getting blocked, and now all of a sudden, you're sitting there 0-for-2 going into the end of the game. That can really start to play mind games on you if you're not capable of getting that out of your head and just moving forward."

Izzo had a theory as to why Vinatieri started this Super Bowl with a pair of missed kicks. It stemmed from a bizarre injury to the team's long snapper. Brian Kinchen accidentally cut his hand with a steak knife during the pregame meal, forcing him to wear a large bandage on his hand during Super Bowl XXXVIII.

"You're wondering how he is going to snap," Izzo said. "During the game, he's rolling these punt snaps back to the punter. Ken Walter had to play shortstop. It was a factor in Adam's miss and Adam's block was a bad snap."

While the Patriots were denied a pair of early scoring chances, the Panthers could do little against the New England Defense. Quarterback Jake Delhomme went 1-for-9 to start the game and was sacked three times. One of the sacks was by Linebacker Mike Vrabel, which forced a fumble by Delhomme in Carolina territory. Defensive Lineman Richard Seymour recovered the ball at the 20, and New England was in position to draw first blood.

"We were a ball-control offense," Proehl said. "We were having trouble running the football. When we tried to throw it, we were struggling as well. It was a chess match at that point."

Four plays after the fumble, Brady found Branch open for a five-yard touchdown pass, and New England had a 7–0 lead. Brady's play-action drew the aggressive Carolina linebackers away from the goal line, allowing Branch to find a clear path over the middle.

"Carolina had a very tough defense," Branch said. "But they were vulnerable because they were so aggressive. All 11 guys want to be the guy to make the play. That's a great thing but sometimes, that can harm you."

The touchdown was the spark which set off a series of scores late in the second quarter. Carolina responded with a 95-yard drive, capped off by a 39-yard touchdown catch by Steve Smith. New England got the ball back with 1:07 left in the half and quickly regained the lead. Brady connected with Branch for a 52-yard gain to the Carolina 14. Two plays later, Brady hit David Givens in the end zone to put his team back on top with 18 seconds remaining in the quarter. It appeared the Patriots would head to the locker room up by seven, but a squib kick was returned by Kris Magnum to the Carolina 47. A draw play to Running Back Stephen Davis put the ball on the 32, and John Kasay's 50-yard field goal cut the New England lead to four. It also gave the Panthers plenty of momentum at halftime.

"It was huge," said Proehl. "I think the big thing was they tried to squib it after they scored. They think we're probably going to take a knee, but Dan Henning, who was one of the most intelligent offensive coordinators of my time, calls the draw play."

The defenses regained control in the third quarter, as both teams were held off the board. However, the Patriots put together a drive late in the period. On the second play of the fourth quarter, Antowain Smith scored on a two-yard run to increase New England's lead to 21–10. It would be a prelude to one of the wildest finishes in Super Bowl history.

"The game started out so slow," said Branch. "At some point, the game was going to pick up. When we started to get things going, they picked it up as well. It was almost like both defenses were pretty tired for going so long. It was almost like somebody had to make a play."

Carolina responded on the ensuing drive, and a 33-yard run by DeShaun Foster pulled the Panthers to within five after the two-point conversion try failed. New England answered with a drive to the Carolina nine, but Reggie Howard intercepted Brady in the end zone. Delhomme would later be faced with a third down on his own 15, but the Carolina quarterback connected with Wide Receiver Muhsin Muhammad for an 85-yard touchdown. It was the longest score from scrimmage in Super Bowl history, and it gave the Panthers a 22–21 lead with 6:53 remaining.

"I think they looked at us as a joke and that they were going to come in and run all over us," Proehl said. "When they went up 21–10, they're laughing at us. The next thing you know, we go up, 22–21, and they're cussing each other out and fighting."

As the teams traded touchdowns, Vinatieri was waiting on the sidelines for another chance after a difficult first half.

"It's such a mental and physical drain on you the week before and the week of the game and the game itself," said Vinatieri. "When you have a game that goes back and forth, it really does play a lot on your emotions and the adrenalin that runs through your body. That game was absolutely no different."

It would be New England's turn to answer after the Muhammad touchdown. A 68-yard drive ended when Brady found Vrabel in the end zone. The linebacker had been used on offense in goal line situations in the past, and had lined up as an extra tight end. Kevin Faulk added a two-point conversion to increase the lead to 29–22, but Branch could sense the game was far from over.

"The fourth quarter was the same as the second quarter," said Branch. "There were just fireworks all over the place."

The fireworks continued on Carolina's next possession. The Panthers took over on their own 19 with 2:44 to play. Delhomme once again drove his team down the field, and the Panthers were faced with a third down from the New England 12. Delhomme found Proehl in the right side of the end zone, and Super Bowl XXXVIII was tied with 1:08 remaining.

"They came hard," Proehl said. "It looked like they had some miscommunication. Jake stayed in there and gets rid of it. That ball was in the air for what seemed like 30 seconds. You can see when I catch it, I wasn't aware that I was that wide open. That ball took forever. I could read the ball and see the laces spinning. It was like slow motion."

The two teams appeared to be headed for the first overtime in Super Bowl history, but a mistake by Kasay would help determine the outcome in regulation. The Carolina kicker booted the ball out of bounds, giving the Patriots the ball on their own 40. Brady still had 1:08 remaining and a kicker who had already booted a game-winning Super Bowl field goal.

"This thing was already written for us," said Branch. "Everyone always says you have to get to the 35. For Adam, we were thinking 'Just get it to the 40. We're good.' Let's just get 20 yards, and the game was over. We were going to win or lose with Adam kicking the field goal."

Vinatieri realized he would have a chance to kick the game winner in another Super Bowl, but the kicker sympathized with Kasay after watching the kickoff drift out of bounds.

"It's a break for us," said Vinatieri. "We get the ball at the 40-yard line. You give Tom Brady the ball at the 40-yard line and you're going to score points pretty much every time. I felt happy for us and bad for him. If I had been just watching that game as a bystander, I would have been really, really sick about it."

It was a bad break for the Panthers, who knew they were in dire straits after Casey's kickoff gave Brady a short field to work with.

"I felt really good about it until the ball is kicked out of bounds," Proehl said. "You watch the ball go out of bounds and you bite your lips and try not to say something you regret, but you go to the bench and you wonder what the hell just happened. That was as painful a feeling as I've ever felt. A minute now is an eternity with Tom Brady."

Brady quickly moved the Patriots to the Carolina 40. Branch came up big once again as his 17-yard catch put New England well within Vinatieri's range.

"We always talked about attention to detail," said Branch. Here's another clear cut case where we practiced situational football all season. We knew we had to draw up our best four plays to get into field goal range. There are the things that we practiced that weren't seen by the fans. We've played a game before we get to the game."

For the second time in three years, the Patriots hopes for a world championship rested on the foot of Vinatieri. The kicker trotted out to attempt a

41-yarder as he looked to erase the memory of his first two attempts in the first half.

"It's easier said than done getting bad thoughts out of your head," Vinatieri said. "But that was purely a time that I know as the game progressed, I said 'This is going to come back down to you again.'"

Nine seconds remained in regulation. After a perfect snap by Kinchen, Vinatieri launched the ball towards the goal posts. The ball split the uprights perfectly, and Vinatieri had his second game-winning Super Bowl kick.

"I don't want to call it a déjà vu feeling," said Vinatieri. "But it was to get this through the uprights, and everything else is water under the bridge. We as a group all zoned back in. Brian Kinchen was our long snapper at the time and Ken Walter was our holder and they did a great job, and the guys up front did a fabulous job."

New England's 32–29 victory was capped off by one of the greatest quarters in history. The two teams had combined for Super Bowl record 37 points in the final period. The last three came off the foot of Vinatieri, who was a Super Bowl hero once again.

"That was more of a relief after I kicked that one," recalled Vinatieri. "It felt good leaving my foot. I looked up and saw it going down the middle, and thought 'Oh, thank God.'"

While the Patriots celebrated their second Super Bowl title, the valiant Panthers were left heartbroken after coming so close to their first ever championship.

"They were going to take a knee," said Proehl. "Jon kicks it out of bounds, and the rest is history."

Many consider Super Bowl XXXVIII to be one of the greatest Super Bowls of all time. It was clear that both sides had emptied the tank, and jubilation soon gave way to exhaustion for the Patriots.

"I was emotionally spent and physically done," recalled Branch. "It was probably the most physical game I've ever been a part of. I went to dinner with my family after the game. It was probably my worst dinner ever despite the fact I was so happy. My head was banging and my body was aching the entire time, but I was so excited for my family."

Even the New England kicker was drained after the frantic finish, but Vinatieri had taken his place in Super Bowl history with two game-winning kicks in three years.

"We were favored in that game," Vinatieri said. "In the Rams game, we were big time underdogs. In this game, we were expected to win. I think everybody was a little relieved and overjoyed."

XXXIX
Three Out of Four

It would be dynasty versus destiny in Super Bowl XXXIX.

The New England Patriots arrived in Jacksonville looking for their third world championship in four years. A victory would put the Pats in the company of teams which had carved their place among the best Super Bowl teams of all time. New England rolled to another impressive season and finished with a record of 14–2. In the playoffs, the Patriots smothered Peyton Manning and the Colts before beating the Steelers in Pittsburgh to claim another AFC crown. While many of the Patriots were looking for their third Super Bowl ring, Deion Branch was hoping to capture his second. The talented wide receiver knew the Pats were set up for another Super Bowl run at the start of the 2004 campaign with Tom Brady back at the helm.

"The sky was the limit," said Branch. "We knew we had pretty much the same team coming back. We had another Super Bowl under our belts. It was another year with Tom and we started to hit our stride."

The sky always seemed to be the limit in Philadelphia, but the Eagles had paid their dues before reaching pro football's ultimate game. Head Coach Andy Reid had built the franchise into a consistent contender, but Philadelphia had lost three straight NFC Championship games heading into the 2004 season. This time, the crown finally fit as Philadelphia rolled past Atlanta in the NFC Championship. Eagles Linebacker and Special Teams Captain Ike Reese was happy to finally put the ghosts of playoff failures to rest.

"It was a relief," said Reese. "You get somewhat of a pass the first year we went. The next two were very disappointing at home. They were just heartbreaking losses."

One of the big reasons for Philadelphia's success in 2004 was the acquisition of Terrell Owens. The talented but enigmatic wide receiver provided a huge boost to the Eagles' offense. However, Owens suffered a broken leg against Dallas late in the season and was forced to miss both of Philadelphia's playoff games. Many did not expect Owens to return for the Super Bowl and even his own teammates were kept in the dark the week after the NFC title game. Reese finally got a chance to check on Owens' progress as he worked with trainer Rick Burkholder.

"We caught the end of Rick and T.O. rehabbing," Reese said. "It was the first time we saw him do anything other than limp around. He was still hobbling, but we hadn't seen him move or jog. He didn't look good."

Owens was determined to play, and his progress improved as Super

Sunday drew closer. However, Owens would play at his own risk. The Eagles forced him to sign a waiver since the team had not given Owens medical clearance.

"There were only a few of us who knew about the waiver thing before the game," said Reese. "I can still remember sitting down in the hotel in our makeshift training room. T.O. happens to be hanging in there with us one night. He kind of brought it up then. He said he had to sign a waiver to release the Eagles of any responsibility if something happens to him on the field. They weren't going to let him play unless he signed it. Part of me was thinking, "Are you crazy?""

Fellow wide receiver Greg Lewis was preparing for extra snaps due to Owens' injury, but wasn't surprised to see Owens suit up for the Super Bowl.

"I wasn't surprised at all that he was going to play in that game," said Lewis. "When he got hurt in the Dallas game that year, he said 'Just get us to the Super Bowl and I'll be there.'"

As the drama surrounding Owens captured much of the pregame headlines, the Patriots were going about their business like a team accustomed to the Super Bowl spotlight. Branch and his teammates heard plenty of noise from their opponents throughout the week, but weren't about to be intimidated by an Eagles' team making its first Super Bowl appearance in 24 years.

"We kind of expected that from those guys," Branch said. "Leading up to the Super Bowl, there was a lot of trash talking going on. They had a lot of 'mc' guys on that team, so you've got to expect that type of stuff to come from them. We just stayed under the radar. That's the type of guys we had on our team."

Staying under the radar in Jacksonville wasn't easy. Philadelphia's rabid fan base had taken over the town. Reese and his teammates were greeted with thunderous ovations every time they returned to their hotel rooms. Jacksonville had been painted green, and Eagles fans clearly outnumbered Patriots followers at this Super Bowl.

"I said we were going down to Jacksonville to turn it into Phillyville," said Reese. That's exactly what we did. It wasn't 'we' as in the players. It was 'we' as in the city of Philadelphia, the Delaware Valley, and Eagles fans everywhere. They had waited so long to get back to that game. There had been a lot of disappointments since the last time they were there. They embraced it."

Eagles fans may have gotten ahead of themselves. On the morning of the Super Bowl, Patriots Coach Bill Belichick told his team the details of a victory parade planned in Philadelphia two days after the Super Bowl. Players such as special teams ace Larry Izzo took notice.

"That's just the perfect type of motivation for that game," said Izzo.

"You've still got a few hours before the game and a bunch of emotions are going to go up and down prior to when you're actually playing, but it was a perfect ending for the last team meeting of the year."

One Patriot used to being front and center in victory parades was Adam Vinatieri. The Patriots kicker booted game-winning field goals at the end of the last two New England Super Bowls, and Vinatieri was well aware the outcome of this Super Bowl could once again ride on his right foot.

"I was very much anticipating it coming down to the end," said Vinatieri. "Two of the last three years, it came down to my foot, so I had better be ready again."

Neither offense appeared to be ready at the start of Super Bowl XXXIX, although the Eagles had their share of scoring chances. On Philadelphia's fourth possession, Quarterback Donovan McNabb connected with Owens on a 30-yard pass. An interception was wiped out by a penalty, but McNabb's second chance was also picked off in the end zone by Rodney Harrison. Philadelphia moved the ball to the New England 38 on its next possession, but a fumble by Tight End L.J. Smith gave the ball back to the Patriots. The Eagles had let a pair of early opportunities slip away.

"They were slow out of the gate offensively," said Reese. "We were moving the ball. We just kept shooting ourselves in the foot. You know against a Belichick-coached team and a Tom Brady team, you had better take advantage of mistakes early. You know that team will make adjustments and make a run in the end."

Meanwhile, the New England Offense could do little in the first quarter. Branch and the Patriots were facing a much different type of defense than the one they had faced in Super Bowl XXXVIII.

"They had the numbers over Carolina," Branch said. "Carolina was just way more physical. Philadelphia's defense had a few physical guys in Brian Dawkins and a couple of their linebackers. After that, it was pretty much a very athletic team. These guys didn't make a lot of mistakes. They were always around the football and they had some great corners."

After another New England punt, the Eagles put together the first scoring drive of the game. McNabb marched his offense 81 yards, and his six-yard pass to Smith gave Philadelphia a 7–0 lead early in the second quarter. New England would move the ball on its next possession, but Darwin Walker recovered a Brady fumble inside the five. The Patriots got another chance on their next drive, and Brady connected with David Givens on a four-yard scoring strike with 1:10 remaining in the second quarter.

"We had a great game plan going in," recalled Branch. "It just took us a little while to get into it. That's what you'd expect out of a Super Bowl."

While the Patriots believed their game plan was falling into place, the Eagles were lamenting their missed opportunities over the first two quarters.

"I can remember thinking that we left a lot of plays out there on the field," Reese said. "You know that team isn't going to play that way for 60 minutes. When you don't take advantage of it in the first half, they're going to collect themselves and play much better in the second half, and that's what they did."

The Patriots had plenty of time to collect themselves. New England had been used to the long Super Bowl halftime. Reese and the Eagles were not, and the linebacker watched a former Beatle exit the field as he came out of the tunnel for the second half.

"We weren't ready to handle that long halftime," said Reese. "You've got a lot of time to sit there and think about missed opportunities. By the time we hit the field, there was two minutes left before kickoff and they were still getting Paul McCartney off the stage."

Branch and the Patriots quickly went to work on their first possession of the second half. The receiver made four catches for 71 yards on the drive, with the final reception putting New England at the Philadelphia two-yard line. In came Linebacker Mike Vrabel, who the Patriots had used as a tight end in goal-line situations.

"I'll never forget going off the field," recalled Branch. "He was laughing. I'm coming off and he's yelling 'Goal line!' and he's just laughing. Everybody had so much fun and just to see that from our guys and how excited they were going in, he knew he was going to do something special."

Vrabel did indeed do something special, as his juggling two-yard touchdown catch gave the Patriots a 14–7 lead.

"There were so many different mismatches," said Branch. "Vrabel was our outside linebacker, but ran like a receiver, and he's going against a linebacker. It was just a complete mismatch."

"They made great adjustments at halftime," recalled Reese. "I didn't think we did our best job of making adjustments. It took us a little while to figure out what they were trying to do to us."

After punting on the ensuing possession, the Philadelphia Offense did some adjusting of its own. The Eagles drove to the New England ten, and McNabb threw a perfect strike over the middle to Brian Westbrook to tie the score at 14–14. For the first time in Super Bowl history, the game was tied heading into the final quarter.

As they had in two previous Super Bowl appearances, New England found a way when the game was on the line. The Patriots used screen passes and misdirection plays against the aggressive Eagles Defense as they moved deep into Philadelphia territory.

"It was a different wrinkle that they had shown," Reese said. "What else would you expect from those guys? They really used our strength against us. We were an attacking-style defense, so what they would do is get in formations where we would bring in our nickel defense. They would either dump the ball short with Kevin Faulk, or they would run the ball out of a three wide receiver formation and give it to Corey Dillon. We didn't have our big people in the game."

Dillon ended the drive with a two-yard touchdown run to put New England ahead, 21–14. After forcing another Philadelphia punt, New England marched back into Eagles territory with the help of another big catch by Branch. The receiver was well covered by Cornerback Sheldon Brown, but Branch somehow managed to reach above Brown and take the ball away for one of the game's biggest receptions.

"It's called a ten route," said Branch. "I was the slot guy. We needed that play badly. It was a coverage where I never thought Tom would throw it to me. Tom didn't go through his first two reads. He went straight to me. In that coverage, it's mainly designed for your running back or your tight end."

It is a catch Brown is forced to relive on a yearly basis each time he has the opportunity to talk with Branch.

"Sheldon and I have the same agent," Branch said. "We still talk about that play to this day. Every time we get together every year, he just looks at me like 'How did you make that catch?' Tom put it exactly where it needed to be. Tom did his job, and it was up to me to do mine. You couldn't have played any better defense than that."

The Patriots moved closer before sending out Vinatieri for a 22-yard attempt. The man who had kicked game-winning field goals in the closing seconds of the past two New England Super Bowls faced far less pressure in Super Bowl XXXIX. Vinatieri connected on his only field goal opportunity of the game to stretch New England's lead to 24–14.

"My mindset is exactly the same every time I step onto the field," said Vinatieri. "The time that you think a 22-yarder or a 30-yarder is the time you lose concentration and lose focus, and things happen the wrong way. I try to approach a 22-yarder the same as a 50-yarder."

Another McNabb interception followed by a New England punt left 5:40 remaining on the clock. What followed would be one of the most bizarre scoring drives in Super Bowl history. The Eagles moved the ball 79 yards on 13 plays, but showed little urgency. Philadelphia continued to huddle instead of running a hurry-up offense, and precious time began to tick away.

The Patriots weren't complaining.

"It was a little weird for us to see that," said Branch. "We're so used to being on the other side and getting to the line and hurrying up to try and get down and score. These guys were all lethargic, which was great for us."

Reese was on the sidelines with his defensive teammates and watched helplessly as the Eagles lost valuable time late in the fourth quarter.

"I just know we're on the sidelines saying the same things that everyone else is saying," recalled Reese. "We're saying 'Hurry up! What are we doing? Hurry up!' We're watching the clock and we're watching basically how we are taking our time."

The drive ended with a catch by Lewis to cut the lead to 24–21. However, the 3:52 drive left the Eagles with little time. The clock was down to 1:48 after Lewis made his leaping 30-yard grab in the end zone.

"It did take us a long time to get down there," said Lewis. "We just didn't execute at a high level at that time. We got what we wanted which was a touchdown, but we didn't preserve enough time to get ourselves a legitimate chance to come back."

In Philadelphia, there are more conspiracy theories about the drive than the Kennedy Assassination. One rumor involves McNabb suffering from dry heaves during the drive, but Reese believes the pounding his quarterback took in the second half took its toll.

"He took a hit when he tried to run during that drive," Reese said. "I remember him holding his back going back to the huddle. It was almost like he was laboring just a little bit. You could tell the hit had an impact on him."

The score was 24–21, but time was almost up for Philadelphia. While the Eagles were not executing at a high level, Branch and the Patriots were once again seizing the moment.

"It's situational football," Branch said. "I'm pretty sure their coach had them go through this a lot. He's a great coach. It was probably issues with the personnel. Who knows? A lot of guys kind of fold under pressure with certain situations like this. Coach Belichick put us through that time after time every day in practice."

The Eagles elected to try an onside kick, but the Patriots recovered and took more time off the clock with three straight running plays. A punt pinned the Eagles on their own four-yard line with 46 seconds remaining. A desperation pass by McNabb was deflected and intercepted by Harrison, and the Patriots were world champions for the third time in four years. The final minutes capped off a frustrating night for Reese and his teammates, and Reese was not happy about the decision to try an onside kick.

"We've got two timeouts left after we score that touchdown," Reese said. "They're going to run the ball because they want to run the clock out. We've got two timeouts. Say we force them to punt from inside the 30. Maybe we get the ball back at our 35 or 40 yard-line. All we need is a field goal."

Branch was named the game's Most Valuable Player, finishing with 133 receiving yards on 11 catches. Branch was still focused on the sidelines as time expired and didn't realize he had won the award until a teammate asked him to turn around.

"David Patten hit me and the shoulder," Recalled Branch. "He said 'Look behind you.' There were eight guys with suits on. They were standing right behind me as if they were trying to get into our huddle. One of the guys said I was the MVP if we win the game. All of the guys were so excited. That just goes to show you how we value the game and how much love and respect we have for each other."

As is the case with many Super Bowl MVP's, Branch was quick to give credit to his teammates and believes several other Patriots could have won the award. Harrison's two interceptions made the defensive back MVP worthy, and the two former teammates have had plenty of "discussions" about the award.

"Rodney had one interception and he ends the game with another," Branch said. "Every time we talk, he says 'You know you have my trophy.' I tell him it's too bad he waited too late to get his second pick."

The parade plans were cancelled in Philadelphia, and the Eagles' teams of the 2000's would never reach Super Sunday again. Owens did his part in defeat despite his leg injury, finishing with nine catches for 122 yards. At the time, Lewis would have never believed it would be his last Super Bowl appearance as a player.

"I was in the NFC Championship my first year," Lewis said. "The second year, I was in the Super Bowl. I thought that this is how the NFL is and I'm going to be here all the time. Here comes year three, and we weren't good. That's when it hit that it's hard to get to where we've been. It's real hard."

As hard as it was for Reese and his teammates to accept the outcome, the wound would grow deeper nearly a decade later. In 2007, the Patriots were disciplined for videotaping coaching signals by the New York Jets during a 2007 game in a non-designated area. Reports surfaced that the Patriots were using a similar practice since 2000, causing many of the Eagles to wonder if New England had an extra advantage in Super Bowl XXXIX.

"They cheated us," Reese said. "Spygate was real. That happened. The commissioner destroyed the tapes. We don't get to see what the Patriots were actually doing to us and to other teams as well. We lost the game on the field, so it's not as if I would want a championship after the fact. To hear all the allegations afterwards, it makes sense why they've been so damn good for so long."

But history will show the Patriots took their place as one of pro football's all-time great teams. It would be Vinatieri's last Super Bowl with New England before winning another championship in Indianapolis.

"I guess I didn't really realize how good we were," said Vinatieri. "They've done a very good job staying very consistent for a long time. I was fortunate to be with the first half of that. I guess I have a greater appreciation when I step back from it and look back at it."

The Patriots would make three more Super Bowl appearances over the next decade, but the team which took three out of four on Super Bowl Sunday will forever have its place as a dynasty.

"It was a truly great run," Branch said. "It was probably one of the greatest teams in history."

XL
FINALLY ONE FOR THE THUMB

The Pittsburgh Steelers had heard enough about the glory days.

The franchise won four Super Bowls in the 1970's but had played in only one championship game since they last hoisted the Lombardi Trophy. In Super Bowl XXX, The Steelers lost to the Dallas Cowboys, who joined the San Francisco 49ers as the only two franchises to win five Super Bowls.

Pittsburgh's path to another Super Bowl appearance was littered with frustrating road blocks. The Steelers lost three AFC Championship Games, with the most painful defeat coming in 2004. After a 15-1 season and the emergence of rookie Quarterback Ben Roethlisberger, the Steelers were beaten at home by New England. Linebacker James Farrior remembered the aftermath in the locker room and the devastation on the faces of Roethlisberger and Wide Receiver Hines Ward. Farrior also knew Running Back Jerome Bettis was running out of chances to become a champion.

"We were a number one seed," said Farrior. "We were 15-1. We had a lot of expectations and a lot going for us, and we came up short that year. Ben was crying and Hines was crying. Ben was trying to get Jerome back for another season, and he promised him we would get to the Super Bowl."

Roethlisberger and his teammates would fulfill their promise in 2005, but the Steelers would get to Super Bowl XL the hard way. At 7-5, Pittsburgh won its last four regular season games along with three playoff road contests. Victories in Cincinnati, Indianapolis and Denver sent the Steelers to Detroit for the 40th edition of Super Sunday. After falling as a favorite in previous playoff contests, Head Coach Bill Cowher believes the role of road warriors worked to his team's advantage.

"We had to win all of them to get into the playoffs," said Cowher. "I think one thing that happens is you get into a place where it just becomes you against everybody else. We felt like we were kind of on a mission. We liked being on the road. It was kind of like us against everybody."

The Steelers were also on a mission for Bettis, who was expected to retire after the game. The popular running back was honored by his teammates on the flight to Detroit with a special dress code.

"He was so receptive of his role on the team," Cowher said. "He was kind of our closer. Willie Parker was the guy that kind of got us going. On the plane going to Detroit, all of the players showed up in Jerome Bettis jerseys. That spoke volumes for the kind of impact he had on the football team."

Waiting for Bettis and the Steelers were the Seattle Seahawks, who were making their first Super Bowl appearance. Seattle's road to the Super Bowl was less bumpy after a 13–3 season. The Seahawks defeated Washington and Carolina at home to punch their ticket to Detroit. The Super Bowl berth was the third for Head Coach Mike Holmgren, who had guided Green Bay to a pair of championship games. Holmgren's quest for perfection in practice helped mold Seattle into an NFC Champion and brought out the best in players such as Quarterback Matt Hasselbeck.

"Mike Holmgren was the most demanding coach I've ever been around," said Hasselbeck. "The hardest part of the week was playing at a high enough standard for him. Getting to Sundays and playing against the opponent was nothing compared to the challenge of never letting the ball hit the ground in practice the entire week."

Hasselbeck shared time with Trent Dilfer before becoming the full-time starter in 2003. With the help of Running Back Shaun Alexander, Hasselbeck and the Seahawks put together the NFL's top-ranked offense in 2005. Seattle arrived in Detroit with a host of confidence, but Hasselbeck decided to do everything he could in his hotel room to block out any distractions during Super Bowl week.

"It had this huge armoire," said Hasselbeck. "I slid the remote behind it so that I could never get to it. It wasn't like TV was off limits, but if I was going to watch TV, I would have physically had to get up from my bed to manually turn the channel. For me, TV was less of a distraction. I was a little bit of a prisoner in my own hotel room."

Meanwhile, the Steelers wanted to take the same approach to the Super Bowl as they did for their three road victories in the playoffs.

"We had the choice of which jersey we wanted to wear," said Cowher. "We wore our road white jerseys because that's how we got there. I think at that point, that team was such a team of resiliency and a very close football team. It didn't matter where they played."

While much of the attention was on Bettis, the veteran would be playing a supporting role to Parker. The second-year back was now entrenched as the starter, and Parker had a chance to reflect on going from an undrafted free agent to playing in the biggest game of the year.

"We were jacked up," said Parker. "We always dreamed about it growing up as kids. It was really a big moment. I can't even explain the feeling of your first Super Bowl appearance. We had finally made it."

After a slow start by both teams, Seattle was able to move the ball to the Pittsburgh 16. Hasselbeck connected with Darrell Jackson for a touchdown, but the receiver was called for pass interference. Replays showed some contact with Jackson and Safety Chris Hope, but many on the Seattle sideline believed it was not enough to draw a penalty. The Seahawks settled for a field goal, but the penalty against Jackson would be the first of several controversial calls in Super Bowl XL.

"That was a big play for us," Farrior said. "I think it was a little deflating for them. They never really recovered from that."

"There were a couple of penalties on that drive," Hasselbeck said. "We overcame them then we had the touchdown to Darrell Jackson. They threw a flag and called the touchdown off, which was super disappointing. We did everything we could on that opening drive, but we came away with three instead of seven."

The Seahawks still had the lead, and the Steelers could generate little offense in the early stages of the game. Pittsburgh did not pick up a first down in the opening quarter, and started the second period with a punt and an interception. Roethlisberger finally sparked the offense with a 37-yard completion to Hines Ward on 3rd and 28. The catch moved the Steelers to the Seahawks' three.

"That's one of those plays he had been doing," Cowher said. "He got out of the pocket and you say 'no, no, no … oh, great play.' He threw it across the field to Hines and I didn't think it would ever come down."

Three plays later, Roethlisberger dove in from the one for the first touchdown of the game. Replays showed the Pittsburgh quarterback may not have crossed the goal line, but the touchdown stood after a video review. The stunned Seahawks went to the locker room trailing, 7–3, despite having the better of the play throughout much of the first half.

"We were extremely disappointed at halftime," said Hasselbeck. "We didn't at the time know what was wrong. Why weren't we scoring enough points? Looking back, I think we were trying too hard."

While the Seahawks were looking to regroup, the Steelers believed they would be able to correct their mistakes from the first two quarters.

"It was a hard-fought game in the first half on both sides of the ball," Parker said. "We had time at halftime to figure out pretty much what they were good at, and we were able to make the adjustments."

The adjustments paid off for Pittsburgh on the second play from scrimmage in the third quarter. Parker followed a block from Guard Alan Faneca on the right side and raced 75-yards for a touchdown. It was the longest rushing touchdown in Super Bowl history, and it gave the Steelers a 14–3 lead.

"I can't really take all the credit for it," said Parker. "Alan Faneca made a great block. Before that play, he pretty much came to me and painted that picture in my head. I can't ever take full credit for that play."

Cowher also gave credit to Faneca, and it was not uncommon for the left guard to pull to his right to open up a hole for the likes of Parker during the season.

"That's kind of the staple for his career," said Cowher. "He was the kind of guy we ran behind. If we ran left, we ran behind him. If we ran right, we pulled him to run behind him. He was pulling from his left guard position to the right. He got a great block and Willie just made a great run. Once Willie Parker was in the clear, nobody could catch him."

After Seattle's Josh Brown missed a 50-yard field goal, Pittsburgh appeared poised to put the game away. Roethlisberger moved the Steelers to the Seahawks' seven, but a pass to the right side was intercepted by Kelly Herndon. The Seattle cornerback raced 76 yards and set Hasselbeck and the offense up on the Pittsburgh 20. Three plays later, Hasselbeck hit Jerramy Stevens for a 16-yard score, and the Seahawks trailed by four with 6:45 remaining in the third quarter. It remained 14–10 entering the final period, and the Seahawks moved into Pittsburgh territory looking to take the lead. Once again, a controversial call contributed to Seattle's downfall. Hasselbeck completed a pass to Stevens at the Pittsburgh one, but a holding call against Tackle Sean Locklear wiped out the play.

"It was my absolute favorite play that we've ever designed for a red zone opportunity," Hasselbeck said. "It was an absolute touchdown. I was so excited when the play actually got called. I just lost my cool. When they threw the flag, I really thought that it was offside."

The Seahawks' frustration only increased with a look at the replay on the video board. Some believed Locklear did not commit the infraction, but the penalty resulted in a ill-advised call by Hasselbeck and Holmgren three plays later. The result was an interception by Ike Taylor.

"I could not regain my composure," said Hasselbeck. "I was so angry. I was going off on (Referee) Bill Leavy and probably owed him an apology. We called a play with four verticals with everybody going deep. I tried to force the ball to Darrell Jackson again. I lost my focus and he didn't look for the ball. It was really a terrible interception. The blame was mine."

"That kind of set the wheels in motion for us to go ahead and take control of that game," Farrior said.

Taylor returned the ball to the Pittsburgh 29. Hasselbeck made the tackle, but was flagged for a 15-yard penalty. Hasselbeck appeared to be going for Taylor, but the official ruled the Seattle quarterback was diving at the blocker running next to Taylor, which resulted in the infraction.

"I really made one of the best plays I ever made as a defensive player in my life," Hasselbeck said. "They called that penalty."

While the Seahawks were still steaming, the Steelers quickly took advantage of their opportunity. Four plays after the Taylor interception, Wide Receiver Antwaan Randle El threw an option pass to Ward for a 43-yard touchdown to increase Pittsburgh's lead with 8:56 remaining.

"He had been doing that all season," Farrior said. "We had probably done that three or four times during the season. He was a former quarterback at Indiana and they always created some type of play for him. That was definitely the best pass of the game."

Seattle would be shutout the rest of the way. The combination of the controversial calls and the play of the Pittsburgh Defense began to wear on Hasselbeck and his teammates.

"We could sense it as a defense," recalled Farrior. "We didn't hold any reservations of letting them know how things were going and what was going on in the game. We added a little bit of trash talking in there and tried to get them rattled a little bit. I don't know if it really worked or not, but it seems like it could have."

The 21–10 final gave Pittsburgh its fifth Super Bowl title. The first four Lombardi Trophies for the franchise had been presented to longtime owner Art Rooney. Now, it was Dan Rooney's turn 26 years later. The son of the popular Pittsburgh Owner raised the tiffany trophy with thousands of Terrible Towels waving in the background by the legion of Steelers fans.

"The biggest thing is the journey," Cowher said. "You think about the journey that a team takes through the course of the year. For me, to be able to win a championship with the Pittsburgh Steelers and to hand that trophy to Mr. Rooney … that's what made it worthwhile."

It was hardly a worthwhile Super Bowl for the Seahawks, who were still angry at the host of controversial calls. However, time has allowed Hasselbeck to put Super Bowl XL in perspective, and considered the game to be a lesson learned about something far more important than football. Hasselbeck does not blame the officials for the result of the biggest game of his life.

"I refuse to buy into that," said Hasselbeck. "We would have won if we played better, and that's really the truth of it." That's something my kids know is never, ever allowed in our house. You can never talk about or complain about officials after a game. I'm sort of grateful for having that perspective on it having been a dad of kids who are now teenagers."

Bill Leavy would not be assigned a Seattle game to work until after Holmgren retired from coaching. In 2009, Leavy's crew was working a Seattle game in San Francisco, and the referee made it a point to seek out Hasselbeck.

"We got him in '09 in Jim Mora's first year after Mike had left," Hasselbeck said. "He came up to me in pregame with kind of an emotional look on his face. He said 'Young man, I owe you an apology.' It meant a lot to me that he said that. I said to him that I appreciated that but, like me, he's trying to do the best he can."

While the classy Hasselbeck accepted his Super Bowl fate, the Steelers were basking in the franchise's return to glory. After over a quarter of a century of waiting, the Steelers finally had their fifth Super Bowl crown.

"Being part of that Steeler tradition is great," Parker said. "Super Bowl XL was really big for the organization and really big for the city."

XLI
Colts Wash Away Bears

Super Bowl XLI would be a test of wills between the Indianapolis Colts and the Chicago Bears. It would also be a battle with Mother Nature.

As the Colts and Bears headed to Miami for the Super Bowl, little did the two teams know they were about to play in the worst weather conditions in Super Bowl history. The long range forecast mattered little to the two conference champions as they arrived in South Florida to battle for the Vince Lombardi Trophy. The Colts may have been relieved more than ecstatic after finally conquering the mighty Patriots in the AFC Championship game. New England had knocked Indianapolis out of the post season in two of the three previous years. This time, Peyton Manning staged the biggest comeback in conference championship history as the quarterback rallied the Colts past the Patriots and into the Super Bowl. For Defensive Lineman Robert Mathis, the end of the Patriots' mastery over the Colts was a symbol of destiny for his team.

"I think a whole lot of guys on that team would agree that beating the Patriots to get to that Super Bowl kind of meant more than the actual Super Bowl," said Mathis. "It exercised a lot of demons. After we beat them, we were confident we were going to finish the job."

Most of the Colts hadn't experienced the thrill of advancing to the Super Bowl in their careers. Manning and Head Coach Tony Dungy had enjoyed plenty of success in the NFL, but had yet to savor a Super Bowl appearance. It was a different story for their kicker. Adam Vinatieri had been a part of three Super Bowl champions in New England and had booted game winning field goals at the end of two of the victories. Indianapolis had signed Vinatieri at the start of the season, and the clutch kicker was hoping to provide another game-winning boot in Super Bowl XLI.

With much of the pregame attention on Manning's first Super Bowl appearance, the Chicago Bears had given the Windy City its first Super Bowl berth since the legendary 1985 squad. Despite a 13–3 record, the Bears were a seven-point underdog thanks largely to the quarterback comparison. While Manning was carving a path to the Hall of Fame, Chicago Quarterback Rex Grossman had been through a roller coaster season. The former first round pick had thrown 23 touchdown passes in 2006, but had also been picked off 20 times. Chicago's defense had been a big factor in the team's run to the Super Bowl and Cornerback Charles Tillman could sense a lack of respect for his team as the Bears arrived in Miami.

"We were playing Peyton Manning in the Super Bowl," said Tillman. Peyton Manning was still in his prime. Everyone just assumed that the Colts would win because it was Peyton Manning's first Super Bowl. I think it's safe to say we got a sense that we didn't have any respect."

The rest of the NFL had plenty of respect for the Bears. That included the New Orleans Saints, who were beaten by Chicago in the NFC Championship game. After shutting down Drew Brees and the high-powered New Orleans Offense, Tillman and his teammates faced a similar test in Manning.

"You prepared for him like you would Drew Brees," Tillman said. "You know he's going to get some good throws here and there. You just have to limit his big plays down the field."

While the Colts and Bears prepared for each other, the two teams were not prepared for the deluge that was to come on Super Sunday. The rain began to fall early and often and Super Bowl XLI would be played in a steady downpour. After years of Super Bowls under sunny skies and climate controlled domes, this Super Bowl was suitable for Noah's Ark.

"It was something else," recalled Mathis. "It was the first time ever it rained on a Super Bowl. We were thinking we were going to get that nice, sunny Miami weather, but it didn't happen."

"You're in Miami and you're hoping it's going to be 75 and beautiful," said Vinatieri. "Sure enough, it rained the whole time we were there. It was a little bit miserable but if you win at the end, that's all that matters."

While most players weren't thrilled about playing in the rain, Tillman was hoping the weather-tested Bears could use the wet weather as an advantage against a team that called a dome its home during the season.

"We played in Chicago and played in the elements," Tillman said. "As a defensive player, I think it works more in our favor. If you're on offense, running the ball is slippery. Catching the ball as a receiver hinders and hurts you more. I felt like it was going to help us, because they were going to have to slow the ball down and I really loved our front seven."

Vinatieri was not as thrilled as Tillman. The Indianapolis kicker had dealt with his share of bad weather during his days in New England, but wasn't happy about the prospect of dealing with a slick surface at the Super Bowl.

"It was a difficult game," said Vinatieri. "It pretty much rained the whole game. The footing was pretty soft. The balls were wet, so they were pretty hard to catch and kick. You probably saw a few more dropped passes and the ball on the ground a little bit more than you normally would have. You go out there and prepare the best you can."

One player who handled the elements well on the opening kickoff was Devin Hester. The rookie returner took Vinatieri's opening kick 92-yards for a touchdown. The Bears had grabbed the lead and the momentum just 14 seconds into the game.

"We kick it to Devin Hester," Vinatieri said. "A couple of guys go sliding around and the next thing you know, he's going 92 yards for a touchdown. You never know what to expect in a Super Bowl. You just have to react and prepare the best you can."

As the Bears celebrated on the sidelines, Tillman took in the touchdown with cautious optimism. The cornerback knew they were nearly four full quarters of football remaining.

"It was very exciting," recalled Tillman. "But football is a game of momentum. There was so much football left to be played. I was really hoping the rest of the team didn't get caught up just on that one play. I really wanted them to reset."

It was the Colts who would reset after Manning threw an interception on the ensuing drive. On Indianapolis' next possession, Manning threw his first Super Bowl touchdown pass. The quarterback connected with Reggie Wayne for a 53-yard scoring strike to pull Indianapolis to within one. Wayne was wide open inside the 20 and ran in untouched thanks to a communication breakdown in the Chicago secondary. Safety Danieal Manning was supposed to help on the play, but Wayne was free after he got past Tillman before streaking downfield.

"He was in a different coverage," Tillman said. "He didn't get the check. We were in cover two. He was playing cover three, so I jammed Reggie Wayne and tried to funnel him to the safety. I look up as the ball is getting thrown over my head. I'm thinking 'Where's the safety?' They scored the touchdown and it was really a communication breakdown."

Vinatieri never got a chance to tie the game as the snap on the extra point slipped through the hands of holder Hunter Smith. On the ensuing kickoff, Vinatieri was under strict orders not to allow Hester to touch the ball. Vinatieri would use squib kicks each time he was asked to kick off the rest of the game.

"Our coach talked to us after the kickoff return," recalled Vinatieri. "He said 'We're not kicking him the ball ever again in this game.' We basically broke our sword because we said 'do not kick him the ball.' He could single-handedly ruin a game for you."

"We went into the game talking about how he was one of their weapons," Mathis said. "We knew that Devin Hester was a game-changer. From that point on, we were thinking 'don't kick him the ball.'"

The Bears would have to find different ways to score. After the teams exchanged fumbles in the soggy conditions, Chicago Running Back Thomas Jones raced 52 yards to the Indianapolis five-yard line. Three plays later, Grossman connected with Muhsin Muhammad for a four-yard score. Chicago had a 14–6 lead after one quarter of play in Super Bowl XLI. The Bears forced a punt and appeared to be in position to move downfield for another score, but a fumble by Cedric Benson set the Colts up on the Chicago 43.

"It's a shift in momentum," said Tillman. "Those guys are jacked and they're excited. It's the Super Bowl. They got it on their side of the 50 and it's hard to defend. As best, they only get three points, which is still too much. They know they don't have far to travel."

"We had our x-factor," Mathis said. "That was Bob Sanders. We called him the eraser. He forced that fumble and Dwight Freeney recovered it. It got our confidence sky high and it let them know that we belonged there and we just kind of took it from there."

The Bears forced an Indianapolis punt, but the Colts would cut into the lead on their next possession. A 29-yard field goal by Vinatieri made the score 14–9 and the Colts would take the lead the next time they had the football. Manning put together a 58-yard drive and Running Back Dominic Rhodes finished it off with a one-yard touchdown run. Tillman would force a fumble late in the half to thwart another Indianapolis scoring drive, but Grossman would fumble a snap during the ensuing drive to deny Chicago the chance to cut into the lead before halftime. Vinatieri missed a 36-yard attempt in the final seconds and the Indianapolis lead was two at halftime. The teams had each turned the ball over three times, but Mathis believed the worst was over for the Colts.

"The team that protects the ball the most is going to be the team that comes out on top," said Mathis. "We were able to do that. We got the early jitters out of our system and we kind of settled down."

Meanwhile, the Bears were hardly discouraged heading into the locker room. Chicago had made its share of mistakes over the first two quarters, but the team had erased a much larger deficit earlier in the season.

"The guys were calm," Tillman said. "After overcoming a 20-point deficit in Arizona, what we were doing in the Super Bowl was nothing. We were extremely calm. Guys made their adjustments. I felt that we had played well under the bright lights."

Manning was also used to the bright lights and was determined not to waste his first opportunity for a Super Bowl title. Manning engineered a drive which chewed up 7:34 of the clock in the third quarter. Vinatieri capped off the drive with a 24-yard field goal. After Chicago was forced to punt, Vinatieri connected again as he hit from 20 yards out. The Indianapolis lead was now 22–14, but the Colts had taken control of the game in the trenches while protecting the football.

"The offense was good at doing whatever they wanted to do with Peyton leading the charge," said Mathis. "It just gave us time to gather our thoughts and make whatever corrections for whatever we needed to get done."

Chicago would finally get back on track after working with a short field thanks to another squib kick. The drive stalled, but Robbie Gould's 44-yard field goal pulled the Bears to within five. Chicago entered the fourth quarter needing one touchdown to take the lead, but the Indianapolis Defense would all but seal the game early in the final period. Grossman floated a pass to the far side where Kelvin Hayden was waiting for an easy interception. The cornerback tiptoed along the sidelines before racing into the end zone for a 56-yard interception return. The Colts' lead was now at 29–17 with 11:44 remaining in regulation. There was still plenty of time remaining, but the Indianapolis players knew they were closing in on a world championship.

"We could smell it," recalled Mathis. "I think we knew it was game, set and match."

"That was huge," Vinatieri said. "It's never over until the last seconds go, but when he took it back for a touchdown, it was celebration time at that point."

Tillman knew his team still had time, but even the confident cornerback could sense Super Bowl XLI was slipping away from the Bears.

"It's very helpless when you are just sitting there," said Tillman. "You're just thinking 'Somebody tackle him.' I was thinking if someone tackles him that gives us the opportunity to take the ball away. We really thought that we as a defense could change the outcome of a game."

Another Chicago turnover would virtually seal the Bears' fate. Sanders picked off Grossman and returned the ball to the Chicago 41-yard line. After an Indianapolis punt, the Bears moved the ball to their own 47 and elected to gamble on fourth down, but Grossman's pass fell incomplete. Manning went straight to his ground game for eight straight plays and the Bears were left with 1:42 on the clock by the time they got the ball back.

"That's where most games are won and lost," Mathis said. "It's in the trenches. That's where it begins. We were able to do that for the whole playoff run. We played Colts Football with speed and one-gap schemes."

Time would run out on the Bears, and the Colts would celebrate their first Super Bowl title since the franchise called Baltimore its home 36-years prior. Vinatieri had already been through three Super Bowl victories and took in the celebration by the rest of his teammates. Manning and Dungy had their first Super Bowl rings after a host of near misses throughout their careers.

"It was super awesome," recalled Vinatieri. "Whenever you win the Super Bowl, it's exciting. There's nothing like that. The excitement level speaks for itself, but the Colts were an amazing team all those years. To see Dungy and Peyton and all of those other guys that had been there, too, was so much fun."

As the Colts celebrated their Super Bowl title, Tillman and the rest of the Bears had little time to take in the defeat on the field. Tillman quickly learned what happens to the losing team when it came time for the post-game ceremony at a Super Bowl.

"The confetti comes out and everyone ropes you off," Tillman said. "If you lose, the event security comes out so quick and they rope you all off. It's like you're a nobody. It's a terrible feeling."

Tillman said he has yet to watch the rebroadcast of Super Bowl XLI as the pain of falling short in the biggest game of the season still lingers. Tillman had a chance to go to the Super Bowl again as a member of the Panthers, but missed Super Bowl 50 due to a knee injury. Tillman had warned his Carolina teammates before the game to make the most of their opportunity.

"I told all the other guys not to assume we're going to come back here next year," said Tillman. "After Super Bowl XLI, everybody on that team just assumed we were going to come back. The next year, we were absolutely terrible. I was the only one who got back to the Super Bowl from everybody on that team."

Just like the Bears, the Panthers would fall short and Tillman was never able to win a Super Bowl ring. Now a successful broadcaster, Tillman is constantly reminded of his lack of a championship by several former Super Bowl champions who work on the broadcast set with the former corner-back.

"It's probably one of the few regrets I've had in football," said Tillman. "It's not winning a Super Bowl in my career. You work so hard for this freaking ring. I've never won a championship in anything in life and to be so close and to lose just sucks."

It was a different story in Indianapolis, where the Colts were finally champions after a host of playoff heartbreaks. Manning was named the game's Most Valuable Player and Mathis was able to literally soak in the moment as the raindrops kept falling in Miami.

"It was awesome," Mathis said. "The owner gets his first, the G.M. gets his first, the coach gets his first and the franchise quarterback gets his first. There were just a whole lot of firsts and it was our first, too. The guy that already had rings was Vinatieri. He just smiled and watched us enjoy the moment."

XLII
A Giant Upset

The New England Patriots were looking to make history at Super Bowl XLII.

The Patriots had the chance to become just the second team in the Super Bowl era to finish with an unbeaten record. New England went 16–0 in the regular season and advanced to the Super Bowl with wins over Jacksonville and San Diego in the playoffs. Bill Belichick's squad had the first opportunity since the 1972 Dolphins to hoist the Lombardi Trophy unbeaten and the 72' Miami squad accomplished the feat in the days of a 14-game regular season. The Patriots were one victory away from a 19–0 season and football immortality. Special teams standout Larry Izzo insists he and his teammates never looked ahead as they were dominating the rest of the pro football world.

"You respect the opponent and respect what they do and then it's about execution," Izzo said. "I don't think we ever felt like we were invincible. Every week was great because you earned every win. You felt like you should win but you still had to go out and do it."

It was easy to understand why many were calling New England the greatest team of all time. The Patriots scored an NFL record 589 points and averaged 36.8 points per game. The defense gave up the fourth fewest points per game, making New England a complete team throughout the season. The Patriots had blown out most of their opponents during the regular season.

One of the exceptions was the New York Giants.

On the final weekend of the regular season, the Patriots and Giants went down to the wire in North Jersey. New England pulled out a 38–35 victory, but the Giants came away from the loss confident they could beat the mighty Patriots. Wide Receiver David Tyree wasn't surprised to see his team rise to the occasion.

"I don't ever think that we felt like we couldn't go toe-to-toe with anyone," Tyree said. "We felt that way about anybody and that was really an opportunity to prove it. We weren't going to be the ones to lie down for their perfect season. You wanted to play the best and beat the best and really gain some momentum, so we went at it."

Before New York could have its Super Bowl shot against New England, Tom Coughlin's squad had to take the long road to Arizona. The wild card Giants won three road games, including a dramatic overtime victory over

Green Bay in the NFC Championship, to reach the biggest game of the season.

"There was real comradery," said Tyree. "There were some things Coughlin had done earlier in the year with the leadership counsel. It created some avenues to cultivate the relationship that is necessary to have a great team."

When the two teams arrived at the Super Bowl, much of the spotlight fell on the Patriots. Would the 1972 Dolphins, famous for celebrating their perfection, finally have company in the world of unbeaten teams? The Patriots were hardly overconfident as Belichick once again kept his team focused throughout the week. The players had little trouble keeping their mind on their work after squeaking by the Giants at the end of the regular season.

"We knew what type of team they had," said Izzo. "We knew they were well-coached. I knew some of the guys and I had a lot of respect for how they did things there. They played us really tight in that last game. We knew it was going to be another tough game a month later."

The Giants were hardly removed from media attention during Super Bowl week, but the players were both relaxed and focused. Few believed Tyree and his teammates would even reach Super Bowl XLII, so the Giants were able to enjoy their week in Arizona while preparing for the Patriots.

"Coverage is always there when it comes to the Super Bowl," said Tyree. "You're really in the moment. There's part of it that you're really trying to enjoy and there's another part you can't separate that you're there for one specific reason. If you find the right balance to that, you can really have a tremendous week."

One of the best ways to stop Quarterback Tom Brady and the powerful New England Offense was to keep them off the field. New York was able to do just that on the opening drive of the game. Quarterback Eli Manning led the Giants on a 9:59 scoring drive. The drive would stall deep in New England territory, but a 32-yard field goal by Lawrence Tynes gave New York a 3–0 lead.

"The pace of the regular season game was much different," Tyree said. "We really began to realize we had a dominant offensive line. Those guys were just hogs. They got the job done. Football, at the end of the day, is going to be a game about execution. When you're able to put that drive together, it certainly sets the tone."

"They kept the ball for what seemed like forever," said Izzo. "That was not good to have our guys sitting over there on the bench. That's when there was the feeling like it was going to be a tough one. We still felt like we had to just make the plays."

It did not take New England long to respond. Laurence Maroney took the ensuing kickoff 43 yards to his team's 44 and Brady quickly went to work.

A pass interference penalty on New York Linebacker Antonio Pierce put New England on the one. On the first play of the second quarter, Maroney reached the end zone to give the Patriots a 7–3 lead.

"I think we got into some rhythm," Izzo said. "Initially, it was not the best start for us. We got into a flow."

The Giants quickly moved into the red zone on their next possession, but a pass by Manning went through the hands of Wide Receiver Steve Smith and into the hands of New England Cornerback Ellis Hobbs. The Giants would get to the Patriots' 25 late in the period, but a sack and a penalty forced another punt. Brady would get another chance before the half as he brought his offense to the New York 44, but a sack by Defensive Lineman Justin Tuck forced a fumble and fellow lineman Osi Umenyiora recovered the ball. The Patriots went to the locker room at halftime with the lead, but all indications were that Super Bowl XLII would feature a dramatic second half.

"Knowing that you're right there is good," said Tyree. "You don't want to be two or three touchdowns down. We knew we had a long half. You really had to focus during the long halftime. We realized we were right where we needed to be to put ourselves in a position to win the game."

The game would remain 7–3 heading into the final quarter as both defenses dug in during the third period. The Patriots had the only scoring chance of the third quarter, but a fourth down pass from the New York 31 fell incomplete.

The Giants took over on their own 20 eight seconds into the fourth quarter. A 45-yard catch and run by Tight End Kevin Boss sparked the Giants on their first play of the drive. Manning would take his team to the five-yard line. On second down, Manning fired a strike to Tyree over the middle in the end zone. With 11:07 to play, the Giants had taken a 10–7 lead.

"It was a perfectly scripted play," Tyree said. "If there was an opportunity for a receiver to do some dirty work, I was the guy who was called on. I was always a candidate for what we called the pop pass. It was just set up perfectly with a hard play action at the goal line. Eli hung that thing in there."

Both teams would punt on their next possessions before Brady and his teammates got the ball back on their own 20 with just under eight minutes to play. New England ran nine plays with seven being Brady completions to move the ball to the New York six. Two straight incompletions set up a third and goal. Brady looked to the right of the end zone where Giants Cornerback Corey Webster had slipped. The quarterback threw to a wide-open Randy Moss and the receiver's fifth reception of the game gave New England a 14–10 lead. The Patriots were 2:42 away from a perfect season

"The last quarter was back and forth," said Izzo. "You knew it was going to be like that. You go into all of those with the assumption that it's not going to be easy."

But the Giants had put together several fourth comebacks during the season, so Tyree and his teammates were hardly discouraged as they took over after the kickoff on their own 17.

"I don't think there was a panic whatsoever," said Tyree. "We had been in similar situations in the past and we were kind of watching Eli grow up before our eyes. It was an opportunity knowing you were down by four and you need a touchdown."

An 11-yard pass to Amani Toomer was followed by a pair of incompletions. Another catch by Toomer set up a fourth and one and Brandon Jacobs kept the drive alive with a two-yard run. A five-yard run by Manning was followed by a near interception by Cornerback Asante Samuel. On third down with 1:15 remaining, Manning dropped back to throw under heavy pressure. Jarvis Green and Richard Seymour both got their hands on the quarterback, but Manning somehow managed to escape and avoid a sack. Manning then ran to his right and flung the ball deep downfield.

"I'm on a post-route," Tyree said. "As you look back and see the melee, I was just trained like most players to keep the play going. For me, it was just really about finding that green grass and putting myself in a position where as he was coming out of that play to give him a target down the field."

Manning threw in the direction of Tyree, who was in the middle of the field near the New England 24.

"He rolled right," recalled Tyree. "I felt that moment of locking eyes. The ball was in the air with 'Chariots of Fire' playing in the background."

Safety Rodney Harrison was covering Tyree, who leaped into the air. Harrison got his hand on Tyree's right shoulder as the ball arrived, but the receiver managed to keep his arms up in the air. Tyree grabbed the ball with his right hand and pulled it against his helmet as he fell to the ground and secured it with his left hand. Tyree kept possession even with Harrison getting a hand near the ball and the Giants had a first down with 59 seconds remaining.

"I went up with two hands," said Tyree. "I remember touching it. Rodney came in and I was expecting for someone to come in and contest the ball knowing how long it had been up there. I didn't know where the ball was. I just knew I wasn't letting it go."

"I was right there watching it from field level," Izzo said. "It was one of those great individual plays that will go down in history with the determination it took for him to hold onto that ball. Rodney's clawing at it. You hope it's just going to fall off to the ground when he hits the ground and it doesn't."

It would go down as one of the greatest catches in NFL history and it would also open the door to the end zone. First, the Giants would need another key third down conversion. Two plays after the Tyree catch, Manning hit Smith along the right sideline for 12 yards. On the next play, Manning floated a pass to the left side of the end zone, where Wide Receiver Plaxico Burress was wide open. His touchdown catch put the Giants ahead, 17–14, with 35 seconds remaining in regulation. New England's dreams of a perfect season appeared to be over, but Brady would get one last chance after a kickoff return put the Patriots on their own 26 with 29 seconds remaining.

"You knew that Tom was going to have a chance at the end," Izzo said. "Even when he was hailing those balls down the field, you're thinking Randy's going to catch them."

But there would be no miracle finish for Brady and the Patriots in this Super Bowl. After an incomplete pass, Brady was sacked by Jay Alford. On third down, Brady's deep pass to Moss was broken up by Webster. With ten seconds left, Brady heaved up one more desperation throw, but it was batted away and fell harmlessly to the ground. One second remained on the clock as the Giants took over on offense to take a knee. By then, Belichick had already congratulated Coughlin and was headed to the New England locker room. The dream of a perfect season had ended.

"That was a difficult loss," said Izzo. "Losing in the Super Bowl is a tough deal. You get so far and then you have all of the other outside things going on. You have a lot at stake then you don't get it done. It's hard to take that."

As the Patriots dealt with their first loss of the season at the worst time, the Giants celebrated one of the biggest upsets in Super Bowl history.

"The only word I could use to describe what I was experiencing was awe," said Tyree. "It encompasses every emotion you can experience. You're reflecting on your team's journey and I'm sure everybody's reflecting on their own personal journeys. It was a lot."

The New York Super Bowl victory may not have happened if it hadn't been for Tyree's incredible catch on the game-winning drive. The receiver would never play another snap for the Giants after injuring his knee in training camp the following season. After a year in Baltimore, Tyree retired and eventually returned to the Giants as director of player personnel. However, Tyree will forever take his place in football immortality with his "helmet catch" in Super Bowl XLII.

"I don't allow people to call it lucky," Tyree said. "Lucky is finding $20 on the street. This was a moment of providence that was just kind of set in order. You couldn't make a better defensive play. It was great for me to be the recipient of it."

Izzo would return to the next Patriots Super Bowl, but as a member of the Giants coaching staff when the teams met again in Super Bowl XLVI. Despite the devastating defeat, Izzo was able to put the game in proper perspective when comparing life with football.

"It's not life or death," Izzo said. "You keep things in perspective. It kind of reminded me of the year that I lost my dad. At the end of the day, life and death is one thing. You lose this big game, so you say 'let's get it done next year.'"

After a half century of Super Bowls, only the 1972 Dolphins can still claim perfection. For Tyree and his teammates, toppling the unbeaten Patriots made Super Bowl XLII one of the most memorable championship games ever played.

"It's really humbling," Tyree said. "Everybody plays the game or lives life to leave a mark. For me, it's humbling because I knew it was something that God had done for me in my personal life. For me, it was something of a heart desire that I knew only God could only accomplish for me. Having the opportunity to be a part of the game and the history of the game is really humbling."

XLIII
ONE FOR THE OTHER THUMB

There could be no greater contrast in franchises heading into Super Bowl XLIII.

The AFC representatives would be the Pittsburgh Steelers, a franchise which was no stranger to Super Bowls. This would be Pittsburgh's seventh appearance on Super Sunday and the men from the Steel City would be looking for their sixth Super Bowl title. While four of Pittsburgh's Super Bowl appearances came during the 1970's, many of the players had been a part of the Steelers' championship team from Super Bowl XL. With only three years removed from the Super Bowl spotlight, players such as Linebacker James Farrior were well-prepared for the hype surrounding the biggest game of the season.

"It was a totally different feeling," said Farrior. "We kind of knew what to expect. We knew what the rundown was going to be the week of the Super Bowl leading up to the game. We kind of used that to our advantage. That was Arizona's first time in the Super Bowl."

The Arizona Cardinals were not expected to be making their first Super Bowl appearance in the 2008 season. The Cardinals captured the AFC West title but did so with an unimpressive 9–7 record. However, everything came together for this long-suffering franchise during the post-season. The Cardinals defeated Atlanta at home before blowing out Carolina on the road. After the Eagles upset the top-seeded Giants, Arizona got past Philadelphia in the NFC Championship game. For the first time in franchise history, the Cardinals were Super Bowl bound. Defensive Lineman Bertrand Berry was part of an Arizona Defense which peaked at the right time of the season. Berry first came into the league in 1997 and had a sense the Cardinals were ready for a deep run after the regular season came to an end.

"We knew we had a good football team," said Berry. "We didn't have a great regular season. The one thing that we wanted to accomplish first was to win the division. We did that. Once everything started happening and the playoffs started, all we had to do was just keep winning and keep putting people behind us."

While Berry and his defensive teammates did their part, the big story behind Arizona's sudden surge was their veteran quarterback. Kurt Warner's best days appeared to be behind him after leading the Rams to two Super Bowls. Warner went to the Giants before arriving in Arizona, where he was expected to serve as a backup for Matt Leinart. However, the 2006 first-round pick could not hold on to the starting job and Warner took over the role at the start of the 2008 season. Warner regained his Pro Bowl form and his veteran presence served as an emotional boost for the entire roster.

"You had a veteran quarterback who had been to two Super Bowls," Berry said. "He knew how to navigate through the playoffs and having a guy who had a point to prove during that time in his career was really a key for our growth and development as a team."

As kickoff approached, the Steelers remained loose and confident. In addition to Farrior and the defense, the offense had been rolling behind Quarterback Ben Roethlisberger. Farrior was expecting to have second a Super Bowl ring by the end of the night in Tampa.

"I remember talking with Larry Foote," recalled Farrior. "We were joking around and he was saying we had been here before and those guys have never been, so we might be up at halftime. By the time they figure out what's going on, the game may be over."

However, the Cardinals were more relaxed than many other first-time Super Bowl participants. In addition to Warner and a select handful of other Cardinals, several members of the Arizona coaching staff had been a part of Super Bowls past. Head Coach Ken Whisenhunt had served as an assistant on the Pittsburgh team which captured Super Bowl XL.

"We had a coaching staff that was full of guys who had either coached in a Super Bowl or played in a Super Bowl," said Berry. "We were pretty well-versed. We didn't know what we didn't know. There were a few guys sprinkled in that had been to Super Bowls before. It wasn't as if the entire team was completely new to the whole situation."

Pittsburgh took the opening kickoff and marched to the Arizona one-yard line. On third down, Roethlisberger was stopped at the goal line. Steelers

Head Coach Mike Tomlin did not want to come away empty on the opening drive and Jeff Reed's 18-yard field goal gave Pittsburgh the first points of the game. After forcing the Cardinals to punt, the Steelers would increase their lead on their second drive. With the help of a 25-yard catch by Santonio Holmes, Pittsburgh quickly moved into Arizona territory. Running back Gary Russell scored from one-yard out, and the Steelers had jumped out to a 10–0 lead in the opening minute of the second quarter. The touchdown drive had taken 7:34 off the clock.

"Our offense was clicking," Farrior said. "They were doing a good job of moving the ball and it's always more fun watching the offense play than being out there playing. When they're out there, we know that something's going good. The more they're out there the better it is for the defense."

The Arizona Offense finally put together a scoring drive on the ensuing possession. A 45-yard strike from Warner to Wide Receiver Anquan Boldin put Arizona at the Pittsburgh one. Warner capped of the drive with a touchdown pass to Tight End Ben Patrick to pull his team to within three. The Arizona Defense followed with a pair of stops as Berry and his teammates forced a punt and an interception. For the first time in the game, the Cardinals were also getting pressure on Roethlisberger.

"I really felt like we got into a groove," Berry said. "We got some hits on him and got some sacks on him. We got some three and outs as well. After that first onslaught, we were able to gather ourselves and play some really, really good football."

It appeared the game was turning in Arizona's favor and the Cardinals were poised to take the lead in the closing seconds of the first half. Warner moved his team inside the Pittsburgh two with 18 seconds remaining. The quarterback dropped back to throw as the Steelers called an all-out blitz. Warner's quick pass went into the hands of James Harrison. The Pittsburgh linebacker headed for the near sidelines and eluded a mass of humanity looking for daylight.

"I definitely know that James Harrison was supposed to be rushing," said Farrior. "He saw it was a quick, short drop back and he didn't think he could get there. To his credit, he used his football sense and made one of the biggest plays in the game."

Farrior eventually made it to the end zone as time expired in the half and his 100-yard return gave the Steelers a 17–7 lead after two quarters. Farrior was one of the first Steelers to greet Harrison in the end zone.

"He didn't say anything," Farrior said. "He was so tired and out of breath. We were just so happy that he got in the end zone. I don't think anybody on the field at the time figured he could get to the end zone. I was hoping he would run out of bounds so we would have time to kick the field goal."

The touchdown appeared to be deflating for Arizona. The Cardinals were less than two yards away from taking the lead but instead faced a double digit deficit. However, Berry insists there was no panic in the Arizona locker room.

"It was right at the half," said Berry. "We went in at the half feeling really good about the way we played. You don't anticipate that being something that happens on a normal basis. It was a huge momentum shift at the end of the half, but we feel like we knew what they were going to try and do."

Even if Berry and his teammates knew what was coming at the start of the half, they weren't able to slow down the Steelers. Roethlisberger took his team on an 8:39 drive in the third quarter. The Arizona Defense stiffened in the red zone, but a 21-yard field goal by Reed increased Pittsburgh's lead to 20–7. The lead stayed at 13 for Pittsburgh as the two teams entered the fourth quarter, but Berry still believed the Cardinals were well within striking distance.

"We played with a lot of confidence," Berry said. "We played really loose like we had played during the whole playoff stretch. We put ourselves in a position to win the game."

The Cardinals would draw closer after an impressive drive engineered by Warner. Arizona went 87 yards and Warner found his top receiver, Larry Fitzgerald, from one yard out. With 7:33 remaining, the Cardinals were within six points. The deficit would shrink to four with 2:58 remaining. Berry and his teammates were finally getting pressure on Roethlisberger and a holding penalty in the end zone on Pittsburgh Center Justin Hartwig resulted in a safety.

"Big Ben was definitely a point of concern," said Berry. "Not only is he a big guy, but he was pretty mobile at the time. He was known for getting out of the pocket. As pass rushers, we wanted to make sure we didn't get out of our rush lanes. If we could get outside and extend plays, then that's when he's the most dangerous."

The Cardinals took the free kick and began their next drive at their own 36. After an incompletion, Warner threw a strike over the middle to Fitzgerald. The receiver caught the ball near his own 45, split two defenders and raced for the go-ahead score. Arizona was 2:37 away from its first Super Bowl title. Farrior and the Steelers realized they may have just let Super Bowl XLIII slip away.

"It ended up being a perfect play for them," said Farrior. "When we saw him running down the field to score that touchdown, all we could think on the defensive side was how we had such a great season leading up to that point. Our defense was very stellar that year. To get in this game and blow it at the end was really tough on us. We were on the sidelines thinking 'How could we let this slip away from us?'"

One man who was forced to temper his excitement over Fitzgerald's touchdown was the wide receiver's father. Larry Fitzgerald, Sr., was working in the press box as a writer for the *Minnesota Spokesman-Recorder* and followed the "no cheering" rule in the press box. The elder Fitzgerald is the first sports reporter to cover his son in a Super Bowl. Fitzgerald's father may have been celebrating on the inside, but the Arizona bench was in the midst of an open celebration. However, Berry knew the defense still had a job to do with plenty of time on the clock for Roethlisberger.

"I had been in the league for 12 years," said Berry. "The first thing I did when I saw Larry streaking down the field was look up at the clock. I said that we were going to have to go out and win this thing. I had felt it was going to be up to the defense. This is what the season had come down to. We needed to make a play."

Roethlisberger started the next drive on his own 22. Despite a holding penalty to start the drive, Roethlisberger was able to move his offense down the field. A key third down catch by Holmes two plays after the penalty moved the ball up to the 39. Three plays later, Holmes struck again as his 40-yard catch and run brought the ball to the Arizona six. After an incompletion to Holmes in the left corner of the end zone, Roethlisberger tried a similar play to the right side. Surrounded by three Cardinals, Holmes leaped into the air to catch the pass then put both of his tiptoes down in the end zone before falling out of bounds. With the help of a replay confirmation, The Steelers had the go-ahead touchdown with 35 seconds left.

"I thought the ball was too high and he couldn't get his feet in bounds," Farrior said. "They called it a touchdown and I didn't celebrate or get up. I was just waiting for the replay. Once the replay came through and they called it an official touchdown, we started celebrating."

"The play before was the exact same play to the other side," recalled Berry. "We had three guys around Santonio Holmes. It was a great play by Ben and Santonio Holmes. You've got to tip your hat to them."

Holmes' heroics had the Steelers on the verge of their record-setting sixth Super Bowl title, but there were still 35 seconds left on the clock. Farrior was not about to celebrate with Warner and Fitzgerald heading back onto the field.

"We knew that Kurt Warner had a strong arm," said Farrior. "We knew that Fitzgerald would be the jump ball guy, so our whole goal going into that last 30 seconds was to try not to let him get to the 40 or 50 yard line."

Catches by Fitzgerald and J.J. Arlington moved the ball to the Pittsburgh 44. Arizona's last hope was snuffed out by LaMarr Woodley. The linebacker sacked Warner and forced a fumble that was recovered by Defensive End Brett Keisel. Roethlisberger returned to the field to take a knee and the Steelers had held off the valiant Cardinals to capture their sixth Super Bowl crown.

"It was a great game," Berry said. "I'm always going to be proud to have been a part of such a highly-contested game. At the very least, you don't want to embarrass yourself. You don't want to have one of those lopsided games when it gets away from you early. As a team, we really represented ourselves. We showed that we weren't a fluke."

The Cardinals were far from a fluke. Despite the loss, NFL Football in Arizona would never be the same. Once a franchise searching for an identity, the Cardinals now have strong support in the desert.

"I'll always be proud of that," said Berry. "I was part of a team that did something that had never been done in franchise history. We got there and put the Cardinals on the map and no matter what they can never take that away from us. That group will always have that bond."

The Steelers had seen their share of dramatic Super Bowls, which included several legendary battles with the Cowboys. However, Super Bowl XLIII's frantic finish has put the game in the discussion of being one of the best Super Bowls ever played. Farrior is hard pressed to find a better game as a participant in his 15-year career.

"No doubt about it," Farrior said. "The emotions of that game were just up and down at the end. We went from being the scapegoats of the game to winning the game."

XLIV
THE SAINTS AND THE CITY

Super Bowl XLIV was the first championship game appearance for the New Orleans Saints, but there was more than football on the minds of the players and the coaches.

The Saints were playing in the Super Bowl just four years after the New Orleans area was devastated by Hurricane Katrina. The monster storm was one of the worst natural disasters in American history, and scars from Katrina remained as the Saints took the field in 2009. The area was still rebuilding in some sections, and a franchise which had been one of the least successful in NFL history was uplifting the spirits of the region. The surprising Saints finished with a 13–3 record and headed to Miami for their first chance at a world championship.

Cornerback Tracy Porter was drafted by the Saints in 2008 and wasn't with the franchise the year Katrina ravaged the city and its surroundings. However, the Port Allen, Louisiana native was all too familiar with storm and knew the Saints Super Bowl run was having an emotional impact on residents all across the region. He also knew from the start of the off-season workouts that the Saints had something special heading into the 2009 campaign.

"I could tell with the whole preparation that we did in the off-season," said Porter. "It's just a feeling that I had going into the year. From OTAs leading into training camp, leading into the preseason and the regular season, I knew and the guys in the locker room knew that we had something special going that year."

There was someone special leading the way for the Saints' Super Bowl opponents. The Indianapolis Colts reached the title game for the second time in four years thanks largely to the arm of Peyton Manning. The Colts quarterback earned MVP honors in the regular season by throwing for 4,500 yards and 33 touchdowns and arrived in Miami looking for his second Super Bowl ring. However there was more than Manning when it came to the success of the Colts, who finished with a regular season record of 14–2. Indianapolis had its share of stars on defense, and one of the standouts was Defensive End Robert Mathis. The seven-year veteran recorded 9.5 sacks to go along with five forced fumbles. Mathis was not taking his second Super Bowl appearance for granted.

"It's so tough to get to that game," said Mathis. "You just enjoy every moment. You kind of seize the moment and take in the sights. Instead of being uptight, you just enjoy the moment a little bit more."

The quarterbacks were taking center stage throughout the week leading up to the Super Bowl. While Manning was preparing to face the New Orleans Defense, the Indianapolis defenders also faced a difficult test. Drew Brees had the NFL's highest quarterback rating in 2009, and the Saints Quarterback led his team to an average of 32 points per game. Mathis and his teammates knew Brees had the potential to put together an MVP performance on Super Sunday.

"He has great awareness," said Mathis. "He's just a great game manager, a leader, and a field general."

Indianapolis had its own field general in Manning, whose brains added to his brilliance at quarterback. Manning's ability to read defenses and make adjustments as well as any quarterback ever to play the game was the ultimate challenge for a defense. Porter knew preparing for Manning was like preparing for an extra coach on the field.

"He can adapt to defense," said Porter. We had to disguise our defense and come up with different game plans quarter by quarter and half by half just to keep him on his toes. It was pretty much a game of chess that we were playing with him."

The Saints defense would be ready on Super Sunday, but the New Orleans defenders had spent much of the season flying under the radar. Just like with Manning in Indianapolis, the impressive offensive numbers by Brees put the spotlight on the offense. However, the New Orleans Defense was third in the NFL in takeaways with 39. Porter had four of the team's 26 interceptions.

"I was confident all season," Porter said. "The defense had a big emphasis of forcing turnovers. Once you get that mentality going into the post-season, you want to continue that. It was kind of a knack we had for getting our hands on the ball."

The New Orleans Defense was on the field after the game's first possession when Brees and the offense suffered an opening three and out. Manning quickly went to work on Indianapolis' first opportunity. It took ten plays for the Colts to get to the New Orleans 20-yard line, where Matt Stover's 38-yard field goal gave Indianapolis the first points of the game. The Saints were forced to punt again on the ensuing possession, but a punt by Thomas Morstead pinned Indianapolis on its own four. Manning was unfazed by the poor field position as he led his team on a 96-yard scoring drive, which matched the longest in Super Bowl history. The masterful Manning mixed the run and pass well throughout the drive, and Running Back Joseph Addai's 53 yards on three carries helped the Colts move closer to the end zone. Manning capped off the drive with a 19-yard touchdown pass to Pierre Garçon. The Colts had held the ball for over ten minutes of the first quarter and had seized a 10–0 lead.

Linebacker Jonathan Vilma attempted to settle down the defense on the New Orleans sideline.

"We were kind of unsettled and little bit rattled in the beginning," Porter said. "Vilma took the lead and put us in the proper positions. Once we settled down and got a couple of stops, we got our feet under us. We were able to play the game with them."

The offense also settled down on the next possession, which carried over into the second quarter. Three completions by Brees moved the Saints into scoring range. A sack by Dwight Freeney pushed New Orleans back to the 29, but a 46-yard field goal by Garrett Hartley gave the Saints their first points of the game. After forcing an Indianapolis punt, the Saints again moved into scoring range. New Orleans reached the Indianapolis three and was eventually faced with a fourth and goal from just outside the one. Saints Coach Sean Payton elected to go for the end zone, but Pierre Thomas was stuffed by Gary Brackett at the line of scrimmage. The Colts had the momentum, and Manning was content to try and run out the time in the first half with only 1:49 remaining on the clock. However, the Saints would force another punt and take over on their own 48 with 35 seconds remaining. Three completions by Brees brought Hartley back on for a 44-yard attempt. Hartley split the uprights as time expired. The Saints trailed, 10–6, at the half, but had momentum after controlling much of the second quarter.

"That's a momentum booster not only for the offense but for the team," said Porter. "It showed that our offense can move the ball down the field and get us in a position where our defense can get our offense the ball back. It gave us a little confidence going into the half, and you knew it was going to be a long, tough battle."

The Colts had been in complete control after the first 15 minutes, but Mathis could sense the momentum swing by the time he reached locker room at halftime.

"We kind of had them off balance in the first half," recalled Mathis. "We kind of did whatever we wanted to do. They made the necessary adjustments."

There would be a special adjustment at halftime in the New Orleans locker room. The Saints would be kicking off to start the second half, but Payton decided to call "Ambush." It was a play in which the Saints would surprise the Colts with an onside kick. Morstead bounced a kick to the left side of the field and off the hands of Indianapolis' Hank Baskett. A mass of humanity piled onto the area of the football just inside New Orleans' territory. It took over a minute for the officials to uncover the pile of players from both sides. Jonathan Casillas was credited with the recovery, and the Saints had the ball along with the momentum to start the second half.

"I think the turning point was the onside kick that we had," Porter said. "We talked about it all week during practice. At halftime, Sean told us we were going to do this onside kick. He said 'I need you guys to make me right and pretty much make me look like a genius.' He came out bold like he was all season, and we executed."

While the Saints celebrated on the sidelines, Mathis insisted the surprise onside kick did not throw the Colts off their game.

"A lot of people make more of it than it really was," Mathis said. "In the first half, we were kind of controlling the flow defensively. It was a desperation move. They rolled the dice and came up big on it."

But Mathis and his teammates were unable to stop the Saints after the kick recovery. Brees marched his team 58 yards for the go-ahead score. Brees threw a short pass to Thomas, who followed his blocks brilliantly for a 16-yard scamper into the end zone. The onside kick had set up the Saints' first touchdown of the game. It would now be up to Porter and the defense to slow down Manning.

"We had two game plans going in," Porter said. "We had one for the first half and one for the second half because Peyton is a guy that can adapt. He can read hand signals. He can read defenses. We had to practice and be prepared to switch our entire game plan and hand signals at halftime."

But the second game plan could not stop the Colts from regaining the lead on the ensuing possession. Indianapolis went 76 yards in ten plays with the help of three catches for 45 yards by Tight End Dallas Clark. The drive ended with Adddai's four-yard touchdown run to put the Colts back on top, 17–13. It would be the Saints turn to score on the next possession as Hartley's 47-yard field goal brought New Orleans to within one after three quarters. Manning and Brees continued their back and forth affair as the final quarter got underway. Manning once again drove his team into scoring position, but this time Indianapolis would come up empty. Stover missed from 51-yards out, and the Saints had the ball back with plenty of time to erase a one-point deficit.

"That was huge," said Porter. "Anytime you put a team in difficult field position where they have to kick a long field goal and they miss and you take points away from a team, that takes the momentum from those guys and it gets us where we need to be."

The long miss gave the Saints the ball on their own 41. Brees put the ball in the hands of seven different players on the drive. The last one to touch the ball was Jeremy Shockey, and the tight end's two-yard catch followed by a two-point conversion put New Orleans ahead, 24–17. There was still 5:35 on the clock, which left plenty of time for an Indianapolis Offense which had put together seven fourth quarter comebacks during the season. It appeared Manning was on track for his eighth as he quickly moved the Colts back into New Orleans territory. With just over three minutes remaining, Indianapolis faced a third and five from the New Orleans 31-yard-line. Manning took a three-step drop and threw to his left for Reggie Wayne.

Porter was waiting.

"We spent a lot of time studying going against the Colts and Peyton Manning," Porter said. "He's a first-ballot Half of Fame quarterback and he had great receivers as well. We had spent extra time in the film room preparing for him. We were able to execute once that time came."

Porter picked off Manning's pass and raced 74-yards for a touchdown. The pick-six increased the New Orleans lead to 31–17 with 3:12 remaining, and Saints fans were just moments away from celebrating their first ever Super Bowl title.

"It was pretty much smooth sailing once I got past Peyton," Porter said. "I was looking at the fans. It was just an unbelievable experience."

With Saints fans outnumbering Colts fans in the stadium, Porter had a chance to savor the moment with the New Orleans faithful as he completed his journey into the end zone.

"I'm looking at the crowd and pointing at the crowd," recalled Porter. "There's just a sea of black and gold. I could see fans cheering and screaming as I'm jumping into the end zone."

Porter's big play had all but ended the game just when it seemed as if the Colts were close to pulling even in the final minutes. Mathis could only watch helplessly as Porter took the ball into the end zone.

"It was extremely helpless," said Mathis. "It was new life. They kind of smelled that the blood was in the water."

Porter wasted little time refocusing on the task at hand. The game was virtually wrapped up, but the Saints still had to finish off the Colts on the ensuing drive. Manning guided his team to the New Orleans three, but the Saints kept the Colts out of the end zone. New Orleans took over with 44 seconds remaining, and Porter could finally savor his Super Bowl moment.

"I'm thinking we have to get right back on the field and Peyton Manning gets the ball again," said Porter. "That was my whole mindset, but once we stopped them on fourth and goal and they turned the ball over and our offense took the field, that's when everything hit me. I caught an interception in the biggest game of my career. Everything just hit me at once."

Four years after being devastated by Katrina, the city of New Orleans had persevered. The Saints had done their part to provide an emotional boost for the region, and the Vince Lombardi Trophy was heading to Bourbon Street. Porter understood the city of New Orleans as well as several other parts of the surrounding area were still recovering from Katrina. The Saints had more than done their part.

"I know the difficulty they had in that area," Porter said. "You had the entire Gulf Coast. You had Mississippi, Alabama, and a little bit of Florida. We had pretty much three or four different states that were behind us."

Meanwhile, Mathis and his teammates were forced to deal with the sting of a Super Bowl defeat. Three years ago on the same field, the Colts became world champions. This time, they were forced to watch their opponents celebrate. For Mathis, the appreciation of reaching football's biggest game was overshadowed by a painful defeat.

"Getting to the Super Bowl is a tremendous feat," Mathis said. "It's nothing to sneeze at, but losing the Super Bowl is kind of the valley low in my career versus winning the Super Bowl, which is the mountain high. To get that far and come up short was very deflating. At the same time, you can't really sneeze at the accomplishments you made that year."

Meanwhile, Mardi Gras began early in New Orleans. Floats from the annual celebration were part of the Saints' victory parade. The franchise which was once a laughing stock was now on top of the football world.

"They were the 'Aints," said Porter. "Fans were wearing paper bags over their heads and were embarrassed by their team. Now, they were proud of their team. I know it was an unbelievable experience for those fans as well. They were excited and I'm just glad I could be part of bringing it back to my home state."

XLV
Mr. Rodgers' Neighborhood

The Green Bay Packers and Pittsburgh Steelers were no strangers to Super Bowls.

The two franchises had combined for 11 Super Bowl appearances. Both had a rich tradition filled with Hall of Fame coaches and players. Pittsburgh and Green Bay both advanced to Super Bowl XLV setting up a Super Sunday in Arlington splattered with nostalgia. The Steelers would be going for a record seventh Super Bowl victory, while the Packers were looking for their fourth. The Packers had to get to the Super Bowl the hard way. Green Bay went into the playoffs as a six seed in the NFC and needed road wins at Philadelphia, Atlanta and Chicago to make it to Arlington, Texas.

One player who knew both teams well was John Kuhn. The Green Bay Fullback had been with the Steelers organization as a practice squad member when Pittsburgh captured Super Bowl XL. Now, Kuhn would have a chance to line up against his former team in Super Bowl XLV.

"I enjoyed that experience so much," said Kuhn. "That was the end of my first season, so it was a magical season my rookie year to be on the practice squad and go to the Super Bowl, but being on the sidelines was one of the things that drove me to want to get back and actually play in the game myself."

Few were surprised to see Pittsburgh reach its eighth Super Bowl. The Steelers finished at 12–4 before surviving two close playoff contests at home against the Ravens and Jets. For the Steelers who played in Super Bowls XL and XLIII, this would be a third opportunity for a ring. The Super Bowl XL champions had advanced as a six seed so players such as Linebacker James Farrior could relate to the Green Bay playoff run.

"We felt that way going into the game," said Farrior. "They had a lot of things going for them that we did in our first Super Bowl. They were a hot team and they got on a roll. They looked like they were unstoppable. We definitely felt they had the momentum going for them."

"We felt very confident," Kuhn said. "We did not feel like a six seed. We went through a stretch where we felt like we were the best team in the league. There were a couple of other guys who were injured. Getting those guys back was going to be huge."

The Packers were led by Quarterback Aaron Rodgers, who appeared to be at the top of his game heading into Super Bowl XLV. After being forced to sit behind Brett Favre for the first three years of his career, Rodgers was thriving in his third season as a starter. He returned from an injury for the final two games of the 2010 season and led the Packers into the playoffs. Rodgers finished the regular season with 3,922 passing yards and 28 touchdown tosses.

The arrival of the Packers and the Steelers also meant the arrival of two large fan bases. Both teams had loyal followers who traveled well and "Terrible Towels" along with "Cheeseheads" could be found throughout the region during Super Bowl week.

"It was definitely one of those throwback Super Bowls," said Kuhn. "You had people talking about what it was like in the 70's and what it was like in the 60's. Both of these franchises had pretty much owned a decade in the past, but the Steelers had won it in 2005 and 2008. The Packers had won one in the 90's, but had a 14-year drought."

Neither side would have much to cheer about early in the game as the two teams combined for three punts on the first three possessions. However, Green Bay would seize the early lead as well as the momentum with two plays. Rodgers got the Green Bay Offense moving on the team's second drive. The Packers went 80 yards on nine plays capped off by a 29-yard touchdown catch by Jordy Nelson. The receiver broke free along the right side after a Rodgers play-action on third and one. On the first play from scrimmage by Pittsburgh after the ensuing kickoff, Quarterback Ben Roethlisberger lofted a pass to the left side. Safety Nick Collins intercepted the pass at the Steelers' 37 and reached the end zone. The Packers had struck twice in a span of 24 seconds to take a 14–0 lead late in the first quarter.

"That was big," recalled Kuhn. "When you get a turnover, then that's big. When a turnover turns into points, then that's as big as it gets. We knew we were playing with house money at that point in time."

Green Bay had scored on both offense and defense, but it was clear that Rodgers was starting to get into the type of rhythm which made him one of the top quarterbacks in the NFL.

"They had showed us some things," said Farrior. "We had studied those guys a lot. They came out with a good game plan against us. I don't know exactly what happened in the first half, but they were moving the ball pretty well. We were very frustrated."

Some of the frustration was alleviated on Pittsburgh's next drive, which carried into the second quarter. With the help of an 18-yard third-down run by Roethlisberger, the Steelers moved into Green Bay territory. When the drive stalled, Shaun Suisham booted a 33-yard field goal to cut the Green Bay lead to 14–3. After forcing a Packer punt, Roethlisberger brought his team to the Green Bay 49, but another interception would put the Packers back in control. The man known as "Big Ben" was intercepted by Jarrett Bush on a short pass over the middle and Rodgers and his offensive teammates quickly took advantage. After moving to the Pittsburgh 21, Rodgers fired a strike in the middle of the end zone to Greg Jennings to increase the Green Bay lead to 21–3. The receiver had lined up in the slot and Farrior was left to deal with one-on-one coverage before it was too late for help to arrive.

"They had a masterful game plan," Farrior said. "They kind of took our pass rushers out of the game. They took the linebackers out of the game and they were throwing the ball around on us pretty much at will."

The early Green Bay onslaught had also forced the aggressive Pittsburgh Defense to play more cautiously throughout the rest of the game.

"They pressured us pretty heavily early in the game," said Kuhn. "As the game wore on, they kind of laid back more so than what they did in the first half."

With just 2:18 remaining in the half, the Steelers needed a drive to stop the bleeding. Roethlisberger shook off his early interceptions and took his team on a 77-yard scoring drive. The drive ended with a pair of passes to Hines Ward. The first put Pittsburgh on the Green Bay seven. The second got the Steelers back in the game as Ward found an open spot on the right side of the end zone. Pittsburgh had life, but Green Bay led, 21–10, after 30 minutes of football.

"It was very frustrating at first," said Farrior. "We thought that we got our feet up under us. After halftime, we thought we could make a run."

While the Packers were pleased with how much of the first half went, Kuhn and his teammates knew Roethlisberger was starting to heat up after a slow start.

"We weren't shaken," recalled Kuhn. "But we knew with that late touchdown that they were still in the ball game and they were dangerous. We knew we had to go out there and just execute, but we felt that little bit of momentum swing as we were going in at halftime. I'd be lying if I said we weren't just a little bit worried to see them finally get their offense kick-started."

The Packers would be shorthanded to start the second half thanks to a pair of key injuries. Wide Receiver Donald Driver and Defensive Back Charles Woodson were both sidelined for the rest of the game and the Steelers quickly took advantage. Pittsburgh forced Green Bay to punt on the first possession of the second half. The Steelers took over at midfield with the help of a facemask penalty on the punt return. Pittsburgh went to the ground game and called five straight runs, with the first by Rashard Mendenhall going for 17 yards. The last run of the drive came from Mendenhall again as his eight-yard scamper up the middle cut the Green Bay lead to 21–17. After being on the ropes in the first half, the Steelers were alive and well.

Both teams would dig in defensively as the game moved to the fourth quarter, but the first play of the final period would result in another turnover by Pittsburgh. With the ball on the Green Bay 33, Mendenhall ran right and was hit by Clay Mathews and Ryan Pickett. The ball popped loose and Desmond Bishop recovered the ball at the Green Bay 45. The Steelers had turned the ball over for the third time in the game and the Packers had regained the momentum in Super Bowl XLV.

Rodgers moved the Packers to the Pittsburgh 40 where he was faced with a third and ten. The quarterback fired a pass over the middle to Nelson who raced down the left side to the Pittsburgh two. After a sack, Rodgers found Jennings open on the right side of the end zone for his second touchdown as the Packers increased their lead to 28–17.

"That was a specialty red zone play for them," recalled Farrior. "We had practiced a similar play to that. I kind of was left in no man's land. It was pretty much all the receivers on one side. It was a three wide receiver strong and the back was over there, too. They caught me in a moment where I was unsure of what to do."

The Steelers weren't going away. Pittsburgh responded with a touchdown drive on the ensuing possession. Roethlisberger was sharp as he completed six of seven passes on the drive. The last pass was a perfect throw along the left side from 25 yards out to Mike Wallace for a Pittsburgh touchdown. The Steelers added a two-point conversion as Roethlisberger made a perfect pitch to Antwaan Randle El. With 7:34 left to play in regulation, Super Bowl XLV was a three-point game.

It appeared the Packers would quickly give the ball back to the Steelers. Green Bay was faced with a third and ten after two plays and a penalty, but Rodgers delivered with a strike over the middle to Jennings for a 31-yard gain. Green Bay would keep the clock moving before the drive stalled at the five. Mason Crosby came on for a 23-yard field goal to increase the Packer lead to 31–25. Only 2:07 remained on the clock.

"We had to keep the ball," said Kuhn. "Those guys were scoring and were very dangerous. Taking time off the clock was probably just as important as the three points we got."

"I thought we still had a chance at the end of the game," Farrior said. "Big Ben had the ball and we would have another heroic moment and another Super Bowl victory, but it just didn't end up working out that way."

Roethlisberger took over at his own 13 with 1:59 left. He hit Heath Miller for a 15-yard gain and followed with a five-yard pass to Ward. Two incompletions later, The Steelers were faced with fourth down. Roethlisberger threw for Wallace, but Tramon Williams broke up the pass to seal the victory for Green Bay.

"He always seemed to come up with big plays at huge times," Kuhn said. "That was just another one. That was one of those great Tramon Williams plays. It was a big play at a big time. I can remember as soon as that happened just hugging my teammates and the jubilation on the sidelines."

Rodgers and the offense ran out the clock and the Packers were Super Bowl champions for the fourth time in their history. The Packers went into a victory formation on the final play and Kuhn was standing next to Rodgers as he took the final snap.

"It was fantastic," said Kuhn. "Coming into Green Bay, Aaron definitely had to fight out of a shadow with Brett Favre. There was a period in 2008 when people didn't agree with the move that the team made. There was a divide in the Green Bay fan base. When we were coming out of the huddle for the last snap, I said 'You did it, man. You got the monkey off your back.'"

It was only the second Super Bowl defeat in eight trips to the big game for Pittsburgh. For most of these Steelers, it was the first loss on Super Sunday after wins in Super Bowls XL and XLIII. Despite two Super Bowl victories, the pain of the loss in Super Bowl XLV still stings for Farrior.

"That's the one I remember the most," said Farrior. "The longest Super Bowl was the one that we lost. I think a lot of players had that same sentiment. Winning them is great and you have that great feeling. It's a totally different feeling and it lasts. It lasts with you a lot longer when you lose that game."

It was a different feeling for the Packers, who were Super Bowl champions for the fourth time in their illustrious history. Kuhn did much of the dirty work as a blocker throughout the game, but said the blue-collar members of the Packers had played a huge part in Green Bay's road to another Lombardi Trophy.

"I'm very proud of that," Kuhn said. "That was something that we looked at going into the playoff run for what we needed. It was kind of a character build that made us the team that we were."

XLVI
NEW YORK, NEW YORK

There is no love lost between Boston and New York when it comes to sports.

The two northeastern cities have a history of deep-seeded rivalries with their various sports teams. The most heated takes place in baseball, where the Yankees and Red Sox have put together generations of memorable moments. The Bruins and Rangers have had their share of ice wars which peaked in the early 1970's while the Celtics and Knicks have battled for decades on the NBA hardwood. By the turn of the century, football had joined the party as the bad blood rose in both towns.

With the emergence of the Patriots as a 21st century powerhouse, the New York Jets became New England's top rival. The tide would turn in favor of the Patriots a majority of the time, but another New York team had spoiled a chance at perfection for the Patriots. The Giants had upset unbeaten New England in Super Bowl XLII and the two teams would meet again at Super Bowl XLVI in Indianapolis. While the Giants and Patriots rarely faced each other in the regular season, players such as Jake Ballard quickly learned about the intensity of the rivalry. The New York tight end compared the feelings of animosity towards the Patriots to a team he faced in his college days at Ohio State.

"Our biggest rival was Michigan," said Ballard. "It almost felt like that around the facility. There was this dislike for the Patriots and they were our enemy. We knew they were a very talented team and well-coached. If we didn't come out and play our best, they were going to beat us."

While many of the Giants would get a chance at a second ring against the Patriots, Ballard would be looking for his first. The undrafted free agent had taken the long road to the NFL but became a key contributor for the Giants during the 2011 season. Ballard had 38 receptions for 604 yards and the Ohio State product was not taking his Super Bowl appearance for granted, especially after an off-season which featured a league lockout during a labor dispute which threatened the season.

"It was a very surreal moment," said Ballard. "Being undrafted and being on the practice squad the year before for half a year before making the active roster. With the lockout, we didn't have an off-season and I was in there getting reps every week. It was like a dream come true."

Few were surprised to see the Patriots reach the Super Bowl for the fifth time in eleven years. New England rolled to a 13–3 record and the top seed in the AFC. Bill Belichick's squad advanced to the Super Bowl with playoff wins over the Broncos and Ravens. The Patriots were no doubt eager for revenge with the Giants waiting in Indianapolis.

New York's resume was a bit less impressive. The Giants became just the third team to reach the Super Bowl with a 9–7 record. However, many believed Tom Coughlin's team was far better than its record and that the Giants were peaking at the right time of the season.

"We knew we had talent everywhere," Ballard said. "Offensively, we could run the ball and we could throw the ball. We had three great receivers. Defensively, our secondary was at the top of the league and our D-linemen were very impressive. We just got hot at the right time and we knew we just needed an opportunity. We felt like no one wanted to play us."

The Patriots seemed to have few complaints about facing the Giants, but New York had beaten New England in Foxboro earlier in the season. The Giants picked up right where they left off at the start of Super Bowl XLVI.

After New York moved to the New England 33 on the opening drive, a sack by Mark Anderson forced the Giants to punt. However, the Patriots started on their own six thanks to a 36-yard punt by Steve Weatherford. On New England's first play from scrimmage, Quarterback Tom Brady dropped back into the end zone and faced a heavy rush from New York Defensive Lineman Justin Tuck. Brady unloaded a pass over the middle, but none of his receivers were in the vicinity of the ball. Brady was called for intentional grounding in the end zone and the safety gave the Giants an early 2–0 lead. New York took the free kick and embarked on the first touchdown drive of the game. Quarterback Eli Manning led his team 78 yards on nine plays. Running Back Ahmad Bradshaw's 24-yard run moved New York to the New England 33. A fumble by Wide Receiver Victor Cruz was nullified by a 12 men on the field penalty and the Giants moved to the six-yard line. After a four-yard run by Bradshaw, Manning hit Cruz for a two-yard strike in the end zone to give the Giants a 9–0 lead. New York had seized the early advantage.

"I think it was huge for the momentum," Ballard said. "We came out doing what we wanted to do. We felt like we were in control of the game. No matter what they did, it was our game to win or lose."

The Patriots would get on the board on their ensuing drive. As the second quarter began, New England had moved to the New York 17. After two plays combining for six yards, Brady's third down pass fell incomplete. Stephen Gostkowski booted a 29-yard field goal to cut the Giants' lead to 9–3. It was the start of a role reversal for the rest of the first half as the Giants began to make the mistakes the Patriots had made in the opening quarter. After an exchange of punts, the Giants began to move towards midfield, but a holding penalty nullified a first down run by Brandon Jacobs. The Patriots got the ball back on their own four after a punt and would embark on a Super Bowl-tying record 96-yard scoring drive. Brady was razor sharp as he completed all 11 of his passes on the scoring march. The last pass went to Running Back Danny Woodhead for a four-yard touchdown with 15 seconds left in the half. New York had scored the game's first nine points, but New England had answered with ten of its own to take a one-point lead at halftime.

"There were some adjustments that had to be made," Ballard said. "But there was no panic. It was more of a sense of urgency thinking we have to get together. We had one half of football for the rest of our lives right now. Let's go out there and get it done."

Ballard had plenty of confidence that his defensive teammates would give the offense more opportunities. Just like in Super Bowl XLII, the Giants front line was getting plenty of pressure on Brady.

"That was huge," Ballard said. "I was lucky every day to practice against probably the best defensive ends in the league. I was going against Osi Umenyiora, Justin Tuck, Jason Pierre-Paul and Mathias Kiwanuka. That got me ready week to week."

The Patriots started out strong in the second half. New England received the opening kickoff of the third quarter and Brady started at his own 21. The New England quarterback was perfect on the drive once again as he hit on all five of his passes. The Patriots would also get 21 yards on the ground in the drive from BenJarvus Green-Ellis. Brady capped off the drive with a touchdown pass to Aaron Hernandez and New England had surged to a 17–9 lead. The Giants appeared to be on the ropes and needed to respond quickly and Manning answered with a scoring drive of his own after the Hernandez touchdown. New York moved from its own 35 to the New England 20. The Patriots' Defense dug in and the drive came to a halt. Lawrence Tynes kicked a 38-yard field goal to make the score 17–12. After forcing a New England punt, the Giants would add three more points on the ensuing drive. Tynes' second straight kick cut the Patriots' lead to 17–15. New York had been kept out of the end zone twice, but the drives had slowed New England's momentum as the fourth quarter approached.

"We were frustrated we didn't punch it in," said Ballard. "We'll take any points we can in the biggest game of the year. We knew we could move the ball on them. We just had to execute."

It appeared the Patriots were ready to add to their lead early in the fourth quarter, but Brady's deep pass was intercepted by Linebacker Chase Blackburn at the New York eight. Both teams would be forced to punt on their next drives after moving near midfield and the Giants would get the ball back on their own 12 with 3:46 remaining.

Ballard would not be around for the frantic finish.

Earlier in the quarter, Ballard tried to break free from Linebacker Brandon Spikes at the line of scrimmage. As Ballard tried to break inside, he slanted his left leg trying to go to his right.

"He's pushing me straight forward," Ballard said. "My knee just kind of twisted and I tore my ACL right there."

Ballard did not know he had torn his ACL. When he reached the New York sideline, Ballard was hoping to have a chance to get back into the game.

"The team doc and trainer came over," said Ballard. "They're doing a stability test and they seemed to think my ACL was intact. We got to the sideline and they did it again and felt it was still there. They thought it was my meniscus. I said I could play with a torn meniscus. We had seven minutes left in a Super Bowl."

To see if he could return, Ballard decided to test his knee along the sidelines. The tight end planted his left knee and the results were disastrous.

"I start running back and forth on the sidelines," Ballard said. "My knee does not feel good at all. It feels unstable and it was definitely not a normal feeling. I went to plant and I just crumbled. It ended up causing more damage in the long run than it should have."

While Ballard was sent to the locker room, his teammates had just under four minutes to retake the lead. New York only needed a field goal, but would be forced to start on its own 12-yard line. On the first play of the drive, Manning delivered a perfect pass along the far sideline to Mario Manningham. The receiver managed to make the catch with two defenders nearby while keeping his feet inbounds. The Giants were now at midfield with more than enough time on the clock.

After an incompletion, Manning would find Manningham two straight times for a total of 18 yards followed by a pass to Hakeem Nicks for 14 more yards. After three more plays, the Giants were on the seven-yard line of the Patriots. With 1:09 left and only one time out remaining for New England, New York had the chance to take most of the time off the clock before a potential game-winning field goal. Bradshaw took the handoff and burst up the middle with the help of a defense that had elected to let Bradshaw score to give Brady time for one more chance. Bradshaw tried to stop at the one, but his momentum carried him into the end zone. Despite a running back not wanting to score and a defense willing to let him do so, the Giants had a 21–17 lead with just over a minute to play in Super Bowl XLVI.

"I start hopping down the hallway on one leg trying to get out to the field," said Ballard. "The doctor kept yelling at me. He went and got me a golf cart and we got out onto the side of the field."

Brady would get one more chance and would have to lead his offense 80 yards in 57 seconds. Two incompletions and a sack by Tuck resulted in a 4th and 16. Brady kept the drive alive with a 19-yard pass to Deion Branch, but time was the ally of the Giants. An 11-yard completion to Hernandez inbounds forced Brady to spike the ball with 19 seconds remaining. After a penalty and another incompletion, Brady was on his own 49 with five seconds left in regulation. Brady fired a Hail Mary pass into the end zone, but the ball was batted away as time ran out. For the second time in five seasons, the Giants had beaten the Patriots in the Super Bowl.

"I got out there right before the last play before Tom chucked it downfield," Ballard said. "I'm sitting in the golf cart watching this play happen and praying that they drop this ball. I see the ball hit the ground and I told the guy on the golf cart to floor it and we just drove right onto the field."

The celebration was on for the Giants, but Ballard was just as busy fighting off the pain in his knee as he was savoring a Super Bowl win.

"It was definitely a very bittersweet moment for me," said Ballard. We had just won the Super Bowl but I didn't know what was going on with my knee. The one thing I do regret is that I never got to go up onto the stage and hold the trophy, but I was just happy that we won."

Manning picked up his second straight Super Bowl MVP trophy as he finished with 296 passing yards. Manning and his teammates were welcomed with another victory parade in New York upon their return to the Big Apple. Ballard joined the parade on crutches and was placed on injured reserved during the off-season. Players on injured reserve can be claimed by other teams when the season is not underway. Many expected Ballard to be back with the Giants, but Ballard was claimed by none other than the New England Patriots. The team that had been his "sworn enemy" in New York was now giving Ballard another chance to play football. Ballard was placed in the physically unable to perform list before the start of the season and never played a down for the Patriots. However, Ballard did get stuck in an awkward moment with his new team after he first arrived in New England.

"They're getting their AFC Championship rings," said Ballard. "Bill is giving this meeting and dismisses everyone who wasn't on the team last year. I go out in the locker room and I see them bringing the cart full of rings. In my head, I am thinking 'this is so awkward.' Bobby Carpenter asks me to show everyone the real ring. Brady smiles and says 'Too soon, Bob … too soon.'"

XLVII
LIGHTS OUT PERFORMANCE

The Super Bowl was about to become a sibling rivalry.

Super Bowl XLVII would feature a battle of brothers. The AFC Champion Baltimore Ravens headed to the Super Bowl led by Head Coach John Harbaugh. The NFC Champion San Francisco 49ers reached the championship game for the first time in 18 years with Jim Harbaugh at the helm. It would be the first time a Super Bowl would feature two family members as head coaches on opposite sidelines. The "Harbaugh Bowl" put the spotlight on the two head coaches as the players prepared for the biggest game of their lives.

As the week leading up to the Super Bowl progressed, players were pelted with questions about a brother battle in New Orleans. Baltimore Center Matt Birk says the Ravens were locked in on the task at hand and had already experienced the hype of a Harbaugh Bowl the previous season.

"We were really not affected at all," Birk said. "The year before, we had played them on Thanksgiving. That was the first time the Harbaugh Brothers coached against each other, so we had kind of been through that."

While John Harbaugh kept his team's eyes on the prize, Jim Harbaugh took a similar approach with the 49ers. San Francisco Linebacker Patrick Willis says his head coach was all business during the week with the challenge of a surging Ravens' squad awaiting on Sunday.

"He didn't talk too much about it," recalled Willis. "Coach Harbaugh was always about our team. We never really talked about the outside at all. We focused on us pretty much the whole week. Nothing really changed."

Baltimore's run to the Super Bowl came 12 months after falling just short of Super Bowl XVLI in heartbreaking fashion. A dropped pass and a missed field goal at the end of the AFC Championship game in New England sent the Ravens down to defeat. One year later, Baltimore advanced to Super Bowl XLVII with a victory over the Patriots.

"It's almost kind of how you would draw it up," said Birk. "It was as heartbreaking a loss as I've ever been a part of in the 2011 AFC Championship game in New England. You go through a three-game losing streak in December and we weather that and then to go into the playoffs and go on the run and have the road go through New England. Not just winning that game but winning it very convincingly was quite satisfying."

San Francisco needed to pull out a dramatic come from behind victory over Atlanta in the NFC Championship game to advance to the Super Bowl. Trailing 17–0, the 49ers stormed back for a 28–24 win. The comeback gave San Francisco an opportunity for a sixth Super Bowl championship.

"That game was tough," Willis said. "It took everything we had to pull that game out. Everybody was just selling out to get there. It was remarkable to be a part of it."

The two teams had a healthy respect for each other after doing battle on Thanksgiving night the previous season. Baltimore won the first Harbaugh Bowl, 16–6, but Birk knew the 49ers would be a formidable foe on Super Sunday.

"It was like watching a horror show when you put the film on," recalled Birk. "They were so strong. We had played them the year before. I came out of that game and I said many times publicly and privately that's the best front seven I've ever played against."

When Sunday finally arrived, the Harbaugh hype was still going strong in New Orleans. For the players, it was easy to put aside the off-the-field distractions on game day, but Birk understood the significance of the game for the family of the two head coaches.

"What an amazing time for the Harbaugh Family," said Birk. "At the same time, this is the Super Bowl. Everybody knows this is an opportunity that if you're lucky, comes around once in a career. Whether it was the Harbaugh Brothers or just all the other stuff that goes on around the Super Bowl, it was more like just pushing all that stuff aside and focusing on the game."

For Willis, the arrival of Super Sunday was literally a dream come true.

"One of the things I remember about the Super Bowl was in the morning when I woke up," said Willis. "I remember thinking 'The day is here.' And thinking now that the day is here, I have to go capitalize and make it happen. You just couldn't believe it."

San Francisco got off to a sloppy Super Bowl start and the opportunistic Ravens quickly took advantage. After the 49ers were forced to punt on their opening drive, Baltimore marched into the red zone. A third down pass by Quarterback Joe Flacco fell incomplete, but an offside penalty gave the Ravens another chance. Flacco made the most of his second chance and fired a 13-yard touchdown pass to Anquan Boldin to give Baltimore the early lead.

"I thought we had a great game plan going in," Birk said. "We decided to spread them out a little bit and get them out of their base package. They were so strong against the run and they were great against the pass, too. We felt we had a better chance of success if we spread them out a little bit and let Joe throw the ball."

It was the continuation of an impressive post-season run for Flacco, who had also thrown 22 touchdown passes in the regular season. Birk wasn't surprised to see how Flacco's calm and cool demeanor served him well under the Super Bowl spotlight.

"That's Joe," said Birk. "He's really low key and that works well for a quarterback in the Super Bowl."

San Francisco responded with a 62-yard drive on its next possession which set up a 36-yard field goal by David Akers. However, the Ravens took advantage of another 49er mistake early in the second quarter. Arthur Jones recovered a LaMichael James fumble on the Baltimore 25. Flacco took the Ravens down the field for a 75-yard drive and Dennis Pitta's one-yard catch increased Baltimore's lead to 14–3. A facemask penalty on San Francisco's Donte Whitner had helped move the Ravens closer to the end zone.

"I felt like our defense was really just giving up some big plays," said Willis. "They were things that were uncharacteristic of our defense."

Meanwhile, the game plan was quickly falling into place for Baltimore and Birk and his teammates had kept their focus to help build the early lead.

"You always want to start fast," said Birk. "The Super Bowl is no different. Once the game starts, it's just the game. It's almost like a relief and I know a lot of people say that, but it really is. Your mind just goes crazy the two weeks leading up to it."

A fake field goal attempt by the Ravens was snuffed out by the 49ers, but Baltimore would still add to its lead before the end of the half. With just under two minutes to play, Flacco threw a deep pass to Jacoby Jones. The receiver made a diving reception untouched inside the ten and was able to get up and spin away from two defenders before diving into the end zone. Akers would add another field goal on the final play of the half, but Baltimore headed to the locker room with a 21–6 lead. The Harbaugh Bowl appeared to be on the verge of a Harbaugh blowout. For Willis and the 49ers, it would be an uphill battle in the second half.

"We had to get back to playing 49er football," Willis said. "We had to get back to playing that 49er defense. When you have it, you always know you can tap into it. It can be done. We had done it before."

Baltimore was in complete control after 30 minutes of football, but Birk knew there was still work to be done as he and his teammates waited for the start of the third quarter.

"We were a veteran team," Birk said. "We knew how to focus for 60 minutes. Halftime at the Super Bowl is excruciatingly long because of the halftime show. It's a little bit different, but we talked about it and we were prepared for it. You leave the locker room up, 21–6. You have 30 minutes left to a world championship. That was a good situation to be in."

The Ravens were in a better situation at the start of the second half thanks to the longest play in Super Bowl history. Jones caught the opening kickoff eight yards deep in the end zone. Jones elected to bring the ball out and flew down the field for a 108-yard kickoff return for a touchdown. The electrifying run increased Baltimore's lead to 28–6.

"I knew nobody was catching Jacoby Jones that year," said Birk. "I know Jacoby Jones is fast but it seemed like that year when he'd get that lane, nobody ever caught Jacoby that whole year."

It seemed nothing could stop Baltimore from finishing off the 49ers and claiming its second Super Bowl Trophy. San Francisco took over after the kickoff return and ran three plays to reach its own 40. On third down, the 49ers were getting ready to run their next play, but the Super Bowl suddenly came to a grinding halt.

A power failure in the Superdome resulted in a Super Bowl blackout. The lights went out throughout half of the stadium and the game was delayed for 34 minutes. For the players, the sudden stoppage was difficult considering the level of concentration by both sides on the task at hand. However, there was little panic on either sideline.

"I didn't sense any of that on the sidelines," Birk said. "You are so locked in. I don't think that anything would phase your concentration at that point.

An elephant could have popped out at the 50-yard line. You're just so focused on the goal."

"This was crazy," said Willis. "You think about this happening watching movies and stuff and it isn't supposed to happen in real life. They were out for a while. You were at a point where it's just thinking 'when the hell do they come back on?' Then, the lights came back on and it was time to play ball again."

The Ravens had been rolling before the power failure, so the 49ers were hoping the delay would give them a chance to regroup and get back into game with nearly a whole half still remaining.

"I felt like it did," Willis said. "I felt we got some kind of momentum from somewhere. We were able to ride it."

The Ravens did not sense any issues with momentum when play resumed, but the 49ers suddenly surged back into the game. Quarterback Colin Kaepernick put together an 80-yard drive later in the period and connected with Michael Crabtree on a 31-yard scoring strike. After forcing a Baltimore punt, San Francisco struck again as Frank Gore's six-yard touchdown run cut the deficit to 28–20. A game which appeared to be one-sided at the start of the second half was suddenly a tight contest and Birk realized the power outage may have worked to San Francisco's advantage.

"I didn't think it was that big of a deal," said Birk. "I really expected us to come out of it okay. I thought it would just help us and we would just continue to roll. Boy, was I wrong."

The 49ers were not done with their third quarter scoring. A Ray Rice fumble was recovered by Tarell Brown. The Baltimore Defense kept San Francisco out of the end zone, but another field goal by Akers cut the Ravens lead to 28–23 early in the fourth quarter.

"You expect yourself to play at a certain level," said Willis. "When you play at that level, it doesn't surprise you. For us, that's the way that game was supposed to be. That's the way we should have been playing. If anything, the game shouldn't have been close like that."

Baltimore's offense finally got back on track. Flacco led his offense on a 5:16 drive that ended with a 19-yard field goal by Justin Tucker. San Francisco was still within striking distance, but the scoring drive had helped the Ravens settle back into their game.

"We knew we absolutely needed it," said Birk. "We wanted seven, but to come away with three was huge."

The 49ers got the ball back with 12:47 to go and needed just five plays to find the end zone. Kaepernick rolled left and raced 15 yards for a touchdown with just under ten minutes remaining. The two point conversion failed, but San Francisco was within two with plenty of time remaining in Super Bowl XLVII. Another Baltimore field goal put the Ravens back up by five, but San Francisco stormed back and reached the Baltimore seven with the help of a 33-yard run by Gore.

"It's tough because you can't influence it anymore," Birk said. "It's also tough because those are your guys. Those are your brothers out there battling and giving it everything they have. You just have to sit there and watch."

Birk and his offensive teammates watched the 49ers gain two yards on three plays, which set up a fourth and goal with 1:50 remaining.

"I don't think you're ever out until the clock strikes zero," said Willis. "For us, there was still an opportunity. We knew our guys at any given time could pop one."

"I remember thinking this is essentially it," recalled Birk. "This one play is going to determine the outcome of the game. To some degree, this play is going to define my career to a certain extent. It was a big moment."

Kaepernick threw a pass to the right side of the end zone for Crabtree, but the pass floated over the receiver and fell incomplete. There was some contact between Crabtree and Defensive back Jimmy Smith, but not enough to draw a penalty on San Francisco's best chance to take the lead.

Willis would have preferred to see Gore's number called with the go-ahead score only five yards away.

"I don't think they should have been throwing that ball," Willis said. "With Frank Gore in the backfield like that, that's not even a question. To be on the five-yard line after he helped get us all the way down there like that and to not hand it to him three times in a row and to have the offensive line we had, there's no way we couldn't have gotten the five yards to score in three plays with our offensive line."

Baltimore was stopped short of a first down on the ensuing possession before punter Sam Koch purposely took a safety to take more time off the clock. Only four seconds remained when Ted Ginn, Jr., fielded the ensuing free kick and was stopped after a 31-yard return. The Ravens had held on for a 34–31 victory and Birk was a champion in his final game in the NFL.

"It was just pure joy," said Birk. "It was my 15th year. There are just times you wonder and say maybe it's not in the cards for me. Every team that wins the Super Bowl is a special team and it's a special journey."

It was an extra special Super Bowl title for the Ravens organization. The team played the 2012 campaign in memory of Owner Art Modell, who died before the season opener. It would also be the last game for Linebacker Ray Lewis who was set to join Birk in retirement. As for Birk, the longtime center from Harvard had a chance to savor the moment as he left the field for the final time.

"There are no guarantees in life that things are going to work out like that and you're going to have a storybook ending," Birk said. "Normally, they don't, but it was nice to be a part of something like that where it did work out. For me, it ended up being my last game. I'd say that was a hell of a way to go out."

XLVIII
THE SEAHAWKS FREEZE THE BRONCOS

There was little chance for the participants of Super Bowl XLVIII to get distracted by warm weather.

The 48th edition of Super Sunday would be played in a cold weather city for the first time in the history of the game. The New York area was selected as the site, and the Seattle Seahawks and Denver Broncos would meet in East Rutherford, New Jersey. The coldest kickoff for a Super Bowl had taken place in New Orleans for Super Bowl VI at 39 degrees, but that kickoff occurred during the daytime in a traditionally warmer climate. An abnormally colder and snowier winter in New York at the start of 2014 prompted fears of an icy climate for the biggest game of the year. Even though the Broncos were used to playing in cold weather, Defensive Lineman Malik Jackson knew this was a different type of cold along the east coast.

"I think you can never get used to the cold," Jackson said. "You just have to tough it out and play in it, but that mountain cold is different than that water cold. Playing in that cold was just a whole other story. It was a beautiful day that day but we were practicing in the cold all week."

While some players prepared for a Freezer Bowl instead of a Super Bowl, others embraced the New York area spotlight. For Seattle Linebacker K.J. Wright, a trip to the east coast gave him an opportunity to see one of the most popular cities in the world.

"I loved it," Wright said. "At first, I was a little concerned that it might be cold, but that weather was absolutely perfect with clear skies. It was fun to go out to the east coast. I always dreamed of going to New York and checking out the city, so I got to do that during the week."

"Perfect" may not have been the word many of the other players would use, but the region did catch a break from Old Man Winter for Super Sunday. Contingency plans had been made to move the Super Bowl to a Monday or Tuesday if nasty winter weather arrived. There was indeed a storm heading for the east coast, but it did not reach the region until several hours after the Super Bowl. The day of the game remained on Sunday, and the temperature would be 49 degrees at kickoff time.

In Super Bowl XL, Seattle was denied the chance at its first ever NFL title. This time, the Seahawks arrived in North Jersey after a thrilling win over rival San Francisco in the NFC Championship game thanks to a game-saving interception in the closing seconds.

"The 49ers and Seahawks were a big rivalry," said Wright. "The matchup was just incredible. It just came down to the last play. That was a great matchup and a great rivalry game and a big win that got us to the Super Bowl."

The Broncos were making their seventh Super Bowl appearance and their first in 15 years. Denver's top-ranked offense was led by Peyton Manning, who reached his third career Super Bowl and his first as a Bronco. For most defenses, shutting down Manning was a nearly impossible task, but the Seahawks had the best defense in the NFL during the 2013 season. As Wright did his film study with Bobby Wagner and the rest of the Seattle linebackers, they believed they were capable of stopping Manning cold in this cold weather Super Bowl.

"They were the number one offense that year," said Wright. "We knew it would be a challenge but I was watching film and I saw more bad defenses than really good offense, so I was telling Bobby this game doesn't have to be close. I know those guys are good, but if we go out there and play our best, it shouldn't even be a close game."

The Broncos were still a slight favorite heading into Super Bowl XLVIII. In addition to the offense, the Denver Defense was a strong unit throughout much of the season. However, the Broncos were missing star Linebacker Von Miller, who was lost for the season with a torn ACL. The injury meant several other younger Broncos needed to step up and Jackson did his part in his second season with 42 tackles and six sacks.

"It was awesome," said Jackson. "It's what you ask for as a player. You want to be consistent and you want to play at a high level. You want to be mentioned as a top defense and we were that all year."

Still, Jackson knew Miller would be difficult to replace in the biggest game of the season.

"We had a lot of guys missing," Jackson said. "People have to step up. It was different when you have your core group of guys playing. Von is one of the best if not the best defensive players in the league. To not have him was a big deal."

The New York area theme carried over to the kickoff, as former Jet Joe Namath and former Giant Phil Simms came to the middle of the field for the coin toss. Namath did the honors wearing his trademark fur coat.

Broadway Joe and the rest of the crowd barely had time to settle into their seats when the first score of Super Bowl XLVIII occurred. Seattle won the toss and elected to kickoff. On the first play from scrimmage, Manning began shifting to his left in the shotgun. Center Manny Ramirez snapped the ball to the right of Manning and into the end zone for a safety. Just 12 seconds into the game, the Seahawks had a 2–0 lead. It was the quickest points ever scored at the start of a Super Bowl and the safety gave Seattle a wave of momentum which would carry over through four quarters.

"That just really set the game off right there," said Wright. "We got some points up on the board. We got the momentum and we got the crowd cheering. The next drive, we go out there and force a punt, so it started out really good for us and we never looked back."

As exhilarating as the play was for the Seahawks, it was equally deflating for the Broncos.

"It was definitely an eye opener," recalled Jackson. "You're the only game on. You're working so hard and you think you're doing everything right."

The safety turned out to a prelude for what was to come for the rest of Super Bowl XLVIII. Two Seattle field goals by Steven Hauschka sandwiched around a Denver three and out increased the Seahawks' lead to 8–0. Things went from bad to worse for Manning on Denver's next possession. On third down, the quarterback's pass floated over the head of Julius Thomas and into the hands of Seattle's Kam Chancellor at the Broncos' 37. It completed a first quarter for the Denver Offense in which it gained only 11 total yards.

"They were running really basic things," Wright said. "They were just out-executing the defenses. It seemed like every person in that game was having their best game ever. We were locked in together and we were moving together and we were just out there having fun."

The Seahawks quickly moved to the one where Marshawn Lynch crashed into the end zone for the game's first touchdown. With 12 minutes remaining in the first half, this Super Bowl was already turning into a rout. It would continue to go downhill for Denver before the half. The Broncos were finally able to move the ball on the ensuing drive and reach the Seattle 35, but disaster would strike again for Manning on third down. A hit by Cliff Avril on the quarterback forced another floater short and to the right. The ball landed into the waiting arms of Seattle Linebacker Malcolm Smith, whose 69-yard interception return made the score 22–0. The score would remain the same until halftime and the stunned Broncos were forced to regroup facing their largest deficit of the season.

"We're down 22," Jackson said. "You're wondering what happened."

The Seahawks had dominated the first two quarters of Super Bowl XLVIII and appeared to be on their way to victory, but Wright and his teammates weren't about to open the champagne with another half looming against Manning.

"That was not enough points to say that the game was over," said Wright.

"We were confident and we were relaxed, but we came out in the second half to do the same thing. It was just following the details and punishing them."

Any hopes of a Denver comeback were quickly extinguished on the second half kickoff. Once again, it took just 12 seconds for the Seahawks to score. A short kick floated into the arms of Percy Harvin at the 13. Harvin raced 87 yards for a touchdown to increase Seattle's lead to 29–0.

Wright and his teammates weren't surprised to see Harvin go the distance to start the third quarter. The Seahawks had actually predicted the score before they left the locker room at halftime.

"We were sitting in the locker room," recalled Wright. "We knew we were receiving the ball. Everybody in the locker room was thinking we were taking this to the house. I don't know why and I don't know how, but we all said it. They just made a little kick and they didn't have a chance to see Percy all year because he was injured."

Even the Broncos began to realize their Super Bowl dream was slipping away. Denver had the chance to get reorganized at halftime, but Harvin's return was a shock to the system for Denver.

"We go into the locker room and talk it over," Jackson said. "Everybody gets re-energized. Then we get out there and they have a kick return. It was not a good day at all."

The bleeding would continue for the Broncos later in the quarter. After driving into Seattle territory, Byron Maxwell's strip of Demaryius Thomas gave the ball back to Seattle. Quarterback Russell Wilson proceeded to take his team on a 58-yard drive which was capped off by a spectacular catch and run by Jermaine Kearse. The receiver caught a pass over the middle and spun away from four Broncos for a 23-yard touchdown reception. With three minutes to play in the third quarter, the Seahawks were already sizing up their Super Bowl rings. The Seattle offense was as dominant as its vaunted defensive unit.

"Those guys have so much talent," said Wright. "When we are all clicking like that, no one in the league can stop us. It's something we strived to do each and every week and we were all on the same page."

Meanwhile, Jackson and the rest of the talented Denver defensive front were unable to get any pressure on Wilson. The quarterback's mobility and quick passes to avoid the rush left the Broncos frustrated and neutralized throughout much of the game.

"We really had a good D-line that year," said Jackson. "They did a lot of that. They schemed us really well. They had a great game plan and you can't take anything away from those guys."

The fourth quarter would prove to be a prelude to the Seattle celebration. Manning and the Broncos finally got on the board at the end of the third quarter thanks to a 14-yard touchdown catch by Thomas followed by a two-point conversion.

"I was actually mad in that they scored in the second half," Wright said.

However, the Seahawks would recover Denver's onside kick and would find the end zone yet again. Wilson finished the drive with a ten-yard pass to Baldwin to increase Seattle's lead and the Seahawks were 11:45 away from claiming their first Super Bowl. The large lead gave Wright and his teammates the opportunity to savor the moment throughout much of the final quarter.

"I actually liked that better," Wright said. "It gave an opportunity for other guys to get in the game. We watched those guys go out there and have fun, too. We were un-wrapping our tape and taking all the gloves off. We were hugging each other and smiling and celebrating."

The 43–8 victory was a reflection of the dominance of the day by the Seahawks. The Seattle defense finished with four turnovers while Wilson out-dueled Manning with an efficient 18-for-25 passing performance. The franchise which was born into expansion in 1976 was now at the top of the football world.

"It's just the moment you always dreamed of when you were a kid," said Wright. "You're looking up at your family in the stands and telling them to come down. They pass out the trophy at the end and everybody's touching and kissing it. All of your dreams come true and you're just living in the moment."

For the vanquished Broncos, there was little to do but tip their hat to the victors. Denver had been dominated on both sides of the ball. Many of the Broncos would use lessons learned from the defeat to propel them to victory two years later in Super Bowl 50.

But it was Seattle's day on this winter night in New Jersey.

"They were awesome," said Jackson. "They had a great O-line and also a great defense. It was great to watch them. "I think seeing them in person left an impression on me. You want to be that top defense. You want to be running around smacking people and knowing the ball loose and having fun."

The Seattle faithful had finally been rewarded with a world championship. The Seahawks fans have a reputation of being among the most loud and loyal in pro football and had given their team an undeniable home field advantage in the years leading up to Super Bowl XLVIII. The victory set off a celebration unlike any other ever seen in the Emerald City.

"I've been all over the NFL," Wright said. "I've been in a lot of stadiums but I haven't seen fans quite like ours. To bring a championship to that city was amazing. Our parade was just unreal. I felt like the whole city was out there. It was just so good to finally bring one to Seattle."

XLIX
The Butler Did It

There was no questioning the credentials of the two participants of Super Bowl XLIX.

The NFL was experiencing more and more parity as the 21st century progressed. Many teams had made runs to the Super Bowl despite being among the lower seeds in their respective conferences. Such was not the case in the 49th edition of Super Sunday as the NFL's top two teams were set for a showdown in the desert.

Representing the AFC were the New England Patriots, who were making their eighth Super Bowl appearance and sixth under Head Coach Bill Belichick. While the Patriots were no strangers to Super Bowls, Quarterback Tom Brady and his teammates hadn't hoisted the Lombardi Trophy in ten years. Many of the Patriots had lived through the losses in Super Bowls XLII and XLVI and some had even been on the roster the last time the Patriots were crowned champions. One rookie who would be soaking in the Super Bowl spotlight for the first time was Safety Malcolm Butler. The undrafted free agent was receiving more playing time as the season progressed and now was ready to be part of New England's quest for a fourth Super Bowl title.

"It was a great experience," said Butler. "I always wanted to play in the NFL and in any game if I started or not. I was extremely honored to get to play in a Super Bowl. There are players who play for 15 years and never won a Super Bowl or have never even been to a Super Bowl. It's a moment that I'll never forget."

Awaiting Butler and the Patriots in Arizona were the defending-champion Seattle Seahawks. The NFC Champions had become the first team to reach back-to-back Super Bowls since the Patriots during the 2003 and 2004 seasons. The Seahawks had survived several tough tests during the season along with an epic NFC title game against Green Bay. Seattle appeared to be just as strong if not stronger than the team which rolled past Denver in Super Bowl XLVIII. For most of the Seahawks, Super Bowl XLIX would be a chance for a second ring. Wide Receiver Chris Matthews was looking for his first.

"It was definitely amazing," said Matthews. "My pop was always telling me that there are not too many people who can make it to the Super Bowl and it's a very elite group to actually win one. Just getting there was an amazing time for me. I was just trying to soak up every minute of it."

Matthews was off the NFL radar when Seattle was rolling past Denver in the previous Super Bowl. He was working at a Foot Locker store in February of 2014 after spending time in the Canadian Football League. The Seahawks offered Matthews a tryout and he would eventually work his way on to the team's practice squad. By the end of the season, Matthews was placed on the 53-man roster. At the end of the NFC Championship game, Matthews recovered a critical onside kick in Seattle's thrilling comeback victory. Now, it was off to the Super Bowl where the attention to detail put in place by the veterans kept Matthews from being distracted by the hype surrounding America's biggest sporting event. However, the former Foot Locker employee did have a bit of an opportunity during the week to savor the moment.

"Everyone went from practice to meeting to eating to going back to the rooms to study," Matthews said. "That's what really happened with us. At that time, I really wasn't a big factor in the offense. I had a little bit more leeway as far as experiencing the whole Super Bowl process. I felt like I had more of a good time than others."

The game appeared to be evenly matched and the odds makers agreed by making Super Bowl XLIX even on the betting lines. It would be Brady and Belichick against the defending champs and both teams had a healthy respect for each other.

"There was definitely momentum going into it," said Matthews. "Of course, we felt like we were the top dog, but we knew what kind of team they were and how good they were. We took every day, every practice and every meeting as serious as possible."

The defenses would dominate the start of Super Bowl XLIX. Both teams were forced to punt on their first two possessions before the New England offense finally got rolling late in the first quarter. However, Brady was intercepted in the end zone by Jeremy Lane and the Seattle cornerback returned the ball to his own 14. Lane would have little time to savor his Super Bowl moment. He broke his wrist on the return and was done for the rest of the night.

Seattle took over but was once again shut down by the New England Defense. The Patriots forced another punt at the start of the second quarter and both offenses were still trying to figure out a way to the end zone.

"I know we both were playing good defense," Butler said. "We were both competing hard in the first half. It always comes down to a couple of plays."

New England would finally break the scoreless tie early in the second quarter. Brady took his team 65 yards with the help of a key third down catch by Julian Edelman. Brady finished off the drive with an 11-yard touchdown toss to Brandon LaFell as the Patriots grabbed a 7–0 lead. Later in the quarter, Quarterback Russell Wilson was finally able to complete his first pass of the game which kept a Seattle drive alive on third down. Two plays later, Matthews would make his first NFL catch. Matthews streaked down the right side and hauled in a 44-yard pass to put the Seahawks on the New England 11.

"It was an amazing feeling," recalled Matthews. "We planned for that play for two weeks. It was really just a decoy route and it was really for Ricardo Lockette for him to run. It was set up for Doug Baldwin or Jermaine Kearse to get the ball underneath for a quick first down. To be honest, I don't know what drove Russ to throw the ball to me, but I'm happy he did."

Three plays later, Running Back Marshawn Lynch rumbled into the end zone from three yards out. The game was tied at 7–7 with just over two minutes remaining in the half, but neither team was done scoring. New England quickly responded to the Seattle touchdown as Brady completed five passes on the ensuing drive. The last throw went to Tight End Rob Gronkowski for a 22-yard touchdown with 31 seconds remaining in the half. It appeared the Patriots would go into the locker room at halftime with the lead, but Wilson and Matthews had one more chance. The Seahawks started on their own 20 but quickly moved to the New England 11. With six seconds remaining in the half, Seattle Head Coach Pete Carroll gambled on one more play. Wilson lobbed a pass to the left side of the field. Matthews leaped in front of Logan Ryan just inside the goal line and hauled in Wilson's pass for a touchdown.

"It was a quick little jump ball," Matthews said. "There was no way I was going to let him deter me from getting that touchdown."

Super Bowl XLIX was tied at the half and a man who had never made an NFL catch before stepping onto the field in Arizona had two of the biggest receptions of the game. Matthews was thrilled to be making an impact, but even he was surprised to be such an integral part of the offense.

"It was definitely a surprise," said Matthews. "I didn't get into any talks about it. I wasn't a part of the offense at all. I was really just out there to support my team and make an impact on special teams. That was my focal point."

The Patriots were looking to regroup after letting the lead slip away in the final seconds in the first half, but many of the New England veterans were hardly shaken by the turn of events. Butler wasn't surprised to see the game tighten up with the caliber of the opponent on the other side of the field and expected the game would remain close over the final two quarters.

"We were pretty confident," recalled Butler. "We knew the game wouldn't be over until it's over and it would come down to a few plays."

Meanwhile, the Seahawks received an extra jolt of adrenalin thanks to the touchdown by Matthews. The wide receiver was trying to keep his focus with some help from the veterans but could sense his score was a momentum swing in favor of the defending champs.

"I felt like it really did," said Matthews. "Things picked up a lot in the locker room. The leaders led by example and were motivating us. For me, I'm a player that doesn't like to let anything excite me to where I'm just out of my element. I try to keep a level head if things are going good or bad. I kind of just kept quiet."

The Seahawks took the opening kickoff of the second half and embarked on a drive which would give them their first lead of the game. It would be Matthews who would once again come up with the big play on the drive. Wilson fired a deep pass on the left side and Matthews leaped in front of Patriots Cornerback Kyle Arrington for a 45-yard catch. The reception put the ball on the New England 17, but the drive would stall inside the red zone. Steven Hauschka booted a 27-yard field goal to put Seattle ahead, 17–14.

It would not take long for the Seahawks to get the ball back. On the ensuing drive, Brady was intercepted by Linebacker Bobby Wagner and Seattle had the ball at midfield. The drive started with Matthews' fourth catch of the night and ended with Wilson's three-yard touchdown pass to a wide-open Doug Baldwin. The Seahawks had built a 24–14 lead and the score would remain the same heading into the fourth quarter.

Seattle had taken control of the game.

"We settled down and focused," Matthews said. "We wanted to get that ring. That was pretty much what everybody was talking about on the sideline. It was just to stay focused. Russ was being a phenomenal quarterback out there and doing what he was supposed to be doing leading the offense. We all just followed along."

Meanwhile, Butler and the rest of the New England secondary were searching for answers with Wilson heating up after a slow start.

"We gave them everything we had," said Butler. "We gave them man-to-man and everything else that we had. We brought out some of our best plays whatever the situation was. That's how you had to do it against a great team like Seattle."

With 12:10 remaining, Brady and the Patriots would stop the bleeding and cut into the Seattle lead. Brady led his unit on a 68-yard drive and finished it with a four-yard touchdown pass to Danny Amendola. The New England Defense quickly forced a Seattle punt and Brady and the offense took over on their own 36 with 6:52 remaining. After three consecutive completions and a penalty, Brady completed three more passes with the third throw going to Gronkowski at the Seattle 19. Four plays later, Julian Edelman caught a three-yard pass in the left side of the end zone to give New England the lead with 2:02 remaining. As Wilson and the Seattle offense prepared for one last possession, the stage was set for one of the most dramatic finishes in Super Bowl history.

"We weren't worried," said Matthews. "We just knew we had a big task at hand. I think Russell handled it quite well. He did what he was supposed to do. I feel like he had a great second half."

Seattle needed to go 80-yards for the game-winning touchdown. The Seahawks picked up the first 31 yards on the opening play from scrimmage as Lynch made a 31-yard catch down the far sideline. Two straight incompletions set up a third down, but Wilson picked up a fresh set of downs with an 11-yard completion to Lockette. On the next play, Wilson threw a deep pass down the near sideline for Jermaine Kearse. Butler was covering Kearse and stayed with the receiver step for step. As the pass arrived, Butler leaped up and deflected the ball. Kearse was on the ground, but the ball hit the upper part of the receiver's leg and popped up into his hands. The remarkable catch put Seattle on the doorstep of a second straight Super Bowl victory.

"I was actually running down the left side of the field," Matthews said. "He threw the ball and I was gassed. I ran three go's in a row. I'm tired and all I see is him falling and I'm thinking maybe he didn't catch that and we have to get back to the huddle. The next thing I know, the crowd is going wild and he's getting up."

Kearse got up and began to head for the end zone, but Butler has the presence of mind to get up off the ground as well. Butler was able to push Kearse out of bounds at the five before he could reach the goal line.

"I did have good coverage on him," Butler said. "The ball was in the air and I was getting ready to turn around. I'm glad I was able to get up real fast. I turned around and he had the ball in his hands. He caught the ball and I got mad about it. I knew I had to try and push him out of bounds or knock the ball out of his hands."

"I sprinted down there as fast as I could to try and help him out," said Matthews. "That type of catch can only happen in the Super Bowl at the best time with the best players."

Kearse's catch meant Super Bowl XLIX would be decided in the closing seconds. A frustrated Butler had saved the touchdown with his quick thinking but knew his team was on the verge of defeat.

"I came out after that play," said Butler. "I went to the sidelines and it wasn't a great feeling."

Seattle had just over a minute to go five yards. The obvious choice to get to pay dirt appeared to come from the backfield where the bruising Lynch was almost automatic near the opponent's goal line. Lynch carried the ball to the one after the Kearse catch as the clock ran under a minute. The time would go under 30 seconds before Wilson snapped the ball on second and goal. All of America expected Lynch to get another carry, but Wilson took a three-step drop in the shotgun. The quarterback looked to his right and fired in the direction of Lockette. Butler, who had returned to the game after the Lynch run, headed for Lockette.

"I came back in," recalled Butler. "I got beat on the play in practice. I just told myself if Ricardo Lockette sticks his outside leg out first, he's coming back in. Once I saw it, I drove on the ball."

Butler arrived at Lockette at the same time as the ball. He stepped in front of the receiver and intercepted the pass to save the game for the Patriots and secure New England's fourth Super Bowl title. Butler's hard work in practice had paid off.

"They were in the red zone," said Butler. "When I got beat on the play in practice, the coaches told me I had to be there. Just a hair over the goal line in the end zone and it's a touchdown. They told me to drive on the ball whenever I saw the play. I just kept that in mind. I remembered the play and I thought about the same situation during the game. Everything clicked at the right time."

Carroll and his offensive staff would receive a host of criticism in the days following Super Bowl XLIX. Many believed another run by Lynch would have given Seattle the victory. Matthews and his teammates were too stunned by falling one yard short of a championship to argue about the play call.

"I was definitely shocked that we didn't get the touchdown more than anything," Matthews said. "If he had caught the ball and we would have scored, our offensive coordinator would have been a genius. Since it didn't happen that way, everybody's looking down upon it. I felt like regardless of what the call was, if we'd had scored it would have been great."

The Patriots ran out the clock and celebrated their first Super Bowl title in ten years. Brady was named the game's Most Valuable Player for the third time in his career after throwing for 328 yards and four touchdowns. The Super Bowl MVP was awarded a Chevrolet Colorado. Brady decided to give the truck to Butler.

"I still have the truck," said Butler. "That was really great. Not too many quarterbacks in the NFL would give up their Super Bowl MVP truck and it was great. When I came in for the parade, he just looked at me and threw me the sample keys that they had at the Super Bowl. He said 'Enjoy your truck.'"

Butler would also enjoy a whole new world in the spotlight after New England's 28–24 victory. The cornerback emerged as one of the most valuable defensive backs in New England in the years following Super Bowl XLIX and he will forever be remembered for his game-saving interception.

"I get a lot more attention that I had been getting," Butler said. "You've just got to carry yourself in a positive way. You've got to try and be on your Ps and Qs. In the field, some people tell me that they wouldn't know who I was if it weren't for that play. It was a big play and so effective in a couple of

---

seconds. It changed my life and it changed other people's perspective of me. I use it as motivation."

Meanwhile, Matthews would no longer be working at Foot Locker. Despite the defeat, Matthews had found a home in the NFL. He would remain with the Seahawks before his release in November of 2015, but would go on to sign with the Baltimore Ravens. Everything went perfectly for Matthews in the Super Bowl ... except the ending.

"That was definitely the beginning of my career in the NFL," said Matthews. "I felt like if that hadn't happened, I probably wouldn't even be in the NFL right now. I appreciate the Seahawks allowing me to play in that game and do the things that I was able to do and showcase my talents, but I really wish I had that game back."

50
DEFENSE WINS CHAMPIONSHIPS

Super Bowl 50 would provide a contrast in styles, beginning with its designation using the Arabic numeral "50." Under the traditional Roman numbering, it would have been billed as "Super Bowl L."

The dynamic Carolina Panthers rolled into Santa Clara after posting a 15–1 record in the regular season. Carolina disposed of Seattle and Arizona in the playoffs, and were favorites heading into the golden anniversary Super Bowl. The Panthers were led by Quarterback Cam Newton, the NFL's Most Valuable Player in 2015. Newton's 3,837 yards passing and 636 yards rushing made him one of the top dual threats in the NFL.

Newton's skills would face a true test against the Denver Broncos. Even with legendary Peyton Manning at the helm of the offense, it was no secret the Denver Defense was the reason for the Broncos' birth in Super Bowl 50. Denver's defenders gave up the fewest yards in the NFL during the 2015 season, and Defensive Coordinator Wade Phillips was receiving high praise for his work. Defensive Tackle Malik Jackson was one player who raised his game to a higher level under Phillips.

"It was a blessing with Coach Wade," said Jackson. "He has so much knowledge. It was great to work with someone who has been around for a while, who knows what he's doing and knows how to coach players and put them in the right position. We were a read and react. When he came in, it was get up and go."

Denver Head Coach Gary Kubiak put his trust in Phillips to run the defense. Trust was something Ron Rivera was quite familiar with. The

Carolina head coach had brought his team to the Super Bowl after surviving a rough start to his tenure. Rivera won just 13 games over his first two seasons, which often spelled doom with other coaches in the modern world of the impatient NFL. The era of free agency had put more pressure on coaches to produce immediate success. However, Carolina Owner Jerry Richardson believed in Rivera, and it would not be long before Richardson was rewarded. Rivera won three straight division titles and put together a spectacular season in 2015.

Rivera was happy to repay Richardson's loyalty.

"You've got to build and develop and grow as a football team," said Rivera. "That's the beauty of it. My owner, Mr. Richardson, gave me the opportunity and so many times, you don't see that. You see a lot of impatience. We've become a society of instant gratification. People want it now, now, now instead of realizing you've got to work for it. There's a commitment and sacrifice that goes along with what you've got to do."

Rivera was making his first trip to the Super Bowl as a head coach. His first Super Sunday came as a player for the Chicago Bears in Super Bowl XX. Rivera served as a valuable backup for one of the greatest defenses of all time. He also had the opportunity to get a taste of what Super Bowl hype was all about as part of one of the most colorful teams in NFL history.

"I came to the realization that the Super Bowl is really two things," Rivera said. "It's an event and then it's a game. I was part of Super Bowl XX that was probably the first rock star Super Bowl."

Rivera had the support of his 1985 teammates as the Panthers prepared for the Super Bowl 30 years after Rivera and the Bears reigned supreme with one of the most dominating teams of all time.

"It was great," said Rivera. "They had a Super Bowl reunion party the week before. They had it on a day we played, so I couldn't make it. I actually called in and they put a speaker next to the phone. I certainly do relish the fact that I was fortunate to be a part of that."

Rivera was also quite familiar with Phillips' system thanks to a stop in San Diego as an assistant.

"We knew they had a good pass rush and that was the bottom line," said Rivera. "I knew a little about Wade Phillips. I got to go to San Diego and basically work on the defense that he installed. I think we had an understanding and a feel for who they were."

The Panthers knew the Denver Defense would present a tough test, but much of the pregame hype centered on a member of the Denver Offense. Manning was making his fourth Super Bowl appearance, and the man considered by many to be one of the best quarterbacks of all-time was expected to retire after the Super Bowl. For Jackson, the extra attention on Manning hardly served as a distraction.

"We just really looked at it as a team thing," said Jackson. "We knew Peyton was a legend in the game. We were all pretty sure it was going to be his last game. We didn't want to take anything away from him. On that defense, we had a lot of unselfish guys."

It was easy to understand why Jackson and his defensive teammates were able to maintain their focus leading up to Super Bowl 50. Many of the same Broncos had left the field in humiliation two years prior thanks to a 43–8 loss to Seattle in Super Bowl XLVIII. Jackson believes the Broncos were better prepared for the Super Bowl atmosphere when they arrived in California.

"We were able to go to Super Bowl XLVIII and see how the media can get in your head," Jackson said. "We didn't want that to happen. Having Coach Wade and Coach Kubiak have us doing the right things and having our mindset right helped us a lot."

The Panthers were hoping one of their top defensive players would be available despite a serious injury. Linebacker Thomas Davis suffered a broken arm in the NFC Championship game, but courageously found his way onto the field for Super Bowl 50.

"He willed himself," said Rivera. "You go back and look at Thomas' history and you understand what he had gone through. He had the three ACL injuries and surgeries and coming back from that, I don't think a simple broken arm was going to stop him."

Thomas and his defensive teammates were focused on stopping Manning. For Jackson and the Denver Defense, it was all about slowing down Newton, the man who triggered the success of the entire team.

"He's a great player," Jackson said. "They scheme very well. They had a great defense. We knew they wanted to run the ball and then let their defense do the rest."

Before the Panthers and Broncos took the field, the 43 MVP's of past Super Bowls were honored. The late Harvey Marvin was recognized, and Bart Starr and Chuck Howley were at their homes and acknowledged via satellite. The other 40 MVP's were in attendance as the Super Bowl celebrated its golden anniversary.

The Broncos struck first on the game's opening possession. Manning connected on three of his first four passes as he moved Denver into the red zone, but the Panthers stopped the Broncos at the 17. Brandon McManus kicked a 34-yard field goal to give Denver the early lead.

"For the offense to go down the field and get any points was awesome," said Jackson. "We knew there was a lot of pressure on them, especially after Super Bowl XLVIII. They kind of had to redeem themselves. We were happy. We knew we had some wiggle room to work with. It's good to see when the offense is doing their job, and it just gives us motivation to do ours."

It would be Jackson who would increase the lead later in the period.

Newton was sacked on his own four-yard line by Von Miller. The ball came loose, and Jackson has the first fumble recovery for a touchdown in a Super Bowl in 22 years. Jackson was able to beat Left Tackle Michael Oher as Miller stripped the football.

"I saw him get the sack," Jackson recalled. "I saw the ball come out and I just shot past him. It was definitely the play of my career to get the fumble recovery for a touchdown, and I can thank Von for that."

Jackson had a chance to savor the moment as he headed back to the Denver sidelines. The man selected 137th overall in the 2012 NFL Draft had the first touchdown of Super Bowl 50.

"It was awesome," said Jackson. "It was really disbelief. I wish I was able to pick up the ball and run 100 yards. It was awesome to get the first touchdown of the game. Just to be able to contribute to the team was all you can ask for."

The Carolina offense finally got in gear late in the opening period. By the time the second quarter arrived, the Panthers were closing in on their first score. They reached the one where Jonathan Stewart hurdled into the end zone, and the Denver lead was cut to three. After a slow start, it appeared the Panthers were finally ready to roll.

"You could feel it," Recalled Rivera. "You could feel the energy."

But the Broncos would regain the momentum thanks to a controversial special teams play. Denver's Jordan Norwood took back a punt 61 yard for the longest punt return in Super Bowl history. The return put the Broncos on the Carolina 14, but the Panthers initially thought Norwood had called for a fair catch. The hesitation by the Carolina tacklers allowed Norwood to break free.

"They felt it was going to be a fair catch," Rivera said. "One guy tried to avoid him because he didn't know if he had caught the ball. Before you know it, it turned into an unfortunate big play for them."

The Carolina Defense kept Denver out of the end zone, but another field goal by McManus increased the lead to 13–7. The teams traded turnovers before the Panthers moved to midfield in the closing seconds of the half, but Newton was sacked by DeMarcus Ware to end the Carolina scoring threat. The Broncos led by six at the half, and a Panthers' squad that had put up 80 points combined in their two previous playoff games was left searching for answers at halftime.

"We knew they couldn't run on us," said Jackson. "They had to pass. We had the dogs on that d-line that could go out there and hunt, and it helped we had a back seven where the d-backs and the linebackers did a damn good job of covering and knowing where they were supposed to be at. Once we got up and we knew they had to throw the ball, they definitely couldn't beat us."

Carolina did indeed go to the air at the start of the third quarter. A 45-yard pass from Newton to Ted Ginn, Jr., put the Panthers on the Denver 35. Carolina would move nine yards closer, but a 44-yard field goal try by Graham Gano bounced off the top of the right upright. Manning moved the ball on the ensuing drive with a pair of passes to Emanuel Sanders. The completions put Denver in field goal range, and McManus connected on his third field goal of the game to increase the lead to 16–7. The score would remain the same heading into the fourth quarter as a Newton interception on the ensuing drive resulted in the third turnover of the game for Carolina.

"The biggest disappointment was we turned the ball over as much as we did," Rivera said. "Michael Tolbert hadn't fumbled all year and fumbled twice in a Super Bowl. We threw an interception when we drove down towards the red zone. We missed a field goal. There were a lot of things that played into the game."

Still, the Panthers were far from finished. Kony Ealy stripped the ball from Manning, and Carolina took over at midfield. Newton drove his team into field goal range once again. This time, Gano connected from 39-yards out to bring Carolina to within six. Despite Denver's domination on defense, the Panthers were a touchdown away from taking the lead.

But the Broncos had been used to tight contests throughout much of the 2015 season.

"There was no panic," Jackson said. "We had been there all year with close games. Nobody was overly excited or overly nervous. We knew we had to go out there and be where we were supposed to be and do what we were supposed to do."

The defense would have to win this championship for Denver as the Broncos' offense continued to struggle. The Panthers forced punts on two straight Denver possessions, and Carolina got the ball back on its own 24 with 4:51 remaining. On third down, Miller stripped the ball from Newton. The Carolina quarterback hesitated to fall on the loose football, and Safety T.J. Ward recovered on the Panthers' four-yard line. The Broncos were about to wrap up their third Super Bowl title, and Newton would face heavy criticism for not diving onto the football in one of the game's critical moments.

"Defenders are fearless," Jackson said. We already have shoulders and wrist and ankle problems. To go down there to get a ball really doesn't bother us. People kind of got on Cam for not diving on it, but to me, he's a quarterback. I don't know too many quarterbacks who would dive on the ball when eleven defensive players coming at you trying to kill you for the ball."

The Panthers had turned the ball over for the fourth time, and Miller's strip capped off a dominating day which earned the linebacker MVP honors.

"It was cool to have a front row seat for that," said Jackson. "He battled his butt off. You sit there and watch him do what he does and take notes and try and mimic his game as much as I can."

C.J. Anderson's two-yard touchdown run followed by a Bennie Fowler two-point conversion catch increased Denver's lead to 24–10. The Panthers had two more chances on offense, but picked up only one first down. The Broncos were world champions, and the Panthers left the field beaten despite outgaining Denver, 315–194.

"It's part of the game," said Rivera. "It's very easy to say we didn't play to our abilities, but they played well. The team that played better won, and I can't take anything away from them. We were just disappointed in ourselves and our performance."

For Jackson and many of his teammates, the victory in Super Bowl 50 wiped away the painful memory of Super Bowl XLVIII.

"It was awesome," recalled Jackson. "Going into that game, you really think about what happened the years prior. You sit there and tell yourself you don't want that to happen again. That was devastating to do the things we did and then just get trashed. The guys that were there really made sure it didn't happen again."

Bibliography

NFL.com (for statistics), http://www.nfl.com/.

NFL Films (Super Bowl Highlight Videos and "America's Game" Super Bowl Series).

NFL on YouTube (full games of Super Bowls to review for accuracy of plays), https://www.youtube.com/user/NFL.

Pro Football Reference, http://www.pro-football-reference.com/.

Wikipedia.com (for background information on players and coaches along with Super Bowl information), https://www.wikipedia.org/.

Index

Lott, Ronnie 86
Louisiana Superdome 60
Lynch, Jim 22
Lynch, John 204
Lynch, Marshawn 261, 266
Lytle, Rob 61

Mackbee, Earsell 22
Mackey, John 26
Madden, John 53, 55, 98, 196
Magnum, Kris 206
Malavasi, Ray 74
Mandela, Nelson 198
Manders, Dave 28
Mandich, Jim 36
Manley, Dexter 87, 118
Mann, Charles 118
Mann, Errol 57
Manning, Danieal 225
Manning, Eli 229, 250
Manning, Peyton 177, 210, 224, 223, 239, 243, 245, 260, 270
Manningham, Mario 252
Mara, Wellington 110
Mardi Gras 245
Marino, Dan 99, 103
Maroney, Laurence 229
Marshall, Jim 20, 40, 43, 56
Marshall, Wilbur 106
Martin, Curtis 167
Martin, George 110
Martin, Rod 75, 93
Marvin, Harvey 273
Marvin, Mickey 81
Mathews, Clay 248
Mathis, Robert 224, 239
Mathis, Terance 177
Matte, Tom 17
Matthews, Chris 265
Maxwell, Byron 263
McAlister, Chris 190
McCardell, Keenan 201
McCartney, Paul 214
McClanahan, Brent 55
McClinton, Curtis 8
McConkey, Phil 110
McCutheon, Lawrence 74
McGee, Max 7, 8, 13
McGinest, Willie 196
McGrew, Larry 106
McIntyre, Guy 101, 123, 127
McMahon, Jim 104
McManus, Brandon 273
McMichael, Steve 106
McNabb, Donovan 213
McNair, Steve 185

McNeal, Don 90
McNeill, Fred 55
Meadowlands 132
Means, Natrone 157
Mendenhall, Rashard 246
Mercer, Mike 8
Meredith, Don 29
Miami 10, 11, 16, 15, 20, 24, 25, 30, 29, 30, 31, 32, 33, 35, 36, 38, 37, 38, 40, 42, 50, 63, 90, 87, 89, 91, 90, 91, 99, 101, 102, 103, 104, 105, 123, 143, 154, 155, 177, 179, 180, 224, 223, 228, 229, 241, 239
Miami Dolphins 30, 32, 37, 90, 99, 101, 104
Michaels, Lou 16
Michigan 82, 83, 193, 249
Middle East 132
Millen, Matt 96, 100
Miller, Bill 13
Miller, Heath 248
Miller, Von 260, 275
Milloy, Lawyer 205
Mills, Ernie 162
Minneapolis 138
Minnesota 20, 22, 37, 38, 40, 42, 43, 45, 46, 48, 47, 53, 55, 57, 58, 59, 57, 123, 130, 177, 178, 189, 239
Minnesota Vikings 20, 22, 37, 40, 43, 53, 57, 178, 189
Mississippi 118, 245
Mitchell, Tom 16
Mitchell, Willie 8
Mobley, John 171, 177
Modell, Art 192, 258
Monk, Art 139
Monroe, Carl 102
Monsters of the Midway 104
Montana, Joe 81, 99, 103, 126, 129, 154
Montgomery, Wilbert 79
Moody, Keith 81
Moore, Nat 101
Mora, Jim 222
Morrall, Earl 15, 16, 26, 29, 35, 90
Morris, Bam 163
Morris, Joe 114
Morstead, Thomas 241
Morton, Craig 26, 30, 59, 61, 60
Moseley, Mark 89, 96
Moss, Randy 230
Mother Nature 4, 45, 224
Mowatt, Zeke 113
Muhammad, Muhsin 207, 226
Mullins, Gerry 43, 49, 64, 71
Murray, Eddie 150
Musburger, Brent 88, 129
Music City Miracle 185